MERRY CHRISTMAS!.

I FINALLY FOUND THE COOKBOOK THAT WE
WERE LOOKING AT IN GREECE. NOW WE
CAN MAKE ALL OUR FAVORITE DISHES —
THE ONES WHICH WE HAD AT ALMOST
EVERY MEAL (TO VARYING DEGREES OF
QUALITY).

> TZATZIKI : CUCUMBER, YOGHURT & GARLIC SALAD
> MELITZANOSALATA : EGGPLANT PUREE SALAD
> TOMATO & CUCUMBER SALAD
> DOLMATHAKIA : STUFFED GRAPEVINE LEAVES
> DOMATES KE PIPERIES YIEMISTES ME RYZI :
>   STUFFED TOMATOES & GREEN PEPPERS
> DOMATOKEFTETHES : TOMATO BALLS / PATTIES
> KALAMARAKIA TIGANITA : FRIED CALAMARI
> MOUSSAKA

I HAD SUCH A WONDERFUL TIME WITH YOU
ON THIS TRIP — EFHAREESTO!

I LOVE YOU.

ALWAYS,
LAURA

GREEK FOOD

GREEK FOOD

An Affectionate Celebration of Traditional Recipes

Rena Salaman

HarperCollins*Publishers*

For my mother

and for Graeme and
our lovely daughters,
Alexandra and Sophia

First published in this revised and updated hardback edition by HarperCollins
Publishers 1993

Originally published by Fontana Paperbacks 1983

Editor: Barbara Dixon
Designers: Claire Neal and Joan Curtis

A catalogue record for this book is available from the British Library

ISBN 0 00 412917 2

Printed and bound in Great Britain by The Bath Press, Bath

Contents

Τὴ γλώσσα μοῦ ἔδωσαν ἑλληνική.
Τὸ σπίτι φτωχικὸ στὶζ ἀμμουδιές του Ὁμήρου.

(''Τα Πάθη'' ἀπὸ τὸ ''˜Αξιον Ἐστί''
τού Ὀδυσσέα Ἐλύτη)

'The language, they gave me Greek;
The house, poor on Homer's beaches.'

('The Passion' from *the Axion Esti*
by Odysseus Elytis)

Acknowledgements

Primarily I owe this book to the women of my family: my grandmother and my mother, who miraculously managed to give me a warm, happy and colourful childhood, despite the horrors of the German occupation and the Civil War that followed, which threw Greece into despair; also to my two lovely sisters, Sally Calder and Maria Metilia, who shared this childhood and my nostalgia for it and who reminded me of a lot of forgotten instances.

Even with this background, I would not have been able to write this book without the unique enthusiasm and encouragement (even occasional gentle nagging) of my husband, Graeme, who became my source of inspiration at all stages. He guided me and criticized the project and more practically gave me time to work on the book by taking our daughters for seemingly endless visits to the British Museum and on country picnics.

I also owe it to the enthusiasm of all our friends for the surprises of Greek food that they tried in our house. Particularly I would like to thank Gavin and M.M. Mackenzie for their unparalleled support which helped this project to become viable. Our friend Sami Zubaida read my manuscript and made a number of useful comments. More importantly he was so warmly positive about it, even if he did occasionally tease me about my incipient chauvinism.

I would also like to thank our friends Diana and Nigel Miller for adopting Greek cuisine totally, even down to the last detail of collecting Greek herbs at the height of a hot day on top of a mountain, and for cooking most of my recipes.

Also my friends Manouella Pantazithou and Petro Seleli, for endless discussions on their balcony in Athens which helped to fill some gaps in the book and for our wonderful fishing expeditions, and Maria Pantazithou in Kriti, for making our last visit to the island so memorable.

Most of all I have a lot of gratitude for all our friends on the island of Alonnisos; particularly our dear friends Mitso and Maria Karakatsani and their daughter Anna and her husband Panayioti Anagnostou; also Stavro and Nina Athanasiou and their children; and many more Alonnisians whose names I cannot mention individually, but who have provided me with a plethora of folklore material as well as warm memories, over the years.

I am also grateful to Richard Clogg of the Department of Byzantine and Modern Greek studies at King's College, London, for guiding me to the relevant bibliography of the Gennadios Library, Athens, for the historical references. I am indebted to Alan Davidson for his *Mediterranean*

Seafood where I found a lot of the scientific names of fish, which I took the liberty of using in my fish chapter.

I am grateful to Vivian Haywood who had the colossal task of typing my manuscript.

Lastly, how could I forget to thank especially some very dear friends who extended their warmth and moral support before and during this project, from near and far, Renate and Russell Miller, Dionysis Glykopantis and Manos Kalogridis.

London, November 1982.

Ten Years Later

I feel very fortunate to be able to update and enlarge *Greek Food*, which was my very first and most favourite book. The missing chapters of Cakes, Pastries and Preserves, Coffee, and Herbs, Tisanes and Medicines have been reinstated, and new classic recipes added. The whole conception of its updating and its current good looks is all owed to Barbara Dixon of HarperCollins who has placed enthusiasm, faith and commitment in the rebirth of the book. Without her this handsome volume would not exist.

I also feel very proud to have Alan Davidson's support so explicitly in his Foreword. As well as being an inspiration to me throughout my writing years, Alan has also been a generous and warm presence.

The rather glamorous photograph on the back cover is totally owed to the alchemist's qualities that my friend Anthony Blake bestows to his art.

My knowledge on culinary matters in ancient Greece is owed completely to three people. First to Aspasia Miha-Lambaki in Athens for her wonderfully comprehensive book *The Diet of the Ancient Greeks* which opened totally new horizons for me, and subsequently to two classicist friends in London, John Wilkins and Andrew Dalby.

Ten years on and revising *Greek Food* has made me realise the great change that has swept through eating patterns in the West, not only in the appreciation of the so-called Mediterranean diet but also in the availability of ingredients. However, the biggest change accounts for the rehabilitation of olive oil, now considered a healthy and desirable prerequisite to our diet. Notions of 'oiliness' do not arise as people's palates are becoming accustomed to the liquid gold of the Mediterranean. Bread dipped in olive oil and sprinkled with herbs, which we as children used to eat for snacks, is now *de rigueur* in trendy restaurants.

Fresh vegetables, salad greens and herbs are now all easily available throughout the year – rocket, dill, fresh peas, courgettes, olives of all kinds, wonderful olive oils and *fyllo* pastry are all there. As is a wider variety of fish and seafood such as squid, cuttlefish, John Dory and even occasionally scorpion fish and fresh anchovies. Free-range chicken is also a great improvement on the characterless birds of the late 1970s.

Changes have also happened in Greece itself – and not always for the best. A number of the old Athenian establishments mentioned in this book have now closed down – for instance, places such as the famous bar Orfanidis in Panepistimiou Street and the old Doris in Praxitelous Street where we used to go for delicious *loukoumathes*. Half of the wonderful *zaharoplastia* (cake shops) around Kolonaki Square have been eclipsed by shoe shops. (Greeks – including myself – are passionate about shoes, like centipedes.) However, some excellent, new food haunts have been added to the Athenian scene, such as the Fresh cake shop off Kolonaki Square, and restaurants such as Vlassis in Armatolon & Klefton Street, Lykavittos, in the winter, Symposio in Erehthiou Street, and Irodio in Propylaion & Agelikara Street in the summer, both these latter in close proximity to the Akropolis. The main markets and street markets are in full swing as always.

Most importantly, however, the Greek culinary spirit has remained unfaltering and the Greeks are as passionate about their food as ever. Distance or labour are no obstacles to them when embarking on a quest for culinary gratification. Theirs is a constant journey in search of a culinary Ithaca.

Rena Salaman
November 1993

Foreword

For a former classical scholar such as myself there is just one answer to the question, where did it all begin? Whether 'it' is the philosophy, sculpture, literature, or cookery of Europe, the answer has to be: Greece of classical times.

Rome and its empire, themselves so permeated by Greek culture, served but to fortify this line of descent; the Dark Ages cast no more than a partial veil over it, dissipated in mediaeval times so that the bright light of the Renaissance could illuminate and reaffirm it for all of us who have come after.

So, for European food and cookery and the manner in which they are embedded in European culture, the basic reference work should be Greek? Yes, I would have replied a dozen years ago, but the work does not exist – compilations of recipes, Greek or English, I have, but nothing which treats the subject in all its aspects, nothing which does justice to its Numero Uno status.

Then, suddenly, when Rena Salaman's book came out as a paperback in 1983, the rectangular void on shelf 1 of bookcase A was at last occupied. How one rejoiced! And yet...I knew that parts of the book had been trimmed by editorial shears; and I could feel that the paper would soon grow brittle and start to brown, and that with frequent handling the unstitched binding would come apart.

The reappearance of the book, in more handsome and permanent form, with the 'cuts' restored – and these include vital material on herbs and cakes – is therefore a cause for even better, because unqualified, rejoicing. Ignite the fireworks, let them soar over the hillside where the author gathers her thyme, and over the Athenian markets which she so vividly and evocatively describes.

Alan Davidson
1993

Introduction

Whoever does not wish to see Athens, is foolish; he who sees it and is not pleased with it, is more foolish; but the climax of folly is to have seen it, to be pleased with it, and yet to leave it.

('Ancient Author', from Modern Greece, Henry Baird, New York, 1856, p. 13.)

You can sense a special intimate nostalgia when expatriates talk about their national food. This is particularly true of Greeks who cling to their traditions and to their food. One may ask a simple question, about a herb that goes into a particular dish, for example, and immediately a whole world unfolds. The eyes sparkle, the faces become animated, the hands gesticulate, the memory flows and the story begins. The enthusiasm is often not restricted to the dish in question but will extend to other dishes that traditionally are served together, the particular qualities of the ingredients, the customs attached to the setting of the table and, more important, traditions. A thousand and one details unfold; a journey into the past, a nostalgic search, very often back into one's childhood, where memories seem to imprint more colourful impressions, where parental associations drift in and out of the image and a whole world is intimately reconstructed – a world where everything is brighter, colours more vivid, the taste of dishes more tantalizing, and their spices and smells sharper and infinitely more aromatic.

Food is a strong factor for causing sentimentality. I, like other Greeks living in London, experience homesickness for our neighbourhood *koutouki* (a small, normally very cheap, homely *taverna*), and its basic simple dishes that one would associate with a proper *koutouki*, such as *fasolatha* (thick haricot bean soup), or *revithia* (chick pea soup), or cummin-scented *soutzoukakia* (meat rissoles highly spiced with garlic and cummin), or even the luxury of a *yiouvetsi* (lamb roasted with fresh tomatoes and pasta). And inevitably one misses the things that go with these dishes: the weather, the brilliant light, the colours, the Mediterranean, the beautiful jasmine-scented evenings ...

Greek food abroad can evoke such images. But, alas, judging by the majority of Greek restaurants in London there must be the widespread view of the whole Greek nation surviving on kebabs and salad or, to be more precise, on small pieces of dried-up, overcooked meat, usually pork – which would be unheard of in Greece – served on a bed of miserable cabbage salad! It is a strange thing, with almost a million British holiday-makers visiting Greece every year and with a remarkable increase in the numbers and popularity of Greek restaurants in Britain, that real Greek cooking is still almost completely unknown in this country. In fact, as the experience of tourists in Greece will confirm, Greek cooking is not easy for the tourist to find even in Greece. A strange, highly limited form of 'internationalized' Greek cuisine has emerged which is composed of such specialities as kebabs, more kebabs and maybe, if one is lucky, a selection of *meze* – starters such as *taramosalata*, *tzatziki* and *melitzanosalata*, an aubergine purée – and it bears little resemblance to the ways we cook at home in Greece. What has happened to Greek restaurants in this country is a result of this vicious circle: restaurateurs offer a bowdlerized, simpli-fied and enormously restricted selection of dishes because they think that is what the customers expect. After all they eat it. The customers on the other hand accept this menu because they think it constitutes real Greek food. Sometimes it becomes obvious that the cook is not even Greek, as I found when I was served *dolmathes* (stuffed vine leaves) in a well-known Greek restaurant in Camden High Street. These were covered in a dubi-ous, watery, tomato sauce and with tomato purée in their stuffing – a sac-rilege to a Greek! *Dolmathes* are always made with lemon, and either they are served with *avgolemono* (an egg and lemon sauce) or alone, but never with tomatoes. And to crown it all they were served on a bed of boiled, cracked wheat! An Arab influence in the kitchen of this particular restau-rant perhaps?

This book is an effort to awaken the potential enthusiasts to the delights of a cuisine which they have, as yet, only sampled. By explaining the various dishes carefully and simply I have tried to make the essential-ly simple Greek cuisine as straightforward as possible, so that even the results of a newcomer must be successful.

HEALTHY ASPECTS

In the west we are increasingly conscious of the way in which our bodies can be poisoned by the foods we eat. Our reliance upon processed food, food with added preservatives and other chemicals, dairy products, ani-mal fats and excessive quantities of meat, have all been shown in their dif-ferent ways to be responsible for specific digestive and circulatory disorders, which are becoming more and more common. Greek cuisine, on the other hand, as well as being delicious, is one of the healthiest, as it never employs processed and canned foods, relies enormously on season-al vegetables and, in the winter, on pulses. It does not make use of animal fats, but on the best olive oil, since Greece is one of the major producers of high quality olive oil. And while it uses some limited quantities of meat, it relies more on fish and enormous quantities of fresh vegetables and lemons – my husband is still surprised at the number of lemons we buy in the market every week – and a lot of fresh salads, spring onions, radishes, etc. The way we cook our vegetables is also more nutritious; they are almost never boiled – which destroys their best nutritive qualities – but are cooked in very little water with olive oil and various sauces. Our treatment of vegetables is altogether different and it produces exciting and delicious wholly vegetarian dishes – try artichokes and broad beans together, or fresh peas in tomato sauce, or spinach with fried onion, or a pilau with leeks. For the health-food-oriented, the vegetarian, or even those simply concerned to eat more healthily, this is the moment to discover the joys of the cooking of Greece.

CULTURAL CONTEXT

Cooking and food are very important to Greeks. Of course, in a minimal way, food is important to everyone. But as we know, the value that is attached to this necessary activity, the time that people are prepared to devote to it and the significance they place on *enjoying it*, vary enormously. For the Greeks, food is a constant physical reminder of who they are and where they come from. Cooking for Greeks, at least until very recently, was, at the same time, highly prescribed but hardly at all written down. It was prescribed because Greek cooking, despite its eternal variety of ingredients, procedures and so on, was a finite and known system. Everyone knew the dishes; everyone knew or claimed to know how they were prepared and cooked; everyone knew how they varied with season, religious calendar, family occasion; everyone knew which dishes accompanied each other. Everybody in short knew the rules: there was little room for choice, for cooking followed the seasons, the time of the year and so on. Thus, the Greek cuisine represented, and still represents, a major element of the Greek's identity: a shared world. As such, there was hardly any need for it to be written down. Recipes were passed down from mother to daughter, or more commonly from grandmother to granddaughter, in a practical way ... over a hot stove. Dishes that represented something new, a regional variation perhaps, would be discussed by the women over a small cup of black coffee. Cookery books were not known and hardly existed in Athens until the early 1960s, but even then were hardly used.

Greek cooking, not surprisingly in view of Greek history and geography, has given and has taken a lot of influences to and from other countries – there are strong Middle Eastern, Turkish and even Italian leanings. But the main influence on Greek cuisine has been the country's rural peasant background. Greek cooking is not aristocratic; it reflects not the European tastes of the élite, nor their metropolitan preferences, but the traditions and resources of a rural people. Greek cooking is the people's: simple and straightforward.

THE STREET VENDORS

All aspects of food are important to a Greek: the planning, shopping, preparation, cooking and, of course, eating. It is very noticeable that in Greece all these things, while the responsibility of each family, are done in a sense collectively. I can remember as a child how the shopping and even preparation were shared activities. The various vendors with their loaded, donkey-driven carts would miraculously appear in the neighbourhood at a specific time, each one singing the praise of the goods he had that day, at the top of his voice. First and most important, the vegetable and fruit man, who in a few minutes would have all the women of the neighbourhood swarming and dancing like bees around his cart, testing and handling vegetables, consulting each other, often criticizing the vendor quite openly for some sad and droopy vegetables that he had the temerity to exhibit among his colourful goods. Remarks like: 'This is fit for your donkey to eat', or even more severe: 'Why don't you throw this into the sea?', would be made to the general amusement of the female party. The older the women, the more outspoken they would be. Finally each one would retreat back to her own house carrying in her apron the prospective meal of the day, having socialized in quite a big way and, of course, having made plans about who was to help whom that day. Peas to be podded, green beans to be topped and tailed, okra to be cleaned, and artichokes and broad beans to be shelled would be the most deserving cases as kilos and kilos were required to feed the large families and extra helping hands were very welcome.

In the winter and the spring there was a particular lady who came around with huge baskets loaded on either side of her donkey selling wild, hand-picked greens (*agria horta ke radikia tou vounou*) from the nearby mountains around Athens. These would sometimes resemble dandelions, or in the spring she would have *vrouves*, a tiny plant that grows in the fields and eventually bursts into tiny yellow flowers. You are supposed to pick them just before they flower, and they must be boiled, drained and then dressed with olive oil and lemon. These have quite a sharp acid-bitter taste and they were highly regarded by the adults but not by us children. They would always be accompanied by fried squid or fried *marida*, a delicious small fish resembling whitebait, and together these would constitute a full meal.

Then the fishmonger would announce himself in his hoarse voice from miles away, carrying his huge, shallow, flat basket on his head and singing: '*Maritha tou Falirou spartaristi*', meaning 'Alive and jumping whitebait from Faliro', Faliro being the beautiful bay just round the corner from Piraeus which was not yet polluted. No one in their proper senses would eat anything that came from Faliro nowadays ...

At about lunchtime and again in the early afternoon in spring and summer the ice-cream vendor would come pushing his white contraption. For a small coin, not only would he give us a cone filled with his delicious homemade ice-cream but also recite a little poem containing the child's name and make some funny remark about a well-shaven boy's head to make him blush or about a little girl's dark brown eyes that are driving boys crazy, or a beautiful brand new pair of shoes that a child would proudly wear. He was the most successful ice-cream seller that I have ever known. Then, in the early evening the yoghurt seller would appear, carrying a long round stick on his shoulders, with ropes about a metre long hanging down on either side, and at the end of these ropes balancing wonderfully, two large round shallow earthenware pots (*yiouvetsi*), full of his homemade yoghurt. He would sell it by cutting out a piece and weighing it. When he stopped he would bend his legs forward, until the *yiouvetsi* reached the ground, where he would rest them, then he would take the stick off his shoulders, rest it on the ground and he would proceed to conduct his business. I always thought there was something melancholic about his voice and his appearance; perhaps his shadow in the dusk and his serious moustached face, unlike the other light-hearted sellers of the daytime, made this particular impression on our childhood.

Lastly, the milkman would come in the evening with huge aluminium containers on the back of his mule-driven cart. One had the choice of either cow's milk or goat's milk, all milked by hand from his own small farm two or three miles away. This fresh milk had to be boiled to kill any possible bacteria. I can still remember our milkman coming round at his precise time daily, even Sundays, since fridges were very rare then, until about 1965. Of course, by then his mule had been replaced by an old and tired-looking motorcycle, and finally he was replaced altogether by pasteurized milk. Yet another sacrifice to civilization ...

The neighbourhood was dotted by tiny grocer shops run by families in the front rooms of their houses. They would all sell on credit or by weekly instalments and sometimes they would extend credit for months to a family whose father was out of work so that his family could at least obtain their staples like pulses, rice and olive oil and survive the catastrophe until a job was found. However, jobs were hard to find in the 1950s, people were suffering from the aftermath of the long German occupation and from the ravages of the civil war which did not end until 1949.

Butcher's shops existed, but not in abundance since they were not often needed. Meat would be eaten rarely, on Sundays and perhaps once more in the week, but even then it would probably be mince. In any case, if a special occasion called for it, a family celebration perhaps or a religious festive day, then one would venture a trip to the big, nearby market in Piraeus, between the main harbour on one side and the railway station on the other, or the wonderful central market in Athens, running parallel on either side of Athinas Street almost all the way from Omonia Square and ending at Monastiraki at the far end. Unfortunately the market in Piraeus was bulldozed over as it was declared unsightly but all the old-fashioned shops remain in the area, still effusing a sharp, slightly mothball-like aroma which one can nostalgically sense in the atmosphere.

Luckily, the central market in Athens has survived almost intact to this day. Meat displayed on marble slabs can be poked and sniffed and argued about by the potential customer. In fact it does not sound very different from the bazaar of 1855 as described humorously by Edmond About. Nor is there much difference in the importance that the Greeks then and now attach to their everyday shopping, illustriously incongruous when done in a glib supermarket in the west:

> The bazaar is perhaps the most frequented part of the town. In the morning, all the people of the town, of whatever rank, go themselves to market. If you wish to see a senator carrying kidneys in one hand, and salad in the other, go to the bazaar at eight in the morning. The maid-servants of Landernau will never be able to gossip so unceasingly as these right honourables making their bargains. They walk from shop to shop, getting information as to the price of apples and onions, or giving an account of their vote the day before to some money-changer, who stops them as they go by. The money-changer has, as formerly, his shop in the market-place. The ancients called him *trapezitis* – the man with the table. He has changed neither his name nor his occupation nor his table, since the days of Aristophanes ... (E.F.V. About, *Greece and the Greeks of the Present Day*, 1855, pp. 280–1.)

In fact he had changed none until the late 1950s, and I have a very clear picture of the same *trapezites*, with their small tables in the streets surrounding the Athens market and particularly round the Plateia Kotzia, the square where the old central post office used to be. I remember going there as a child in the late 1940s and early 1950s, with my mother, in order to change some very exotic-looking notes with foreign writing on them.

We would walk hand-in-hand, from money-changer to money-changer, trying to get an improvement on the ludicrous rate already quoted for our Turkish liras that my grandfather occasionally sent to us from Constantinople.

Back to About's bazaar:

> At eight o'clock in the evening, in summer, the bazaar has really an enchanted aspect. It is the hour when the workmen, the servants, the soldiers, come to buy their provisions for supper. The more dainty divide among seven or eight a sheep's head for sixpence; the frugal men buy a slice of watermelon, or a large cucumber, which they bite at, like an apple. The shopkeepers, from the midst of their vegetables and their fruits, call the buyers with loud cries; large lamps, full of olive oil, throw a fine red light on the heaps of figs, pomegranates, melons and grapes. In this confusion, all these things appear brilliant; discordant sounds become harmonious; you do not perceive that you are paddling in black mud and hardly smell the nauseous odours with which the bazaar is infected. (About, p. 281.)

About was quite sharp in his opinions on Greece and the Greeks of 1855, and when his book was published it caused quite a stir among the Philellenes in the western world; but many of his remarks are humorous and apt.

One can still easily recognize the modern *agora* (market-place) in Athens, now lacking the 'black mud' and the 'nauseous odours' in his description. In fact, if you do not mind the blood-dripping carcasses, then behind them and among the sheep's heads, you can find two wonderfully colourful restaurants bustling with noise and huge steaming pots. This is where the market people and particularly the butchers go for their lunch and their substantial very early 'breakfast'; Sideris, one of the restaurants, opens at one in the morning with traditional, rough and nourishing soups, such as *patsas* – tripe soup – and beef knuckle soup, for late partygoers or early-market workers, and stays open all day.

All the contents of the pots can be inspected as one goes through the entrance where they are steaming on top of the black old-fashioned range, frying or grilling, with the large sweaty cook presiding right behind them. It is here that one may find a genuine *stifatho* – tender pieces of beef cooked with quantities of small and sweet onions; a *yiouvetsi* – lamb cooked with pasta and fresh tomatoes in the oven; or a plate of green *horta* or *vlita*, according to the season, dressed with olive oil and lemon; or such genuine treats like crispy fried *gavros* – slim, silvery, fresh anchovies, a deliciously appetizing addition to our lunches at home, unfortunately too cheap and humble to make it to the more genteel restaurants of the city. In the same restaurants, as indeed in other restaurants in Greece, one will probably see overcooked spaghetti and rice being served; these are to be avoided as they are regarded as 'soft' food for those with ailing teeth and gaping elderly mouths and as a result they are invariably overcooked for the benefit of their special clientele.

Retsina wine comes to the table from the barrels like in the old days, in the special measures – copper containers of a *katostaraki* – almost two glasses, or half a kilo. For those who are unfamiliar with *retsina* William Miller describes how the Bavarian royal court, who had installed themselves in Greece in the late nineteenth century, used to serve resinated wine in their palace, 'to the unsuspecting "European" visitor, who fancies at the first draught, that he has swallowed a dose of furniture polish by mistake.' (W. Miller, *Greek Life in Town and Country*, London 1905, p. 298.) With this in mind, be cautious until you establish a taste for it.

But the most exciting place for us, the children, was the fish market, contained and surrounded by the meat market. Ferocious-looking octopus, long-beaked *zarganes* (garfish), or huge shell-cupped *pinnes* (fan mussels), smelling amazingly strongly of iodine, would make our childish spines shiver. On the other hand we would be amused and delighted by silver-threaded *gavros* (anchovies), by tiny brown *maritha* (young picarel), by glistening pink *barbounia* (red mullet) and by various severe or innocent-looking fish that we would try to relate to similar-looking friends, relatives or even teachers and giggle behind our mother's back. It is still a treat for me to visit the fish market in Athens, though sadly it now contains quite a lot of frozen blocks of fish from Japan or the African coast and most of the shellfish have disappeared due to the pollution in Saronikos bay. We are lucky enough though to be able to get an abundance of beautiful fresh fish and huge but tender and succulent squid in our island in the summer.

It was a treat to be taken on these special trips to the central market in Athens by our mother, but it was a bigger treat that awaited us at the end of the shopping expedition. Then we would be taken to what looked like a very grand building, a *zaharoplastio* (a sweet pastry shop), with high corniced ceilings and heavy cast iron small tables with cool white marble tops. It was called Krinos (the Lily), and its speciality was hot *loukoumades* (a doughy, puffed, rounded pastry ball immersed in boiling hot oil, covered in wonderful scented honey and sprinkled with cinnamon). Krinos is still to be found in its original building in Aiolou Street, round the corner from the old central post office, rather decaying in its grandeur but still busy serving wonderful *loukoumades* to us and other enthusiasts.

Or sometimes we would venture slightly further into Praxitelous Street to the old Doris shop, a similar kind of establishment which served in its old-fashioned style, apart from *loukoumades*, really wholesome, thick and rich-tasting farm yoghurt with or without the inevitable Attika honey on top. Or we would walk down Evripithou Street on the other side of the meat market, crossing the main Athinas Street, and pay visits to dark, strange basement shops with hundreds of herbs and tisanes, piled in baskets and hessian sacks all intermingling their strong aromas, with strange little tags explaining the remedial qualities of each one: chamomile and *frascomilo* (a wild sage) for the stomach and insomnia, something different for the pile sufferer, something else for the kidney and gallstone sufferer, and so on. Despite the recent widespread use of antibiotics, a lot of people in Greece still believe and practise these herbal remedies and shops of the same kind are still to be found in the same street.

Of course, the mobile donkey-carted vendors have long disappeared but in their place another colourful custom has emerged: the mobile fruit-vegetable-groceries street market – *laiki*, as it is called, meaning the popular market or the people's market. These *laikes* move daily to different neighbourhoods, to pre-specified streets, of course. There, mostly spread on rugs on the ground, mountains of the freshest seasonal vegetables, fresh herbs, fruit, and even nursery seedlings and plants for the garden are exhibited. Further down will be various assortments of olives – always present at a Greek's table – olive oil, eggs, pulses and even toiletries. A lot of the growers themselves bring their own produce down from nearby provinces. In the spring there are always firm and tight-looking globe artichokes of both varieties, green as well as purple, from Corinth and Loutraki, fresh spinach and *vlita* (another kind of greens with an earthy crunchy taste) from Megara, and so on. In the summer there are every shade of purple and all shapes of *melitzanes* (aubergines) as well as the famous sweet melons from Argos. This kind of market takes place throughout the year in all the suburbs of Athens and Piraeus but also right in the middle of Athens wherever there are residential districts. It even takes place in middle-class strongholds in Athens such as Kolonaki, where one can find the folkloric jumble assembled along Xenokratous Street on Fridays.

So, each household has the choice of at least three street markets per week in the vicinity to shop and socialize in, for, of course, trips are still organized in little groups of friends and relatives in the neighbourhood.

RITUAL AND FOLKLORE

Once the food is cooked it is customary for neighbours to exchange small samples. So, one will see small or, more often, large plates of some speciality of a particular household being taken to a neighbour or a relative.

In a shy but obviously pleased manner the giver will claim that it is only a very small *meze*, or sometimes the giver will claim apologetically that since the aroma of her frying must have been, as we say, 'piercing the neighbour's nostrils', to take a small sample is the least she could do. So, back and forth go the plates of *keftedes* (fried, herby hamburgers) or aromatic *soutzoukakia* (cummin-scented meat rissoles in tomato sauce) or *skorthalia* (a kind of garlic paste or sauce) with fried young marrows or fried salted cod, or a couple of pieces of spinach and cheese pie.

In fact there is an even stronger belief attached to the custom of cooking smells. If a pregnant woman ever smells any food, it is essential that she be given a taste of it if she is not to miscarry. So, neighbours will be even more liberal and justified in their *meze*-giving to the household of the pregnant lady. But if the smell has not come from the immediate neighbourhood, the pregnant woman has the right to go in search of it, virtually sniffing all the way to the culprit's door, then knocking and demanding some. Of course, she will be received with great reverence and hospitality and she will receive endless but humble and well-meaning, sincere apologies for not offering her some initially. But what if the smell cannot be traced? Do not despair! There is a remedy if this problem arises. The remedy is an octopus dried in the sun and hung by an external door. A piece is cut and scorched over a flame at the end of a fork, then munched by the pregnant lady. I can still smell its overpowering aroma lingering from the past, when my grandmother was performing this ritual for my mother just before my youngest sister was born. I suppose that the overpowering smell and taste of the octopus is meant to kill any other possible craving and thus prevent a miscarriage.

SECRETS OF THE BAKER'S OVEN

Until the early 1960s most Greek homes had quite primitive means of cooking. Small Primus stoves were the usual thing in the cities and even today the corner hearth is in full use in most village dwellings. So, baking at home in the cities was impossible. The answer to the baking problem can still be seen being acted out any day in any Greek town and village big enough to have a baker's shop: by paying a few pence, people can have their dishes cooked in the baker's oven with the bread. Twice a day, in any neighbourhood, you can see people walking to and from the baker's carrying enormous shallow aluminium dishes either round or oblong, filled with stuffed tomatoes and peppers, or roast lamb and potatoes, or a cheese and spinach pie and other delights. On delivery, in the morning, the family's name will be scribbled on the container and a time for collection will be assigned, usually between noon and 2 p.m. If one is cooking a *yiou-*

vetsi which requires the addition of pasta at some stage during the cooking, then a packet of pasta will be taken along to the baker's and he will add it to the dish at the required time as well as water, salt and pepper. Apart from saving on electricity, this is a wonderful way to do one's cooking and be able completely to forget about it!

Very often, to this day, we will deliver our dish early in the morning, then go off swimming and at lunchtime collect it on our way back home. I still find walking into a baker's, particularly on a Sunday lunchtime, a wonderful experience. There one can see the colourful spread of innumerable dishes waiting for collection, while the warm air is filled with the cooking aromas mixed with the familiar homely smell of the freshly baked bread. Of course, the baker needs to test and try some dishes in order to check on their cooking progress! My grandmother was always convinced that the prime piece would end up on the baker's table and that if we were to drop by his home on a Sunday lunch, we would find a Lucullian spread made out of all the varying dishes of his customers! The temptation is hard to suppress even for me, let alone the baker ...

Almost every urban household now possesses an electric cooker, but these are very often exhibited in the kitchen as prize pieces while people cook on camping-gas stoves – for possessing an electric cooker is a status symbol. One has to show that one can afford it, but actually using it is a completely different matter! First, electricity has always been very expensive in Greece. Secondly, there is still some doubt about the taste of things cooked with electricity; but thirdly and most importantly our roots are stronger than we realize. My mother has covered her electric cooker with one of her prettiest and frilliest dainty handmade linens and there it stands: a shrine to modernity!

Peasant households and village communities still cook and bake in the corner hearth. Very often they build a clay, beehive-shaped contraption in the yard for summer cooking when it can get too hot for cooking indoors. These ovens work by lighting a pile of dried sticks inside which produce an intense heat. After about half an hour, when the clay has got really hot, the embers are scraped out and the dish is put inside, while the embers are kept burning just outside the semi-circular opening. In the island where we live in the summer, the women have even got a rota system whereby three or four families get together and bake their bread in a communal oven twice a week.

HOSPITALITY

One of the delights and surprises that awaits the visitor to Greece is the discovery of Greek hospitality. Even the eccentric Scot William Lithgow, travelling to Greece in the early seventeenth century, could not but comment on the hospitality he was given: 'For these Athenians or Greeks, exceeding kindly banqueted me four days, and furnished me with necessary provision for my voyage to Creta; and also transported me by sea in a brigandino freely, and on their own charges to Serigo, being forty-four miles distant.' (William Lithgow, *Travels and Voyages Through Europe, Asia and Africa for Nineteen Years*, 1797, p. 64.)

Greeks are hospitable by nature; they are open and friendly, and find it hard to treat people as strangers – even when they are strangers. There is nothing secretive about any aspect of a Greek's life, from the food they eat daily to the vote they cast every four years for their favourite political party. Indeed, discussion, quite often heated, is a way of life, a way of entertainment. Every afternoon one will see small groups of people sitting outside their houses talking and drinking small cups of black coffee. More people will join the group in the course of the afternoon, sometimes bringing their own stools or chairs to the small assembly, while others fall out. In the early evening *ouzo* or *tsipouro* (homemade spirit from fermented grape skins after they have been pressed for wine) will be offered to the men, perhaps with a small plate of olives, slices of cucumber or some white feta cheese, while the women may have soft drinks. During the course of the evening, some of the men may decide to take a stroll to their local *kafenion*, where groups of men only can be seen sitting round small tables having a drink and joining in the discussion or concentrating on a game of backgammon. No matter how many people fall in and out of the group, the small nucleus will be kept alive and going until late in the night.

In the winter, friends and neighbours will drop by for a chat, always without any prearranged invitations, and the rules of hospitality that are felt so strongly in Greece demand that they be offered a small coffee (*ena kafedaki*), at least. If you happen to drop by at the time that the family is having their meal, it will be difficult not to join in, as people push their chairs out of the way, making space for the visitor and an extra plate and glass are immediately brought to the table. It makes no difference what kind of food they are having; it may just be 'bread and olives' as the saying goes in Greece, but they would still like you to share it with them and their pride would be hurt if one tried not to. Henry Miller said: 'Charity, generosity, kindness, sympathy, spontaneity, are virtues which the Greeks as a whole possess to a high degree.' Well, when it comes to sharing a Greek's food you will find these virtues in abundant supply.

If visitors are expected for a meal a lot of excitement prevails in its planning and preparation. Only the best is considered. This is not the time to make do; to cut corners, to serve that wine left over from last week. On the contrary, the family may skimp on their meals throughout the week, perhaps have one extra vegetable soup, in order to enrich their table with only the choicest dishes and best cuts of meat for their visitor's table. And everything will be in abundance, for it would be regarded a humiliation if they were to be caught short of something. Those bottles of wine will come out, even that treasured bottle of *prephylloxera* wine could not find a better occasion! This is the time for display. The greater the hospitality, the greater the honour to both the householder as well as the visitor. At the receiving end, it may be an old friend or a new one, a Greek or a foreigner, it makes no difference. Once you are identified as a guest you will be showered with hospitality, almost aggressively. And most importantly, there are never expectations of reciprocity. In fact, they rather you didn't try to reciprocate, since to do so diminishes the original gesture.

Greek table manners rely on demonstration of enjoyment, on giving, on sociability: people offer each other choice bits at the end of their forks or with their fingers, they serve each other wine, they toast each other continuously; and as the hours pass and more wine is consumed, the toasts will become more humorous and exuberant, the level of noise will rise, songs will be sung and the whole neighbourhood will know you are having a party. Celebratory meals can go on for hours, people are not expected to eat and then get up for the table to be cleared; and if spirits are high enough one meal will sometimes extend to include the next.

When Greeks eat together, their behaviour celebrates what it is they share: an extravagant generosity, a highly developed sense of honour – the famous *philotimo* – an impatience with the formal or the bureaucratic, an enthusiasm for the direct, the personal, the emotional.

CELEBRATORY MEALS

For Greeks there are the usual family occasions which require celebration and communal eating: engagements, weddings, namedays, the birth of a child, particularly the first born (and particularly when it's a boy!). But apart from these there are also a considerable number of regular, annual, prescribed feasts, with a religious, and sometimes a markedly pre-Christian, origin: Easter, New Year's Eve and New Year's Day, *Kathari Deftera* (literally 'Clean Monday'), the First of May, the Fifteenth of August (the Virgin Mary's Day) or *Panagia*, Ascension Day and various saints' days. On the islands and in the country, the saints' days are taken particularly seriously. Different places tend to value different saints. In Alonnisos, the island which we visit every summer, the day of the prophet Elia is a major occasion for the community.

The most important of all these, throughout Greece, is Lent, starting with the celebrations of *Kathari Deftera*, to mark the beginning of Lent, and ending with the religious celebrations of Easter week, which reach their climax on Easter Sunday. Lent is an important religious period in

Greece. It has a traditional pattern of diet. Its main feature is a stress on abstention from all animal products – meat, butter, cheese, eggs and even milk – on certain days of each week and for the whole of Easter week. The Lent diet is recognized by many people as a wise way of giving the human system a rest from rich and cholesterol-loaded foods. In many ways this is a celebration of vegetarianism before the movement or even the word was conceived. A vegetarian festival, called for by the Gospels!

Kathari Deftera is traditionally always celebrated in the open air, ideally in the open countryside, but if not then in any small garden. Every vehicle will be mobilized. In the 1950s and early 1960s even the donkey-driven carts could be seen, packed with people and provisions, leaving Athens for the nearest open countryside. Nowadays, every car will set off, packed with friends and relatives. At the other end, colourful tablecloths will be spread on the grass, among the wild flowers, or tables will come out in small gardens, and the various traditional dishes will be unpacked: *taramosalata*, or even *tarama*, which people sometimes spread on slices of bread with some lemon squeezed on it; spring onions, and fresh green garlic, mixed pickles, olives of every variety, green, black, purple or brown, in abundance; lettuce leaves, red radishes, fresh shellfish, particularly *ahinous* (shiny black-purply sea urchins) and the most wonderful of all, delicious sea-tasting *kidonia* (sea quinces), boiled shrimps, perhaps dressed with the best-tasting olive oil, some boiled octopus dressed with olive oil and a little vinegar; and delicious shiny green *dolmadakia* (small stuffed vine leaves, vegetarian for the occasion, stuffed with rice, spring onions and a lot of dill and cooked in olive oil). I can remember in the 1950s, driving out of Athens on *Kathari Deftera*, one could see along the coastal roads fishermen with huge baskets wrapped around with seaweed, selling their freshly caught shellfish and shrimps or waving octopus at the passing cars, trying to attract attention. For the more affluent there would be *brique* (a kind of cheap red caviar) and for the rich there would be *avgotaraho apo to Messolonghi* (botargo, salted and pressed roes of the grey mullet, resembling two sausages stuck side by side and coated in a thick layer of beeswax for preserving purposes). Messolonghi, on the west coast of Greece, is famed for its *avgotaraho*.

But the most traditional hallmark of *Kathari Deftera* is the special unleavened flat bread which is covered with roasted sesame seeds, the *lagana* as it is called, and which is only produced on this one day of the year. The *laganes* would fill the houses with their nutty hot smell as people rushed to the local baker's early in the morning in order to get it hot as it came out of the oven and ensure that they had enough for the day before the baker ran out of it. I can still remember being wakened early in the morning by its unmistakable aroma mingling with my dreams, as my grandmother would have already been to the baker's by seven o'clock.

The other ritualistic feature of *Kathari Deftera* is the kite-flying. Every family will fly at least one colourful kite, in order to keep with the custom of the day. Greeks, being extremely superstitious, believe that keeping the tradition is for the welfare of the family. '*Yia to kalo tis meras,*' as they say, which, loosely translated, means 'for the happy outcome of the occasion'. The children would put a lot of thought into planning the kite-making, and buying the materials. Excitedly they would work away for weeks in advance, sometimes with some help from the adults. Whose kite was going to be the most unusual shape or colour? Or, most important, fly highest and be admired most? The result was a wonderfully coloured dotted sky, resembling a vast outdoor artistic exhibition.

And the people will nibble all day, filling their glasses with wine and toasting each other continuously with '*Kali Saracosti ke Kalo Pascha*' ('Have a good Lent and a happy Easter').

Lent, of course, with its fasting and churchgoing, is a build-up for the major occasion of Easter. Each household reaches an almost frenzied level of activity in preparation for Easter Sunday and the first celebratory meal after the week's fasting, which takes place after the midnight liturgy on Saturday night celebrating the resurrection of Christ. Various shapes of *koulouria* (small cakes of the shortbread variety) will be made during Easter week and sent to the local baker's in huge, flat, shallow dishes which are lent out by the baker. Always there will be some made specially for the children in the shape of rabbits or hens or fish, with shiny bright red eggs stuck in the middle of their tummies. These hardboiled and dyed red eggs are traditionally prepared on Good Friday, but they should never be touched before Saturday midnight.

On Easter Saturday, we would walk to our local church, St George's, with our next-door neighbours, in time to find a good place in the square in front of the church, so that we could watch the celebratory liturgy at midnight. Everyone carried a white candle, plain for the adults, but particularly large and pretty fluted ones, with large pink and white or gold-threaded ribbons tied in bows around the top of the candles, for the children. Everyone also had a red egg in their pockets, specially selected from among the pyramid of red hardboiled eggs at home.

A little before midnight, the assembly of richly gold-draped priests and their faithful congregation would come out to celebrate the Resurrection in the open air. The first words of *Hristos Anesti* (Christ has risen) would be sung by the priests in the warm spring night on the specially erected wooden platform in the middle of the square. At midnight, the bells of the church would join in a pandemonium of excitement. Everyone would start singing, fireworks would be lit, people would light their candles from each other's (the original light having come from the special candles of the priests on the platform), friends and relatives hugged and kissed each other on both cheeks and finally cracked each other's eggs and eat them. Everybody would then walk home in small groups, carefully carrying their lit candles, and before entering the house the head of the family would mark the sign of the cross on the lintel of the front door with the flame of the candle which would leave a smoked mark of a cross.

My grandmother would always stay behind, fussing about her cooking and having everything ready for our arrival. The table would have been prepared, covered with the best white linen tablecloth, and on it a small feast would have been laid: various *meze*, to be followed by a traditional soup called *mayiritsa*, made by boiling the cleaned intestines of the young spring lamb and adding to it a large quantity of fried spring onions and dill and a few small fried pieces of the liver. This would have an *avgole-mono* (egg and lemon) sauce added to it at the last minute, just before it was served. *Mayiritsa* would be followed by plates of freshly fried liver and lights, as well as the heart of the lamb, and large bowls of salad, with thinly shredded cos lettuce, spring onions and dill, dressed with olive oil and lemon.

One can imagine what wonderful moments these were for the children! The whole colourful ritual would be awaited, talked about and dreamed of for the rest of the year. This is the evening I missed most when I left Greece.

On Easter Sunday, every family with a small garden or patio would roast a young lamb outdoors. In and around Athens, of course, with most people living in flats, that has become impossible for many people nowadays, but they still drive out to a friend's or relative's house with a garden to celebrate, roasting two or even three lambs sometimes. We used to buy our lamb alive at the beginning of Easter week. I remember going to Piraeus, where, by the *gefyra* (railway bridge), the shepherds used to bring their flocks for sale. Lambs and more lambs marked with a stripe of various colours, so that each vendor could distinguish his animals, were creating havoc with their noise in this impromptu market. Then the lamb would be slaughtered on the Thursday by some dexterous neighbour and it would be hung until Easter Sunday. A charcoal fire would be started early in the morning and the lamb would be roasted slowly by being turned almost continuously over it and sprinkled with hand-picked mountain herbs. Once you try a young spring lamb cooked in this manner, lamb will never taste the same again.

I remember at least on one occasion, spirits being particularly high, my father insisting that we should all eat the roasted lamb like the ancient Greeks used to do. Of course he wasn't claiming that they were also celebrating Easter! Anyway, he stripped the table of its white tablecloth, cut the treasured large shiny green leaves of the *Monstera* plants – to my grandmother's horror – lined the table with these, then laid the whole roasted lamb on top of the leaves and urged all of us to attack it with our fingers at any point and angle favoured, plates not being allowed.

On our island, each family fattens one or two small baby goats especially for Easter. The celebrations there are still to this day very colourful and high spirited and feel more traditional than they now are in urban Athens.

The First of May is the other major occasion for outdoor celebrations and picnics. This is the day when spring is at its best in Greece. The village is surrounded by hillsides, blazing with colour. Whole bright red fields covered with poppies are intermingled with huge white and yellow patches created by thousands of wild daisies and, wherever small gardens exist, dotted by the purple heads of artichokes. Wild strong-scented fennel is growing everywhere and the never-ending fields of soft chamomile fill the air with their sweet smell. In fact I cannot imagine a First of May outing without the familiar beautiful aroma of the chamomile intermingling with the tantalizing smells of lamb or goat being barbecued.

Traditionally, people must go to the open countryside on the First of May to welcome spring and, of course, to feast and drink all day. They pick and make bunches or wreaths of wild flowers, which are then brought back home and hung outside their front door. Most important, fresh garlic has to be added on the wreath or bunch of flowers before it is hung, in order to avert the 'evil eye'. (The 'evil eye' theory figures a lot in everyday life. A guarantee against it, as well as garlic, are round blue beads.) These wreaths or bunches would hang there until the other traditional day, the day of St John, which called for the wreaths to be burned outdoors in the street or in a garden while family members jumped over the fire three times. A very exciting night for us children, who would visit as many neighbourhoods as we could and jump over as many fires as we could find.

We have celebrated the First of May on a couple of occasions in our village on the island and they were really very memorable occasions. Almost all the families in the village walked to a tiny, whitewashed church, crouched on top of a small hill, surrounded by overgrown fields, just on the outskirts of the village. Each family carried their pots of food, usually roast goat and baskets of *meze*, their own homemade goat cheese, home-produced olives, freshly made large loaves of bread, perhaps some fried fish, or special stuffed vine leaves (stuffed with spinach and rice as well as onions and wild-growing fennel). Red wine and water, with rugs and blankets to be spread on the ground, were also carried. We cooked, together with our neighbours, in our outdoor beehive-shaped oven, a huge wonderful *yiouvetsi* (young goat cooked with tomatoes and small pasta), our neighbours and friends prepared their delicious special cheese pies, rolled in a spiral shape and fried in olive oil, and off we went.

Some families were roasting whole goats when we arrived and some had prepared *kokoretsi* (a large sausage on a skewer, assembled from small pieces of liver, lights, spleen, the heart and sweetbreads of the goat, highly seasoned and spiced and wrapped around with the intestine), which they were roasting over a slow wood fire. An almost communal table was made out of the various rugs spread on the terrace of the church and the adjoining fields. People were offering and being offered favoured bits from the amazing variety of wonderful dishes, plates started travelling from one end of the table to the other, families with their homemade red wine urging others to try it and proudly waiting for the inevitable praise. As the afternoon proceeded and spirits rose higher and higher, everybody joined in the singing and dancing. Eventually those who got tired or drunk receded under the trees for a nap, the young girls went chamomile- and flower-picking, the women gossiped and made black coffee over small fires and the day did not end until sunset when we all walked home, longing for the next occasion for such a magical outing.

EPILOGUE

There are a lot more occasions when Greeks eat communally either outdoors or indoors and there are a lot more colourful customs attached to different occasions, but the ones I describe are the most important and most representative of our traditions in Greece. My hope is to give a more complete picture to the enthusiast of not only how the food is prepared, but also in what spirit it is being consumed. And so you can begin to understand what I mean when I say that for Greeks food and cooking and eating are, at least on occasion, things of excitement, exuberance and, just possibly, magic.

My intention is not to collect every existing Greek recipe and then describe three or four variations of it, but to give you the best and the most common dishes that are being cooked every day in every household in Greece: dishes that have been cooked in my family for three generations or more, and which I know work. I have not collected these recipes in order to construct this book, rather the book contains what I, like any other Greek, have been brought up on, and taught to perform. I hope that through these recipes you can begin to share not only the wonders of Greek food, but also the intensity of the people and the places.

Helping the Reader
with Quantities

Most of the quantities in the recipes of this book are intended for feeding four people, perhaps a little generously, taking account also for the unexpected visitor in typical Greek fashion. Wherever the nature of the dish is unsuitable for small gatherings, such as in the typical Greek pies – spinach, cheese or meat – it has been indicated, with the number of portions stated. Also, most of the roast meat recipes, *yiouvetsi* for example, call for a shoulder or leg of lamb and are intended for six people.

MEZETHES
Appetizers

A *meze* or a *mezethaki*, a little *meze* (the addition of the ending *-aki* suggests the diminutive form of things), are words that one hears often in Greece. A visitor, and particularly a male one, cannot be acknowledged in a more honoured way than to be urged to stay and participate in a *mezethaki* and a drink that is quickly assembled from whatever suitable candidates the household possesses. The simple ones which will always be found in Greek houses are olives and feta, white sheep or goat cheese, which is always homemade in the countryside.

But there are variations even in these simple commodities according to different traditions and places. If in Kriti, you will be offered their small, tight, sharp olives and their delicious homemade, white, unsalted cheese, the *myzithra*. Kriti *myzithra* is made from sheep's milk, which is brought

31

to the boil and then fresh lemon juice added which causes it to curdle and thicken. It is as rich and delicious as their sheep's yoghurt. But in most of the Aegean islands the olives will be round, large and fleshy and the goat cheese salted and lighter and lacking the creamy texture of the sheep's cheese.

To accompany these, a plate with quarters of freshly peeled cucumber and quartered firm round tomatoes may appear, or a plate of sharp home-pickled tiny aubergines. In the winter there will almost certainly be one variety or another of salted fish; *lakertha* (slices of tuna fish kept in brine), a favourite of my father, or salted anchovies which have to be rinsed well first and then dressed with a lot of olive oil. This is a favourite of my mother. Or it may be the dried, long, slim *tsirous* which are the young mackerels that have spawned in the spring; these, which resemble the Bombay ducks of India, are firstly cleaned, kept in brine then dried in the sun. They are held over a flame until their skin starts to blister; they are then skinned and filleted into small thin portions, which are served on a shallow plate, dressed with a lot of olive oil and, for those who like it, a little vinegar. On top there is freshly chopped dill sprinkled all over and this is a *tsirosalata*, which was our favourite when we were children.

Living in Bombay for a few months, seeing the Bombay ducks, row after row, hanging on washing lines drying in the sun in Kolaba's fishing community, made me so homesick for the *tsirous* of my childhood that we bought a packet in the fish market and returned home. There our cook took one horrified look at these dried fish and obviously thought we had made some terrible mistake, whereupon he quietly put them aside until he could discreetly deposit them in his dustbin. They were never seen again.

A *meze* in Greece is offered with a drink, as Greeks never drink without eating at the same time, unlike western habits. The drink may be a small square glass of *ouzo* offered with a glass of water separately, in case the visitor wishes to dilute it, a glass of homemade *tsipouro*, much stronger than ordinary *ouzo*, a glass of wine or a glass of cold lager in the summer. Having a drink *xerosfyri* (*xeros* means 'dried', and *sfyri* is 'a hammer') is a word pronounced with horror, mixed with contempt. It is uttered at a glance of a table with drinks but no plates of *mezethes* which is exactly the situation it metaphorically describes. It goes without saying that there are no places such as bars or pubs in Greece where one can only have a drink and nothing to eat. Places like that, which are completely contrary to Greek traditions and habits, could not survive, as the Greeks are good eaters but no big drinkers. As E.F.V. About rightly observed in 1855, 'Drunkenness, so common in cold countries, is a rare vice with the

Greeks; they are great drinkers, but water drinkers. They would have scruples about passing by a fountain without drinking at it, but if they enter a tavern, it is to chatter.' (E.F.V. About, *Greece and the Greeks of the Present Day*, 1855, p. 33.) Drunkenness is so rare in Greece largely because of the national custom of *mezethes*.

A *meze* may be a small portion of whatever is being cooked in the large saucepan in the kitchen for the meal of the day or, indeed, if the visitor arrives near or during a meal time a *mezethaki* might well mean a full plate of the meal that the family is eating, but it is called this in order not to embarrass the visitor. My husband and I have had a lot of experience of this as on numerous occasions on the island we have been persuaded to have a full meal offered under the pretence of a *mezethaki*. I must add they were always very pleasurable experiences. A word of caution: whatever you cannot consume of the offered *mezethaki* may be neatly parcelled up for you to take home.

A more desirable *meze* is crispy fried rings of *kalamarakia* (squid), *soupies* (cuttlefish) and any of the tiny fish mentioned in the fish chapter (pages 189–238), such as sardines, little fresh anchovies, etc., which would be served fried, as whitebait is served in England.

Alternatively, any of the lamb's intestines including liver, lights, fries, the Greek *ameleteta* – the 'unmentionables', as they are known – sweet-breads and other such delicacies that are described in the meat chapter (pages 239–283) are highly desirable.

Thin slices of courgettes, home-grown baby marrows, which are deli-ciously sweet, or aubergines are often fried and served with *tzatziki* (cucumber and yoghurt salad) or *skorthalia* (garlic paste). Slices of *kefalotyri* or *graviera kritis* are often fried and served under the name of *saganaki* (fried cheese). The giant haricot-type beans belong to the *meze* tradition, as do small round *keftethes* (minced meat hamburgers heavily scented with traditional Greek herbs of oregano – *rigani*, thyme – *thy-mari*, and occasionally fresh mint) and, of course, the more elaborate *meze* of stuffed squid or any of the savoury pies such as *spanakopitta* (spinach pie), *tyropitta* (cheese pie) in varying shapes and sizes. Sometimes these would be individually wrapped with crisp *fyllo* pastry, in triangular shapes or in round elongated shapes, and either fried or baked; other times they would be made into a large pie, cut and divided into attractive diamond shapes.

Dolmathes (stuffed vine leaves) used to be made particularly thin when we were expecting visitors at home. Each vine leaf was cut in two, so one can imagine the work involved. The smaller the *dolmathes* or *keftethes* or little pies, the more honoured the visitor, since there were no grounds left for doubt as to the decorum attached to the gesture.

It is the image and the connotations attached to a *meze* that are important. A little round or square tin table, painted blue, the Greek colour *par excellence*, placed in a courtyard surrounded by pots of scarlet carnations and aromatic basil and shaded by an ageing vine, or simply outside a decaying old *taverna* with an anomalous whitewashed wall as a brilliant background, with a couple of small glasses on the table and a frugal plate of shining black olives is enough to inspire the participants, and exhilarate the spirits.

At the other end of the spectrum one should go through the kitchen-entrance of *taverna* Kostoyiannis in Zaimi Street in Athens where there is an amazing collection of *mezethes* to titillate the eyes. Container after aluminium container of freshly cooked, delicious dishes, almost everything mentioned in this chapter, make one of the most pleasing and satisfying images. In fact, they make the most appropriate introduction to Greek *mezethes* without any verbal elaborations needed.

AMIGTHALA ALATISMENA

Salted Almonds

Almonds treated in this manner have a beguiling, almost wicked taste, which captures people instantly. Their profoundly sour-salty taste and their crunchy texture can easily keep one addicted to their charm.

In Greece one can buy almonds already salted in this manner in the shops, but most people I know used to make their own at home, particularly people who owned even one single almond tree somewhere or had relatives who did. At the right time of the year, normally late July–August, they would receive offerings in the shape of freshly picked almonds.

We always prepared them at home, and my mother still does every year. Normally she prepares quite large quantities, then they are sent in their sparkling aluminium round dish to the local baker's.

Almonds should be kept in tightly screwed jars and they are at their best when eaten within two months, in my experience. After that they get a faintly old, slightly damp taste. This can be remedied by putting them in the oven again for ten minutes which refreshes them, but in any case they should not be kept for much longer. They make the perfect accompaniment to drinks and are an ideal appetizer.

1 kg/2 lbs shelled almonds,
   left in their brown skins
55 g/2 oz citric acid
   (*lemontozou*), obtainable
   from the chemist

150 ml/¼ pint cold water
25 g/1 oz table salt

Spread the almonds in a large, flat container, such as an oven dish. Mix the citric acid with the water until completely diluted. Sprinkle this liquid all over the almonds, stir so they are well soaked in it, leave for 10 minutes and then drain in order to get rid of any excess liquid. Put them back into the container, spread them out and sprinkle with half the salt. Shake the pan and sprinkle on the rest of the salt. Put them in a pre-heated oven, gas no. 4 (350°F/180°C), for 30 minutes, stirring them twice, at least, until they are turning nicely brown and crisp. Let them cool before you store them in jars.

MELITZANOSALATA

Aubergine Purée Salad

With a touch of exoticism in its taste, this dish makes an unusual starter. It can be prepared the day before and served cold with a green salad. In fact, it lasts perfectly well in the fridge, when properly covered to prevent it from drying, for 3-4 days. Very simple to prepare but make sure the aubergines are properly cooked. Traditionally the aubergines are cooked on charcoal and bear that unmistakable scorched aroma in the dish.

450 g/1 lb aubergines (1–2 large aubergines)
1 small onion, thinly sliced
1 clove garlic, peeled and crushed
60 ml/2 fl. oz olive oil
juice of ½ lemon, or 1 teaspoon vinegar

1 tablespoon mayonnaise (optional)
salt and freshly ground black pepper
parsley
olives, to garnish

Choose large aubergines for your own convenience (less peeling). Prick them with a fork. Put them in the oven, gas no. 4 (350°F/180°C), on the high shelf for approximately 1 hour. Rest them on the oven shelves and turn them round occasionally. When cold enough to handle, peel them. Chop the flesh on a wooden board (so extra juices run) and put in a liquidizer with all the other ingredients, apart from the parsley and olives, and blend well. Serve in a bowl, sprinkle the chopped parsley on top and garnish with a few olives.

If you do not have a liquidizer, mash the aubergines with a fork in a bowl, add the other ingredients and blend well by hand. In any case, traditionally in Greece, this is always done in a wooden mortar, a *goudi* as it is called, and the women pride themselves on beating for hours and making the texture as fine as it can be.

TZATZIKI

Cucumber and Yoghurt Salad

A wonderful refreshing summer dish. It is used mostly as meze, when people dip pieces of bread into a common bowl. Very often it is served with crispy fried elongated slices of courgettes, or slices of fried aubergines, in which case the crisp vegetable is dipped into the white tzatziki first and then eaten in an unusual combination of hot and cold, sweet and sour, or it can be served as an accompaniment to roast lamb or roast chicken. It is an easy dish to make and it adds a lot to a meal or a party.

1 tablespoon olive oil
1 teaspoon vinegar
1 clove garlic, peeled and
  crushed
225 g/8 oz Greek or Greek-
  style natural yoghurt
17-cm/7-in piece cucumber,
  peeled and coarsely grated
  or finely diced

5–6 fresh mint leaves, rinsed
  and finely chopped, or a
  pinch of dried mint
a little salt and pepper black
  olives, to garnish

Mix the olive oil, vinegar and garlic in a small bowl. Add the yoghurt and mix well. Drain the cucumber and add to the yoghurt with the mint, the salt and pepper and mix again. Garnish with a few black olives. Serve lightly chilled.

FASOLIA GIGANTES PLAKI

Giant Beans Baked in the Oven

A sensational dish. Splendidly vegetarian, luxuriously rich, it makes one of the best main meals served in Greek homes and it is customarily served as an appetizer in *tavernas*.

The satisfactory supple texture of the beans, wrapped in their luscious olive oil and tomato sauce, melts in candied waves, slowly, in the recipient's mouth. The nearest to these fleshy huge haricot-type beans in the west are butter beans but they are not the equivalent in taste. Butter beans are flatter, they tend to get waterlogged and they lack the sugary taste of *fasolia gigantes*. Unfortunately *fasolia gigantes* are still very hard to come by in this country, so we have to import them from Greece ourselves through a network of friends and relatives.

Our English friends who have become converts to this dish and find the butter bean version unsatisfactory do exactly the same and bring them back from their Greek summer holidays. Their price matches their taste, so they are more expensive than ordinary beans. They are grown mostly in the north of Greece and the fresh supplies arrive in the shops in early September. Their taste varies a lot, as with ordinary beans, and people go a long way to their favourite outlet in order to get a tasty variety.

The versions of this dish one gets in restaurants seem to lack the piquancy and poignancy of the home versions, particularly when they have a watery tendency, but they are still worth sampling. *Fasolia gigantes* are often cooked with pork in a baked version and as they supremely match and complement the taste of each other, the final result is outstanding.

Gigantes plaki *make an excellent and appetizing first course for six with the quantities given here, or a main course for four, supplemented with a fresh green salad, some feta cheese and some fresh bread.*

450 g/1 lb Greek *fasolia gigantes*, or butter beans
150 ml/5 fl. oz olive oil
285 g/10 oz onions, finely sliced
3 cloves garlic, peeled and finely sliced
1 tablespoon oregano
1 teaspoon thyme

2 396-g/14-oz cans tomatoes, or 1 kg/2 lbs fresh ripe tomatoes
1 tablespoon tomato purée
1 teaspoon sugar
salt and freshly ground black pepper
3 tablespoons finely chopped parsley

Pick the beans clean from stones and grit and soak them in cold water in an earthenware bowl overnight. Drain and rinse them in a colander, put into a large saucepan or a pressure cooker, cover with plenty of cold water and boil them until they are cooked but still a little hard. This type of bean cooks quickly, so be aware until you get used to them. They take hardly 2 minutes in a pressure cooker and about 30–40 minutes otherwise. If they get overcooked, they get mushy and soggy and they don't taste at their best. This first step then is also the most important in this recipe.

Drain the beans through a colander and keep aside. In the same saucepan, heat the olive oil and fry the onions, the garlic and the dried herbs, until they start turning pale golden. Add the tomatoes with all the juice from the cans or, if fresh tomatoes are used, add 150 ml/¼ pint water. Then add the tomato purée and sugar, break up the mixture with a fork, season with salt and pepper, cover and cook for 30 minutes or until the sauce thickens.

Mix the parsley into the tomato sauce, add the beans and mix well. Spread the beans in an oven dish, preferably a decorative one so they can be taken straight to the table in it. A large cast iron frying pan serves this purpose perfectly. Sprinkle a little oregano and black pepper on the top and cook in a pre-heated oven, gas no. 4 (350°F/180°C), for 30 minutes, without stirring, until they look slightly crisp on top and quite dry.

Alternatively, add the beans to the tomato sauce, mix well, cover and simmer for 10–15 minutes.

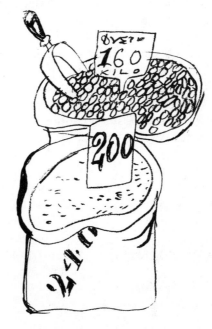

DOMATOKEFTETHES

Santorinian Tomato Rissoles

I shall never forget the animated discussion this created in the little court-yard in Oia: Should one put soda in the mixture? Or soaked stale bread as well as flour, as Katina tou Lambrou, who runs the charming little restaurant on the Ammoudi beach underneath Oia, had told us at lunchtime? Earlier, we had sampled all her delicacies after a swim: sweet beetroot with *skorthalia*, *fasolia gigantes*, a tomato salad with home-grown tiny bright scarlet Santorinian tomatoes, crunchy cucumber – something we used to call *antzouria* but which in Santorini they call *katsounia* – and, of course, *domatokeftethes*, *the* speciality of the island.

One can indulge in the food here as there is no danger of enlarging one's waist, not only because the prime ingredients are so healthy: there are also 276 handsome steps to climb back to Oia in the dazzling heat.

The following day, Maroulia Laoutha, in whose spectacular pension we were staying – practically suspended over the blue sea, announced that she was going to make her *domatokeftethes* specially for us to sample. But first we needed her husband, she said, for the arduous fine chopping of the mound of onions. No, they should not be grated and food processors were an unknown commodity here. Husbands were used instead.

I spotted the loaded donkey meandering down slowly through the cubic clearances of the hillside and suddenly Maroulia's husband had arrived; he unloaded his donkey of the heavy sacks of *fava* (a kind of split pea) from his field and in a little while he had been set on his task in the dark cool kitchen inside their traditional *iposkafo* building. Maroulia and I made for her little patch of earth, where she harvested her brilliantly scarlet tomatoes and I was given the honorary task of harvesting the mint. She had no basil or parsley, as everything had already dried up by early June. Operations were then resumed under the vine on the terrace directly in front of her kitchen.

450 g/1 lb ripe tomatoes, rinsed and dried
2 medium onions, peeled and finely chopped (not grated)
¼ teaspoon paprika
salt and freshly ground black pepper
6 tablespoons fresh mint, finely chopped (about a teacup)
2 tablespoons parsley, finely chopped
1 tablespoon olive oil
150 g/5 oz self-raising flour
sunflower oil, for frying

Once she had rinsed and dried the tomatoes, they were put whole into a large bowl – for she was making a huge quantity in typical Greek fashion – and she squeezed and manipulated them with her hands, until they had turned into a pulpy substance. This is the only way to do it as you need the skins to give some substance. So, no electrical tricks here, but you can chop the onions in a food processor briefly so they do not turn into pulp.

Next, mix all the ingredients together, apart from the flour. Add enough flour gradually to make a thickish but moist paste. You will probably not need all the flour. The mixture can now wait until it is time to be cooked and eaten.

Put about 2.5 cm/1 in oil in a large frying pan. When the oil is hot, but not smoking, drop in tablespoons of the mixture and fry, turning the rissoles over once, until lightly golden all over. Serve immediately.

XYNOGALO

Sour Fresh Cheese

Xynogalo is a sour wobbly cheesy concoction that is mostly made by individual households on the islands and in the countryside in June and July when the goat's milk is at its richest.

Fresh milk is brought to the boil with a little salt. After it has boiled briefly it is drawn off the heat and allowed to get cold. It is then poured into a thick, unbleached cotton bag resembling a small pillow case, its top is strung and tied securely and the bag is hung in the shade in the garden to drain off the whey from the curds. If you walk into a village garden on Alonnisos you see these bags hanging under the ubiquitous mulberry trees. Underneath is placed a container to gather the whey drippings. The external surface of the bag is wiped clean with a wet cloth a couple of times a day to prevent it solidifying. If the fresh air could not get through then its contents would also dry out and solidify.

While the days pass, the curds form in the bag, and after 3–4 days the texture solidifies like that of a very thick knobbly yoghurt. By then it has become sour in taste and it is very appetizing and cooling. Spread on a thick slice of village bread it makes an earthy delight.

Once it has reached the right taste, it must be consumed within 2–3 days. It is inevitable then that small bowls are taken as presents to friends and relatives. And we all rejoice.

TARAMOSALATA

Salted Cod's Roe Dip

One of the most popular and better known Greek specialities, through-out the world. Out of quite humble ingredients a miracle can be produced. The roe of the grey mullet is first dried and salted and then pressed into large wooden barrels. These barrels can be seen in the old-fashioned gro-cer shops in the central market in Athens or the markets of the large provincial towns. *Tarama* itself is cheap and the fact that you need so lit-tle of it for a portion of *taramosalata* makes the dish even cheaper. Very often *taramosalata* accompanies vegetarian meals such as bean soup or chick pea soup which, along with a dish of some variety of Greek olives, produce a full meal. Even though *tarama* can be found all year round, since it is salted, there is still a season for it! It is mostly made in the win-ter and, most particularly, in the spring during Lent. For people who were fasting (and in the old days there used to be quite a lot of them – almost all the adults, otherwise it was a kind of social stigma), it was a delicious alternative. Our old grandmothers were real fanatics on fasting and they would make even us children abstain from meat, butter and eggs on Wednesdays and Fridays during Lent and for the whole Easter week, par-ticularly Good Friday, when only boiled lentils were allowed with spring onions, but certainly no olive oil. So, this is the season that you will find *taramosalata* on almost every table in Greece.

The genuine version is always made with bread soaked in water and not in milk and it contains a tiny bit of grated onion in order to impart a faint onion flavour but it certainly never contains garlic whose strong taste would obscure the almost delicate fishiness of the *tarama*.

In Greece, it is made in large wooden mortars by beating the *tarama* first to soften it, adding a little bit of the olive oil and then beating it again. The soaked bread is then added and pounded again, then the *tarama*, and at this stage are added, alternating them almost drop by drop, the juice of the lemons and the rest of the olive oil. If you find olive oil too heavy you could use groundnut oil or corn oil, or a mixture of olive oil and nut or corn oil. Also there is a version of it where instead of bread you use boiled potatoes mashed up. This produces a firmer texture and blander taste.

Salted tarama is available in Greek shops in small containers or from large department stores. You could use the fresh smoked cod's roe but that is quite expensive and it does not last longer than 4–5 days in my experience, while the salted one keeps in the fridge for months. If you use the smoked roes you should take their skins off first and proceed as for the salted kind, but the quantity should be 110 g/4 oz. I have finally compromised, deserted my wooden mortar and pestle and started using an electric blender, because it is so much easier.

6 medium slices white bread, preferably stale
55 g/2 oz *tarama* (salted), or 110 g/4 oz fresh smoked cod's roe
1 large juicy lemon

1 small shallot, sliced
90 ml/3 fl. oz olive, groundnut or corn oil
chopped parsley and black olives, to garnish

Soak the bread without the crusts in a bowl of water for 10 minutes. You will not be able to put all the ingredients into the blender at once, so you will have to halve them and use the blender twice. Put one tablespoon of *tarama* in the blender first, squeeze most of the water out of the soaked bread (but don't leave it too dry) and add it to the blender, add half of the lemon juice, the shallot, and half of the oil, and blend fast until all the ingredients have been incorporated and a smooth pink creamy paste appears. You can try the taste at this stage and decide if you would like some more lemon in it or perhaps less bread in the second batch. Empty the blender and proceed in the same way with the rest of the ingredients. At the end mix everything together in a bowl or on a platter and garnish with some parsley and a few black olives.

TARAMOKEFTETHES

Salted Cod's Roe Rissoles

An unusual appetizer, mainly eaten during Lent in the spring, when most people in Greece fast (nowadays for tradition's sake and out of habit, rather than for strict religious ritual).

At this time it is also served in various restaurants (unfortunately not the ones included in the tourist trail) but I have never come across a good version of them in a restaurant or one comparable in the least with the excellent home versions.

The home version though, which is quite easy and also delicious, is worth trying any time. If you use the fresh smoked cod's roe, you will have to skin it first, but if you get the potted salted variety which is available in most Greek shops and delicatessens you don't have to do anything in advance.

In Greece, they used to soak the *tarama* for 10 minutes first, in order to get the stringy skin bits away, but the present-day *tarama* is very different and unfortunately too industrialized to contain anything like that, so I don't find the soaking necessary nowadays.

Taramokeftethes *must contain some fresh greenery. In Greece this is always a combination of dill* (anitho) *or wild fennel* (maratho) *and parsley, finely chopped. It is exactly these ingredients they lack in restaurants and they also tend to arrive at the table rather dried, too flat and overcooked.*

In Greece, taramokeftethes *are also served as part of the main course with boiled cauliflower salad, or hand-picked mountain greens* (horta) *boiled and dressed with olive oil and lemon, and a green salad, or as an accompaniment to our traditional soups, particularly the bean soup,* fasolatha.

1 large onion, finely sliced
vegetable oil, for deep-frying
75 g/3 oz *tarama* (the salted variety), or 170 g/6 oz fresh smoked cod's roe
4 medium slices white bread, crusts removed, soaked in water and squeezed dry
1 tablespoon lemon juice
25 g/1 oz flour

½ teaspoon baking powder
1 teacup (approximately) mixed parsley and dill, finely chopped, or just parsley
freshly ground black pepper
55 g/2 oz flour, for coating
chopped parsley and quartered lemons, to garnish

Sauté the onion in a little oil until it becomes light golden. Place the *tarama* (or roe) in a blender or a food processor with the crustless and squeezed bread and the lemon juice. Blend well until it all looks amalgamated. (Women in Greece pound the *tarama* in wooden mortars first and then add the bread and pound them together, by hand, even to the present day.)

Take the mixture out of the blender and put it in a bowl. Add the fried onion, 25 g/1 oz flour, the baking powder, parsley and, of course, dill if you have it as it is very characteristic of the dish, some freshly ground pepper and mix well by hand.

If you find your mixture too liquid, you can always add a little more flour as a remedial measure. Too much flour though alters tastes drastically.

Make small, round, slightly flat (not too flat) shapes, roll them lightly in flour and deep-fry them in hot oil for 2–3 minutes until they look pale golden.

In Greece, they are shallow-fried still as most people stick stubbornly to the old traditional method. If you shallow-fry them they have to be turned over individually until golden on both sides.

Drain on kitchen paper, spread them on a flat platter, sprinkle some parsley over them and serve with some quartered lemons to be squeezed on, according to individual tastes.

SPETZOFAI PILIORITIKO

Casserole of Country Sausages and Sweet Green Peppers

This is the speciality of the mountain villages in Pilion, on the east coast of central Greece.

According to our mythology it was in Pilion's dramatic high ravines and mountain tops, in Pliassithi which is the highest, in Xeforti and Golgothas, that the mythic centaurs – strong and wild half-horse half-human creatures – lived and had their monumental fight with the Lapithes, over the bride Ippodamia. On the day of her wedding to Pirithous, king of the Lapithes, one of the more lively centaurs tried to abduct her. As a result of his impertinence, the libidinal centaur Evrition had his ears and nose cut off.

Outraged by the insult, the centaurs descended heavy-handed or rather heavy-footed from their mountain-top caves, over the mountain water-falls, armed with the monumental trunks of the wild horse-chestnuts, and took their revenge by killing the Lapithes men and carrying away their women.

The last word, though, lay with the Lapithes who, with the help of the Athenian hero Thiseas, finally attacked and drove the centaurs out of the mountainous range of Pilion into the even wilder mountains of Pinthos in central western Greece, making sure they got their women back first.

Pilion is also supposed to have been the original home of the magnificent horse-chestnut trees that are abundant here; they were sent from here to most European countries around the middle of the sixteenth century. It was also from the feet of Pilion, where the ancient city of Iolkos was, that Iason – the mythic Jason – and his crew sailed in his *Argo* on the dreamy journey to distant, foreign Kolhis in order to search for the allegorical Golden Fleece.

It is in the villages of Pilion that you will find *spetzofai*: in the village of Portaria almost suspended between the blue of the sky and the green of the mountainside, lost in its eternal huge plane trees and cascading waters; or in the village of Makrinitsa, with its stately decaying houses, nesting like a proud eagle in its lofty ambience, commanding a sweeping view over the Pagasitikos bay as far as the Cape of Trikeri and even misty Evia, on the horizon, luxuriously outstretched on the clouds like a voluptuous lizard.

In Hánia, when skiing in the winter, we were given another speciality apart from *spetzofai*: *fasolia gigantes*, the gigantic haricot beans intermingled with hot, spicy, rough homemade sausages, in a rich, wonderfully warming dish resembling the French *cassoulet*; or you might find it in Zagora, famous for its traditional, architectural style, its apples, its chestnuts and its hazelnuts and choked in pastel pink apple blossom in April; or in the melancholy, leafy village of Tsangaratha, with its tiny village gardens effusing the aromas of creamy, velvety gardenias mingled in the pastel shades of hydrangeas; or by the diaphanous blue sea in the village of Horefto, through orchards of apples and pears and dense walnut trees.

This is the home of *spetzofai*, and the images it evokes at Greek tables, whenever it is served as one of the most piquant *mezes*.

The best sausages to use, if you can't get home-made Greek ones, are the rough, meaty spicy sausages in Greek or Italian shops; and since the particular long, round, pale green sweet peppers cannot be found here, I suggest our green sweet peppers as a substitute. When in Greece, though, look out for these beautifully green peppers, particularly in the area of the island of Evia, the islands of Sporathes, in Athens and, of course, in Pilion. If you find yourself in Pilion you can try the authentic dish, in its even more authentic, astounding setting.

675 g/1½ lbs sweet green or
   red peppers
60 ml/2 fl. oz olive oil, or
   good vegetable oil
1 teaspoon oregano
450 g/1 lb country-style
   sausages, such as Italian,
   Toulouse or Greek

225 g/8 oz fresh tomatoes,
   peeled and sliced, or
1 227-g/8-oz can
   tomatoes, chopped
salt and freshly ground
   black pepper

Rinse, core and slice the peppers into 4 large pieces. The elongated, slim peppers used in Greece are normally sliced into two, lengthways.

In a saucepan, sauté the peppers in the olive oil and the oregano. Slice the sausages thickly and fry them in a frying pan for 4–5 minutes. Sausages of this kind exude quite a lot of oil or fat, so avoid any additional oil. Using a slotted spoon, lift the sausages into the saucepan with the peppers, add the sliced tomatoes, stir, season, cover and simmer for 20 minutes. Do not add water unless the fresh tomatoes (if used) are not very juicy. In the latter case, add tiny amounts of water when needed. The sauce should be thick and oily. As this dish is quite rich, a small amount is enough.

ELIOPSOMO

Olive Bread

This is a delicious bread, full of robust tastes and the aromas of the fresh greenery. A real representative of the Mediterranean. It is a variation of a recipe by my friend Vera Kyriakou.

Use an oily type of olive such as the small Kretan variety or that from Kerkyra, and not sharp olives soaked in vinegar, such as the Greek kalamata *variety.* Eliopsomo *is baked in individual rolls which are delicious fresh but which can also be frozen once baked. Take them out of the freezer as needed, defrost for a couple of hours and then warm them in the oven. The following quantities will produce approximately 22 rolls.*

450 g/1 lb fresh spinach, trimmed and rinsed properly
3–4 tablespoons flat-leaved parsley, rinsed and drained
2–3 tablespoons fresh mint, rinsed and drained
2–3 tablespoons fresh coriander, rinsed and drained

225 g/8 oz onions, or 2 bunches spring onions
450 g/1 lb oily olives, preferably stoned
25 g/1 oz fresh yeast
600 ml/1 pint warm water
1 kg/2 lbs wholemeal or plain flour
150 ml/¼ pt olive oil
a little salt

Chop all the drained and prepared vegetables finely, including the onions. The olives can be used with the stone but warn people about them. Otherwise, stone the olives or buy an already stoned variety. If the olives have been kept in brine and they are salty rinse them briefly first.

Crumble the yeast into half the warm water and dissolve it. Mix the flour, salt and olive oil and rub together. Add the dissolved yeast, mix well and knead it for 10 minutes. Keep adding more of the warm water as necessary. You may not need all of it even though the dough should be quite wet and sticky.

Mix in a separate bowl all the chopped vegetables and herbs with the olives and a little salt. Add these to the dough, mix well and knead it again until the greenery is well incorporated. Cover with a clean cloth and let it rest in a warm place for approximately 45 minutes or until it is well risen.

Oil a baking tray with vegetable oil, and also oil your hands to prevent the dough from sticking. Make large, well-oiled rolls approximately

8 cm/3 inch in diameter (keep oiling your hands as you make each roll) and place them on the baking tray.

Pre-heat the oven to gas no. 7 (425°F/225°C) and place the baking tray in the middle. Cook for 15 minutes, then turn the heat down to gas no. 5 (375°F/190°C) and cook for a further 15 minutes, until the rolls are nicely brown. Continue cooking each batch in the same way until they are all finished.

SAGANAKI

Fried Cheese

This is considered very appetizing, particularly when it is made with slices of sharp, salty *kefalotyri*. It takes its name from the little round aluminium frying pan with two black, semi-circular handles, one on either side. It is cooked and served piping hot in the same container as it comes off the heat. The heat of the 'dish' causes some urgency sometimes and occasionally makes the waiter run.

It has always been served (and still is) in the small square of Dexameni at the foot of Lycabettus, and I always associate it with cool evenings under the dense foliage of the trees in the square, and sunny autumnal or winter days with everybody seeking the sun.

For saganaki, *thin, long slices of* kaseri, kefalotyri *or* graviera kritis *are used, basically all hard cheeses but with some bite in them and very tasty.*

225 g/8 oz any hard cheese, kefalotyri, *Parmesan*, *Gruyère or Greek Cypriot* haloumi	55 g/ 2 oz butter a little fresh lemon juice freshly ground black pepper

Cut the cheese into 1-cm/½-in thick slices. Heat the butter in a frying pan and put the slices in. Turn the heat down a little and let it cook for 1–2 minutes until it bubbles. It should not turn brown, but should look creamy and sticky. This is the reason the cheese is cooked in small frying pans, so they can be taken straight to the table. Sprinkle a little lemon juice on top and some black pepper and offer it with fresh bread, letting people eat it as they prefer to.

KEFTETHES

Fried Minced Balls with Herbs

This is one of the most common and most popular dishes among Greeks. Its name comes from the Greek verb *kopto*, to mince or to chop. The same name or almost the same is used throughout the Middle East, as well as India and Pakistan, as *kofta*.

It is a very easy standby dish to have with any of the vegetable casseroles. They should be eaten hot as they come out of the frying pan. They also make an excellent *meze* for a dinner party.

Every Greek cook has a favourite method for keftethes. *The best I have ever eaten were in a* taverna *in Psychiko, but I think this recipe is as good.*

2 medium slices of white or
   brown bread, crusts
   removed, soaked in water
   for 10 minutes
450 g/1 lb minced beef or
   lean lamb
1 medium onion, grated
1 egg
a squeeze of lemon
1 tablespoon each thyme and
   oregano

2 tablespoons fresh mint, or
   a pinch of dried mint
salt and freshly ground
   black pepper
3 tablespoons vegetable oil,
   for frying
55 g/2 oz flour, for coating
2 tablespoons chopped
   parsley

Squeeze most of the water out of the bread, then mix with the meat, onion, egg, lemon juice, herbs (except the parsley) and seasoning in a large bowl, either with a fork or, even better, by hand, making sure in particular that the bread is well incorporated. Let this mixture stand for 30 minutes if you can. Of course, this can be prepared in advance and left in the fridge.

When ready to fry, mould the mixture with your hands into small squashed round shapes; the size can vary according to the amount of time you want to spend frying, but the smaller they are the more presentable. My grandmother used to make them the size of a small walnut for family parties, but much bigger when they were just intended for the children.

Put some oil in a shallow frying pan (3 tablespoons is enough) and when it is hot, coat each *kefte* lightly in flour and put in the frying pan. Fry on medium heat for about 3 minutes on each side, turning once, and when they are crisp all over, take out. Sprinkle some parsley over them and serve.

KOLOKYTHAKIA TIGANITA ME TZATZIKI

Fried Courgettes with Cucumber and Yoghurt

A light and refreshing dish which is served almost all year round in restaurants and *tavernas* in Greece. On some islands and villages it is served with *skorthalia* (garlic paste) instead of *tzatziki* (cucumber and yoghurt salad). Alonnisos is included in this category. There, people serve their own home-grown baby marrows, pale striped green and white and ravishingly enticing; these are the sweetest and most delicious type of courgette that we have ever eaten. They are harvested when they are quite stout and they weigh roughly 450 g/ 1 lb each, so it is not their size that makes them so delicate and delicious. They are sliced in thick rounds, coated lightly with flour and fried in olive oil. Seeds are religiously kept by the people on the island at the end of every summer for the next year's planting season.

*Choose fresh and firm courgettes, otherwise they look and taste
'droopy', once they have been fried. They can be either deep-fried
or shallow-fried.*

3–4 courgettes, about 450 g/1 lb	55 g/2 oz flour, for coating
salt and freshly ground black pepper	vegetable oil, for frying
	tzatziki, to serve (page 37)

Top and tail the courgettes. Lightly scrape them under running water. Slice them lengthways in medium slices, about 3–4 slices each courgette. Some people and some restaurants, like Kostoyiannis in Zaimi Street in Athens, slice them paper thin and deep-fry them, so they become very crisp. Personally I prefer them a little thicker and still juicy in the middle. Spread them out and sprinkle salt and pepper over them. Coat them lightly in flour and fry briefly in hot oil, turning them once, if they are being shallow-fried, so they acquire a light golden colour on both sides. They should be served very hot and eaten after having being dipped in the *tzatziki*.

OMELETTA ME DOMATES
(Kerkyraiki Strapatsatha)

Omelette with Fresh Tomatoes

I have very fond memories of this dish; of the innumerable summer lunches under the shade of the dense vines in our small back garden, with the huge, rough, blackened frying pan set in the middle of the small, square, blue tin table, and with the ravishing whirls of the aroma of sugary ripe tomatoes rising in the hot, still air. It has become a kind of ritual by now that my sisters and I have to perform at least once in the summer when we all meet in Greece. This omelette is quite often made impromptu and offered as *mezethaki* with a small glass of *ouzo*. Greek tomatoes are large, beautifully uneven and sugary, one has to remember; in any case the combination of any fresh tomatoes with eggs is a quite astonishingly successful one and has to be experienced. The same dish is known on the Ionian island of Corfu under the eccentric name of *strapatsatha*, from the Italian verb *strapazzare*, to beat.

This is a very simple dish to make, basically an omelette with fresh tomatoes and olive oil, but with the right tomatoes it can be absolutely delicious and very appetizing.

3 tablespoons olive oil
450 g/1 lb ripe tomatoes,
  peeled and chopped
½ teaspoon oregano, thyme
  or fresh basil

salt and freshly ground
  black pepper
pinch sugar
4 eggs, beaten a little with a
  fork

Heat the olive oil in a large frying pan and add the prepared tomatoes and the herbs. Stir a little and let them cook gently for 5–8 minutes until all the liquid evaporates. Stir in some seasoning and the sugar and add the seasoned beaten eggs, pouring them evenly all over the tomatoes. Stir gently with a fork and cook slowly for 3–4 minutes until the eggs are cooked but not too solid. Take it to the table in the frying pan and let people dip in it or serve themselves. The consistency of the dish should resemble scrambled eggs.

SKORTHALIA

Thick Garlic Sauce

Skorthalia is a simple but very appetizing dish and is assembled from very earthy ingredients – bread, garlic, olive oil and a little vinegar. The recipe dates back to the ancient Greeks as it was a favourite of Athenians at the time, who called it *Skorothalmi*. It travelled with them all around the Mediterranean, where variations of it can be found nowadays, even as far as Andalucia in Spain, where the cold summer soup called *gazpacho blanco* seems identical to a diluted *skorthalia*.

Skorthalia *is routinely served, particularly in the countryside, mountain villages or islands, with fried vegetables such as slices of courgettes or aubergines, with fried fish or sometimes with boiled chicken. Its sharpness varies according to the amount of garlic, from mild to really hot and burning.*

4 medium slices stale bread, crusts removed, soaked in water for 10 minutes
4 cloves garlic, peeled and sliced
2 tablespoons wine vinegar

4–5 tablespoons olive oil
salt
1–2 tablespoons water, if necessary
55 g/2 oz finely crushed walnuts (optional)

Squeeze excess water from the bread, but do not leave it too dry; it should be moist. Put the bread, garlic and vinegar in the liquidizer and blend well; add the olive oil a little at a time and blend. Season with salt. If the mixture appears too dry, add the water. Personally I don't like the addition of walnuts, but this is a matter of taste. If you are using them, add at the end and blend well. The sauce should be of a runny consistency by the time it is finished. Serve separately in a bowl, for people to either serve themselves or to dip vegetables into.

AVGOLEMONO
Egg and Lemon Sauce

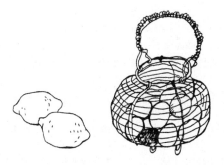

Avgolemono is a sauce made with egg (*avgo* in Greek) and lemon (*lemoni*) as the word suggests. It is added to soups or casseroles in order to provide body and flavour at the same time. It is light and delicate and highly regarded and much loved by Greeks. It also gives them a chance to exercise their passion for the abundant, golden, juicy fruit of the land, the lemon. Some Greek cooks, as a result, make it very sharp and lemony by adding 2–3 lemons in a casserole for an average family; others prefer to make it more rich and velvety by putting more eggs in it.

Whenever I make an *avgolemono* sauce I remember one occasion that has stuck in my mind from my childhood. When an elderly lady across the road died from a heart attack, my grandmother came back with the news regarding the case and exclaimed: 'Do you know how many eggs she had put in the *avgolemono* for the fricassee she made today? Four eggs! That did it!' And all the other women nodded in agreement. Since that moment, when, rarely, I add three eggs to an *avgolemono* I then worry about people just nodding off the table with heart attacks in the middle of dinner!

Avgolemono can be added to more or less anything that has been cooked *au naturel*, that is without tomatoes and definitely without even a hint of garlic. It can miraculously transform a particularly thin soup and disguise its faults. Primarily it is added to fish soups, chicken soups and tripe soup, or to casseroles like lamb fricassee (lamb cooked with quantities of shredded cos lettuces, spring onions and dill), lamb with fresh green peas, pork with celery, stuffed courgettes, *dolmathes*, most of the globe artichoke dishes, etc.

There are various ways of making *avgolemono*, with each cook claiming that his or her method is better; with some adding cornflour to make it thicker, some adding a tablespoon of milk to make it whiter and all of them worrying about the one important point: to safeguard the eggs from cooking! Keeping that in mind, one can make an *avgolemono* sauce very easily and in very little time.

Never add a boiling hot sauce into the egg-and-lemon mixture or the other way round as the egg will cook; always let the saucepan stand away from the heat for at least 5 minutes before proceeding with the *avgolemono*. Once you have added the *avgolemono*, never let the dish boil.

The average quantities for *avgolemono* are 2 eggs to 1–2 lemons. The quantity of lemons depends on the nature of the main ingredients of the casserole; *dolmathes*, made with vine leaves, which by nature are sharp and lemony in taste, require less lemon, otherwise one is running the risk of making them too acid; *arnaki fricassee* or stuffed cabbage leaves, on the other hand, which are very mild in taste if not bland, benefit enormously from a sharp lemon taste. Here are the basic methods of *avgolemono*:

THE EASIEST AND MOST COMMON METHOD
2 eggs
juice of 1–2 lemons

With a fork, beat the 2 eggs with a tablespoon of cold water for 2–3 minutes; add the lemon juice and beat it together for about 1 minute. Start introducing, slowly, tablespoons of the hot (but not boiling) sauce from the casserole or soup that the *avgolemono* is intended for, beating at the same time. Once 4–5 tablespoons have been added we assume that the *avgolemono* has acquired a mild warmth, and we can add it to the saucepan. It should be poured in very slowly, while stirring with a wooden spoon at the same time. If it is a casserole with fragile contents like artichokes, pour the *avgolemono* sauce slowly all over and immediately rotate the saucepan and keep the sauce moving for 1–2 minutes. This should always be done away from heat. Return the saucepan on very gentle heat for a few seconds, in order to thicken the egg a little. Keep stirring or rotating in the meantime.

This version that contains the egg whites is also the more dangerous. The egg whites run the risk of getting slightly cooked at any stage. Even if they do, though, as long as it is slightly, it does not mean the end of the world. The advantage of this version is that it produces a whiter result and so is prettier than the next version. Whenever the addition of cornflour is indispensable for thickening, it is given separately under the particular recipe. The cornflour should first be diluted in 3–4 tablespoons of cold water and then beaten into the eggs.

A SAFER VERSION

Separate the eggs and use only the egg yolks. Beat the egg yolks with a tablespoon of water for 1–2 minutes, add the lemon and continue as in the previous basic method. It is in this method that sometimes it is advisable to add an extra egg yolk if there is a considerable amount of food that the sauce has to cover. This version does not become light and fluffy as the previous one does. It is thicker and creamier.

A REFINED VERSION

Separate the eggs and beat the eggs whites until they stay in soft peaks. Add the egg yolks and beat together for 2 minutes until well amalgamated. Add the lemon juice, beat together a little and start adding tablespoons of the hot sauce or soup as described in the first method. This method results in the lightest and fluffier appearance and is preferred for soups as it makes them look frothy. Beating the egg whites first safeguards them also against the heat.

SOUPES KAI OSPRIA
Soups and Pulses

A peasant can always gain his drachma per day; out of which he will buy an oker of bread (two pounds and a half), which will cost him twenty-four leptas; he will then purchase five leptas' worth of olives; and will make a soup out of five leptas' worth of *beans and garlic*.
(George Cochrane, *Wanderings in Greece*, Vol. I, London, 1837, p. 296.)

If one was to summarize a cuisine by its soups Greece would be under the heading 'Beans and Lentils'. Literally these are soups at the very basis of the cuisine and what the nation has always relied on in harsh winters, religious fasting periods and times of frugality.

Olive oil which exists in great abundance in Greece is, of course, the magic ingredient that brings these soups to life. And for frivolity there are the dried mountain herbs that will enhance flavour as well as aroma.

FASOLIA SOUPA

Cannellini Bean Soup

'*Fasolatha pou trefi tin Ellada*' is a popular saying virtually meaning that the whole of Greece is brought up on *fasolia* (bean soup). This is our 'national' dish; if anything is brought up on it, my family was. A wholly vegetarian meal, it is so nourishing that we used to have it at least three times a week. Sometimes at suppertime a luxurious note was added in the form of crispy fried squid or tiny *marida* (picarel), a fish that resembles whitebait in this country, which were served alongside the soup. When we started serving it to our English friends, it obtained a real following, with everyone asking for the recipe. The 'health-food'-oriented friends were especially enthusiastic.

Fasolia Soupa is a straightforward dish with no secrets, apart from soaking the beans overnight in cold water and making sure you add the salt at the end (otherwise the beans become tough and leathery) and do not be mean with the olive oil. This is one of the most important ingredients. Fresh bread, preferably brown or wholemeal, matches it perfectly.

225 g/8 oz cannellini beans
2 carrots, scraped, rinsed and
  thinly sliced
1 stick celery, trimmed,
  rinsed and thinly sliced
1 large onion, finely sliced
150 ml/¼ pint olive oil

1 396-g/14-oz can tomatoes
1 tablespoon tomato purée
1 teaspoon oregano
some chopped parsley
freshly ground black pepper
salt

Pick out any stones or grit from the beans and soak them in cold water overnight. Rinse, cover with cold water and bring slowly to the boil. Allow to boil for 2–3 minutes, then drain and cover with fresh water. Bring to the boil, add all the vegetables, the olive oil, tomatoes, tomato purée, oregano and half of the chopped parsley. Add pepper but no salt at this stage and simmer for about 1¼ hours, or if using a pressure cooker 6–8 minutes. When cooked, add salt and the rest of the parsley. It should have the consistency of thick soup.

REVITHIA SOUPA
Chick Pea Soup

This is another great favourite with Greeks. Indeed, when we talk of soups we basically mean the bean soup, or the lentil soup or the chick pea soup. Of course, there are other soups, special ones for the sick, or Lent, or midnight Easter Saturday supper, the traditional *mayiritsa*, but these three are the staple ones that poor households used to survive on. *Revithia* was a real favourite of our school years, when we went home for lunch, red-nosed and frozen to the bone in the winter months.

Even though a wholly vegetarian soup, the combination of olive oil with the rich taste of the chick peas produces a chicken-flavoured soup. Chick peas take a long time to cook and you can virtually never overcook them. They must *always* be soaked overnight.

Revithia cooked in a more esoteric manner is also the traditional dish of the island of Sifnos in the Kyklathes. On Sifnos it is always served as a first course in the various *panegiris* – religious festivals of eponymous saints that take place in the actual location of the chapel. This may be located on a stony hillside, suspended from the rocks between the blue of the sky and the blue of the sea, like the chapels of the Prophet Elias always are. It may be a little chapel dedicated to Agia Marina, dazzling with white colour in rivalry with its tall white halcyon-like, winged companions – the windmills that shed their summery charm so characteristically over the island; or it may be the monastery of Hrysopigi (Golden Spring), perched on the granitic rocks of a little island that looks as if it has just been split away from its other half that still lies on the narrow mainland peninsula and is miraculously bridged over in a charming reunion by a thin white-walled bridge. The celebrations of the most important religious festivals are financed and catered for by one member of the community or a group of members, that differs every year; a custom similar to the *Horigies* of ancient Greece. (*Horigos* was the man who financed the chorus in ancient theatre.) During these celebrations *in situ*, *revithia* is the first course served to all the visitors, followed by roast goat and roast potatoes and washed down with local red wine, all free of charge.

Alternatively, *revithia* is the Sifnos Sunday lunch *par excellence*. They start to soak the chick peas on Friday afternoon and they stay soaking for twenty-four hours, with the water being changed a couple of times. Then, on Saturday afternoon, they are put into the special two-handled, earth-enware, brick-coloured pot with pretty white linear patterns, with quite a lot of olive oil and an onion peeled but left whole and taken to the local baker's. The baker adds the required water (here lies one of the Sifnos *revithia* secrets), from a water tank that gathers only rain water, and he then puts all the pots into a communal oven, where they stay until Sunday lunchtime, simmering slowly, melting and amalgamating into a wonderful profusion by the time they are ready. (The slow, long cooking in the primitive oven is the other secret of this delicious dish.)

What really makes this soup is the olive oil and the fresh lemon juice added at the end. Greeks with their passion for lemons add quite a lot of it, usually the juice of 2 lemons. Without this the soup tastes a little bland.

350 g/12 oz chick peas
150 ml/¼ pint olive oil
2 medium onions, thinly
   chopped
1 cup chopped parsley
4 whole peppercorns

salt and freshly ground black
   pepper
juice of 1 lemon
1 tablespoon flour dissolved
   in a little water

First check the chick peas and remove any stones, then soak the chick peas overnight in an earthenware bowl. Next day, drain and rinse. Put the chick peas in a saucepan, cover with water to about 2.5 cm/1 in above them, bring to the boil and skim with a slotted spoon until the water is clear. Then add the olive oil, onion, half of the parsley, and the peppercorns and simmer for about 1½ hours or until the chick peas are very soft. Add salt and black pepper, the lemon juice, the rest of the parsley, stir and serve. If a pressure cooker is used then cooking time is about 20 minutes.

My grandmother used to dissolve a tablespoon of flour in a little water, then add it to the soup, simmer for 5 minutes and serve it. This made it thicker and more filling as a result, which I suspect was her motive.

FAKI SOUPA

Lentil Soup

Not finding Mr Bell [a British Naval Officer] at home, I entered a cottage near his residence, which I found inhabited by a man and his wife, two children and two of his more distant relations. They were partaking of a repast, consisting of hard brown bread and a soup made of beans, lentils and garlic.

(George Cochrane, *Wanderings in Greece*, London, 1837, p. 281.)

The great taste of this humble and insignificant-looking pulse is quite striking. It has a nutty taste that combines excellently with garlic, onions, tomatoes and olive oil, in particular, to produce this thick peasant soup that one will find eaten all over Greece, winter and summer, from mountain villages to island communities, particularly during Lent.

There are several types of lentils, but the small brown ones are the most popular in Greece. Lentils are an easy and plentiful crop; this is the quality that makes them a favourite with village communities who keep them as a delicious standby during the isolating winter months.

On Alonnisos, most of the people grow their own lentils, a particularly small variety but extremely tasty. When the short plants turn yellow towards the end of June, they are harvested with menacing-looking, half-moon-shaped scythes, used only by the experienced; while for people like me there are slower but safer implements, my hands. Once cut, the plants are gathered and tied into neat bundles which are left in the sun in order to dry completely.

A few days later, when the weather is suitable (there should be a slight wind, neither too windy nor too calm), the bundles are taken to the threshing floors. These round threshing stone floors are located high up in exposed but also breathtaking spots overlooking the sea, in order to catch the sun as well as the wind. The stone floor is swept first, then the bundles untied and spread all over it. There, with the help of a mule or a horse that is tied to the middle wooden pole and goes round in circles, some in one direction and some in the opposite direction, the golden paper-like stems are trodden on for hours upon hours until it is decided that all the brown crop of the tiny lentils has fallen underneath.

At this point the empty husks are pushed into piles with a long wooden fork, whereupon we all take armfuls of them and throw them overboard into the field where later they are again made into neat bundles and kept for the mules' meals in the winter. Taking armfuls of the papery golden husks is everyone's favourite task as it is easy and permeates one's clothes and hair with their satisfying, dry, sunny aroma. When almost all the empty husks have gone, a ritualistic invisible cross is drawn on the threshing floor with the long wooden fork, before the next stage of the work starts.

This is the iconographic image of the thresher, throwing heaps of the dried-out husks into the air with the help of the long wooden fork, so that the wind catches the feathery husks and blows them away, while the heavier lentils are separated and fall clear on to the stony ground.

There is a pristine and dramatic quality in this solitary figure standing, almost at the edge of a precipice above the sea, with his calm, rhythmical movement undistracted by the blazing midday sun, in complete silence; a silence, uninterrupted even by the cicadas, that feels ripe and impregnated with life; an image that can grip a spectator and keep him captive in its soporific spell for hours. At the end, the crop of lentils is swept into heaps and collected. Later, at home, the brown lentils are spread in the sun in order to dry completely before they are stored for the winter.

A very elderly lady in the village recalled that in the old days they used to spread a coat of olive oil on the lentils before they were spread in the sunshine to dry, in order to prevent and discourage moths nesting in them; a habit now eclipsed probably because of the more resistant modern crops which have been introduced since.

On the island of Kriti they talk of 'wedded lentils' (*fakés pantreménes*) which could totally confuse the uninitiated. In a folkoric way the Kretans wed their lentils with rice, a dish very reminiscent of the Middle Eastern 'kedgeree'. Once the lentil soup has been made as described below and most of it has been consumed for lunch, a handful of rice is thrown in with the lentils in the evening and simmers slowly in their juices, thus stretching quantities. Lastly, traditionally boiled 'sad' and strict-looking brown lentils are eaten by all Hellenes on Good Friday, with not even a drop of olive oil permitted, in order to match the sad spirit of the day.

Lentils do not need to be soaked and they cook much quicker than either beans or chick peas, so care should be taken not to overcook them, which gives them a mushy appearance. They are not suitable for cooking in a pressure cooker as the lentils get mushy. This quantity will serve six people.

225 g/8 oz brown lentils	1 tablespoon tomato purée
1 litre/1¾ pints water	1 bay leaf
1 medium onion, thinly sliced	1 tablespoon oregano
3 cloves garlic, peeled and thinly sliced	a tiny bunch rosemary (optional)
150 ml/¼ pint olive oil	freshly ground black pepper
1 396-g/14-oz can tomatoes, or 450 g/1 lb fresh tomatoes, sliced	salt
	1 tablespoon wine vinegar (optional)

Pick out any grit from the lentils. Rinse them well in a strainer, put in a saucepan, cover with water and slowly bring to the boil. Allow to boil for 2–3 minutes, then drain. Put the lentils back in the saucepan, cover them with the water, add the onions, garlic, olive oil, tomatoes, tomato purée, the herbs and pepper and simmer for 30 minutes. Add salt at the end.

Traditionally a little vinegar is mixed into the soup at the every end, before it is served; a habit more of the older generation school. I much prefer the taste of lentils, though, in pure form.

KOTOPOULO SOUPA AVGOLEMONO

Egg and Lemon Chicken Soup

Abroad, at least, this is the best known of the Greek soups. It is a very light soup, so it is often given to somebody who is recovering from an illness. The connotations attached to this side of the soup are so strongly embedded in me that I cannot bring myself to make it for an otherwise ordinary occasion. There is a Greek saying that goes: '*E palia kotta ehi to zoumi*' ('An old hen makes the best soup') – as a result, a boiling fowl is preferred for making the soup as it makes it much more flavoursome.

There are various ways of serving this dish, once the original cooking has been done. Some of the chicken meat can be added into the avgolemono *soup, and the rest can be served separately and on a different occasion with a* skorthalia; *or a clear* avgolemono *soup can be made with the broth, or some of the broth can also be used for making tasty rice.*

1 boiling fowl, or chicken	salt
1.5 litres/2½ pints water	*Avgolemono soup*
2–3 carrots	2 eggs, separated
2 medium onions	2 lemons
2 sticks celery, sliced	55 /2 oz rice, rinsed and
6 black peppercorns	drained (optional)
1 bay leaf	

Rinse the bird, put it into a large saucepan and cover with the water. Add all the vegetables, peppercorns, bay leaf and salt. Cover and bring to the boil. Skim until the water appears clear, then cover and cook for 1–1½ hours according to the size of the bird. When the leg comes easily away from the body, it is done. Take the chicken out, drain the broth and discard the vegetables.

Make the *avgolemono* sauce as described on page 57, preferably according to the third method; but the first one could also be used. Add it to the soup slowly. Put the soup back on a very low heat for 1–2 minutes and serve immediately.

For a more substantial soup, add the rice to the drained broth and/or some small chicken pieces, taken off the bone and skinned, and cook for 6–8 minutes then proceed with the *avgolemono* sauce as above. I personally prefer the soup plain, or occasionally with some rice added, but never with the chicken in it.

MAYIRITSA

Midnight Easter Soup

Mayiritsa is the soup that Greeks break their fasting with after the midnight liturgy on Easter Saturday, as I have described it in the Introduction. It is made traditionally with the intestines of the milk-fed lamb that each family prepares for roasting on a spit outdoors for the following morning, on Easter Sunday: its liver, lights and the heart. Quantities of spring greens, such as spring onions, dill or fennel, are added to it. My grandmother, who used to prepare the best *mayiritsa* I have ever eaten, used also to add shredded hearts from cos lettuces. The last time she prepared it for all the family, a few years ago, just before she died, it had lost some of its edge and taste but somewhat understandably, as by then she was ninety and had lost some of her *brio*. People who have an aversion for intestines omit them altogether and use the rest of the ingredients. Others who prefer a stronger tasting broth or make *mayiritsa* for large numbers of family, prepare broth in advance by boiling 2–3 small lambs' heads first; when cooked the meat is taken off the bone and added to the rest of the ingredients. It is more unusual to add the tripe of the animal as well.

I have a passion for *mayiritsa* and I long for it all year round; I don't make it on other occasions apart from Easter as I am afraid that this magic spell that binds us with our childhood, our families and our tradition may break; so, I long and wait. When we were spending Easter in a small village in Kriti, recently, with family and friends, I had three large soup plates of it and I still craved for it even though I felt absolutely bloated. This *mayiritsa*, which was made by a local family, was very rich and tasty and rougher, as it contained almost everything that I have already mentioned above, including a lot of tripe.

I have described the way to clean and prepare intestines for those who can find and use them. Without the intestines genuine mayiritsa *cannot be made, but with fresh ingredients you can make a good substitute. It is wise to prepare an enriched broth in advance if you are not using intestines; use a lamb's head, or lambs' bones, or 2–3 pieces from the shoulder, trimmed of all the fat first. Strain through a fine strainer, once the meat is cooked. Take the meat off the bones, cut it into mouthful portions and keep aside; discard the bones or inedible parts. The following quantity will serve six people.*

lamb's intestines (or replace with 1 kg/2 lbs shoulder on the bone, sliced neatly into 2–3 large portions, trimmed of all the fat and boiled)

1 kg/2 lbs lambs' liver, lights and heart (or whatever one can find)

6–7 spring onions, trimmed, rinsed and finely sliced, greens and all

25 g/1 oz butter

2 cos lettuces, trimmed, shredded and rinsed carefully (use only their young leaves and hearts)

fresh dill or fennel, rinsed and finely chopped (about a teacupful), or parsley

1.15 litres/2 pints broth, or hot water

salt and freshly ground black pepper

55 g/2 oz rice, rinsed

Avgolemono sauce

2–3 eggs

2 lemons

Rinse all the meat. Turn the intestines inside out with the help of a thin long stick and rinse them thoroughly. Plunge the intestines into boiling water for a few minutes. Drain them and cut into small portions. Plunge the liver, lights and heart into boiling water and drain immediately. This step gets rid of any overpowering odours. Cube them into small portions.

In a large saucepan, sauté the onions in the butter, until they start to change colour. Add all the chopped meat (intestines, liver, lights, heart or meat), fry together for a few minutes, stirring. Add the shredded lettuces and all the fresh herbs and sauté for a few more minutes. Add the broth or hot water, and seasoning, cover and cook for 30 minutes. Then add the rice and cook for a further 6–8 minutes. Remove from the heat and let it stand for at least 5 minutes, before proceeding with the *avgolemono* sauce.

Make the *avgolemono* sauce as described on page 57 (third method), and add it to the soup, stirring vigorously with a wooden spoon. Return to a very gentle heat for 1–2 minutes, stirring at the same time. It should be quite a thick soup by now with a lot of greenery interrupting the whiteness of the *avgolemono*.

PATSAS SOUPA

Tripe Soup

Since Greece, as a poor country, has never relied on meat, cheap cuts such as tripe and trotters, either sheep or pork ones, constituted a substantial part of the Greek diet. The particularly nourishing qualities of this soup made it traditionally a worker's breakfast, especially for people who started work very early in the morning, at three or four o'clock, who by seven were ready with a Lucullian appetite for a full meal. Restaurants specializing in this type of 'breakfast', similar to the triperies in Paris, developed round the port and railway station in Piraeus, and round the two big markets: the main meat market in Sfagia and the big central market in Athens, as these were the places where working life was bustling at full swing by four o'clock in the morning. Thessaloniki, also, is a very good place to sample the real tripe soup.

The two wonderful *tavernas* that I describe on page 17, located right in the heart of the meat market in central Athens, are the exact places that one will still find *patsas soupa* served as a substantial breakfast to the early workers, or as a nourishing 'sober-up' course to late-night partygoers. Either way, it is a magical place to be in the middle of the night, at two or three a.m., or in the early morning, whichever way one would like to think of it, with an eerie silence oozing from the dark empty alleys of the market, the closed accordion-like shutters expressing a definite sense of terminability with their huge, heart-shaped, old-fashioned tin locks firmly in place, and the iron hooks and decorative balustrades, normally covered with all types of meat hanging from them, naked to the voyeur's eye for the first time. A wonderfully interesting *mélange* of people unite there over bowls of this hot steamy soup.

In the winter, this soup constituted a good part of our diet at home. The time being of a Primus-type paraffin cooker and six of us to feed, the substantial-sized pot with its ingredients was ceremonially started to simmer the night before by our grandmother. It was left on the stove all night and by twelve o'clock the lingering smell could hardly keep us away.
It was served in varied ways, but the one favoured by us, the children, was plain with lots of lemon juice. The adults preferred a more 'beastly' dressing, we thought at the time, of vinegar and chopped raw garlic (called skorthostoubi). *Another way of serving it was with the traditional Greek* avgolemono, *a mixture of beaten eggs and lemon added at the end.*

450 g/1 lb tripe, cut into	juice of 1 lemon, or 2
small pieces	tablespoons vinegar and 1
2–3 pig's trotters	clove crushed garlic
salt	

Rinse the tripe thoroughly. Singe the hair of the trotters on top of a gas cooker. Drop the tripe and trotters into boiling water for 2–3 minutes then drain. This process will ensure that they are thoroughly clean. Cover with cold water, bring slowly to the boil, and skim until no more froth is produced. Add salt, cover and let it simmer for at least 3 hours, or if you are using a pressure cooker for 40 minutes. Then remove the feet, take the meat off the bone, cut it into small pieces, and return it to the soup. Serve with either lemon juice (or vinegar mixed with the clove of squeezed garlic), or with an *avgolemono*, as described on page 56.

ARNAKI SOUPA AVGOLEMONO

Egg and Lemon Soup with Lamb

Unglamorously boiled goat, sheep or lamb is strangely enough the traditional dish of Kriti. In a similar ritual such as the *Hirosfayia* (slaughtering the family pig in November) in the Kyklathes, it is served to friends and relatives during work days when communal help is required, such as the sheep-shearing season, or just during national holidays or family celebratory meals such as weddings (when the dish appropriately is then called *nyfiatiko*), baptisms, etc. But there is a difference in the way it is served in Kriti. Once the meat has been cooked to the point where it is almost dropping off the bone, it is taken out and an enormous pilafi with rice is made in the tasty broth. It is served not as a soup, as in the rest of Greece, but as a pilau with meat.

More characteristic of the place is the accompanying communal enjoyment with the special Kretan instruments – the Kretan lyre (the *santouri*) and the more esoteric *askomantoura* and the *thiamboli* – as well as the other ordinary instruments of Greek peasant music, the clarinets, the violas, the guitars, the drums, all wailing in high-pitched notes in expressions of sadness or reaching climactic outbursts accompanied by the frantic dancing of the black-booted men with the traditional black, lacy, short headscarves worn round the head and over one eye, and shots fired in the air. All this to a background of folkloric songs, indigenous to the island, some well known all over Greece, such as '*Pote tha kami xasteria, pote tha Flevarisi ...*' in which the bandit is longing for the starlit crisp nights of February, so that he can get down from his mountain hideout to the Kretan plains with his best treasured gun as his only companion.

In fact, the saying about February in Greece is '*O Flevaris kian Flevisi, kalokairi tha mirisi*', which reaffirms the song in that even when February plays his worst Februarian tricks with cold or even snow, one can still smell the summer.

It is around the middle of February that the almond trees start to blossom all over Greece and one can have the magnificent spectacle of a whole plain of dense white or ivory blooms that cannot be surpassed in beauty by anything else.

For this soup, it is best to have lean pieces of lamb such as shoulder for a better occasion, or neck if one is aiming for the soup and not the meat. Quite often in Greece the soup used to be made for ailing children by boiling the sheep's head or small lamb's head.

1–2 lambs' heads, or	2–3 potatoes, peeled whole
1 kg/2 lbs shoulder, cut	white pepper
into pieces	55 g/2 oz rice, rinsed and
salt	drained
3–4 carrots	*Avgolemono sauce*
2 onions	2 eggs
1–2 sticks celery, sliced	1–2 lemons

Rinse the meat, place it in a large saucepan and cover with cold water. Add some rock salt and bring to the boil. Skim it until it appears clear, cover and cook for about 50 minutes. Add the vegetables and pepper and cook for a further 20 minutes. Take the meat and vegetables out and keep them warm on a platter. Drain the broth, add the rice and some more water for the soup if needed, and cook for 8–10 minutes.

Prepare the *avgolemono* in one of the ways described on pages 56–7. Return to a very low heat for 2–3 minutes, stirring constantly. Serve the soup immediately, followed by the meat and vegetables.

A bowl with a vinaigrette can be served with the meat. Alternatively, do as the Kretans and make a rice in the broth instead of the soup. In this case you serve the meat on a bed of rice.

FAVA
Yellow Split Pea Salad

Fava is a frugal dish associated with winter, Lent and the war. It is a very old favourite – dating back a couple of thousand years perhaps – as it is probably the same dish mentioned by Aristophanes as *Etnos*, a kind of pulse porridge with olive oil, which was sold in the streets of ancient Athens and which, acording to the same source, was a favourite of Hercules. Current trends towards traditional food have made it rather fashionable again, so it is to be found among the *mezethes* in Athenian *tavernas* throughout the year. It is served at room temperature but I prefer it warm, about half an hour after it has been cooked. In ancient Greece it was served hot.

Fava *is made with a yellow split pea which is smaller than ordinary yellow peas, and light yellow rather than bright orange in colour. It is also sweeter in taste and not as solid in texture once cooked. The* fava *from the island of Santorini is excellent. However, if one cannot find the Greek* fava *then split peas can be used instead. Use 150 g/5 oz yellow split peas but keep the same quantities of the remaining ingredients and cook 5 minutes longer.*

225 g/8 oz *fava*, or Greek
   Cypriot *louvana*
1 litre/1¾ pints water
½ medium onion, finely
   chopped
salt

1–2 shallots, finely sliced
5–6 tablespoons good olive
   oil
freshly ground black pepper
lemon wedges, for serving

Pick the *fava* clean of grit and soak it in cold water for 30 minutes. Rinse in several changes of water. Place the *fava* in a saucepan and cover with the cold water. Bring to the boil and skim until clear. Add the onion and simmer uncovered for 45–50 minutes, stirring occasionally. Add salt to taste halfway through. By the end it should look mushy. Mash it further, using a potato masher, or put it through a food processor. It will appear quite liquid but it solidifies as it cools down. Spread it immediately on a small platter before it solidifies. Garnish with the shallots, dribble the olive oil on top and sprinkle with black pepper. Serve with lemon wedges.

KOUKIA KSERA

Dried Broad Beans

These beans can be obtained at Greek or Italian shops and they are the whole ones with dried brown skins and not the split yellow ones without their skins. They are quite hard to cook, so they need soaking overnight before anything else can be done to them. They look very humble and they cost very little but if treated rightly they produce an amazingly tasty, earthy result.

225 g/8 oz dried broad
  beans, soaked overnight
150 ml/¼ pint olive oil
1–2 medium onions, chopped
3 cloves garlic, peeled and
  finely chopped
1 396-g/14-oz can tomatoes

1 teaspoon tomato purée
1 tablespoon oregano and
  thyme, mixed
1 bay leaf
450 ml/¾ pint water
freshly ground black pepper
salt

Soak the beans overnight. Rinse and drain them. Cover with cold water, boil for 5 minutes, then drain. Add olive oil to the saucepan and fry the onion and garlic until golden, then add the broad beans and fry together for 5 minutes. Add the tomatoes, tomato purée, herbs, bay leaf, water and some pepper and stir. Cover and cook slowly for about 1½ hours. If a pressure cooker is used, cook for 20 minutes. Add salt to taste at the end.

DOLMATHES KAI YIEMISTA
Stuffed Vegetables

Intricate, colourful and aromatic are the combinations that make stuffed vegetables such a favourite. In a country which relies primarily on vegetables it is natural that different methods are explored for new and tempting ways to cook and serve vegetables. Rice, pinenuts, almonds, walnuts and, of course, other vegetables help to serve the purpose and the results can be mouthwatering – from the stuffed vine leaves of ancient Greece to the colourful containers with stuffed vegetables that fill the local bakers of each neighbourhood with their aromas at lunchtime.

THRIA, THE DOLMATHES OF THE ANCIENT GREEKS

Stuffed Vine Leaves

Stuffed vine leaves originated in ancient Greece and from all accounts it was an Athenian dish. In order to put the record straight, one has to turn to the ancient authors. For this purpose I quote from a short article in *Petits Propos Culinaires* 31 (Prospect Books, March 1989) by classicist Andrew Dalby.

> *Thria* in ancient Greek meant "fig leaves". These were listed among other culinary ingredients in Anaxandrides' play, *Protesilaus* (Athens, 370BC) quoted by Athenaeus in his *Deipnosophists 131 a–f*.
>
> Thria were also a dish – stuffed fig leaves – and they were already known by the 5th century BC: they might be stuffed with beef fat (Aristophanes, *Knights* 954) or with pickled fish (*Acharnians* 1101) or with brains (*Frogs* 134). There are mentions in the ancient authors of professional cooks being called to prepare them and they were also popular in Thebes before the city was destroyed by Alexander the Great in 336BC. There is a recipe given by Pollux – the 2nd century AD author – in his *Onomasticon* (thesaurus):
>
>> Take hard pig-fat boiled and mix with milk and thick grain of wheat [possibly bulgur or boiled barley grains]. Combine with soft fresh cheese and egg yolks and surround with a fragrant fig leaf. Boil in chicken or kid stock. Discard the leaf and drop in a pot of boiling honey [possibly mixed with water]. The name of the dish is derived from the leaf.

Andrew Dalby's research has brought him a step further and nearer to the modern equivalent. 'Pollux', he says, 'aimed to explain the vocabulary of the Athenian comic authors. In the fifth century AD, the lexicographer Hesychius, who had many other sources of information, gives the definition of *thria*: "Fig or vine leaves; also foodstuffs wrapped in these." It is obvious from these that people had discovered by the 5th century AD at least that *thria*, although originally made with fig leaves, when made with vine leaves made a much more tasty alternative.

Stuffed vine leaves are still the crown of Greek cuisine. Either vegetarian or with meat, they are always deliciously aromatic and hardly need any additions. In fact additions such as garlic, tomatoes or spices would distract from, if not destroy, their delicate taste. Vine leaves are best when left alone. I always think of it as a 'purist's' dish if ever there was one! So, tomatoes and, even worse, garlic and spices are sacrilege to a Greek and I think rightly so. I have had *dolmathes* all over Greece in restaurants and private homes, some more exquisite than others. I came across a stunning variation of the dish in the spring some years ago while having lunch with a local family in the old village on our island. They had used fresh spinach from their garden for the stuffing as well as rice and onions, which are the usual ingredients in the rest of Greece. Undoubtedly this was the most delicious version I have ever had.

Dolmathes, like most other Greek dishes, is a seasonal dish because of the fresh vine leaves. They have to be small, young and tender in order to be utterly delicious. So, spring and early summer is the season.

Vines grow in abundance in Greece. They are used for shading court-yards, cobbled village alleys and gardens; they are used for their fruit and, of course, for their precious leaves for cooking. Whenever there is a tiny space for a so-called garden, a Greek will immediately plant a vine. We had two small gardens, one at the front and one at the back of our house, and my grandmother had planted three vines long before I was born. By the time I can remember them they were shading both gardens beautiful-ly so we would always have our lunch underneath them and they would also be a good protection against the early morning sun when we slept outside in the hot summer months. Their trunks had gone a very dark brown colour and they were almost beautifully knotted in their old age, resembling my grandmother's hands I always thought. Anyway, every year she delighted, and so did I, in the early spring, bringing out the lad-der and harvesting the first young leaves for our *dolmathes*. I would stand underneath trying to catch them in my skirt as she threw them towards me one by one, making a game of it.

My parents' house does not have a garden any more; instead my father proudly possesses a garage for his car and my grandmother is dead now, otherwise no doubt she would have planted a vine on their roof terrace. But you only have to go a little out of Athens and you still find vines every-where. So, friends as well as relatives are always bringing fresh vine leaves from their own gardens as token presents whenever they visit my parents and, of course, you can buy them in every greengrocer and the *laiki* mar-ket in abundance.

At about the middle of April, fresh vine leaves start arriving in London from Cyprus by air. You can see them in all the Greek shops but even bet-ter at about the beginning of June we start harvesting the young leaves from our own vine in a small London garden and that is really exciting. If you don't have a vine, why not plant one? They do well in England without much expertise or care, and we go on harvesting the leaves throughout the summer as the sun here is quite gentle so they don't become hard and scorched as happens in the summer months in Greece.

Alternatively, of course, you can buy the preserved ones from any delicatessen. They come in glass jars, plastic air-sealed packets or cans from Greece or Cyprus, and they can wait, unlike the fresh ones that have to be used within 2–3 days, until you are in the mood to exercise your fingers rolling them. Here are some useful hints on how to prepare your leaves.

If it is served as a main meal you must allow at least 8–10 *dolmathes* per person as they are small and light and, of course, delicious so no one ever turns them down. You will have approximately 45–48 leaves in 225 g/8 oz of fresh vine leaves. Also, there is the same number in an 225-g/8-oz packet of preserved leaves.

You always need a few leaves for lining the bottom of the saucepan so the *dolmathes* don't stick. You can sort out any damaged leaves for this purpose and you do not need to plunge these ones, instead you can use them raw.

If you are using fresh leaves rinse them first. Have a saucepan with boiling water and a little salt ready on the heat, and plunge the leaves in bunches into the water. Boil for 1 minute. Take them out at once with a slotted spoon and put them in a strainer for a few minutes, then transfer them to a plate. Be careful not to let them boil or cook in the water at this stage, just plunge them quickly in and out, otherwise they disintegrate and become difficult to handle as a result. Most important though, they lose much of their lovely fresh taste. If the vine leaves are not young, plunge them for a little longer. If you are using preserved leaves, rinse them first, plunge them in a bowl of boiling water, leave for 5 minutes then transfer into a bowl or a sink with cold water, rinse them and put in a strainer. They must be rinsed properly otherwise they can be salty. It is a great help if, at this stage, you have somebody to help you by stretching out each leaf carefully on to a table or work surface, while you can proceed with the stuffing and their rolling for which various recipes follow.

DOLMATHES AVGOLEMONO

Vine Leaves with Meat Stuffing and Egg and Lemon Sauce

This is very delicate and one of the most delicious dishes. Mostly when an avgolemono *sauce is served with* dolmathes, *it means that this is a non-vegetarian version and the stuffing contains minced meat. Rarely in Greece will one find the vegetarian version of them served with the egg and lemon sauce.*

Meat stuffing
225 g/8 oz fresh vine leaves, or a jar of preserved ones
110 g/4 oz long-grain or Patna rice
675 g/1½ lbs minced lamb, or beef
1 large onion, grated
4–5 spring onions, finely chopped (optional)
½ cup chopped dill, or fennel
½ cup chopped parsley

juice of ½ lemon
2 egg whites, lightly beaten
600 ml/1 pint hot water
salt and freshly ground black pepper
25 g/1 oz butter
Avgolemono sauce
300 ml/½ pint cooking liquid
3 egg yolks
juice of 1 lemon
1 tablespoon cornflour
salt and white pepper

Prepare the vine leaves as described on page 76. Soak the rice in a bowl of cold water for 10 minutes. Drain, rinse, and drain again for at least 10 minutes. Mix all the stuffing ingredients, apart from the vine leaves and butter, together in a large bowl. If you cannot get dill or fennel, don't worry. The most efficient way of mixing everything properly is to do it by hand. Line the base of a large saucepan with 3–4 vine leaves.

Spread a vine leaf out on a chopping board or a plate, uneven side upwards. Often there is a little stalk at the base of the leaf. Nip this off with your fingers. Take about a teaspoon of the stuffing, unless the vine leaf is a large one in which case you take a tablespoon, and place it near the base of the leaf at the stem end. Press the stuffing into a small sausage-like shape and fold over it the stem end of the vine leaf. Then fold inwards both edges of the leaf towards the middle, and roll into a sausage-like shape. Rolling them can be rather awkward to start with but if you persist you will find it much easier until, after a few sessions, it becomes second nature.

Lay each *dolma* on the spread leaves at the bottom of the saucepan, trapping the folded edge of the leaf underneath, tightly together in circles.

When one layer is finished, start a new one on top and continue in the same fashion until all the mixture is finished. Sprinkle some salt and pepper on each layer and dot the top layer with the butter.

Place a small inverted plate on the top layer, in order to keep them in place while they are cooking, pour 600 ml/1 pint hot water in the saucepan, cover and cook slowly for approximately 50–60 minutes. Take a *dolma* out and try it in order to make sure that they are cooked to your taste.

A little more water may be added if needed, it all depends on the absorbent qualities of the rice. As soon as they are cooked, their cooking liquid must be emptied into another saucepan, otherwise it will be absorbed if they remain in it.

Next, make the sauce. Holding the saucepan with one hand and pressing the plate on the *dolmathes* with the other, lift and, carefully and slowly, pour all the liquid into a small saucepan. There should be approximately just under 300 ml/½ pint. Measure it if you feel uncertain to judge by eye and make it up with hot water if there is less. Let it stand for at least 5 minutes, so that it cools down, before you proceed with the sauce.

Beat the egg yolks with the lemon juice. Add the cornflour and beat until the cornflour has completely dissolved. Then add a tablespoon of the hot sauce slowly, while you beat. You must make sure at this stage that your egg mixture does not cook. Add a few more spoonfuls of the sauce in the same manner and then pour this mixture into the small saucepan with the rest of the strained sauce, stirring continuously. Season with salt and white pepper.

Once this is done, put the saucepan on a very low heat for 2–3 minutes only, so that the sauce thickens up and the cornflour is not prominent, but on no account should you let it boil. Stir continuously at this stage.

Serve at least 8 *dolmathes* per person for a main course and pour 2–3 tablespoons of the sauce over them. The contrast of the yellow velvety sauce on the bright green leaves is strikingly pretty but subtle.

In Greece, the sauce is sometimes poured over the *dolmathes* in their saucepan, the pan is shaken so that the egg and lemon sauce gets well amalgamated, and then the *dolmathes* are served. I personally prefer to have the sauce separately so that none is wasted and because of the prettier appearance on the plate. Let me confess though that this was the way my grandmother always served them, so how could I betray her steps?

DOLMATHAKIA LATHERA OR SARAKOSTIANA

Vegetarian Stuffed Vine Leaves

This is undoubtedly my favourite dish. It has a 'homecoming' aura about it. I feel I have travelled a long way when I end up in front of a plate of these vegetarian stuffed vine leaves in Athens at my parents' home.

Their wonderful amalgamation of fresh summer herbs fills me with a definite sense of continuity, of a 'here I am again ...' feeling, as if nothing has changed and time has stopped. All this, despite the fact that it tends to be an overcooked plate of stuffed vine leaves. My mother's mistake is that she gets a 'brace' of friends in for the rolling session and as the morning proceeds they enjoy themselves so much that they cannot stop themselves rolling! So, more and more *dolmathes* are piled into the saucepan, layer upon layer, until it is full to the brim and this is where the mistake lies. By the time such a large quantity is covered with enough water to cook the ones at the top, the bottom ones are sadly falling apart! Of course, various excuses are made for the vast quantities, mainly pity for us 'poor things living in London' being deprived of such delicacies. Last summer I watched such a session. A good friend of my mother's had just flown back from her house on the Aegean island of Limnos, bringing with her a huge quantity of admittedly beautifully young and fresh vine leaves from her vines. There was virtually a green mountain lying there on the table in front of them! To waste the leaves would be real anathema to all three of them, so, on went the rolling until we had enough overcooked *dolmathes* to feed Piraeus as well as its suburbs.

There are variations of this delicious dish and differences of opinion as to the preparation of the stuffing. Basically there is the faction that believes in sautéeing the onion and the rice (but not the herbs) for 3–4 minutes only, and the other faction that uses them raw.

No one, as far as I know, ever really cooks the stuffing beforehand. That would obviously be a real mistake as then you would end up with overcooked *dolmathes* and much of their flavour lost and taste altered. The rice should be a bit hard when cooked and the herbs will obviously be more aromatic when not completely 'killed' by overcooking.

It is absolutely essential that good quality olive oil is used; these *dolmathes* derive their name from the olive oil, *lathera*, or *Sarakostiana*, *Sarakosti* being the forty-day period of Lent before Easter.

Their taste also relies on the amount of fresh green herbs used, dill being the main participant, with fresh mint, parsley and an abundance of spring onions and, of course, lemons.

DOLMATHES KAI YIEMISTA

79

On the island and particularly around the village there is an abundance of strongly scented wild-growing fennel, so this is what everybody uses instead of dill. This is regarded as normal as they hardly know dill. By June, and particularly July, when we are there, even wild fennel gets scorched by the sun so we have to search for nice green patches of it. Luckily, our local friends are very concerned that we get the right ingredients, particularly the lovely eccentric lady with the herd of goats, *Lenaki* as she is called, or '*Yiayia Katsiki*' as our children call her (the granny with goats). She gives us the tip that in the middle of such and such field there is still a lot of green fennel and she promises not to let her goats have a go at it, or she simply arrives with huge bunches of long-stemmed feathery fennel, which she knows I also love to dry so I can take it back to England with me.

If you cannot find fresh dill, replace with fresh or dried fennel. If you cannot find either, alas, replace it with a larger quantity of fresh parsley and perhaps some fresh thyme. If you cannot find fresh mint replace with a tablespoon of dried mint. You must though have some fresh herbs otherwise it is not worth making this dish. Wait for next spring or summer instead if you want to go for authenticity. This is undoubtedly one of the most excellent dishes for a picnic: it can be prepared the day before, it is dry so there is no danger of spilt sauces, it can be eaten by hand without being messy and, most important, it is delicious.

225 g/8 oz fresh or preserved
  vine leaves
150 g/5 oz Patna or long-
  grain rice
350 g/12 oz onions, or
  225 g/8 oz onions and
  1 bunch spring onions
¾ teacup dill, or fennel
3 tablespoons chopped fresh
  mint

½ teacup chopped parsley
150 ml/¼ pint good quality
  olive oil
salt and freshly ground black
  pepper
juice of 1 lemon
300 ml/½ pint hot water

Prepare the vine leaves as described on page 76. Soak the rice in cold water for 15 minutes then rinse and drain well. Cut the onions in tiny pieces – it may take some time but you must cut them and not grate them or, worse, liquidize them. You need their volume for lightness and balance in each *dolma*. If you grate them they disintegrate and, although the taste is evident, their volume is not there to keep the rice apart. So you end up with a thick ball of rice. Quite undesirable!

In a large bowl, mix together the rice, onions, herbs, half the olive oil, salt and pepper and half the lemon juice. Line the bottom of a wide saucepan with vine leaves. Place a teaspoon of the stuffing on a vine leaf and roll as described on page 77. Arrange in circles in the saucepan, tightly together, until all the vine leaves are used. Pour the rest of the olive oil, as well as the lemon juice, on top of the *dolmathes*.

Put a small inverted plate on top of them in order to keep them in place, carefully add the hot water (they should not be covered but they should sit in it) and cook very slowly, covered, for 50 minutes. After 50 minutes take one out and try it: if a little too crunchy, cook it or a few more minutes. A lot depends on how young the vine leaves are if they are fresh. A little more water may be needed.

You can serve them hot, or when cold they can be arranged on a pretty platter, on a bed of raw vine leaves, and served with quartered lemons. Pick them up individually by hand in order to arrange them so that their appearance is not spoilt.

In Greece, they are very often served with a bowl of plain yoghurt at the table which people either serve on the side of their plates or even spoon on top of their *dolmathes*.

LAHANODOLMATHES

Stuffed Cabbage Leaves with Egg and Lemon Sauce

A frugal dish but with its taste superseding its frugality. The egg and lemon sauce that characterizes it complements the taste of the usually bland cabbage and renders the dish luxurious, new and totally unexpected. It always contains a meat stuffing, indeed a pork stuffing is preferred, but it is not indispensable and, unlike Greek habits, it is always cooked with butter.

All in all, a winter dish; I remember our next-door neighbours would join my grandmother and my mother on dark winter mornings with all the women stuffing the cabbage leaves, round huge pots on the kitchen table, in a joint effort to prepare the dish for both households, and turning their task into a very pleasant and chatty morning, as we went off to school and left them in peace.

Lahanodolmathes *is an ideal dish for England with the abundance of the (notorious) English green cabbage, which at last can serve a more worthwhile purpose than usual! Even though in Greece the white Dutch cabbage is used, the same variety here seems to be much harder and woody and it does not make a good candidate for stuffing. The stuffing is always used raw, even though occasionally some people prefer to sauté the chopped or grated onions first. These quantities will give approximately 25 dolmathes, or more if you make them smaller.*

1 large green cabbage, between 1.5–2 kg/3–4 lbs
450 g/1 lb minced lamb, veal, beef or pork
2 tablespoons olive oil
110 g/4 oz long-grain or Patna rice, soaked, rinsed and drained
2 large onions, finely sliced or thickly grated
3 tablespoons chopped parsley

1 tablespoon chopped fresh dill, or fennel (if possible)
salt and white pepper
2 egg whites, lightly beaten (keep the yolks for the sauce)
55 g/2 oz butter
Avgolemono sauce
150 ml/¼ pint cooking liquid
3 egg yolks
juice of 1 large lemon
25 g/1 oz cornflour

Core the cabbage, keep the outer leaves for lining the saucepan once they have been rinsed. Start peeling off each layer of leaves carefully. Cut more of the core off as you proceed in order to make the peeling easier. When you reach the tight hard centre, stop, as it is easier to blanch this part intact and then peel the leaves off.

Rinse the stripped leaves in a sink of cold water. Blanch them in small bunches in boiling salted water for 1–2 minutes, according to their hardness. Take out with a slotted spoon and drain in a colander. As one bunch is taken out, dip another one in the boiling water. At the end put in the heart of the cabbage unstripped and let it boil slightly longer. Be careful not to overboil the cabbage as it will make it difficult to handle and it may fall apart during the cooking. Also its taste will suffer. The leaves only need to soften slightly in this preliminary step and not to cook.

In a large bowl, mix all the remaining ingredients, except the butter, together including the egg whites, and add a generous amount of seasoning to counterbalance the blandness of the cabbage.

Cut the large outer leaves in two and also trim any hard ends and veins, in order to make them pliable for the rolling. The stuffed cabbage leaves are much larger than stuffed vine leaves and not so gracious, so one does not have to worry about their size or shape, even though, in general, they should resemble fat cigars.

Place a tablespoon of stuffing at one end of each leaf, fold the leaf over it in the shape of a short fat cigar, fold the two ends in towards the centre, securely trapping the stuffing, and roll it tightly, but bearing in mind that the rice will need room to expand. Always place the stuffing in the inner surface of the leaves, following their original shape, packed round the central head, as it will make it easier than trying to roll them in a totally opposite manner.

Carefully strip as many leaves as possible from the heart of the cabbage, and stuff them individually. Leave the inner heart intact, open the leaves on the top, and put some stuffing in it, too.

Prepare a large saucepan, lined with the uncooked outer leaves in order to prevent the *dolmathes* from sticking. Layer them tightly together in circles. Try not to place more than 2–3 layers at the most in one saucepan as one runs the risk of having the lower layer invariably overcooked, if not disintegrating. Season each layer with salt and white pepper and scatter small knobs of butter all over it. Any stuffing left over at the end can be shaped into round small balls and cooked on top of the rest in the saucepan. Trimmings from the cabbage can also go in as they add to the flavour. Place an inverted small plate on the last layer, in order to keep them down and prevent them from bubbling and unfolding. Pour about 600 ml/1 pint hot water all around, or enough water to barely, but not completely, cover the top layer.

Keep in mind that you will need at least 150 ml/¼ pint of liquid sauce at the end of their cooking in order to make the egg and lemon sauce. Some people like to squeeze a little lemon juice in the saucepan, but a lot depends on how lemony you prefer them as Greeks can overdo it sometimes. Cover and cook gently for about 50 minutes.

As soon as they are cooked, lift up the saucepan and, holding the plate down firmly over the *dolmathes*, tilt it and empty almost all the liquid into a bowl. Make it up to at least 150 ml/¼ pint with hot water, if there is not enough. Beat the egg yolks a little, add the lemon juice and beat them together with a fork for a few minutes. Mix the cornflour in 2 tablespoons of water, making sure all the lumps are diluted. Add it to the egg mixture and beat together. Start adding tablespoons of the hot liquid sauce from the *dolmathes*, while you are beating all the time. Once 4–5 tablespoons have been added, the sauce should have acquired the right warmth in order to be used. Pour it all over the *dolmathes* and rotate the saucepan. When it has been well incorporated, return on a very gentle heat for 3–4 minutes, rotating the saucepan occasionally.

DOLMATHES KAI YIEMISTA

YIEMISTA

Stuffed Vegetables

It is difficult even for the visitor in the summer in Greece not to notice the round or oblong aluminium containers, dazzling with colour and exuding exoticism from their bright stuffed-vegetable contents, on their way to the local baker's in the morning or on the way back around noon, with their good looks slightly dampened this time, or on the serving counter of a restaurant. They invariably attract one's eyes.

In monochromatic hues of red, of solitary tomatoes, or more commonly coupled with vibrant green peppers and, in the home versions, accentuated by the lustrous mauve tones of the elongated aubergines or stripy green courgettes, these stuffed vegetables have become an *epigramma* to Greek summer life. *Yiemista* literally means 'filled up', from the verb *yiemizo* (to fill). In varied versions they may contain a totally glorious vegetarian stuffing of rice, a quantity of onions and fresh herbs, such as fresh mint and parsley, or dill and parsley, and a lot of fragrant olive oil. It is in this version that pine nuts and a handful of raisins are sometimes added, mostly by Greeks whose origins lay in Asia Minor.

Greeks, particularly the islanders, prefer their tastes pure and sharp and they are not terribly keen on mixing sweet and savoury, as happens further east; they have their main courses and their *mezethes* sharply accentuated, and their coffee and desserts accentuated sweet.

The simple vegetarian stuffing is almost always used uncooked to stuff the vegetables; some people though, particularly on the islands, fry the onions first which results in a more piquant and heavier dish.

In the Aegean islands they include a small aubergine, cubed, some garlic, a small courgette and a green, soft-skinned pepper, also cubed.

There is an even more exotic and unusual version of stuffed vegetables when we use the simple vegetarian stuffing of rice, onions and fresh herbs for stuffing the flowers of the courgette. This results in one of the most voluptuous and aromatic dishes one can experience.

Kolokythokorfathes, as these flowers are called (*kolokythi* being a courgette), are rather special and time-consuming; therefore, the likelihood of stumbling across the dish in a restaurant in Greece is slight. It is worth looking out for in Kriti, or in large cities like Iraklion, where they cater for local people, or in one of the small mountain villages. Some years ago my sisters and I had some outstanding versions of it there that have left their taste in our mouths, as well as in our hearts, ever since.

A more luxurious meat filling makes a Sunday version which is not necessarily the most favoured by Greeks, though it is certainly the one favoured by all children. Occasionally fried aubergine pulp is used to stuff tomatoes, along with grated cheese, beaten eggs and some breadcrumbs. This, though, is more of a party version than the usual *yiemista* of Greek families. The essence of *yiemista* lies in the fusion of fresh herbs with the onions and olive oil. The urban Greek housewife will search in her local street market (*Iaiki*) for the possible but indispensable candidates: spring onions, feathery bunches of dill, dense bunches of flat-leafed parsley, small bunches of strong-scented mint, all crowned by fresh leaves from the inevitable basil plants that every Greek household possesses.

The Greek woman of the country or the islands will either take a walk to the periphery of her village herself, or otherwise will send her daughter in order to gather the greenest sprigs of wild fennel, wild mint, fresh oregano and anything else she might decide beneficial to the aroma of the dish; she, too, will supplement this with a few fresh leaves of her basil plants, from her colourful, whitewashed courtyard. And perhaps some of her spring onions, too, if they are still young and slender and have not been scorced by the brilliantly hot sun.

For the purpose of stuffing, vegetables should be selected for their shape, good looks and freshness; tomatoes are selected round, large and not over-ripe; green peppers should be thin-skinned and symmetrical, so that they can sit upright; the aubergines should be from the long, thin, sweet varieties like the *argitikes*.

Yiemista are almost always sent to the local baker's, but occasionally they are also cooked in a casserole at home. Special aluminium round containers, which resemble a deep roasting dish with a lid, are used for the latter. Any large saucepan, though, will do as long as it can contain them in one single layer.

When they are sent to the baker's, they always contain some thick slices of potatoes which are wedged in between the various vegetables to fill the spaces and help to keep them upright. These potatoes are delicious as they get impregnated with the aromatic juices. They are peeled, cut in half lengthways and sliced, resembling quarter-moon shapes (*kithonates*).

Stuffed vegetables, in particular tomatoes and green peppers, and especially when using the uncooked vegetarian stuffing, are terribly easy to make. Bear in mind that like all Greek vegetable dishes, they rely primarily on olive oil for their rich taste; particularly so in their vegetarian version. It is not wise to economize on the quantity of the olive oil; it is a healthy and natural ingredient, after all. Another important point is to try to have the rice slightly hard at the end of the cooking. With this objective in mind, try not to waterlog either the stuffing or the finished product in its baking dish or saucepan. There are tomatoes and masses of chopped or grated onions and, of course, there is olive oil in the various stuffings;

DOLMATHES KAI YIEMISTA

the rice will absorb the moisture required for its expansion from these ingredients, and later on from the basting, during cooking.

Waterlogged and overcooked rice gives the dish a completely different texture and taste. It is best to use a long-grain variety such as Patna rice with a smaller and more slender grain rather than the hard round Italian variety. If the Uncle Ben variety is used, remember to make the stuffing more moist and add another 5 minutes to the cooking.

The Indian variety of the aromatic Basmati rice can be used, although one will never come across it in Greece. It is always best to soak the rice for at least 10 minutes in cold water, and then to rinse it under running water and drain it, in order to get rid of the excess starch.

When the dish is baked in Greece, it is never covered, so inevitably the tops of the stuffed vegetables become slightly scorched; these scorched ones are particularly sought after as they are considered a delicacy.

The quantities I give are for four people, allowing two pieces of vegetables per person, such as a tomato and a pepper, which supplemented by a few potatoes and a salad or some cheese will make a main course. Alternatively, serve one per person for a first course and wait for the reaction. They are quite light, so there won't be any problem with the rest.

DOMATES KE PIPERIES YIEMISTES ME RYZI

Tomatoes and Green Peppers Stuffed with Rice (Vegetarian Version)

Stuffing 1

4 large tomatoes

4 medium green peppers

150 g/5 oz Patna rice, rinsed and drained

2 large onions, about 350 g/12 oz, skinned and thickly grated (3–4 spring onions, finely chopped, add to the taste)

1 teacup chopped fresh parsley

4 tablespoons fresh chopped mint, or 1 teacup finely chopped fresh dill

a few fresh basil leaves (optional)

150 ml/¼ pint olive oil

salt and freshly ground black pepper

2–3 medium-sized potatoes, peeled and sliced *kithonates*, as described on page 85 (optional)

½ teaspoon sugar

225 g/8 oz fresh tomatoes, peeled and thickly grated, mixed with 150 ml/¼ pint water

This is the most common stuffing in Greece. Rinse the tomatoes and peppers. With a small sharp knife, cut a thin, round slice off the top, stem end of each one and keep aside. Remove the seeds from the peppers. Place the tomatoes open-side down on a plate, in order to drain them. Reserve their juice for the stuffing. Using a teaspoon, scoop most of the tomato pulp out, put it on a wooden board, and shred it finely.

Place the rice in a bowl. Add the onions (or chopped spring onions) to the rice. Add the fresh herbs – parsley and mint, or parsley and dill, or whatever other aromatic herbs you have available, if not the above. Make sure, though, that you always use a large amount of parsley. Dried mint can replace the fresh mint if need be, in a smaller quantity (1 tablespoon). Add the shredded tomato pulp and any reserved tomato juices, half the olive oil, season with salt and freshly ground pepper and mix well.

Place the prepared tomatoes and peppers in a deep baking dish, tightly packed. Insert a few thick slices of potatoes in between to pack any empty spaces and in order to keep the peppers upright. Sprinkle a little sugar into each tomato to counterbalance their slight acidity, and a little salt into all the vegetables. Fill each vegetable with the prepared stuffing, but only three-quarters full, leaving room for the uncooked rice to expand. Cover with the reserved sliced round tops. Pour the rest of the olive oil on top of each vegetable. Pour into the bottom of the dish the grated fresh tomatoes, mixed with the water, season with salt and pepper all over and bake in a pre-heated oven, gas no. 5 (375°F/190°C), for 1½ hours.

Baste the vegetables at least twice, in order to keep them moist on the top. Some people sprinkle some fresh breadcrumbs on top of the vegetables in order to give them a crustier top.

DOLMATHES KAI YIEMISTA

YIEMISI ME KOUKOUNARIA

A Vegetarian Stuffing with Pine Nuts and Raisins

Stuffing 2
8 large tomatoes, or 4
    tomatoes and 4 peppers
1 large onion, finely sliced or
    thickly grated
150 ml/¼ pint olive oil
55 g/2 oz pine nuts
25 g/1 oz blanched and
    skinned almonds
110 g/4 oz Patna rice, rinsed
    and drained
salt and freshly ground black
    pepper

1 teacup parsley, finely
    chopped
25 g/1 oz raisins, rinsed and
    drained
450 g/1 lb potatoes, peeled
    and quartered (optional)
½ teaspoon sugar
1 tablespoon tomato purée
    diluted in 150 ml/¼ pint
    water

Prepare the tomatoes and peppers (if using) as in the previous recipe. Sauté the onion in half the olive oil in a frying pan. When slightly golden, add all the nuts and rice and sauté together for a few more minutes until the nuts start to change colour. Add the reserved shredded tomato pulp. If there are 8 tomatoes to be stuffed, keep some of the pulp for the baking dish and do not add it all into the frying pan. Add 3 tablespoons water, season and simmer for 2–3 minutes. Mix the parsley and the raisins into the stuffing as soon as it comes off the heat.

Place the tomatoes, or tomatoes and peppers, in a baking dish. A few sliced potatoes can be lodged in between them. Sprinkle a little sugar into each tomato, and a little salt into all the vegetables.

Fill them three-quarters full with the above stuffing, cover them with the reserved round tops, and pour the rest of the olive oil over them. Pour the diluted tomato purée into the bottom of the dish along with any reserved tomato pulp.

Cook in a pre-heated oven, gas no. 5 (375°F/190°C), for 1½ hours, basting occasionally as in the original recipe.

NISIOTIKO

Island Stuffing

Stuffing 3
4 large tomatoes
4 green peppers
1 small courgette, sliced into
tiny pieces
1 small aubergine, sliced into
tiny pieces
1 very small green pepper,
cored and sliced into tiny
pieces
225 g/8 oz fresh tomatoes,
peeled and thickly grated,
mixed with 150 ml/¼ pint
water
1 large onion, about 225 g/
8 oz, peeled and finely
chopped, or grated thickly

2 cloves garlic, peeled and
sliced
salt and freshly ground black
pepper
150 ml/¼ pint olive oil
110 g/4 oz Patna rice, rinsed
and drained
a few fresh basil leaves
2 tablespoons fresh mint, or 1
tablespoon dried mint
1 teacup chopped parsley
½ teaspoon sugar

Rinse and prepare all the vegetables as described on page 87. Place the shredded pulp you get from the 4 large tomatoes into a frying pan, along with the onion, garlic, seasoning and 3 tablespoons of water. Stir for a few minutes until all the water evaporates, add half of the olive oil and sauté for a few minutes. Add the tiny pieces of courgette, aubergine, green pepper, the rice and the herbs and stir for a few more minutes, until the rice looks glistening, but it should on no account cook. If the rice cooks at this stage, by the time the stuffed vegetables come out of the oven, the rice will have become a soggy, overcooked mass.

Sprinkle a little sugar into each tomato and, using a teaspoon, fill the vegetables three-quarters full with the above stuffing. Cover them with the reserved round tops, pour the remaining olive oil all over them, pour the grated fresh tomatoes mixed with the water into the bottom of the dish and cook in a pre-heated oven, gas no. 5 (375°F/190°C), for 1½ hours. Baste them from time to time, as in the previous recipe.

YIEMISTA ME KREAS

Meat Stuffing

Stuffing 4

8 large tomatoes, or 4
  tomatoes and 4 green
  sweet peppers
1 medium onion, finely sliced
4 tablespoons good vegetable
  or olive oil
350 g/12 oz minced lamb, or
  beef
salt and freshly ground black
  pepper
2 tablespoons fresh chopped
  mint, or 1 tablespoon
  mixed oregano and thyme

3 tablespoons chopped
  parsley
55 g/2 oz Patna or other
  long-grain rice, rinsed and
  drained
½ teaspoon sugar
1 tablespoon tomato purée
  diluted in 150 ml/¼ pint
  water

This is the second most common stuffing in Greece. Prepare the tomatoes and peppers (if using) as on page 87. Sauté the onion gently in half the oil, until it becomes translucent. Add the minced meat and fry together, stirring with a wooden spoon and breaking up any lumps. Once the moisture from the meat has evaporated and the meat has acquired a brown colour, add the tomato pulp reserved from the scooped tomatoes. If you are using only tomatoes, keep some of the pulp for the bottom of the baking dish, in order to make their sauce tastier. Season, add 150 ml/¼ pint water, cover and cook gently until the meat is tender, approximately 30 minutes. Add all the herbs at the end, together with the rice, and a little more water if it looks too dry. Stir together and cook gently for a further 2–3 minutes only.

Sprinkle a little sugar into each tomato and, using a teaspoon, fill them three-quarters full with the stuffing. Seal them with the reserved tops. Pour a little of the reserved olive oil on each stuffed vegetable, pour the diluted tomato purée into the bottom of the dish and bake as before, basting them occasionally.

MELITZANES KE KOLOKYTHAKIA YIEMISTA

Stuffed Aubergines and Courgettes

It is quite common to stuff aubergines and courgettes with any of the first four stuffings: a simple rice and onion vegetarian stuffing, with or without pine nuts and raisins, or a meat stuffing. The most common, though, is the island-type stuffing. The reason is that almost always the pulp extracted from the vegetables is shredded and used in the stuffing, either wholly or partly. The amount of rice is then reduced slightly; and I find that sautéeing the onions and the vegetable pulp first, particularly for aubergines, results in a more tasty dish.

The aubergines should ideally be of the long thin variety – either the pale striped ones (*argitikes*) or the dark, lustrous purple ones. Sometimes the aubergines are too long, particularly in the latter variety, or the courgettes may be too long; then it is better to cut them in half, otherwise the task of scooping them and later filling them with the stuffing can become arduous. Scooping aubergines and courgettes is not as simple as with tomatoes; it requires some patience, at least at the beginning. An apple corer, a strong teaspoon, or a small sharp knife may be used for the purpose.

Rinse the aubergines and courgettes first (roughly one of each per person). Cut a thick round slice off the stem end and keep it for sealing the stuffed vegetables later. Slowly and carefully start scooping out the middle fleshy part, with short circular movements. The further down you go, the more difficult it becomes. One end ideally should remain intact. Fill them with your favourite stuffing, lay them on a roasting dish and bake as described for the other stuffed vegetables for 1 hour and 20 minutes.

KOLOKYTHAKIA YIEMISTA AVGOLEMONO

Stuffed Courgettes with Egg and Lemon Sauce

A deliciously delicate and light dish, and a particular favourite of all our family, which includes three generations at the moment and not so long ago four. It can be made with either of the first two vegetarian raw stuffings (pages 86–8) but with any hint of tomatoes omitted; instead the juice of half a lemon should be added in the stuffing. Also a large amount of fresh dill or fennel is always added to the dish along with the freshly chopped parsley. Dill, in particular, seems to have an affinity with courgettes. Also a little fresh mint may be added.

In the meat version, which makes an outstanding dish, a little grated cheese is sometimes added, either kefalotyri *or* Parmesan. *In both versions, the whites of the eggs are added to the stuffing, once they have been slightly beaten, and also some of the courgette pulp that has been extracted is shredded finely and added. Courgettes can be substituted by marrows very successfully in this dish; in fact, it is one of the most successful ways that marrow can be consumed. Allowing 2 courgettes per person, I shall give the recipe for the meat stuffing with the* avgolemono *sauce added at the end, and any vegetarian alternatives can easily be adapted to this recipe and description.*

8 medium-sized courgettes,
about 1 kg/2 lbs at least
3–4 spring onions, finely
sliced
1 medium onion, finely sliced
55 g/2 oz butter
225 g/8 oz lean minced lamb,
beef or veal
a squeeze of lemon juice
300 ml/½ pint water
salt and freshly ground black
pepper
55 g/2 oz long-grain rice,
rinsed and drained

3 tablespoons chopped fresh
parsley
3 tablespoons chopped fresh
dill, or fennel
1 tablespoon chopped fresh
basil
55 g/2 oz cheese, grated
(optional)
2 egg whites (keep yolks for
the sauce)
Avgolemono sauce
2–3 egg yolks
1 large and juicy lemon
salt and white pepper

Rinse the courgettes under running water, scraping them a little with a sharp knife, in order to dislodge any grit. Cut off the stem end and discard. Scoop out their middle fleshy part, with circular, short movements, being careful not to damage their skin. (Not too serious if you do.) Continue as far down as you can reach but do not pierce the other end. Some people, in fact, cut both ends and scoop them from both sides, in order to make this task easier. If this method is adopted, one has to be careful when filling them to keep them horizontal at all times. (Treat like an Italian canelloni.) If the courgettes are too long, cut them in two to make the task easier. Place the courgettes in a bowl of cold water as you finish scooping each one.

Prepare the stuffing by softening the onions in half the butter, until they become glistening. Add the minced meat and half the shredded courgette pulp and sauté together, stirring and breaking any lumps, until the meat looks slightly brown. Squeeze on a little lemon juice, but reserve most of it for the *avgolemono*. Add 150 ml/¼ pint water and seasoning, and simmer for about 15 minutes. Add the rice for the last 3–4 minutes. Remove from the heat, add the freshly chopped herbs and, when slightly cooler, the cheese, if used, and the slightly beaten whites of the eggs. Mix well and, using a teaspoon, fill the courgettes three-quarters full with this mixture. Leave them aside.

Melt the rest of the butter in a sauté pan or a large frying pan with a lid, large enough to take the courgettes lying horizontally in a single layer.

Add the rest of the shredded courgette pulp to the pan and turn it about to sweat a little. Add the remaining 150 ml/¼ pint water, bring to the boil and lower the stuffed courgettes into it. Sprinkle in a little more lemon juice and season with salt and white pepper. The courgettes should not be covered with the cooking liquid, they should be half-immersed in it, otherwise their stuffing will run out. Cover and cook gently, approximately 30 minutes, basting them occasionally. Add a little more water if needed, keeping in mind that they should not dry out completely as some liquid is needed at the end in order to make the sauce. Remove from heat and let stand for 5 minutes before adding the *avgolemono* sauce.

Make the egg and lemon sauce by beating the egg yolks as described on page 56. Pour this mixture over the courgettes in the saucepan but away from the heat, rotating the pan at the same time. Return it to a very low heat for 2–3 minutes in order to thicken the egg slightly, shaking the pan occasionally in order to prevent the egg curdling. Serve hot, with a fresh green salad, with plenty of fresh dill and spring onions if possible, and fresh bread for the wonderful sauce.

AN EASY ALTERNATIVE

An easier but also lighter alternative is to use the above meat stuffing raw. In this case just mix all the stuffing ingredients, onions, rice, meat, herbs, cheese, egg whites, a little lemon juice, half of the courgette pulp, seasoning and add 2 tablespoons of olive oil or vegetable oil, in a large bowl. Fill the prepared courgettes and cook them as above, melting all 55 g/2 oz butter in the saucepan. Add the *avgolemono* sauce exactly as above.

DOLMATHES KAI YIEMISTA

ELIES KAI LATHI
Olive Trees and Olive Oil

The almond trees are in blossom; the anemones spring up by thousands in the fields; the air is divine; everything speaks of spring. People are at work already in the vineyards and are digging deep circles round the roots of the olive trees, in order that the rain water, when rain comes, may collect there.

'Give my roots plenty of water and I will give thee jars full of oil,' says the olive tree according to a Greek proverb.

It is quite affecting to observe how much the olive tree is to the country people. Its fruit supplies them with food, medicine and light; its leaves, winter fodder for the goats and sheep; it is their shelter from the heat and its branches and roots supply them with firewood.

The olive tree is the peasant's all in all.

(Frederica Bremer, *The Narrative of a Winter Residence and Summer Travel in Greece and Its Islands*, London, 1863, p. 213.)

According to myth, it was the goddess Athena in her strife with Poseidon over the patronage of the city of Athens who produced the first olive tree and so won the contest by outdoing the miracles Poseidon performed. So, she became the patron goddess of Athens and was worshipped not only in Attica and Boeotia, but also in various places in Greece, its islands and its colonies. Also various coins exist, and in particular a silver tetradrachm of Athens in 440BC, with a sprig of olive and the owl as the symbols of the goddess.

For factual information the *Oxford Classical Dictionary* says: 'We know from finds that olives were grown in the Mediterranean area and Minoan Crete during the Neolithic Age. Plantations are mentioned by Homer and oil was exported from Attica before, and after, the time of Solon (the Athenian legislator 638–559BC). As soon as it became possible by imports of grain to satisfy most of the requirements of the Greek people, crops such as olives and grapes took the place of grain and were very widely cultivated in Greece during the classical age.'

Sophocles, the great dramatist (496?–406), in his *Oedepus epi Kolono*, praises the Athenian olive tree as 'γηγενὲς', literally meaning, self-sprung from the earth.

Peisistratos, the Athenian tyrant (560–527), is supposed to have had a special fund which was distributed to people in order to promote and encourage the cultivation of more olive trees, and the athletes who participated in public occasions such as the *Panathenaea*, the four-yearly tribute in honour of the patron-goddess of their city, Athena (the *Panathenaea* were introduced and organized by Peisistratos), rubbed their bodies with olive oil and an olive branch was given to the victors.

But the olive was not only the symbol of victory (*niki*) but also the symbol of peace (*eirene*), so, according to history, when the messengers of Aeneas came to ask for their dead, after the battle in Latium, they were carrying olive branches (Virgil, *Aeneid*, Books 7 and 8). An olive branch was also held by Orestes, when he comes as a suppliant to Apollo (Aeschylus, *Eumenithes*, line 43).

Plato's Academy was located near the river Ilissos at Keramikos, amidst olive groves it seems, and when later his best pupil, Aristotle, introduced the famous Peripatetic school of philosophy, he and his pupils took their *peripatoi* (strolls) under the coolness of the olive trees. Milton spells an air of wonder when, inspired by this exact spot, he writes:

> See there the olive grove of Academe,
> Plato's retirement, where the Attic bird
> Thrills her thick-warbled notes the summer long

Tradition has it that one of these olive trees from Plato's Academy is still surviving to this day. It is a huge tree with a knotted trunk full of cavities with a metal sign '*Elea tou Platonos*' – Plato's olive tree – and a square iron balustrade to mark it. Its shape, its size, its history and the conductor's voice shouting '*Acadimia Platonos*', for the bus stop, every time the bus approached it, used always to fill me with awe as a child.

The scientific, Latin name of the olive tree (*Olea europea*) is derived from the Greek *elaia*. When I asked a local friend and experienced grower on Alonnisos, Mitsos, how long an olive tree can survive, his face became very serious and with a typical Greek hand movement, circling in the air above his head, he replied, 'Over a thousand years,' and he himself seemed to be awe-struck by this statement.

Olive trees are virtually everywhere in Greece. One can find them in small gardens, public squares and even sometimes planted along pavements on busy streets. But most common of all in the countryside and islands is the sight of whole hillsides that seem to sway in a silvery cloak of blades under the gentle breeze. Most importantly, the olive trees are very hardy and will grow almost everywhere, on stony ground, exposed to the sea winds and particularly the notorious Aegean *meltemi*, the north-eastern wind. They will grow on almost vertical slopes and arid spots where other trees would shrivel. The olive trees grow old in a gentle fashion; they wrinkle with grace but they do not die.

Olive trees in Greece usually bear fruit every second year because they do not get enough water. Olive groves that have irrigation systems bear fruit every year. It is not unusual in Greece to have no rain at all for four to five months in the spring and summer. In early June everyone worries about the rain. Will it come or not? If it does not then the olive trees drop most of their slim fruit at that stage. Quite often *litanies* are performed by the local priest. With the right amount of rain, the yield can be tremendous and everyone is overjoyed and as a result very generous with their olive oil. Our friends and main suppliers on the island will, on no account, accept money for it and the mother-figure of the household is always encouraging me not to economize but to enjoy it.

Every summer we are given innumerable bottles of olive oil by various families of friends, from the new crop to be sampled. Sometimes if it is early in the morning, the bottle, accompanied by some freshly picked plums or peaches and some garden-grown tomatoes, is left on the front steps or at the table in the garden, a gesture which is particularly moving, since sometimes it is impossible to find out the donor.

Consequently, in the dry summer months on the island, with not a drop of water in the village tank but with plentiful quantities of olive oil, I cannot help thinking: 'Pity we cannot have a shower or wash our hair with olive oil.' Olive oil has always been the main source of fat in Greece. It is a great tradition and in ancient Greece butter was considered food fit only for barbarians. The tradition is so embedded that still very little butter is used in Greek cooking and still none in the Greek countryside.

It is this dietary fact that may account for the long-lived Greek peasantry, as village communities wholly depend and survive on olive oil. Olive oil, of course, is a wonderful commodity. It adds to vegetables the spark and fruitiness that absolutely transforms them. It puts back into pulses the taste and freshness that lies dormant, like no other ingredient can. Where indeed would pulses be without olive oil?

Its nutritious qualities are well known and appreciated in Greece. During the German occupation, 1941–4, whole houses were sometimes exchanged for a few kilos. German propaganda posters stuck on Athenian walls at the same period tried to advertise their good will and innocence to the starving population and focused on the shortage of olive oil. The Germans claimed that since they never ate olives or olive oil, they could not be blamed for the shortages or for the starving population. 'It is the Jews, the British, *provocateurs* and black marketeers that are responsible,' the posters claimed! In this case at least the ancient Greeks were right: 'Butter is food for barbarians.'

A Greek scholar told me that during the German occupation the neutral Turkish Embassy in Athens used to distribute three tablespoons of olive oil along with some rice and small quantities of pulses to Turkish nationals weekly. (My mother also confirmed this later.)

After the war we used to have as mid-morning snacks a slice of brown bread with olive oil and salt and pepper sprinkled on it, as it was considered to be so nutritious.

In Greece, olive oil is used not only for culinary purposes. Soap is made out of it, and in a cup of water and a tiny wick from the flowers of the wild-growing Verbascums, it is still used for lighting and sometimes often one will see it perpetually burning in front of the ikon of the patron saint of the household.

'The streets are lighted with oil, except on the nights on which the light of the moon is reckoned on. If the almanac is wrong, or if the moon hides itself, all Athenians are allowed to break their necks.' (E.F.V. About, *Greece and the Greeks*, 1855, p. 283.)

In Christian Greek baptisms the baby is anointed with olive oil in different parts of its body by the priest, and the olive leaves that are aromatic are used in Greek churches as burning incense. It is used medicinally against constipation, particularly in children; it is used against dandruff when the scalp is massaged with it; it is used for rubbing ailing rheumatic parts of the body or sprained ankles and it is even used in a mild vinaigrette against hair infestation!

Olive oil is also believed to have aphrodisiac qualities and in old folklore the proverb 'Fae lathi k'ela vranthi' in a suggestive way says: 'Eat olive oil and come for the night.'

The best-known areas for their olive oil in Greece are Peloponnisos, with the plain of Kalamata in particular, the island of Lesvos (Mytilene) and the island of Kriti. It is also the main produce of most of the Sporathes islands and particularly Alonnisos, where we feel particularly privileged to have access to one of the best olive oils in Greece.

In a good year each family, on average, produces 900–1200 kg/2000–2650 lbs olive oil. Considering that it takes 5–6 kg/11–13 lbs olives to produce 1 kg/2 lbs olive oil, this will give a fair picture of the amount of olives that have to be gathered and the work involved in the overall process. Each family on the island consumes on average about 250 kg/550 lbs olive oil per year. Their olive oil is dark green, fruity and very fragrant. They store it in huge, very old, Ali-Baba-type earthenware pots which are called *pytharia*. These are inherited from generation to generation and they are treasured by the local people for their usage but also for sentimental memories. We also treasure them for their sometimes slender, sometimes exuberant but always magnificent shapes.

ELIES

Olives and How to Treat Them

'The rich are well satisfied with a dish of vegetables for their meal; the poor with a handful of olives or a piece of salt fish.'

(E.F.V. About, *Greece and the Greeks*, 1855, p. 33.)

As olive trees grow in such abundance in the mild temperate Greek climate, it is inevitable that olives constitute the most common, but the most favoured and treasured commodity of Greek diet. Also one of the cheapest but most nutritious and healthy. They provide the zest and spark to our vegetarian table as well as variety.

My generation was virtually brought up on olives and *fasolatha*, the wonderful bean soup. We were not affluent enough yet to be able to afford the luxury of feta cheese.

Consequently, olives with brown bread was our mid-morning as well as our mid-afternoon snack for a number of years. It was handy too, since it was eaten in the streets without much ceremony and without interrupting our street games. Later on, affluence in the form of *halva* (the solid, sweet, nutty product made with sesame seeds) and *tahini* (the liquid, unsweetened paste extracted from sesame seeds again), appeared and became our favourite diet! Then our snacks were alternated either with brown bread and a piece of *halva* or a slice of bread spread with *tahini* paste and a little sugar sprinkled on top. These provided our main meals on traditional days of fasting. The last dinner of each month, when money simply was not there to be stretched, called for a favourite of my grandmother: hot lemon tea served with a variety of olives called *throumbes* (a mild, slender, almost sweet-tasting, rich, oily, wrinkled variety of warm honey colour) and brown bread. To the peasant attending to his land, olives still constitute a main meal along with cheese or tomatoes and homemade bread.

There are innumerable varieties of olives in Greece, different in size and colour. They can be round, tight and tiny with a strong definite taste, lingering in the mouth long afterwards, pure black and shining like ebony – these are the olives of Kerkyra which are particularly favoured for salads; or they can be round and fleshy, like those from the Sporathes (Skiathos, Skopelos, Alonnisos), ranging from medium size to what in Greece is referred to as 'mammoth', like the olives of Amfissa and Agrinion.

They can be elongated, slender and shrivelled, of a dull black colour but very strong tasting, like those from Megara in Attiki, or the faintly sour ones from the island of Thassos in Makedonia. Or they may be shrivelled and sweet-tasting, soft and consequently favoured by the elderly, displaying all the shades of copper like the renowned *throumbes*, often called *hamades*, from the Aegean island of Samos. Or the best known abroad among all are the almost heart-shaped *kalamata* variety with the sharp sweet-and-sour taste and a beautiful display of mauves and bright violets to dark blues, that originated in Kalamata in Peloponnisos but do not necessarily come from there nowadays as the variety is cultivated in Lakonia, Aetoloakarnania, and also the island of Kriti. Also, there are the equivalents of all the above in green olives, differing in shape and size but with less variation in the way they are prepared. This is just an indication of the enormous variety of the most familiar and best-known types of olives to urban dwellers. And, of course, there are the endless unmentionable and unaccountable permutations of the wonderful homemade and home-consumed varieties of each individual olive grower, according to old family traditions.

One can get an idea of the variety that exists by strolling down the central market in Athens, crossing the main Athinas Street towards the fruit and vegetable stalls where, just behind these stalls in Sokratous Street, the main suppliers of the large bustling capital are located. A number of shops are to be found here specializing in olives and pickles, all of them in their original, gently decaying, old-fashioned, high-ceilinged, open-fronted buildings with accordion-like shutters that roll down in the night.

You will see olives in baskets, in hessian sacks, in wooden barrels and even sometimes in tin drums; olives in every corner of the shop, in the underground-smelling store-rooms, in the wooden mezzanine (*patari*), olives bursting out and taking over the pavements, spreading their slightly fetid unmistakable aroma over the whole area.

In the corner of Sokratous and Theatrou Steet, there is my favourite and one of the oldest establishments. The Apotheki Elaion, Papalexanthri has been there since 1921 and is still run by the same family. Here, apart from the variety of olives in origin and the different ways in which they are prepared, they are also graded into sections and sub-sections according to size and appearance. So there are at least four different grades of *elies kalamon* kept in an olive oil and vinegar solution – their major characteristic, three or four within the Kerkyra (Corfu) variety, four different kinds and grades of green olives and so on.

It is customary for the buyer to try his or her favourite candidates and discuss their aspects favourably, or unfavourably, with the vendor.

In the same shop there are big drums with various sharp pickles: mixed vegetable ones, containing gherkins, cauliflower, red peppers, green elongated peppers; sometimes quite hot ones; plain pepper pickles, or more exotic ones like aubergines, stuffed with carrots, garlic and coriander and tied up with celery stalks.

The rather genteel variety of homogeneous tasteless green olives, stuffed with red peppers – a family accompaniment to western cocktails – are nowhere to be seen here. Those you have to search for in the more metropolitan environment of the Athenian supermarkets.

To conclude, olives are a major feature of Greek life difficult even for the visitor not to notice. They appear at the slightest excuse, and at all times of the day. The most common excuse – the offer of an *ouzaki* – is always accompanied by the traditional plate of olives, embarrassingly difficult to reject as it would be considered ungracious. They are offered as an appetizer before a meal, one or two varieties appear at the table during a meal, they are mixed in salads and often cooked in the main meat course such as *soutzoukakia smyrneika* (cummin-scented rissoles) or with chicken, sometimes with a rabbit casserole, or with Salted Cod.

OLIVES AND HOW TO PICKLE THEM

Olives for eating are favoured when they are still hard, so they have to be collected from the trees before they ripen. Sometimes they are collected when they are still completely green, the familiar green olives which lack the acidity of darker olives, or usually as soon as they are turning brown or black. Sometimes the grower may just miss their turning point by accident and not preference.

It is not unusual for an olive grove nearer the sea or in general with the right climatic conditions to ripen much earlier than usual. In this respect they are like a vineyard – responsive to the weather. Of course, there are certain varieties that require the olives to be ripe or over-ripe, like the *throumbes* from Samos which are also called *hamathes* (*hamo* means on the earth or on the floor) because they are collected after they have fallen.

The ripe olives are always softer, predominantly oily and milder in taste, while the unripe ones are robust and more piquant.

After the olives have been collected in baskets or sacks and brought to the house, they are rinsed with cold water and then they are processed in any one of the following three basic ways, with mild variations. The jars should always be packed tightly with olives in order to prevent too much air flowing around them which encourages the formation of mould; therefore pack 1 kg/2 lbs olives in an appropriately small container.

OLIVES IN BRINE

After they have been rinsed, they are covered with cold water in earthenware jars or cans and they are kept immersed with some weight on top, usually a flat stone. The water is changed every second day, four times. Then they are immersed in a solution of rock salt and water in the proportions of 10 kg/22 lbs olives to 1 kg/2 lbs salt. They are left in this solution for about a month before they are ready to be eaten. If at this stage they still taste too bitter and sharp they should be left undisturbed for slightly longer.

Once they are ready, they still remain in the same solution and are only taken out in small quantities. They are then rinsed with water before they are eaten. Sometimes a little olive oil is poured over them and some oregano sprinkled on top, before they are presented at the table.

In my experience, olives out of their brine will keep covered in a container for about 5–6 days. After that their taste alters and becomes slightly fetid. They do not need to be kept in a fridge. Mould appearing at the top of their solution is of no significance and can be just rinsed away.

ELIES MEGARON KE THASSOU

Dry, Shrivelled Olives

The dry, dark olives, not kept in brine, are magnificently wrinkled all over, and specially selected in order to be processed differently. They are selected more ripe and juicy than olives that go into brine; they are packed in baskets or hessian sacks in layers alternating with rock salt.

A huge weight is then put on top of them; a round grey *mylopetra* (a mill stone) or like the one our friends use, a piece of iron salvaged from a sunken ship, weighing approximately 30 kg/66 lbs.

The basket or sack is put on a slightly elevated, wooden construction made with slats, so that there is space left underneath for the bitter juices to trickle away. The sacks are left in a dark, cool place for at least one month before the olives are ready to be eaten.

Some growers use an alternative method that has almost identical results. As a continuation to the olives in brine method above, they take some olives out of the brine once they are almost ready and process them as above; alternating layers with rock salt and weighted down at the end. This method only needs a week before the olives are ready.

ELIES KAI LATHI

103

Either of these two methods and particularly the first one, results in a more compact, undiluted taste, richer and more oily than any other.

Best representatives of the first method are the black, slim olives from Megara in Attiki, favoured by most customers in street markets, and the olives of the island of Thassos that are slightly bitter.

This method is obviously simpler but also very economical in usage of space; bigger quantities of olives can be processed in very small spaces.

TSAKISTES

Cracked Green Olives

No matter how many different times I have seen green olives being prepared to go into brine in the autumn, the instances that have predominantly stuck in my mind are those when my grandmother used to prepare the olives at home. She used to get all the children involved, so for us it was quite an occasion.

We would all be given marble flat stones for cracking the olives. Each olive had to be put on one small marble flat stone and then hit gently with the other piece of the flat stone, so that the flesh of the olive would crack. Then they were dropped into small *pitharia* (earthenware jars) full of cold water. The rhythmical dull noise of the olive being cracked followed immediately by the ringing clear sound of the marble stones hitting each other echoed and reverberated in the atmosphere for hours, as we were completely absorbed in our task and trying to concentrate in order to avoid hitting our fingers.

One can achieve the same results by cutting a cross on one side of the olive with a sharp knife or, even better, with a razor.

Green olives are mostly bitter, so by opening their flesh they are helped to exude their bitterness. Once this is achieved they tend to taste rather mild if not dull. Of course, the difference between them and their ripe counterparts is that they lack the oiliness and therefore people find them more refreshing.

In order to counterbalance their dullness, various aromatics are then added to them, including garlic. These are not usually added to any other olives. Their water should be changed every second day, four times at least, then they should be put in a solution of water and rock salt with some coriander seeds, peeled cloves of garlic and sprigs of fresh thyme. The proportion of salt to olives is approximately 1 kg/2 lbs to 10 kg/22 lbs, or scaled down:

1 kg/2 lbs green olives
110 g/4 oz rock salt
2 cloves garlic, peeled
   (optional)
25 g/1 oz whole coriander
   seeds

2 bay leaves
2 sprigs thyme
some fennel, or sprigs of dill
3 vine leaves, for sealing the
   surface

Rinse the olives first in case of pesticides. If you are cracking the olives, be careful not to crack their stone; it should be left intact.

Put them in a jar and cover with cold water. Change the water every second day, four times, that is about a week altogether.

Fill a jug about three-quarters full with cold water, add the salt and stir to dilute. In order to check that the brine is the right strength, drop a raw egg in it, in its shell. In Greece they say that when the egg floats to the surface, then the solution is right.

Pack the olives tightly in this with all the aromatics. Of course, if you prefer a plainer taste you can omit the aromatics. Cover with the vine leaves, which should keep the olives immersed as well as adding their faint aroma. Cover the jar and keep in a cool dark place for 3–4 weeks. Take a few olives out at a time, rinse them and try to see if they are ready. To serve, once they have been rinsed, they can be sprinkled with oregano. Take out only as many as you need, the rest will keep in their solution for 5–6 months.

Any mould which has formed at the top bears no significance and it can just be rinsed away or taken out with a slotted spoon.

KALAMATA OLIVES OR XITHATES

The popular *kalamata* olives favoured by most foreigners are called *xithates* in Greece. They are named after the solution that gives them their particular flavour which contains vinegar, *xithi*. Of course, by *xithates* we mean predominantly the particular *kalamata* variety, at least for buying purposes, strangely heart-shaped to my eyes (tear-shaped to my husband's eyes – this is a family argument at the moment).

But despite this, any black olive can be treated in the same manner and indeed they are. In all the islands of the Sporathes and even on the mainland around Volos and Pilion, they make their own large, round, fleshy variety of *xithates*. These are very juicy, fully flavoured and worth trying. Indeed it is worth asking if you can buy their homemade olives even in an ordinary grocer shop wherever you are in Greece.

In many of these islands and other provincial places there are strange grocer shops or *pantopolia* as they are called (meaning selling virtually everything, and this is what they do, from newspapers and paperbacks, shoes and fishing equipment to cheeses, beans, yoghurt and haberdashery) which sell local, mostly homemade olives and olive oil as a matter of course. Quite often this is extended to their local homemade honey, this being particularly true and particularly delicious on the island of Skopelos; their own free-range eggs (more chances of getting those out of season before the crowds descend) and their own homemade goat cheese which is quite different from the creamy French-type goat cheese we are used to in England.

The olives for this recipe should really be hard but slightly ripe, almost black all over. It is unlikely that one would be able to find olives at this particular stage of their life unless one was near an olive-producing area at the right time. One never sees them for sale as I guess they would not survive the travel, unlike unripe green olives. However, any black olives can be used here.

2.25 kg/5 lbs black olives
300 ml/½ pint red wine
    vinegar
225 g/8 oz rock salt

150 ml/¼ pint olive oil
water to cover three-quarters
    of the container

Rinse the olives first because of the various pesticides they are sprayed with. Make three slits lengthways on each olive. There is a special tool for this in Greece that looks like a pencil sharpener. The olive is put through one side and pushed out through the other side, where it appears ready-slit. Otherwise a razor blade is used, as the slits have to be fine and expertly done so the olive does not get bruised or it may go mushy in the solution.

Put the olives in jars or even cans and cover with cold water. Change the water again every second day, four or five times. The olives should be tried at this stage in order to make sure that they are not still exceedingly bitter. If they are, they should be left in water longer. Only when their bitterness is not dominant are they put in the above solution of vinegar, rock salt, olive oil and, of course, water. This should be stirred. The rock salt should go first in the water and be stirred until properly dissolved, then the vinegar and olive oil added and lastly the olives. They should be kept immersed with a flat stone and left for at least a month in a cool place. They should be taken out with a slotted spoon, they do not need rinsing, and a little oregano can be sprinkled on top.

SALATES
Salads

It is inevitable in a country like Greece, where vegetables constitute a major part of the national diet, that salads should be taken for granted as they are. They are as much part of the everyday table as knives and forks. They are not just something to nibble at; on the contrary, very often they are the main course coupled with some delicately fried fish, squid or sweetbreads. Their arrival at the table, even at restaurants, is never questioned; it is expected. Always seasonal, they vary from the most ordinary, such as tomatoes, cucumbers and lettuces, to the most eccentric and esoteric of hand-picked wild greens (*horta* as they are collectively described) from nearby hills and fields, or at their most unusual, made of wild plants which grow in the cracks of gigantic rock formations by the sea. These are called *kritama* in Greek, or rock samphire (*Chritmum maritimum*) as it is known commonly in England. It is a short, soft, fleshy, spiked-leaf plant of a cactaceous appearance and grey-green colour.

Rock samphire was best known as a pickle in seventeenth-century England but was very popular as a vegetable in the nineteenth century, boiled, drained and served with butter. This is very popular on our island. From March onwards the short leaves are collected in quantities and treated like any other wild greens. They are first boiled and then drained and dressed with olive oil and lemon. Apart from valuing it as a salad the local people believe that it also has medicinal qualities against rheumatism. It has quite a definite bitter, slightly sour taste of aniseed and it takes some time to get used to and become a believer. Since I was introduced to it, quite late in my life, I still haven't become one! In the Pilion villages they pickle it and offer it as a *meze* with *ouzo*.

In no other country have I seen such an affinity for wild hand-picked greens as well as their specially cultivated counterparts, as in Greece. '*Agria horta tou vounou*', wild greens from the mountains or '*Imera horta*' (strictly translated, 'tame greens') were street cries that we grew up with.

There is an enormous variety of the wild greens that appear with the first autumnal rains, such as all kinds of dandelions, and then delicious *vrouves* in the spring (a kind of mustard with tiny yellow flowers).

There is a wonderful description of *vrouves* growing in one of the most unlikely places in Athens, none less than the Acropolis, in William Miller's *Greek Life in Town and Country* (p. 194). 'The sacred rock of the Acropolis produces a mustard plant from which an excellent salad is made and in February numbers of women may be seen collecting herbs and digging up roots on the Pnyx and near the monument of Philopappos, which they cook and eat ...'

I am sure *vrouves* as well as the other wild varieties of *horta* are still growing around the foot of the Acropolis and the hill of Philopappos, along with soft carpets of chamomile with the first rays of spring. I am also quite certain that you will not see anyone collecting them, as in the late 1970s the pollution in Athens reached such unacceptable standards that it alarmed even the Greeks, though optimists by nature.

There are also young poppy plants which are collected before they flower and are used not only as a salad like the rest but, on the island, also as a filling for a delicious pie.

Then there are their cultivated counterparts, *radikia*, a spinach-leafed-like plant, and another variety called *italika* which resembles rhubarb plants on a micro-scale, with their unusually red slender stems (perhaps this is the reason I still cannot get used to eating rhubarb as a dessert in any form); there are curly endives (*andithia*) which are also used in a lamb fricassee, and the most delicious of all, *vlita*, which no visitor to Greece should miss an opportunity of trying in the spring and early summer. *Vlita* has a sweet but also faintly sour taste that one can get addicted to. It seeds itself so easily that on our island it is not even cultivated; it just comes back every spring here and there, in people's gardens or disused fields, and there it really thrives unless it is a particularly dry spring and summer. Then consequently all the crops suffer, since most of them do not rely on irrigation systems but on God's good will!

All these greens are always first boiled, covered in salted water, then drained and dressed with a refreshing olive oil and lemon dressing. There is a great tradition of collecting wild greens in Greece, as the extract from W. Miller so picturesquely reaffirms. Very often in the autumn or the spring, a Sunday family outing from Athens would be a *horta*-picking expedition to the nearby countryside of Penteli, Marathon, Tatoi, or slightly further on the way to Delphi, with the breathtaking mountain views and the wonderful amphitheatre along with other archaeological treasures waiting at the end. These outings would always be followed by an exquisite lunch in some small, isolated place with huge barrels of wine and a roaring fire.

Sometimes, one could see hillsides dotted by the colourful *horta* pickers, since whenever a good spot was discovered it would soon attract other cars to stop and join in with singing and joking and laughing echoing and bringing the deserted hillsides to life. Sometimes we would hold competitions among the family of who could collect the largest amount. These were all rituals that brightened our childish lives and gave them a sense of continuity, as all rituals do, and I still get an enormous joy out of similar expeditions.

I remember how proud I was when, while on a school outing for the day, I spent the entire morning gathering *horta* with my little blunt knife and storing them in my jacket and how proud I was when I presented my grandmother with my trove at the end of the day.

During the German occupation and the terrible famine of the years 1943–4, wild greens saved a lot of lives and if the favourites could not be found, there was always an abundance of nettles, which even the Germans could not stop from growing. Friends a little older than myself can clearly remember eating boiled nettles quite often.

In the villages and, of course, in our village on the island, gathering *horta* is done almost routinely at the end of the working day in the fields or the olive groves along with the other essentials – that is a pile of firewood for the home hearth and a huge bunch of greenery for the goats' daily meals. One of the goats' favourite bushes is a large evergreen shrub with small glossy leaves called *koumaria* in Greek, *Arbutus unedo*, or, as it is known commonly in the west, a strawberry tree. This grows wild in abundance in the Greek countryside and on the hillsides of our island. This was also a favourite of our childhood years, not for its shiny leaves but for its bright red-orange and perfect round berries that achieved magical qualities, to our eyes at least, ripening as they were in the autumn amidst a season of discipline and fading colours, coinciding with the opening of our schools. I remember particularly the familiar smell of our brand new books covered neatly in dark blue paper by our mother, our new stiff dark blue uniforms ready for the 'battle' and above all the remote autumnal melancholy that vibrated in the air.

We used to long for the melodic cry of the *koumara* sellers on Sundays, as they went from neighbourhood to neighbourhood carrying a large basket on their arm and we would gather round them waving our coins. They, in return, would make a tiny paper funnel and fill it with their sweet, crunchy, almost exotic berries.

Later, when cars were not such a distant possibility, we were thrilled to discover the 'magical' berries ourselves among the dense, leafy *koumaria* bushes in areas around Athens, such as Marathon or Penteli.

But we were not the only ones to look upon these bushes with wonder. Here is an interesting and humourous description of the same bushes in the same area in Athens in the year 1856.

> Around us we saw many of the shrubs of Greece; among them the oleander and the heather with its copious branches of fresh coloured blossoms. The Arbutus, however, most attracted our attention. The branches were laden partly with clusters of bell-shaped flowers and partly with the yellow or red fruit, which has somewhat the flavour of the strawberry. One of our party, after tasting sufficiently of the pleasant berries, was considerably alarmed when he found that the colour of all was not similar and that the leaves of some were remarkably like those of the laurel. His companions for his edification, cited the famous incident from Xenophon about the soldiers who were poisoned by eating honey made from laurel flowers. Recourse to the guide dispelled these fears and banished all thoughts of emetics. The suspected shrub turned out to be only a variety of the arbutus.
>
> (Henry M. Baird, *Modern Greece*, 1856, p. 300.)

Apart from the cooked 'green salads' that I described, there is a whole range of salads made with haricot beans, black-eyed beans, courgettes, beetroots, cauliflower, etc. Then there are the raw salads made with tomatoes, often mixed with feta cheese and crowned with black, fleshy Greek olives, tasty cucumbers, cos lettuces, etc. Quantities of fresh feathery dill, spring onions and lemons are inevitable.

The 'vinaigrette' is seldom a vinaigrette in Greece but more commonly a combination of olive oil and lemon which I think is much more refreshing anyway. Three parts of olive oil and one of lemon juice constitute a mild balance, even though in Greece a sharper lemony taste is favoured. In the exceptional instances of a vinaigrette, four parts of olive oil and one of wine vinegar is an appropriate formula. Quite often plain, but good quality, olive oil is used.

Crushed garlic is never used in salads as it is more familiarly in the west. Of course, I am only describing for authenticity's sake and not setting any strict code to go by.

Plates of young red radishes, spring onions, rocket leaves (*roka*) and fresh green garlic, when in season, or slices of large white radishes are common finds on a Greek table.

In the autumn there are bunches of *glystrida* (*Portulaca oleracea*), the common purslane plant, whose short branches and tiny succulent leaves are used for a salad or just eaten *au naturel* and which can only be described as a weed. This has a juicy, faintly bitter taste and a crunchy texture. *Glystrida* is supposed to make people over-talkative, so the saying for somebody who chatters incessantly is 'Did you have *glystrida* for breakfast?'

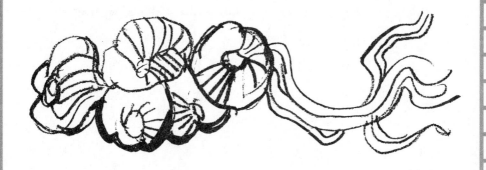

MAROULI SALATA

Cos Lettuce Salad

Cos lettuces are the only variety of lettuce in Greece. Perhaps in fancy supermarkets in areas like Psychiko or Glyfada where a lot of foreign diplomatic personnel live one could find other varieties but this would be strictly foreign influence.
Cos lettuces are also seasonal and are at their best in the spring; by the end of June they are hard and tasteless, until they disappear altogether to be replaced by their summer competitor, the tomato.

1 small cos lettuce	2 tablespoons lemon juice, or
3–4 spring onions	1 tablespoon wine vinegar
a few sprigs fresh dill, about	salt and freshly ground black
3 tablespoons	pepper
4 tablespoons olive oil	

Discard the outer tough leaves of the lettuce, trim the core and plunge each leaf individually in a bowl of cold water or rinse it under running cold water. Put in a colander and drain for at least 1 hour or even better longer, otherwise it will make the salad too watery. Trim and rinse the spring onions. Rinse the dill and press gently to remove excess moisture.

In Greece a lettuce salad is meant to be cut very finely; people in their own homes take pride as to how fine they can shred the lettuce leaves. The finer they are the better the salad, it is considered, unlike western habits of tearing anything green quite roughly. So, take a few leaves at a time, roll them like a cigar and shred them very finely. Cut onions and dill and place everything in a bowl. Mix the dressing and seasoning separately, pour over the salad and toss.

DOMATOSALATA OR HORIATIKI

Tomato or Greek Salad

*This is the summer salad par excellence in Greece, with little
variation. Most commonly it is a combination of tomatoes and
thinly sliced onions and a few black olives. Quite often though it
contains round thin slices of peeled cucumber and/or green pepper.
If, in addition to all the above, slices of white feta cheese are
added, then it is called a peasant salad, or* horiatiki *in Greek. This
last is the most common way served in* tavernas.
*Almost always we dress a tomato salad with plain olive oil and
never with a vinaigrette so don't be surprised at restaurants. It is
simply taken for granted that this is the norm so it arrives already
dressed. Just ask for vinegar if this is the way you prefer it – they
are bound to think you are peculiar but in a good-hearted way!*

225 g/8 oz tomatoes
1 onion, thinly sliced
1 green pepper, cored and
  thinly sliced
½ cucumber, peeled and
  thinly sliced

3–4 tablespoons olive oil
salt and freshly ground black
  pepper
a pinch of oregano
feta cheese and some black
  olives (optional)

Rinse the tomatoes. Cut them in half and take out the black mark at the
top and bottom. Slice in thin quarters. If you want to reduce the sharpness
of the onion, soak it in a little salted water for 5–10 minutes, then take out
and squeeze gently. Add to the tomatoes, the onion, the pepper and
cucumber, or whatever else you decide to use, and dress it with the olive
oil, salt and black pepper and some oregano. If you want a *horiatiki* or a
Greek salad, as it has been renamed, add 3–4 thin slices of white feta
cheese on top, and some black olives.

LAHANO SALATA

Cabbage Salad

This is made with the white 'Dutch' cabbage as it is called in England which unfortunately tends to be rather hard and woody. In Greece the same variety is much more tender. It is an autumn and winter salad when the cabbage is in season in Greece and is very crisp and refreshing.

Cut the cabbage in half, discard the outer leaves and trim the hard stem and core at the bottom. Quarter it, lay each quarter on its side and cut long, but very thin, slices until you reach the central core, which you discard. Put it into a bowl of salted cold water and rinse properly, even though it should be quite clean. Drain in a colander, squeezing it gently, and let it drain for at least 1 hour if you have the time, otherwise place in a cloth and dry. Place in a bowl.

Prepare separately 4 tablespoons olive oil with 2 tablespoons lemon juice, salt and pepper and mix well. Pour over the salad and toss. Sometimes black olives are added. Alternatively use 4 tablespoons olive oil with 1 of wine vinegar. Lemon though is more traditional. In restaurants this salad arrives already dressed with the olive oil and a quarter of lemon on the side of the plate for individual preference.

KOLOKITHAKIA SALATA

Courgette Salad

A very old-fashioned dish, served as an intermediary to richly flavoured sauces, as a calming influence to overworked stomachs and to those on a definite medical diet or recovering from 'hypochondriac' ailments. A definite favourite among the hot 'spa' clientele in summer at Kammena Vourla and the spa of Kaiafa.

Only a very old-fashioned restaurant like that of Xinos in Angelou Geronta Street in Plaka would bother to serve such a dish along with their wonderful egg and lemon fricassee. Under the patriarchal eye of its owner Xinos himself, and amidst the rising horrors of the concrete blocks all around it, this restaurant has survived like an oasis of a Greek 'home' and homely Greek cooking. My sister, who knows the place quite well, tells me that they put great effort into selecting the best of vegetables daily. They are hand-picked and chosen individually.

Quite a plain dish, but refreshingly welcome when served alongside a lamb and lettuce fricassee instead of a salad, or even with a roast of lamb, and even better with some grilled or fried fish. As it is quite plain, you rely upon the tenderness and freshness of the courgettes firstly and the quality of the olive oil secondly. If you cannot get small and firm courgettes it is not worth bothering. Of course, it should not be overcooked and served soggy as the essence of the dish is then completely spoiled. You should allow two small courgettes per person.

675 g/1½ lbs courgettes, small and firm	salt and freshly ground black pepper
4 tablespoons olive oil	oregano, or freshly chopped
juice of ½ lemon	basil (optional)

Scrape and rinse the courgettes. Leave whole. Bring a pan of water to the boil, add some salt and put in the courgettes. Cover and cook rapidly for 6–8 minutes. Test with a knife, making sure that they are still a bit hard. Drain. Place in a platter or an elongated bowl. Mix the olive oil, lemon juice, salt and pepper in a bowl and pour over the hot courgettes. Roll them gently in the dressing so they look glistening. You could add a tiny sprinkling of oregano or a little chopped fresh basil. Offer separate small plates for them so that they do not lose their independent taste by being drowned in an overpowering alien sauce. They are mostly served cold in Greece but I prefer them warm.

KOUNOUPITHI SALATA

Cauliflower Salad

Trim the hard core of the cauliflower and rinse the cauliflower carefully. Scrape lightly any dark blemishes. Boil it whole, core downwards, in salted water for about 6–8 minutes, uncovered, and take out with a slotted spoon. The belief is that if cooked uncovered most of its overpowering smell will evaporate. It should still be a bit hard.

Place the cauliflower in a bowl and pour olive oil and lemon dressing over it. Season with salt and black pepper.

If you prefer, you can either cut the cauliflower into smaller pieces or break it into florets. In this case it should be cooked for a shorter period. Alternatively it can be steamed.

FASOLIA SALATA

Cannellini Bean Salad

This again is quite a substantial dish that can be served as a main course along with fried squid, fried fish, taramosalata *or* keftethes. *It is always served cold in Greece. It makes an unusual salad for a party.*

225 g/8 oz cannellini beans
1 small onion, finely sliced
3 tablespoons chopped
   parsley
salt and freshly ground black
   pepper

6 tablespoons olive oil
1 tablespoon vinegar, or juice
   of ½ lemon
6–8 black olives, to garnish

Soak the beans overnight. Rinse and drain. Cover them with cold water, adding a little salt so that they do not disintegrate, and bring to the boil. Cover and cook for approximately 45 minutes, or 4–5 minutes in a pressure cooker. They should be a little hard and not mushy. Drain through a colander, reserving 3–4 tablespoons of cooking liquid, and place in a bowl. If you want to have a milder-flavoured onion soak it in salted water for about 10 minutes and squeeze it before you add it to the beans. Otherwise just add the onion, parsley and the reserved cooking liquid to the beans and season with salt and black pepper.

Mix the dressing in a bowl with seasoning and pour over the beans. Mix gently with a spoon. Often a sprinkling of oregano, the old Greek favourite, is added and, of course, one can add sliced tomatoes or cucumbers or green peppers. Always garnish with olives and, if you wish, quarters of hardboiled eggs.

FASOLIA MAVROMITIKA

Black-eyed Bean Salad

Made in exactly the same way as the *Fasolia Salata* (Cannellini Bean Salad) above, but these black-eyed beans do not need soaking and they cook much quicker – 30 minutes in an ordinary saucepan. Be careful not to overcook as they become quite mushy.

PATZARIA SALATA

Beetroot Salad

In Greece, beetroot is sold in the markets, raw in bunches. It comes as a whole plant, that is, with its green tops, and everything is eaten. In fact, its green leaves are very tasty. Out of philological interest I shall describe how it is prepared since beetroot in England is mostly sold precooked. I have only seen it raw a few times in provincial town markets. It is definitely a winter salad in Greece. It is always served with a vinaigrette and very often with *skorthalia*, a garlic paste (page 53), which comes to the table separately. On our island though, as an exception to the rule, the *skorthalia* envelops the beetroot salad like a regal cloak, forming iridescent marbling effects as it arrives at the table.

Top and tail the beetroots. Discard the root ends, but keep stalks and green leaves of the top part. Rinse the beetroots, scrubbing their skins properly, and then rinse the leaves. Cover the beetroots with water and slowly bring to the boil. Cover and cook for approximately 40 minutes according to their size. When cooked take out with a slotted spoon and add the stalks and leaves to the pan. Cook for a further 5 minutes. Drain. When cool enough to handle, peel the beetroots with a knife and cut them into thin round slices or thick quarters. Cut the stalks and leaves into 5-cm/2-ins pieces and place everything in a bowl or a on flat platter. Dress generously with a vinaigrette.

LAHANIKA
Vegetables

They eat good bread at about one penny per pound; and their other dishes are generally vegetables, made into soups, four days out of the seven. Olives they eat with their bread. Meat they do not use more than once or twice a week.

(George Cochrane, *Wanderings in Greece in 1826*, Vol. I, 1837, p. 295.)

This is an accurate description of Greek diet at its most fundamental; particularly brilliant as it has been perceived by a foreigner travelling in Greece in 1826, with little knowledge of the language.

If one can keep this picture in mind, one has caught the elementary Greek dietary principles which point even historically towards vegetables, pulses, olives and olive oil as well as bread.

Vegetables become main dishes, quite substantial, nourishing and desirable in their own merit; in colourful combinations, like stuffed tomatoes, peppers and aubergines all in the same baking dish, or a *briami* (potatoes, courgettes, green peppers, green beans and sometimes okra) or artichokes *à la polita* (globe artichoke casserole); in monochromatic combinations with no deviation in taste and not even the familiar parenthesis of the red of the tomatoes, such as fresh peas with artichokes and lemon, or green broad beans with artichokes.

Interchangeable with the word *lahanika* is the word *lathera* – literally meaning oily – because a Greek cannot conceive of vegetables without the thick yellow-green fragrant Greek olive oil. This is considered as a vital ingredient to the taste of the dish and it is therefore used in considerable quantities, not just our usual western, gentle addition of one or two tablespoons.

Dishes that lack in olive oil are spotted immediately by the hawk-eyed Greeks; mouths turned down in a croquet-hoop-style grimace, almost blowing steam with disappointment, the dish is automatically dismissed with one over-exemplified word *nerovrasto* – water boiled or insipid – the ultimate step of degradation for any vegetable to undergo!

A plate of watery courgette casserole, or artichokes and fresh broad beans is pushed away with indignation as the heavy condemnation comes thumping down: *nerovrasto*, the seal of the cognoscenti! Real anathema is a plate of watery *imam bayildi* (baked aubergines) or any of the aubergine dishes, a stigma for a Greek wife to bear.

Vegetables then are highly respected protagonists at a Greek table and they are not thought of as adornments or aides to other dishes. Sometimes they are cooked together with meat or poultry but they are even then treated as equals if not as treasured guests; in *arnaki me anginares* (lamb with globe artichokes) it is the artichokes that are treasured and adorned by the lamb and not the other way round, as the season of the artichokes lasts for only two months in the spring. In *kotopoulo me bamies* (chicken with okra casserole) it is the taste of the okra that is enriched by the chicken flavour and so becomes even more highly desirable.

Vegetables have always been, and still are, seasonal, despite frozen attempts in the modern supermarkets. When we talk of *araka* (peas) we think of the fresh, green young pods that start to appear in the markets in April and continue to do so until the middle of May, when they start to become too full and overgrown and lose their delicate taste and aroma and are undesirable. The essence of *araka*, then, in the mind of a Greek cannot be matched by any parboiled, frozen variety on a supermarket shelf, or even worse in a tepid, chemical liquid in the canned specimens.

The idea of vegetables being seasonal is so well rooted in me that I feel strange eating okra or courgettes in the winter months in London. A specific vegetable always implies a season. Peas, artichokes and broad beans mean spring; green beans and courgettes early summer; aubergines and okra, summer with all its splendour; *horta* and various greens, wild or cultivated, *kounoupithia* (cauliflowers), *prassa* (leeks), and *pantzaria* (beetroot), autumnal melancholy and winter gloom. Large, scarlet, anomalous-shaped tomatoes belonged to the summer, even though their season extended to the end of November and into December sometimes. At the end of August every year, my grandmother would busy herself with bottling the tomatoes and making tomato paste for the winter as, indeed, all our neighbours were. They would not even think of using canned tomatoes. Now this, at least, has changed with modern techniques; tomatoes, and also aubergines, are grown under large cloches in Kriti, in the Ierapetra area, at the southern tip and in Peloponnisos and so they are available fresh all year round at reasonable prices, even though they lack the taste of their summer relatives.

It goes without saying that Greece does not import any vegetables or fruit; modern trends are satisfied by growing the newly desired product in Greece. Recently, they have introduced new varieties of lettuces such as Webbs, and icebergs. Avocados are grown in Kriti with successful results, mangetout are grown in the north of Greece and lastly the unknown commodity of mushrooms – despite the term 'mushrooms à la Grecque'* that makes people assume this is a Greek speciality – has been cultivated and marketed for the past five or six years; I hasten to add without much success; they are not the kind of vegetable one finds in mounds in the local street markets because of their rather expensive price, the heat and also they are not seasonal; these factors automatically exclude and alienate the average Greek woman from new commodities like mushrooms.

The same applies to avocados, even though we saw them in abundance in the wonderful covered old central market, built in 1911, in the centre of Chania, in Kriti. In the same market there was the freshest and the most beautiful collection of vegetables I have ever seen.

In Kriti, also, there is an unusual variety of globe artichokes grown everywhere, resembling more a proper but beautiful thistle. Each leaf of the artichoke ends in a dangerous, strong, prickly spike. In Peloponnisos these are referred to as wild artichokes. They have small round heads, tight like a fist, while the Kretan variety is something to remember; huge

*The French term *à la Grecque* is used in French cuisine to describe almost any vegetable dish cooked in the Greek manner; this is, with olive oil and preferably served at room temperature.

heads, sometimes weighing about 1 kg/2 lbs, with their light green petals opening up like a magnificent rose. The Kretans are proud of them and rightly so; their taste is quite something. Often then, they are eaten raw in Kriti, just sprinkled with lemon.

My sister and I watched a ritualistic performance in a local *taverna* in Agia Galini on the south coast of Kriti late one evening. Six heavily moustached Kretans produced a beautiful huge artichoke and started skilfully peeling its thorny petals and biting each one of them as a *meze* to accompany their red local wine. When they reached the heart, the choke was extracted and thin slivers sliced, rubbed with lemon and offered in turn to all the men; all this under a murmur of singing and the sad tone of the lyre that one of them was playing. This whole performance could not have been more Greek and it shows how seriously and reverentially vegetables can be treated in Greece.

The decision of the daily meal is not made at random by the Greek mother-figure of the household (despite contrary beliefs a fair amount of decisions are made by the women in Greece; matriarchy is a Greek word after all!). A visit to the local street market (*laiki*) is made early in the morning, at least three times a week, with freshness taken into account primarily and cost secondarily, in order to make a decision.

There is no point planning a casserole with green beans (*ambelofassoula*) from Syros, if they look sadly yellow or are too large and stringy on the day; or if the fresh broad beans of Tripoli in Peloponnisos look gigantic an alternative has to be found; beautiful pale striped courgettes can be fried and served with *skorthalia* (garlic paste) or they can be stuffed and casseroled with a splendid *avgolemono* sauce added at the end.

Vegetables and fruit are picked up individually, squeezed and looked at all round by the women before they are approved, while the seller stands by. They are expected to do so; there are no decorative pyramids of polished fruit and vegetables to be destroyed, only colourful piles.

How was I to know the response of the huge red-faced stallholder in Berwick Street Market in Soho, when I tried to handle the courgettes, on my first market outing in England? My impression was that he was going to eat me alive, even though he was lacking a few vital teeth.

Open-air vegetable markets in Greece are crowded by the women. It is a woman's task to choose and decide, as the cooking is wholly a woman's responsibility; men very rarely participate and then it is only in order to carry the goods back home. This early part of the day with the marketing is quite a highlight as it provides the women with a chance to meet their friends and socialize. It is a pleasurable experience done at ease, not a task blighted by pressures and done in haste.

ANGINARES

Globe Artichokes

'Little lambs! Home-raised, tender, milk-drinking lambs!' The basket on his back displays only green stuff; green balls of some sort ornament the rim. They are artichokes, young artichokes, cut probably in the market-gardens which fill a great part of the moat beneath the ancient walls of Constantinople; and the merit of being home-grown, which is insisted upon by all the vendors of spring produce, may be explained by the fact that the greater proportion of the early fruit and vegetables is supplied from Broussa, Smyrna, the Greek islands, and even from Egypt, where they come in much earlier than in this cooler climate, but being gathered too soon and badly packed, they arrive faded and flavourless, very inferior, indeed, in quality to those that are truly 'home-grown'. What is there in the undeveloped artichoke to evoke poetic fancies? In Paris they are offered by the mysterious cry of, '*La tendresse et la verdurette!*' Here they are 'sucking lambs!' We cannot pause to solve the question, for the man has wandered away with his little green 'lambs' and it is again a gardener that follows him down the path.

(Mary Walker, *Eastern Life and Scenery*, London, 1886, p. 80.)

What there was in the 'undeveloped' artichoke of 1886 and there still is in the artichoke of our days is the perfectly delicate, melting taste, matched by a freshness-evoking aroma which takes the uninitiated completely by surprise.

Artichokes figure a lot in Greek cuisine and Greek life. They are a ritual in themselves! One of the first spring vegetables to appear in early March along with fresh broad beans, fresh dill, young cos lettuces and spring onions, so artichokes represent the arrival of spring in Greek homes. They are always associated with Easter and eaten a lot during Lent when people are fasting and meat is forbidden.

In fact, I think they make the most wonderful vegetarian dishes. In western Europe at least, they tend to be eaten *à la vinaigrette*, which is almost 'Philistinism' – and all it achieves is to bring the overpowering tastes of vinegar and garlic to the already sodden droopy head that once had a wonderful taste and texture.

Serving them the Greek way of course involves preparation. The wonderful Greek artichoke dishes that follow involve a little bit of work. But it sounds more difficult than it really is and once you master the art of cleaning or 'undressing' the artichokes (because that is exactly what you do) then the rest is routine. Of course some recipes are more complicated than others and as a result not so popular, like the stuffed artichokes or artichokes fried in egg and flour.

The artichoke plant is perennial and from the way they grow in Greece they must be the crop that never fails! Once planted they need almost no care or attention and they will go on producing their pretty purple heads every spring from about February to June. In our island they are used as a separating hedge between different spring crops on the terraced hills and they are an unusual variety of very dark purple colour and have very small and tight heads. I must also stress how much tastier the purple variety is, even though more expensive.

To prepare artichokes

Here are some general hints about cleaning them. First have a bowl ready filled with cold water, a little salt and the juice of half a lemon. Peel the outer leaves of the artichoke until you reach the tender ones (approximately three-quarters of the artichoke will go or even a bit more). Then, cut off the head of the artichoke, halfway down, leaving the heart with a short collar of tender leaves. At this stage, if you are a beginner, it would be easier to slice them in the middle, so that you can see the hairy 'choke' in the middle of the heart, surrounded by some prickly purple leaves. You can scoop all this out with a teaspoon, being careful not to trim any of the tender heart underneath. When you are more experienced you can leave the artichoke whole and scoop all the middle part out in the same way.

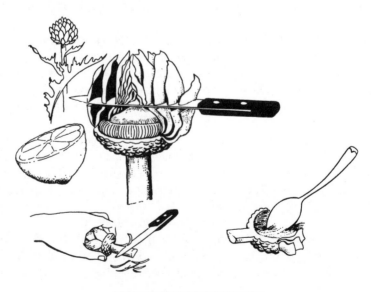

Now, cut the stalk, leaving about 4 cm/1½ ins only attached to the artichoke, and peel its woody outer green surface, leaving the white part only. Trim also the base of the artichoke of its tough green surface, rub the artichoke all over with the other half of the lemon and drop it into the bowl. This process is in order to prevent them from discolouring.

Traditional accompaniments to artichoke dishes are dill in great quantities, spring onions and lemon.

ANGINARES AVGOLEMONO

Artichokes with Egg and Lemon Sauce

Globe artichokes, cooked in this manner, are so fine that they should really be enjoyed unadulterated. The best way to serve this dish is as an outstandingly fine first course.

6 globe artichokes
juice of 1 lemon
2 medium-sized onions,
   thinly sliced
3–4 young carrots, sliced
   (optional)
55 g/2 oz butter
300 ml/½ pint water

3 tablespoons chopped dill
salt and white pepper
3–4 spring onions, sliced
Avgolemono sauce
2 eggs
juice of 1 lemon
1 tablespoon cornflour,
   diluted in a little water

Prepare the artichokes as described on page 124, using the juice of half a lemon for the mixture of water and lemon. Sauté the 2 onions and the carrots in the butter for 2–3 minutes. Add the water and the juice of half a lemon. When this comes to the boil, add most of the dill, the artichokes, salt and freshly ground pepper. Add more water if necessary so that the artichokes are almost covered. Cover and cook on medium heat for about 35 minutes, making sure that you are left with a nice thick buttery sauce. Add the spring onions in the last 5 minutes. Remove the saucepan from the heat and let it stand for at least 5 minutes before you add the *avgolemono* sauce, otherwise the egg will cook.

Then prepare the *avgolemono* sauce as described on page 56 (first method using cornflour). Pour this over the artichokes and rotate the saucepan. Do not stir, as this will break the artichokes. Return the saucepan to a very low heat for 2–3 minutes, shaking it gently and sprinkle some dill on top.

ANGINARES A LA POLITA

Artichokes in the Constantinople Style

This is a speciality of the Greeks who lived in Constantinople, of whom my mother is one, and when cooked well it really is a delicacy. I have an aunt who lived in Constantinople until a few years ago and her version of this recipe is so exceptional that whenever we go to Athens we make a point of being invited to her house for this artichoke meal when the artichokes are in season.

You can have this either as a main meal, in which case you must allow 2 artichokes per person, or as a first course and then 1 artichoke is plenty. It can also be eaten cold, so it can be cooked the day before and either served at room temperature or warmed up first. It is an astoundingly delicious dish, one of the best in Greek cuisine, and the most successful.

4 artichokes
juice of 1½ lemons
1 bunch of spring onions
  when in season, or 1 large
  onion, thinly sliced, or
  225 g/8 oz small pickling
  onions, peeled
150 ml/¼ pint olive oil
3–4 carrots, sliced

3–4 tablespoons fresh dill
300 ml/½ pint water
225 g/8 oz potatoes, peeled
  and sliced, as for roasting,
  or a few small new
  potatoes, whole
salt and freshly ground black
  pepper

Prepare the artichokes as described on page 124, using the juice of half a lemon for the mixture of water and lemon in which you immerse the prepared artichokes. If you are using whole small onions, peel and rinse them.

Heat the olive oil in a large, 25-cm/10-ins wide saucepan. Drop the onions in, either the whole or the sliced spring onions, and sweat them a little, stirring with a wooden spoon. Add the carrots and most of the dill and keep stirring for 2–3 minutes on low heat. Add the water and the juice of 1 lemon and slowly bring to the boil. Then add the potatoes and artichokes. The artichoke hearts should be almost covered with the liquid in the saucepan, so if needed add a little more water. Sprinkle in some salt and black pepper, cover and simmer slowly for 35–40 minutes, according to the size of the artichokes. Sprinkle on a little dill before serving.

ANGINARES ME KOUKIA

Artichokes with Fresh Broad Beans

Fresh broad beans appear in Greece in the spring at the same time as artichokes, dill and cos lettuces, so inevitably they accompany each other in a variety of dishes – with excellent results, particularly at the beginning of the season when the broad beans are young and tender. They start to appear in the Greek shops here in February and are at their best then, dark green and velvety.

This recipe can be cooked with either a lemon sauce or with a tomato sauce. They are both delicious, but personally I prefer the lemon version as I was brought up under my grandmother's disciplinarian wings whose loyalties on this issue lay definitely with the lemon faction! She just would not agree to adding tomatoes to artichokes under any circumstances – she regarded such a thing as sacrilege.

This dish makes an excellent vegetarian main course and either version can be eaten cold – in fact, it is even more delicious. It makes an astonishingly appetizing first course, which is the way we serve it to our friends in this country and they all love it! The following quantities are for either a first course for four or a main course for two.

LEMON VERSION

1 kg/2 lbs fresh broad beans in their shells	150 ml/¼ pint olive oil
4 globe artichokes	450 ml/¾ pint water
juice of 1½ lemons	3 tablespoons dill, or finely chopped parsley
1 medium-sized onion, or a bunch of spring onions, thinly sliced	salt and freshly ground black pepper

Shell the broad beans, discarding the skins of the large ones but keeping most of the smaller and more tender pods. Peel these tender pods by removing the string around them, as you would with green beans, and cut them in two lengthways. Immerse them in a bowl of cold water and rinse them carefully. Repeat the process several times then leave the beans to drain. Prepare the artichokes as described on page 124, using the juice of half a lemon for the mixture of water and lemon in which you immerse the prepared artichokes.

Sauté the onions in the olive oil for 3–4 minutes and add the juice of one lemon. Add the water to the onions and bring to the boil, then add the broad beans, artichokes, dill, or parsley, and salt and pepper. Cover and cook gently for about 45 minutes, shaking the pan occasionally. Sprinkle on a little dill before serving.

TOMATO VERSION

Use the same ingredients as above, but replace the lemon used for cooking with one small can of tomatoes or 3 tablespoons of tomato purée. (You will still need the juice of half a lemon to add to the water in which the artichokes are placed as you prepare them.)

Sauté the onions, add tomatoes or tomato purée and mix well. Add broad beans, artichokes, salt, pepper and dill or parsley. Cover and simmer for about 45 minutes as above.

MELITZANES

Aubergines

Aubergines are the most commonly used vegetable in Greece and the most versatile. They appear in local markets at the beginning of April, these most probably coming from southern places and in particular the island of Kriti. Ierapetra in Kriti supplies most of the markets early in the year, but Peloponnisos is the place most renowned for its aubergines. Most of the large rounded uneven variety, the *tsakonikes* as they are called, come from there and, of course, the most popular of all and the sweetest come from Argos and are consequently called *argitikes*. These are the slim variety, long, pale, purple-white, almost striped sometimes, exclusively used for an *imam bayildi* (baked aubergines) and the stuffed aubergine dishes. These appear later in the summer towards the end of June. I was amazed to find almost the exact variety (perhaps a shade lighter in colour) in the markets in India and I wondered if the mercenary armies of Alexander the Great, compiled from volunteers from all over Greece, having defeated the Indian King Porus, did not bring with them the seeds of the *argitikes* to these distant lands. Too romantic or simply too peaceful a thought for any army?

Another variety, quite long and slim but much bigger than the *argitikes*, comes from the valleys of Thessaly and the area of Volos. These are the darkest in colour, almost blue, and the fiercest in appearance. They look angry and bitter but they are not – they are among the mildest.

Aubergines are still available until November and sometimes December, perhaps a little more expensive at this time, but in the summer they are one of the cheapest vegetables along with courgettes and they are eaten at least twice a week in every Greek home.

Aubergine plants are medium in height, not very bushy, with amazingly pretty, light purple, clematis-like flowers. Basically, they need a lot of sun and water. Aubergines derive their sweetness from the sun like bees do from flowers. Consequently those grown in greenhouses definitely lack taste and have a watery texture and are only a poor relative of a majestic original. Aubergines make the most substantial and mouthwatering wholly vegetarian dishes combined with sweet onions, aromatic garlic, fresh tomatoes and, of course, green peppers and olive oil. They taste infinitely richer if fried first before they are amalgamated into whatever dish they are going to be used. They do tend to absorb a lot of oil so, if you do fry them in advance, use the olive oil in the final dish sparingly. If you do not fry them though, then be generous with it as a watery aubergine dish is far less desirable.

To prepare aubergines

Aubergines tend to have a slightly bitter taste which has to be treated before you embark on their cooking. The only exception to this is the argitikes, which are always mild and sweet. There are two ways to treat their bitterness. The first, which is also my favourite and in my opinion more efficient, is to immerse them in salted water in an earthenware bowl, after slicing them, for at least 30 minutes. Then, rinse them under cold water, squeezing gently at the same time so that a slightly brown water runs away. Then drain them in a colander for at least 30 minutes and pat them dry with a clean tea towel, otherwise they 'spit' when you fry them.

The second method is to slice them and then sprinkle the slices with salt and place them in a colander with a plate on them in order to extract their bitter juices, for one hour. You should again rinse them individually, squeezing them gently and drying them before frying them as, in my experience, the salt makes them even more absorbent to the olive oil. It is not necessary to peel them beforehand as some people believe, otherwise they totally disintegrate and also lose their sparkling, appealing appearance.

What is even more important, though, is choosing them. They should be shiny, firm and tight-skinned, their flesh vibrant and altogether appealing to the eye. The long thin varieties tend to be used for the stuffed aubergine dishes, the imam, and sometimes even the papoutsakia. The large round varieties are used for the moussaka, the melitzanosalata (aubergine dip), etc. Either can be used for the casseroles.

LAHANIKA

MELITZANES IMAM BAYILDI

Baked Aubergines with Tomatoes, Onions and Garlic

This is the most delicious of the aubergine dishes. It derives its Turkish name from the story told from generation to generation about the Turkish priest – the *imam* – who fainted either because of over-indulgence in this quite rich dish or from meanness because of the extravagance with which the olive oil was used in the dish.

The aubergines used for this dish are the slim, elongated, light purple variety from Argos in Peloponnisos, the kingdom of King Agamemnon, the leader of the Greeks in the Trojan war, but more renowned for the dramatically perplexed domestic arrangements in his royal household. Sometimes they are almost striped with white and purple but they are always sweet and they do not have the sharpness and acidity of other varieties. They are called *argitikes*.

An imam *can be cooked the day before and reheated slightly before it is to be served. In fact, its flavour becomes even more memorable when left for twenty-four hours. It is equally delicious cold.*

4 slim, elongated aubergines, about 675 g/1½ lbs	450 g/1 lb fresh tomatoes, peeled and sliced, or 1 396-g/14-oz can tomatoes
150 ml/¼ pint olive oil	
salt and freshly ground black pepper	1 teaspoon each oregano and thyme
450 g/1 lb onions, thinly sliced	1 teaspoon sugar
3–4 cloves garlic, peeled and thinly sliced	2–3 tablespoons chopped parsley

Cut the stalks off the aubergines and rinse them. Using a sharp knife, slit them lengthways on one side only, making sure you do not slit all the way through. They should open like a wallet, so you can put the stuffing in the opening. Pat them dry with a cloth before you fry them. Shallow-fry them gently all around in 4 tablespoons olive oil. If not enough you can add some vegetable oil in the frying pan in order to cut down the expense. (Think of the Turkish *imam*.) Take out and arrange side by side in a small oven dish. Season them.

Put the rest of the olive oil in a saucepan and sauté the onions and garlic in it until they are slightly golden. Add fresh tomatoes and half a cupful of water, or the can of tomatoes and no water. Season. Add the oregano, thyme and sugar and cook gently, covered, for 15 minutes. Add half of the parsley for the last 5 minutes.

With a spoon, fill the aubergines with this stuffing, opening them slightly. They should be quite soft by now so keeping them opened should be no problem. Virtually pile the stuffing in them, filling them generously. Normally they generate enough juices on their own so no addition of liquid is necessary in the oven dish. Cook in a pre-heated oven, gas no. 4 (350°F/180°C), for 40 minutes; baste them once during cooking. Sprinkle with the parsley and serve.

MELITZANES 'ORIENTALE'

Aubergines Oriental Style

I was always fascinated by the name of this dish. I still am! Pronounced the French way, with the accent on the last syllable, it brings a cosmopolitan aura with it – slightly mysterious, slightly naughty. It is reminiscent of an era long gone, bulldozed over by the greed of property developers, at least in Athens, of once elegant, high-ceilinged, corniced establishments, marked by curvilinear bentwood furniture. Elegant but still with their copper implements in sight, like The Oriental restaurant at Omonia Square, in Athens, and the Oriental ice-cream parlour at the beginning of Stadiou Street.

It is dishes like this that could appropriately have been served to elegant, fur-clad, mysterious ladies aboard the Simplon Orient Express as it whistled its way across the Balkans. Ladies elegant but sensuous enough to enjoy their aubergines!

An almost simple but rich dish, with no onions and no garlic, it makes an excellent main course for four, or a starter for six, with the following quantities.

2 medium-sized aubergines, about 675 g/1½ lbs
150 ml/¼ pint vegetable oil
675 g/1½ lbs fresh tomatoes and 150 ml/¼ pint water, or 2 396-g/14-oz cans tomatoes
3 tablespoons olive oil

salt and freshly ground black pepper
1 teaspoon sugar
55 g/2 oz grated Parmesan, Gruyère or Cheddar cheese, or *kefalotyri* for a Greek flavour

Prepare the aubergines as described on page 129. Slice them into rounds and shallow-fry quickly in the hot vegetable oil. Do not burn them, they should get slightly brown.

If you are using fresh tomatoes peel and slice them. You could pour boiling water over them in a colander in order to make peeling easy but if they are ripe summer tomatoes they should peel quite easily. If you are using cans, liquidize their contents, one at a time, quickly so they become pulpy. Put the tomatoes in a saucepan with the olive oil and cook slowly, stirring often so it does not stick. If fresh tomatoes are used, add a cup of water. Cook for 10 minutes, season with salt and black pepper, add the sugar and cook for a further 5 minutes.

Arrange the aubergines in layers in a small oven dish. Coat each layer with the tomato sauce and the cheese. Finish with a layer of tomatoes and cheese and cook in the oven, gas no. 4 (350°F/180°C), for 30 minutes.

MELITZANES STO FOURNO

Aubergines in the Oven

The large, round variety is the best for this wonderful dish. Its rich sweet taste is always an instant success. If prepared in advance, even the day before, and served cold it tastes even better as all the flavours have had the chance to get amalgamated in a splendid profusion. This quality makes it an excellent choice for a large party. Otherwise it can be served hot as it comes out of the oven. In my opinion this is a much more wonderful dish than the overrated moussaka.

3 large aubergines, about
   1 kg/2 lbs or under
150 ml/¼ pint vegetable oil
salt and freshly ground black
   pepper
2 large onions, thinly sliced,
   about 350 g/12 oz
120 ml/4 fl. oz olive oil
2 cloves garlic, peeled and
   thinly sliced
1 tablespoon oregano
1 teaspoon thyme

1 bay leaf
1 396-g/14-oz can tomatoes,
   or 450 g/1 lb fresh
   tomatoes, skinned and
   sliced
1 teaspoon tomato purée
1 teaspoon sugar
1 green pepper, thinly sliced
1 cupful chopped parsley
55 g/2 oz grated cheese,
   either Parmesan, Gruyère
   or Cheddar

Cut off the stalk and bottom end of each aubergine. Rinse and slice them lengthways in medium slices. Immerse in salted water and proceed as described on page 129. Fry them in the vegetable oil, turning once until they are nicely brown but not burnt. Take out each one with a fork and let any excess oil drain. Arrange them, covering the bottom of a 25 × 25-cm/10 x 10-ins oven dish. (A pretty earthenware one is an advantage as it can then be presented at the table.) Sprinkle the aubergines with salt and black pepper.

In the meantime, prepare the sauce. Sauté the onions in the olive oil in a saucepan until they are transparent. Add the garlic and sauté, but do not let it brown as then the dish becomes quite heavy. Add all the herbs, bay leaf, salt and pepper and stir. Add the tomatoes, tomato purée and the sugar. Cover and cook slowly for approximately 15 minutes. Stir with a wooden spoon occasionally to prevent it sticking. If fresh tomatoes are used you should also add about 150 ml/¼ pint water. A few minutes before the end, add the sliced green pepper and half the chopped parsley. Pour this sauce evenly over the aubergines so that it covers them completely; sprinkle over the cheese and bake for 40 minutes at gas. no. 4 (350°F/180°C). Sprinkle with remaining chopped parsley before serving.

MELITZANES ME KOLOKITHAKIA YIAHNI

Aubergine and Courgette Casserole

This is the Greek equivalent of the French ratatouille and it is a very common summer main course in Greece, but we have two versions of it! The common one is where all the vegetables meet in the saucepan raw, apart from the onion and garlic *mélange*. That is the very quick and easy one and is ideal if one is hurrying to save time for swimming or to go off to some outdoor market, or worst of all, if it is washing day. For me, this version is always associated with huge white sheets on the line.

The second version, where the aubergines and courgettes are first fried separately, results in a different dish altogether. The taste of the first could be described as summery and refreshing; that's being generous about it, even when it is not watery, because there is a danger that this dish becomes watery and, even worse, overcooked. The taste of the second, the fried version, is richly supreme and much superior to the first one.

Personally I would always cook the second version, unless I really do not feel like cooking at all on that day. But if you do the first version try not skimp on the olive oil – skimp on the water instead. It really makes all the difference. That and, of course, the freshness of the vegetables and the length of their cooking time. Courgettes, in particular, taste very different if they are still a little hard and have not completely disintegrated into an amorphous coexistence with the rest.

This is the more unusual and elaborate version of the dish, but if you decide to try the first one (described above), just use the same ingredients, add the vegetables raw after you have fried the onion and garlic and sauté them by turning and coating them in the olive oil for 4–5 minutes. Then add the tomatoes and the rest of the ingredients, but no water.

450 g/1 lb aubergines
450 g/1 lb courgettes
150 ml/¼ pint vegetable oil
1–2 green peppers, chopped
1 medium onion, sliced
2 cloves garlic, peeled and
    sliced
4–5 tablespoons olive oil
1 396-g/14-oz can tomatoes,
    or 450 g/1 lb fresh
    tomatoes, sliced, and
    150 ml/¼ pint water

1 tablespoon mixed oregano
    and thyme (fresh
    equivalents from the
    garden are also wonderful)
½ teacup finely chopped
    parsley
salt and freshly ground black
    pepper
pinch of sugar

Prepare the aubergines as described on page 129. Top and tail and rinse the courgettes. Slice the aubergines in round pieces about 1 cm/½ in thick. Slice the courgettes lengthways. Shallow-fry the courgettes in the vegetable oil. In the same frying pan and oil, fry the aubergines. Turn each one over when slightly brown but do not burn. Then sauté the peppers in the same frying pan. Next, sauté the onion and garlic in the olive oil in a large, wide, preferably heavy saucepan until they turn slightly golden. Add the tomatoes. If you are using fresh tomatoes, add just under 150 ml/¼ pint water. Add the oregano and thyme, either fresh or dried, and half of the parsley. Stir slightly, pressing the tomatoes so that they disintegrate. Cover and cook slowly for 15 minutes.

Add the salt, black pepper and sugar, then the fried aubergines, courgettes and peppers. Coat them all with the tomato sauce, stirring gently. Cover and cook very slowly in order to prevent sticking, for approximately 10 minutes. If it looks too dry add a few tablespoons of water. Shake the pan rather than stir at this stage.

Sprinkle with the remaining parsley and serve. It is also delicious served cold, so one could cook it the day before it is to be eaten.

OVEN VERSION

Instead of cooking it in a casserole, spread the aubergines and courgettes in layers in a baking dish, pour the tomato sauce that you have prepared with the onions, garlic and the olive oil all over the top and cook, uncovered, in the oven, gas no. 4 (350°F/180°C), for 30–40 minutes.

MELITZANES PAPOUTSAKIA
Aubergines 'Little Shoes' Style

The funny name of this dish is literally derived from its final appearance. It is unusual but full of flavour, particularly when the minced stuffing has been cooked long enough in order to be tender and to have had its various summery ingredients well amalgamated. In Greece you can have it with a béchamel sauce over each aubergine or without it. We used to have it without the béchamel at home and I still much prefer it like this, as I find the taste of the aubergines entangled with the minced stuffing richer but smoother without the milky interference of the béchamel.

This was undoubtedly the favourite of our childhood. We could hardly wait when the sparkling round aluminium container arrived from the baker's, to sample the sweet taste and smooth texture of the long-simmered and almost melting boat- or shoe-shaped aubergines.

In Greece Melitzanes Papoutsakia *are invariably served as a main course with a tomato or green salad. Allow half an aubergine per person as this is quite a rich dish. A larger variety should be used.*

2 medium-sized aubergines, cut in half lengthways, about 1 kg/2 lbs
150 ml/¼ pint vegetable oil
2 medium onions, thinly sliced
450 g/1 lb minced beef, or lamb
1 227-g/8-oz can tomatoes, or 225 g/8 oz fresh tomatoes, peeled and sliced
salt and freshly ground black pepper

½ cup chopped parsley
25 g/1 oz grated cheese (*kefalotyri* would be used in Greece but Parmesan or Cheddar is fine)
1 tablespoon tomato purée
Béchamel sauce (optional)
25 g/1 oz butter
25 g/1 oz flour
300 ml/½ pint milk
1 egg yolk
salt and white pepper

Trim and rinse the aubergines. Cut them in two, lengthways. Using a spoon, scoop some of their pulp out from the middle so that you have a shape resembling a child's shoe or a little boat. Put all but 2 tablespoons of the vegetable oil in a frying pan and fry the aubergines slowly on both sides until they are nicely brown. Arrange side by side in an oven dish.

Put the 2 tablespoons of vegetable oil in a clean saucepan and sauté the onion in it. Then add the mince and the aubergine pulp and fry until all the lumps have gone. Add the tomatoes, salt, black pepper and most of the parsley. (Keep some of the parsley for garnish when serving.) Cover and simmer for about 20 minutes, stirring occasionally and adding a little water if needed. It should be fairly dry at the end but not sticky.

Fill each aubergine with this mixture. If you are using the béchamel sauce, melt the butter, preferably in a heavy saucepan. Stir in the flour and mix it well with the butter over a gentle heat for about 1 minute. Remove from the heat, add the warmed milk (it should not be boiling hot) and stir, or, even better, whisk vigorously for 1–2 minutes, until they are well amalgamated. Return to the heat and whisk until it starts to boil and thicken up. Let it simmer for 1–2 minutes until a thick consistency has been reached and the flour has cooked. Let it stand for a few minutes, beat the egg yolk slightly and stir it into the sauce. Add salt and white pepper. Cover the top with 2–3 tablespoons of the thick béchamel. Sprinkle some grated cheese on top. If you are not using the béchamel just sprinkle the cheese on top of the stuffing. Dilute the tomato purée in about half a cup of water and pour into the bottom of the oven dish. No oil is needed because the aubergines are quite oily already and they are bound to produce some. The risk with aubergines is making them too oily without realizing it, so it is better to be sparse.

Put them in a medium oven, gas no. 4 (350°F/180°C), for 45 minutes, adding a little water if needed. Take out, sprinkle the rest of the parsley on top and serve immediately.

BRIAMI

Baked Courgettes and Potatoes

A refreshing concoction of summer vegetables, primarily containing potatoes, courgettes, tomatoes, onions and olive oil. Different vegetables are added to the basic ones, according to different regional customs. Sometimes it is only green beans, but on the island of Kriti it is customary to add, apart from the green beans, sliced aubergines and sometimes some okra. We ate it like this with a local family in the village of Mounthros, about an hour's drive from Rethimno, under the coolness of the huge plane trees in their sloping hilly terrace, backed by the monotonous resounding cascading of the cold crystal water of the mountain waterfalls for which the village is well known. People come from distant villages in order to sample and take with them some of its healthy spring water, rumoured to have medicinal qualities.

In Greece this is a main course for ordinary week days, served with white cheese. In Mounthros, it was served with their own delicious homemade soft, white, unsalted sheep's cheese (myzithra), which in this case was deliciously rich and melting in the mouth in a slow process of overlapping waves of pleasing tastes.
Exactly the same dish can be casseroled but I feel the baked version with its slight crispness on the top is infinitely better and more presentable.

675 g/1½ lbs courgettes
450 g/1 lb potatoes, peeled and sliced as for roast potatoes
450 g/1 lb ripe tomatoes, sliced, or 1 396-g/14-oz can tomatoes
1 green pepper, sliced
3 cloves garlic, peeled and sliced
1 medium onion, finely sliced
3 tablespoons parsley, finely chopped
150 ml/¼ pint olive oil

150 ml/¼ pint water
1 teaspoon oregano
salt and freshly ground black pepper
or
Reduce the amount of courgettes and potatoes slightly and add 225 g/8 oz fresh French beans and/or 225 g/8 oz okra and 1–2 green peppers, sliced thickly. An aubergine can also be included.

Scrape the courgettes under running water and slice them in thin round pieces. Prepare each vegetable accordingly and slice in small but thick pieces. Mix all the ingredients together in a large baking dish, sprinkle the oregano on top and season. Cook in a pre-heated oven, gas no. 5 (375°F/190°C), for about 1½ hours. Mix the vegetables gently after 30 minutes and baste 2–3 times. Turn the heat up to gas no. 7 (425°F/220°C) for the last 10 minutes in order to get the potatoes crisp.

BAMIES

Casseroled Okra

Bamies, to my taste, is the queen of the summer vegetables, queenly non-versatile. Strangely shaped (known as 'ladies' fingers' to the Americans), almost uneasily velvety in texture, with a rich, melting, ripe taste, uncommon in the sense that you have to search for it and with a definite exotic nuance about it. After this prelude it is almost needless for me to say that it has to be handled gently throughout its life, as well as in its final cooking hours.

A tall annual, sometimes reaching the height of 2 metres/6 feet, the *bamia* plant (*Abelmoschus esculentus*) has a bushy appearance with large, flat leaves resembling those of the vine, a red trunk and, I was surprised to find when I first saw it growing, it is covered with pretty carnation-like creamy flowers.

In the north of Greece where it is cultivated on a large scale, the *bamia* pickers have to wear gloves or to cover their hands with clothes when harvesting the green pods, in order to protect them from the minute thorn collar of the stems, that can produce quite an unpleasant irritation. A seasonal vegetable in Greece, *bamies* start appearing in the markets around the end of June but at quite high prices for the average household. By the middle of August it becomes cheaper and so more accessible.

The varieties we get here tend to be much larger than the tiny pods that are held in high esteem in Greece. Nevertheless, when they are firm, unwrinkled and unblemished they are equally tasty. They have to be handled gently in order to avoid their glutinous juices pouring out. Top and tail them first. In Greece, the stalk end is taken off with a slanting movement, using a sharp knife, which leaves a small conical head underneath. This requires a bit of expertise and a lot of time! I suspect it also provides the perfect excuse for Greek housewives who love sitting in a shady spot during the summer mornings, executing such arduous tasks communally, helped by numerous small cups of black coffee. It will do if you cut the top off horizontally, but not too deeply, otherwise you run the risk of exposing the little tubes that hold its juices which may result in a messy appearance. Tail them by cutting the tiny pointed end (not so important). Put them in a large bowl of cold water and rinse them gently. Drain.

In Greece the ritual goes on by spreading them on a flat container, sprinkling a couple of spoonfuls of vinegar all over them and leaving them in the sun for about an hour. This apparently makes them hold their juices. Then they are rinsed again and drained. Time, but most importantly, sun being scarce in this country, I do not bother with this last step.

Okra, as indeed most other vegetables, is always cooked with olive oil in Greece and they are delicious served either hot or cold. When cooked with fresh tomatoes they make a wonderful vegetarian meal on their own. Canned okra is quite good but it has to be drained and rinsed with cold water. It also requires very little time for cooking, approximately 10 minutes.

1 kg/2 lbs fresh okra, or 2 400-g/14-oz cans okra
150 ml/¼ pint olive oil
1 large onion, sliced
450 g/1 lb fresh tomatoes, sliced, or 1 396-g/14-oz can tomatoes

some chopped parsley
salt and freshly ground black pepper
pinch of sugar

Prepare the okra as described on page 138. Heat the olive oil in a wide saucepan and sauté the onion until transparent. Add the fresh tomatoes (skinned if you want to be a perfectionist), or the can of tomatoes, and bring to the boil. Add the parsley, salt, pepper and sugar, stir and carefully add the okra, shaking the saucepan so they fall into place. Do not stir once you have added the okra. Try to coat them with the tomatoes and add some water to barely cover them.

Cook slowly for about 30–40 minutes according to size. If using canned okra, let the tomato sauce cook properly for approximately 15 minutes, then add the drained and rinsed okra carefully and cook slowly for about 10 minutes.

Once cooked they should not be floating in water but have an oily sauce. If you realize you are going to be left with too much liquid, cook uncovered.

SPANAKI

Spinach

Fresh spinach is widely used in Greece. It makes a variety of unusual but delicious dishes, either vegetarian or with meat. Most commonly spinach is served in wholly vegetarian casseroles, accompanied by fried squid or fried fish. Added to lamb and served with an egg and lemon sauce, spinach makes a wonderful festive dish fit for a special occasion. Mixed together with cheese and eggs, it produces splendid variations of *spanakopitta*, the lovely Greek spinach pies of all sizes and shapes which are rolled in *fyllo* or homemade pastry, fried individually, baked or fried in large snail-like coils, as on the islands. Of course, when used in stuffings, as in the stunning variation of *dolmathes* (stuffed vine leaves) I found on the island, or in stuffed squid, it renders the dish a quality that can only be described as eternal. Lastly, added to cuttlefish and cooked in white wine or lemon, spinach produces one of the most unusual but definitely Mediterranean-flavoured dishes. Fresh spinach is easily available and quite cheap in this country, so it is sad to see people opting for the frozen packets.

Fresh spinach has a lot more healthier and nutritious qualities, and its taste and texture is millenniums ahead of the frozen stuff. But it does need careful and proper rinsing as there is nothing worse than exercising your teeth like grinding stones. It is no good throwing the whole mass into a bowl of cold water, draining it and thinking it is clean; most certainly it is not.

Sort out any yellow or rotting leaves first, trim the stalks slightly when necessary and then rinse it several times in cold water, taking it out by hand and letting the grit sink to the bottom of the bowl, then replacing with clean water. In Greece we use stalks and all – why not? Drain it, squeeze it gently and ideally let it stand in the strainer for about an hour so you do not end up with a lot of water while cooking it. In order to keep its nutritious qualities you must never strain it after it is cooked. It follows that we never boil it in Greece.

Once it is rinsed and drained you can either chop it roughly, which makes it easier to serve, or cook it whole.

Here is the basic recipe when cooked on its own.

SPANAKI ME LEMONI

Spinach Cooked with Lemon

For four people as an accompaniment to a roast, or served with other dishes such as fried fish or fried liver, or for a vegetarian meal served with sauté potatoes. Or enough for two for a more substantial course.

1 kg/2 lbs fresh spinach	salt and freshly ground black
1 large onion, thinly sliced	pepper
4 tablespoons olive oil, or	juice of ½ lemon
25 g/1 oz butter	

Rinse, drain and shred the spinach as described above. Sauté the onion in the olive oil or the butter until transparent, add the spinach, salt and pepper and stir with a wooden spatula until all the spinach is coated in the oil and looks glistening. Cover and cook gently for 5–7 minutes. Add the lemon juice and serve.

This can easily be prepared in advance, and re-heated before serving. When cooked with olive oil it does not even need re-heating, unless out of preference.

SPANAKORIZO

Spinach with Rice

This dish can be cooked in advance and eaten either cold or warmed up a little before serving. You can have it on its own or serve taramosalata with it, fried keftethes (herby hamburgers), fried squid or fried fish. This quantity will serve four people as a main course.

675 g/1½ lbs fresh spinach
1 large onion
90 ml/3 fl. oz olive oil
salt and freshly ground black
  pepper

150 ml/¼ pint water
juice of ½ lemon
110 g/4 oz long-grain rice

Rinse, drain and shred the spinach as described on page 140. Sauté the onion in the olive oil until transparent, add the spinach, salt and pepper and stir until all the spinach is coated with the oil. Add the water and the lemon juice and bring to the boil. Add the rice, stir, cover and cook slowly for 10 minutes or until the rice is cooked to your taste. If needed, add a little water during cooking, in order to prevent the rice from sticking.

LAHANORIZO

Dutch Cabbage and Rice Casserole

A good vegetable dish very similar to the spinach and rice one, above. It is very sweet and tasty and it can be supplemented with something else, such as keftethes or some fried fish, to provide a more substantial meal. It is the Dutch white cabbage and the olive oil that are used that produce the sweet taste. It can be eaten cold or at room temperature without its taste suffering.

1 kg/2 lbs Dutch white
   cabbage
1 onion, sliced
150 ml/¼ pint olive oil
55 g/2 oz long-grain rice,
   rinsed and drained

2 tablespoons tomato purée
   diluted in 220 ml/7 fl. oz
   water
salt and freshly ground black
   pepper
chopped parsley

Core and shred the cabbage thickly. Immerse it in a bowl of cold water, rinse and drain it. Fry the onion in the olive oil until it is light golden. Add the shredded cabbage and sauté together for a few minutes until the cabbage becomes pliable and glistening. Add the drained rice and stir for 1–2 minutes until it is coated in the olive oil. Add the diluted tomato purée and the seasoning. Stir, cover and simmer very slowly until all the water is absorbed and the rice is soft, about 15 minutes. Withdraw from the heat, sprinkle the chopped parsley on the top and keep covered for 5 minutes before serving.

PRASSORIZO

Leeks with Rice

A good way to serve leeks either on their own as a vegetarian meal with black olives and fresh bread, or with taramosalata *and some cheese. It can also be served as an accompaniment to any kind of meat, particularly roasts and grills. Try to keep some of the green part of the leeks, but make sure they are properly cleaned. One of the most unpleasant characteristics of leeks is when they have not been rinsed properly, as happens with fresh spinach sometimes, and you find yourself exercising your teeth like grinding stones.*

110 g/4 oz long-grain or
   Basmati rice, soaked in
   cold water for 10 minutes
675 g/1½ lbs leeks
1 large onion, sliced
60 ml/ 2 fl. oz olive oil

2 tablespoons lemon juice
300 ml/½ pint hot water
salt and freshly ground black
   pepper
some chopped parsley, about
   2 tablespoons

Rinse and drain the rice. Top and tail the leeks. Discard any coarse or damaged outer leaves, particularly at the green end, but keep the tender green part in the middle. Rinse them. Slice in 1-cm/½-in rings and immerse them in a bowl of cold water for 5 minutes in order to soak any stubborn grit. Pick the pieces up by hand or with a slotted spoon in order to allow grit to sink to the bottom, then drain in a colander. If the leeks are particularly muddy, repeat this process until the water remains clear.

In a saucepan, sauté the onion in the olive oil until transparent, then add the prepared leeks. Sauté together, stirring for a further 5 minutes, until the leeks become soft and glistening, then add the lemon juice. Add the hot water, salt and pepper and bring to the boil. Then add the drained rice, stir, cover and cook slowly for 10–15 minutes. If needed, add a little more water as different qualities of rice have different absorbent capacities, but make sure the rice is not overcooked. Do not forget that it will go on steaming after it has been withdrawn from the heat. Sprinkle parsley on top, cover and let stand for 5 minutes before serving.

TOMATO VERSION OF LEEKS WITH RICE

The tomato version is equally tasty and unusual. Prepare as above but replace the lemon juice with 2 tablespoons tomato purée or 4–5 skinned and sliced fresh tomatoes, or 1 227-g/8-oz can of tomatoes.

KOUNOUPITHI KAPAMA

Cauliflower Casserole

A more interesting alternative to plain boiled cauliflower, and also tastier. This is a recipe that was rumoured to have originated in Peloponnisos and, in particular, in the area of Kalamata. Traditionally it is cooked with olive oil, particularly since Kalamata is one of the most prolific areas renowned for its olive oil and its splendid black olives. Of course, this could be replaced with butter without its taste suffering. Serve as a vegetarian meal in itself or supplement with sauté potatoes, or fried fish or taramosalata. Alternatively, it could accompany anything from grilled lamb chops to a roast of pork.

1 large cauliflower	2–3 tablespoons tomato
juice of ½ lemon	purée
5 tablespoons olive oil, or	salt and freshly ground black
55 g/2 oz butter	pepper
1 medium onion, thinly sliced	2 tablespoons chopped
150 ml/¼ pint water	parsley

Trim the cauliflower from its outer leaves and the hard core at its base. Rinse carefully and dry with a kitchen towel. With a sharp knife, cut it into medium-sized pieces. Sprinkle the lemon juice all over the pieces and leave for 5–10 minutes.

Place the olive oil or butter in a saucepan and sauté the cauliflower pieces, a few at a time, without letting them turn brown. Take out as they are ready. In the same saucepan, sauté the onion gently, then add the water and tomato purée and stir to dilute it. When it comes to the boil, add the cauliflower pieces, salt and pepper, and cover and cook for approximately 7–10 minutes. Sprinkle with the parsley and serve.

PATATES LEMONATES

Potatoes in Lemon Sauce

A simple potato dish but with a surprisingly delicate, winning taste. I had completely forgotten about it when a few years ago it suddenly appeared on our table at an ordinary restaurant in Athens.

The Phillipou restaurant at 35 Xenokratous Street in Kolonaki, at the foot of Lykavittos, is an unpretentious place with genuine home cooking, bustling with the noise of hungry Greeks and busy (sometimes cocky) waiters at lunchtime. This utilitarian, semi-basement restaurant has remained the same for over fifteen years, serving Greeks at lunchtime and undiscovered by the temporary trail of tourists, being out of their main avenue and perhaps difficult to get to. We have surrendered Plaka and the Akropolis to tourism but not Kolonaki! None of the nasty versions of *moussaka* here, or the eternal miserable pork *souvlaki* or the *horiatiki salata* (Greek salad as it has come to be known) appear automatically on the table at the sniff of foreigners around.

The food here follows the calendar as home cooking does, so you will find the wonderful artichoke and meat fricassee dishes in the spring; seasonal vegetables like okra or the various green beans in the summer; always a salad of boiled *horta* or *vlita* (greens); excellent *yiouvetsi* (roast lamb with tomatoes and pasta), etc. The menu is quite limited and the cooking, which is honest, ranges from very good to indifferent, but never bad. Even when it is indifferent, though, it is still honest!

The restaurant is mainly frequented by people who want a quick lunch in order to retire home for the ritualistic Greek siesta, totally undistracted. The clientele ranges from politicians and prime ministers out of office, to actors, students and journalists.

It is a vibrant place to be at lunchtime. I felt excited and sentimental when this potato dish appeared, as it looked exactly as if it had been cooked by our grandmother, with the waxy-looking potatoes (*kithonates*), resembling a quince, thickly quartered lengthways and glistening in their rich buttery sauce. Not only did it have the same appearance, though, but also that particular taste which this dish used to have when we ate it at home; it instantly transported me through taste to the past and made me see my two pretty, dashing sisters sitting across the table with me in Lilliputian, bright blue school uniforms with their well-plaited, disciplined hair just touching their dazzling, stiff white collars.

Most Greek homes own a special, round, aluminium container with handles and a lid, much deeper than a roasting tin and quite large. This is used mostly for dishes that need to be cooked spread in one layer like *bri-*

ami (baked courgettes and potatoes), or stuffed peppers and tomatoes or stuffed courgettes and aubergines, but on top of the cooker, even though the same container can be sent to the local baker's oven without the lid, for a roasting session, if need be. Spread in this manner, potatoes need a minimum of water added to the dish and they all cook in contact with the butter and lemon sauce. They are not crisp as a result, but soft and creamy looking; quite often the same dish is baked in the baker's oven and then they are still delicious, perhaps even more so, but almost a completely different dish to me. Also they can be cooked with olive oil instead of butter for the health-conscious and they are still startling.

A large casserole or large frying pan with a lid will produce basically the same results, as long as the potatoes are not allowed to cook fast and completely disintegrate or overcook. Alternatively, they can be roasted in a slow oven.

My husband, being quite titillated by the Proustian results of this potato dish on all three of us (my sisters and me), was determined, on returning to London, to experiment and find the 'golden formula'. He has been quite successful and here are the results: a casserole and a roasted version.

Served with Greek keftethes *(herby hamburgers) or* taramokeftethes *(salted cod's roe rissoles fried in oil) or a fresh green salad and white cheese, this makes an excellent main course.*

CASSEROLE VERSION

1 kg/2 lbs potatoes	2 tablespoons finely chopped
55 g/2 oz butter	parsley
juice of 1 lemon	300 ml/½ pint hot water
salt and freshly ground black	
pepper	

Peel the potatoes, halve them lengthways, and quarter them, or if very large, slice them, lengthways also. Rinse and drain them. They should roughly resemble a half-moon shape. Melt the butter in a large casserole and sauté the potatoes in it, until they are glistening. Pour the lemon juice over, turn them for a few more minutes with a wooden spoon, sprinkle in seasoning and the parsley and then add the hot water. On no account should they turn brown. Cover them and cook slowly for 25 minutes, shaking the pan occasionally or stirring gently. They should still be a little hard at the end but with no water left in their sauce, just dry and buttery. If there is water still at the end, cook the potatoes a little longer with the dish uncovered.

OVEN VERSION

1 kg/2 lbs potatoes
juice of 1 lemon
75 g/3 oz butter

salt and freshly ground black
pepper
150 ml/¼ pint hot water

Prepare the potatoes in the same manner as above. Spread them in a roasting tin, pour the lemon juice all over them, season and dot them with the butter. Pour the water in a corner of the container and put into a pre-heated oven, gas no. 5 (375°F/190°C), for 1 hour and 20 minutes. Turn the oven up to gas no. 6 (400°F/200°C) for the last 15 minutes. Baste them twice and add a tiny bit of water if needed. They will be delicious.

PATATES YIAHNI

Potato Casserole with Tomatoes

Another vegetarian, simple but tasty potato dish. Sometimes when the potatoes are new and small, they are left whole to cook amid the bright red folds of the ripe tomatoes.

1 kg/2 lbs potatoes
1 medium onion, sliced
90 ml/3 fl. oz olive oil
1 396-g/14-oz can tomatoes,
   or 450 g/1 lb fresh ripe
   tomatoes, sliced

1 tablespoon oregano
salt and freshly ground black
   pepper
2–3 tablespoons chopped
   parsley

Peel, rinse and cut the potatoes as in the previous recipe or leave them whole if small. Fry the onion in hot olive oil until light golden. Add the tomatoes (if fresh ones are used, add 150 ml/¼ pint water), breaking them up with a wooden spoon or fork, and the oregano and, when the mixture is boiling, the potatoes. Season, cover and cook gently for 20–30 minutes. Add the parsley in the last few minutes. Add a little water if needed.

PATATES LATHERES ME LEMONI

Potato Casserole with Olive Oil and Lemon

Deliciously tasty but dangerously sticky. When we gave a *myrothia* (a small sample) to a German family who were renting a house opposite us in the village on the island they got terribly impressed and over-enthusiastic and asked for the recipe. They raved over their results and the taste of their potatoes but they mourned their burnt saucepan, having tried rather overzealously to include as little water as possible, according to our instructions. In fact, this is the trick of the dish. Cook the potatoes with a lot of olive oil and onions and very little water. The more dangerously sticky it will become, the more tasty the results will be.

Even though the ingredients are not very different from Patates Lemonates *on page 145, the essence and the taste of this dish are quite different. Potatoes in Lemon Sauce is rather genteel and light, but this recipe is rather rough, peasanty and sharply appetizing. Both of them are almost strictly vegetarian, basic and easy but totally unlike the insipid taste vegetarian cuisine carries around it like a dark cloud.*

1 kg/2 lbs potatoes	salt and freshly ground black
150 ml/¼ pint olive oil	pepper
1–2 medium onions, sliced	3 tablespoons finely chopped
juice of 1 lemon	parsley
150 ml/¼ pint water	

Peel the potatoes and cut them *kithonates* – like quinces, that is resembling half-moon shapes. Rinse and drain them. Heat the olive oil in a large saucepan and fry the onion in it, until it starts to change colour. Add the potatoes and continue stirring and frying together for a few minutes until the onion becomes light golden. Pour the lemon juice over and, when the steam subsides, add the water. Season, add the parsley, cover and cook very slowly, stirring occasionally in order to prevent the onions sticking. Avoid adding more water unless it is dangerously needed. It can take 30–40 minutes. Watch it, particularly towards the end, in case it sticks or burns, even though a little sticking is inevitable. It should strictly be left in its rich, light green, oily sauce.

PATATOKEFTETHES

Fried Potato Croquettes

*I find it hard not to think of spring when I bring back the taste of
these to mind. Unmistakably, it is the abundance of chopped dill
that my grandmother used to add to them and the spring onions
that I recall. Since then I have always felt that if I cannot get the
fresh dill it is not worth making them, but I know I am wrong as
they are equally delicious with chopped parsley and spring onions.
We used to have these at lunchtime as a main course with a green
cos lettuce salad, or with boiled* horta – *any variety of either wild
or purpose-grown greens, such as dandelions or young mustard
plants* (vrouves), *which are everywhere in the spring.*

675 g/1½ lbs potatoes
2 eggs
75 g/3 oz grated *kefalotyri*
 cheese, or Gruyère, or
 Parmesan and Cheddar
2 spring onions, finely sliced,
 or 1 small onion, finely
 grated almost to a pulp

2–3 tablespoons finely
 chopped dill, or, alas,
 parsley
salt and freshly ground black
 pepper
55 g/2 oz plain flour
55 g/2 oz butter, or 4
 tablespoons olive oil, or a
 mixture of both

Rinse and then boil the potatoes in their skins. They hold their taste, their
firmness and their nutritious qualities this way, otherwise they become
too soggy. When cool enough to handle, but still hot, peel and mash them.
Beat the eggs a little and add them to the potatoes, along with all the other
ingredients apart from the flour and the butter or olive oil. Season and mix
well either with a fork or your hands.

Make small, round, flat shapes about 5 cm/2 ins in diameter, roll them
in flour and fry in hot olive oil or butter on both sides until they are gold-
en. These can be fried in advance and warmed in the oven when needed.

ARAKAS

Fresh Young Peas

Fresh, sweet peas appear in the markets in Greece at the beginning of April and they sustain their delicate taste until the end of May. At this time of the year, one will find them in every Greek household cooked in a number of delicious ways – cooked on their own with olive oil and a little lemon, cooked with tomatoes or combined with artichokes or with spring lamb; undoubtedly they make the most glorious, simple, surprising dishes in Greek cuisine.

I have tried them on most of our friends in England and, with no exception, they all loved them and started cooking them, particularly since they are so easy to make, with no special skills or exotic ingredients required. The most successful dish of all is the casserole with fresh globe artichokes, which combines a number of enticing tastes perfectly blended into one of the most unusual and unexpected combinations.

I recall innumerable happy occasions when we were children helping the adult women to shell the round, sweet pods, a very pleasurable and easy task that I have since found most children love, including my little daughters.

The youngest and the freshest and consequently the sweetest pods we were encouraged to eat on the spot, as was the case with the youngest of the shelled broad beans. Luckily, we start to get the same young sweet peas flown over from Cyprus in all the Greek shops here at about the end of March. By the time their season is over the English peas start to arrive, so we are particularly privileged.

ON FROZEN PEAS

Frozen peas could be used in any of the following recipes with good results as frozen peas go. However, do not expect the delicacy, sweetness and aroma of the fresh peas. Frozen peas, unfortunately, seem to withhold and taste predominantly of water. Keeping this in mind, one could choose a good quality 'garden pea' variety and be careful when adding water. As they normally require very brief cooking, 4–5 minutes, there will only be 2–3 tablespoons of water needed during this period. Otherwise, follow the recipes in exactly the same way, but cook the onions with or without the tomatoes a little longer before adding the peas. You will need a 450-g/1-lb packet of frozen peas.

ARAKAS

Fresh Peas in Tomato Sauce

Peas cooked this way should be young since towards the end of their season they become too large and hard as stones and taste completely different.

1 kg/2 lbs fresh peas in their green pods
1 bunch spring onions, thickly sliced, or 1 large onion, thinly sliced
120 ml/4 fl. oz olive oil

1 227-g/8-oz can tomatoes, or 225 g/8 oz fresh tomatoes
150 ml/¼ pint water
salt and freshly ground black pepper
2–3 tablespoons fresh dill, chopped

Shell the peas. Rinse them in cold water and drain. Sauté the onions in the olive oil until transparent. Add the tomatoes; if using fresh ones they should be sliced finely. Add the water and bring to the boil. Add peas, salt and pepper and the dill, stir and cover. Cook slowly until the peas are tender (they take about 40–50 minutes according to their size). If they are particularly young ones they would take less.

ARAKAS ME LEMONI

Fresh Peas with Lemon Sauce

Most often fresh peas were cooked with lemons instead of tomatoes in our house. So, perhaps out of habit, I feel that lemons have an affinity with peas and do not interfere and distract from their delicate taste.

Often there was an *avgolemono* sauce made at the end and added to this dish, which made it even more delicious. Either way it is very simple to make. It is customary to cook peas in butter if an *avgolemono* is to be added. Use the same ingredients as in the previous recipe of peas with tomatoes, but omit the tomatoes and use the juice of half a lemon instead. Sauté the onions in the olive oil until transparent, add the shelled peas and stir them for a few minutes until they are all coated in the oil. Add most of the dill and 150 ml/¼ pint hot water. It is better to add more water later if needed, little by little. Also 2–3 peeled and sliced carrots may be added. Add some seasoning, cover and cook gently for about 40 minutes, stirring occasionally and checking the water, in case they stick.

They are absolutely delicious like this but in case you decide to add an *avgolemono* sauce, beat an egg, add the juice of the other half of the lemon and proceed as on page 56.

ARAKAS ME ANGINARES

Fresh Peas with Globe Artichokes

The quantities given will either make a vegetarian meal for two or a wonderful first course for a dinner party for four. For the latter purpose, leave the artichokes whole, without slicing them in the middle, after they have been peeled and properly cleaned of their hairy choke in the middle. Serve them resting on their cup, with their stalk upright, in the middle of the plate and surrounded by a ring of peas.

4 artichokes
juice of 1 lemon (use half for
   the peas only, the other
   half for immersing the
   artichokes)
1 kg/2 lbs fresh peas in their
   pods

1 bunch spring onions,
   roughly chopped, or 1
   large onion, thinly sliced
150 ml/¼ pint olive oil
3 tablespoons dill
salt and freshly ground black
   pepper
450 ml/¾ pint water

Clean the artichokes as described on page 124. Put them in a bowl of water with half the lemon juice. Shell the peas. You could keep a few of the pea pods if they are very, very young and tender. Rinse the peas in cold water and drain them.

Sauté the onions in the olive oil and add the remaining lemon juice, most of the dill, salt and pepper and the water. Bring to the boil, add the peas and stir, so they are coated in the oily sauce. Then add the artichokes, cover and cook slowly. During the cooking, gently turn the artichokes round so they do not rest on the same side throughout the cooking period. Do this at least twice. Also stir the peas gently. Cook for about 40 minutes. There should be left at the end hardly any water but a nice, oily-looking sauce. Sprinkle the remaining dill on top and serve.

ARAKAS ME ANGINARES KE DOMATES

Fresh Peas with Artichokes in Tomato Sauce

Make exactly as above, but omit the lemon and add instead 225 g/8 oz fresh tomatoes, sliced thinly, or 1 227-g/8-oz can tomatoes. Bring to the boil and proceed in exactly the same way.

FASOLAKIA

Green Beans in Tomato Sauce

Runner beans do not exist in Greece but if you want to use them in this recipe you can as long as they are young and tender because sometimes they can be gigantic, hard and terrible. Make sure you string them properly all around and then slice them in two lengthways and proceed as above. When beans are expensive and you want to boost the dish up you could add 2 medium potatoes, sliced thickly. Or you can do that anyway as a variation. Alternatively, you can add 2 carrots, sliced thinly.

1 kg/2 lbs French green
   beans, or bobby beans
1 large onion, thinly sliced
150 ml/¼ pint olive oil
1 396-g/14-oz can tomatoes,
   or 450 g/1 lb fresh
   tomatoes, thinly sliced

300 ml/½ pint water, if using
   fresh tomatoes, or 150 ml/
   ¼ pint if a can is used
2 tablespoons finely chopped
   parsley
salt and freshly ground black
   pepper

Have ready a bowl of cold water. Top and tail the beans and drop them into the bowl, if they are very tender, otherwise it is important to cut the stringy edges all around with a sharp knife first.

Sauté the onion in the olive oil in a saucepan until it is transparent. Add the tomatoes and sauté together for a few minutes. Add the water and bring to the boil.

Rinse the beans and drain them. Add them to the saucepan – they should barely be covered by the sauce. Add the parsley, salt and pepper, stir and shake the pan. Cover and cook slowly until tender – approximately 40 minutes. They should have a thick, oily sauce at the end.

PITTES
Pies

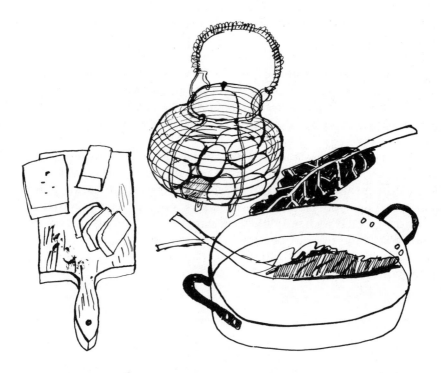

Greek pies constitute a great tradition. They always carry a celebratory nuance. When we were children we could sense the excitement when a pie was announced by our grandmother for the following day. I can still sense the excitement when our local friends on Alonnisos announce that they are planning to make one of their pies. Pie-making on the island is a real art, with huge, flat, round, shallow copper pans and beautifully home-made pastry, involving skilful home-baking.

The pie needs to be miraculously turned over, all in one piece, halfway through the cooking so that both sides are brown and crisp. They use intricate fillings, savoury, vegetarian or sweet. The most delicious and most characteristic of the island is a spring-time filling which requires a lot of fresh herbs collected from fields, including large quantities of young poppy plants before they burst into flower, masses of wild feathery fennel and spring onions. This kind of vegetarian filling, using good quality olive oil, is traditionally made during Lent, on fasting days when even eggs are considered a sacrilege.

Spinach and masses of spring onions and fresh dill make up the urban equivalent which we were used to and eagerly awaited when our fasting spirits were rapidly fading as Easter approached nearer and nearer and fasting became stricter and stricter under my grandmother's disciplinarian eye.

I can still sense the fervour that prevailed the day before pie-making as we collected the quantities of ingredients required and prepared them. The huge shallow round containers (copper ones originally, later replaced by aluminium) had to be cleaned and polished, ready for the assembly of the pies early next morning, after which they were taken to the local baker's at dawn.

Near noon, the crisp and aromatic pies were brought back and samples divided and sent to favoured neighbours – the traditional Greek *myrothia*, literally meaning a 'sniff' but in general terms a small sample, a particular necessity for pregnant neighbours as they run the risk of a miscarriage if left with unfulfilled culinary desires! Since the whole neighbourhood could not escape noticing the triumphant parade of the aromatic containers to and from the baker's, 'samples' or *myrothies* were a built-in must. (They still are.)

SPANAKOTYROPITTA

Spinach and Cheese Pie

The most common and most favoured of all the pies are the spinach pies, with added white feta cheese and eggs; or cheese pies, the famous *tyropittes*, which constitute such a common part of Greek life and can be bought routinely at any street corner and eaten everywhere, in streets, on beaches, on buses, etc. There used to be wandering, white-aproned, cheese-pie sellers (*tyropittathes*) who carried large square tins and glass boxes with handles. They had a built-in shallow tray underneath filled with tiny charcoal that kept the goods warm and appetizing, while the *tyropittathes* aroused the children of the neighbourhood with their cries.

Westernization has almost eclipsed this kind of wandering street-seller, but *tyropittes* can be bought in every small snack-bar all over Greece and good pies can still be found around Constitution Square in Athens as well as Kolonaki Square. Some that are made in the premises are absolutely exquisite; one particularly good place is The Ariston, established in 1911, at 10 Voulis Street, near Syntagma, which emerged with its mouthwatering, crisp, shortcrust pastry *tyropittes* in the early 1960s when I was working just round the corner. I could hardly believe my good luck. It is still going strong, in a slightly genteel, old-fashioned style. More elaborate, more celebratory, but not necessarily more delicious, fillings are used in *kotopittes* (chicken pies) and *kreatopittes* (meat pies).

Nowadays the task has become easier with the exquisitely thin *fyllo* pastry widely available ready-made in Greece and elsewhere. We don't have to slave over pastry-making, at the crack of dawn, like our grandmothers did. *Fyllo* (φυλλο) in Greek means a leaf. It becomes *fylla* in the plural, but when referring to pastry it is always used in the singular.

Greek pies are surprisingly easy to master and very quick to make. One does not have to be absolutely accurate with the quantities of the filling, a few grams of feta cheese more or less won't make much difference and three or four eggs won't change the result either. Later on you can even improvise on the fillings and assemble any favourite alternatives.

Greek *spanakotyropittes* and *tyropittes* are delicious rough, peasant-type food, suitable to be taken to the fields for a day's work; they are not hair-raising French soufflés, so one has nothing to worry about. The main thing is that one needs to catch the essence of the dish, rather than be obsessively accurate about quantities. Needless to say, the essence of a *spanakopitta* or a *spanakotyropitta* is the grandeur of the delicate fresh spinach and if one replaces this with frozen spinach, only one Greek word is a suitable description for the results: *katastrophé.*

PITTES

Fyllo pastry can be frozen but it has to be given time to defrost completely before it can be used successfully. Defrosting takes about two hours in an average warm room. It should be allowed to defrost in its plastic covering; if taken out it will dry and crack. There is some wastage with frozen *fyllo*, as a few leaves of the pastry are bound to crack and become unsuitable but that does not matter as there is plenty anyway.

The other important factor is that spinach has to be cleaned and properly rinsed of any traces of grit. Immerse it in a clean sink, full of water, let the grit sink and lift the spinach out by hand into a colander. Repeat this several times until the water appears perfectly clear. (Read about spinach, pages 139–40, for more information.)

The quantities given here will feed six people as a main course, or up to twelve as an appetizer for a party. (It could feed even more if you cut the pieces smaller.) Choose an oblong-shaped oven dish to make things easier, (since fyllo *pastry comes in an oblong shape), otherwise you will have to patch odd corners. Do not leave* fyllo *pastry uncovered at room temperature or it becomes brittle and unusable.*

1 kg/2 lbs fresh spinach
1 large onion, finely sliced
1 bunch spring onions including their greenery, trimmed, rinsed and finely sliced
3–4 tablespoons olive oil
salt and freshly ground black pepper
4–5 tablespoons finely chopped parsley (try to get the flat-leafed continental variety)

3–4 tablespoons chopped fresh dill, or fennel
225 g/8 oz white feta cheese, crumbled
3–4 eggs, slightly beaten
450-g/1 l-lb packet *fyllo* pastry
110 g/4 oz melted butter, or 150 ml/¼ pint olive oil, for brushing container and pastry

Although not essential, cutting off any rough stalks from the spinach will give a finer result. Clean and rinse the spinach meticulously as described above. Drain well, squeezing it gently by hand. Sauté the onion and spring onions in the olive oil, until they become transparent but not brown. Shred the spinach roughly and add it to the onion. Stir with a wooden spoon over medium heat to get it all coated in the olive oil. It will produce its own moisture so do not add any water. Cover and cook gently for 5–6 minutes. Add salt, pepper, parsley and dill and keep aside to cool down a little.

Crumble the feta cheese into the beaten eggs. If the spinach mixture when cooled has produced a lot of liquid, drain it before adding to the cheese and egg mixture. Season and mix well. Be careful not to add any more salt as feta is quite salty.

The size of the tin I find best to use is approximately 39 × 28 × 8 cm/15 × 11 × 3 ins. A tin is more suitable so that you get the layers of pastry underneath crisp, otherwise they may stay soggy. Even this though is not a strict rule.

Gently unfold the roll of pastry onto a flat surface. Place the container you are going to use on top of it to measure it roughly. Keep in mind that *fyllo* shrinks once cooked, so make an allowance before you cut away the leftover strip, if there is one, with a sharp knife or scissors. Brush the base and sides of the container with oil or melted butter. Coat the uppermost sheet of pastry, lift it carefully and spread it on the bottom of the container, trying to avoid creasing. Oil the next sheet of pastry on top of your pile and spread it on top of the previous one. Place 7–8 layers of *fyllo* pastry in the same fashion on the bottom of the container, then evenly spread on the filling. Cover the filling with 6–7 layers of oiled pastry, without pressing it down. Oil the top layer well, and cut it into diamond or square shapes with a small sharp knife. Be careful to cut only the top layers of pastry and not as far as the bottom ones, otherwise the filling will spill and become messy. Sprinkle tiny drops of cold water on top of the pastry with your fingers, in order to stop the *fyllo* from curling up at the edges.

Place the dish in a pre-heated oven, gas no. 5 (375°F/190°C), for 40 minutes until the pastry puffs up and the top appears lightly golden and crisp. Take it out of the oven, let it stand for 5–10 minutes and then cut the marked pieces all the way down to the bottom of the tin. Lift the pieces out individually and arrange them on a pretty platter. It is equally delicious cold, particularly when no butter is included but olive oil is used instead, but it does go a little soggy after 24 hours.

Alternatively, cook it earlier for a slightly shorter time. Then, just before it is to be eaten, put it back in the oven for 10 minutes in order to get it hot, take it out and cut it as above.

SPANAKOPITTA

Spinach Pie

When the cheese is omitted, but a lot more herbs and spring onions are added, then this is called *spanakopitta*. Additionally, when the eggs are omitted and olive oil only is used it becomes *spanakopitta nistisimi* (fasting spinach pie), or otherwise totally and strictly vegetarian.

ALTERNATIVE SPANAKOPITTA

Any of the above spinach pies can also be made without pre-cooking the spinach or the onions. This results in a lighter pie but it needs longer and slower cooking. Make sure the spinach is shredded finely in this case and that it is also well drained, otherwise it may become too watery. Mix all the ingredients together in a large bowl and proceed as above. Cook in a pre-heated oven, gas no. 4 (350°F/180°C), for about 1 hour.

TYROPITTA

Cheese Pie

A delicious pie and also very quick and easy to make. It needs absolutely no preparation, unlike the spanakopitta. *It is infinitely better when hot, and it will survive re-heating in the oven like the* spanakopitta, *just before it is to be eaten.*
Almost any combination of cheeses is possible, but it must contain the Greek feta, otherwise it lacks the peppery sharpness of the real thing. Cheddar is not suitable as it tends to melt and stay liquid. On the other hand, you could use feta with Parmesan, and feta with cottage cheese is also very good, or feta with Swiss Gruyère is excellent. In Greece they use either wholly feta or combine it with a little kefalotyri.
The quantities given here are for the same size of dish and portions as for the spanakotyropitta, *which will give you at least 12 good-sized pieces.*

3–4 eggs
2 tablespoons milk (optional)
little grated nutmeg
some freshly ground black
  pepper
285–350 g/10–12 oz feta
  cheese

225 g/8 oz cottage cheese, or
  110 g/4 oz thickly grated
  Parmesan or Gruyère
  cheese
2 tablespoons finely chopped
  parsley (optional)
450 g/1 lb *fyllo* pastry
75 g/3 oz melted butter

Beat the eggs (and milk, if using) lightly with a fork, and add the nutmeg and pepper. Roughly crumble the feta cheese in the same bowl, either with your fingers or with a fork. Do not include the liquid which comes with it as it is too salty. Add the other cheese (whichever you are using), the parsley and mix well.

Spread 7–8 layers of *fyllo* on the bottom of a metal oven dish as described in the *Spanakotyropitta* (Spinach and Cheese Pie) on page 157, spread the cheese filling evenly, add 5–6 layers of *fyllo* in the same manner, brushing them with melted butter first. Be more generous with the butter when brushing the last sheet of pastry, so that it becomes crisp and nicely golden when cooked.

Cut the *tyropitta* with a sharp small knife in the shape you have chosen, square or oblong, making sure you only cut the top layers of *fyllo* and not through to the bottom ones.

Using the tips of your fingers, sprinkle a few drops of water all over its surface, in order to prevent the edges of the pastry from curling up, and cook in a pre-heated oven, gas no. 5 (375°F/190°C), for 40 minutes until the top becomes nicely brown.

If it is not to be eaten immediately, cook it 15 minutes less and put it back in the oven for a further 10–15 minutes just before it is to be eaten. Let it stand for 5 minutes and then, just before it is to be served, cut the pre-shaped pieces with a sharp knife, taking each one out as you cut it and arranging them on a flat platter.

KOLOKYTHOPITTA

A Courgette Pie

*This is an alternative pie filling for spring and summer, and it is
both subtle and delicious. It is a variation of a courgette pie made
in the Ionian island of Corfu. This pie will serve six or eight people.*

567 g/1¼ lbs courgettes,
trimmed, rinsed and dried
4 eggs, lightly beaten
4 spring onions, trimmed,
rinsed and sliced finely
110 g/4 oz feta cheese,
crumbled, or 55 g/2 oz
grated Parmesan cheese

4–5 tablespoons chopped
fresh dill
salt and freshly ground black
pepper
Pastry
450 g/1 lb *fyllo* pastry
110 g/4 oz melted butter

Coarsely grate the courgettes through a food processor. Lightly beat the
eggs in a large bowl and add the remaining filling ingredients, including
the courgettes. Mix well.

Butter the base and sides of a medium-size roasting dish and layer the
fyllo and filling as described above.

Bake in a pre-heated oven, gas no. 5 (375°F/190°C), for 45 minutes,
until crisp and light golden. Take out and let it stand for at least 5 minutes
before serving. At its best when served hot or warm, but it can also be
served at room temperature.

KREATOPITTA

Meat Pie

A meat pie constituted a glorious event at home. Glorious were its ingredients and even more glorious was its taste. A small leg of lamb was boned
and roughly minced or cubed by hand; this was the protagonist of the
midday performance with a supporting cast of eggs, onions, grated
cheese, breadcrumbs and a quantity of fresh greenery, parsley and mint.
The whole thing was fragrantly enwrapped with a faint suspicion of the
Orient, from the rich brown bark of cinnamon. Nowadays, minced lamb

is used instead, preferably from a lean leg of lamb; alternatively, minced beef is used as long as it comes from a tender piece of meat, and I find in the west it is excellent with minced veal.

Like all the pies, this is best cooked in a metal container in order to avoid soggy bottom layers of fyllo pastry. It is excellent even cold, taken at a picnic, but it should be covered with foil when cold and left at room temperature rather than in a refrigerator, I find. The quantities will give 10–12 good portions which is enough to feed six people.

2 medium onions, finely
   sliced
4 tablespoons vegetable oil
675 g/1½ lbs lean minced
   lamb, beef or veal
1 glass white wine, or juice of
   ½ lemon
salt and freshly ground black
   pepper
1 stick of cinnamon
½ teaspoon ground allspice
150 ml/¼ pint water
4 tablespoons chopped
   parsley

2 tablespoons fresh mint, or
   ½ teaspoon dried mint
55 g/2 oz fresh breadcrumbs
   (optional, but they do
   result in a lighter stuffing)
55 g/2 oz grated *kefalotyri*,
   Parmesan or Gruyère
   cheese
4 eggs, lightly beaten
450 g/1 lb *fyllo* pastry
110 g/4 oz melted butter

Sauté the onions in the oil until transparent. Add the meat and sauté together, breaking any lumps with a wooden spoon. When the meat looks brown, slowly pour the wine or lemon juice over it. Add some seasoning, the spices, the water and cover and simmer for 30–40 minutes, stirring occasionally until the meat is very tender and quite dry. Withdraw from the heat, discard the cinnamon stick, add the parsley and mint and mix well.

When slightly cooler, add the breadcrumbs, the cheese and the beaten eggs and mix together. Assemble it with the *fyllo* pastry, brushing each sheet with melted butter, exactly the same way as described on page 165.

Cook in a pre-heated oven, gas no. 5 (375°F/190°C), for 35–40 minutes. Take out and let it stand for 10–15 minutes in order to cool a little and set before cutting it into square or oblong portions.

KOTOPITTA

Chicken Pie

Another of these glorious pies that can transform an everyday event into something special and celebratory. Light and delicate, it is perfect for a cool summer evening, contrary to Greek folklore that according to the old proverb it should be eaten in January: '*Kotta pitta ton Yienari, peteino ton Alonari*' ('Hen made into a pie eaten in January and cockerel in July'). I don't know if hens have some special hidden flavoursome quality in January thus becoming more desirable by Greeks, but I do know that the long slow simmering session of a hen with masses of pulpy onions is definitely connected with the rather more primitive forms of cooking: the home hearths in peasant households even nowadays and Primus stoves in urban ones not so long ago; the long simmering required doubled up as a form of heating too, steaming the room up and creating a welcoming homely mood.

Since we are talking of 'glorious pies', I shall give the recipe for one that subsequently could feed four to six people as a main meal with a salad and I will not go into the subject of leftover chicken. Leftovers are leftovers, no matter how well disguised they may be. The form and texture of the pie make it a delicious candidate for a picnic, and it is best kept covered with foil at room temperature and not placed in a refrigerator unless one is dealing with specially hot summer weather. Otherwise it can be cooked slightly shorter in advance and put in the oven for 10 minutes just before it is to be eaten, like the spinach and cheese pies. Once taken out of the oven, let it stand for 10–15 minutes in order to cool slightly and set, before cutting it into individual portions.

1 1.5 kg/3 lbs, free-range chicken, or a good boiling fowl (not one of those slim miserable boilers)	55 g/2 oz grated Greek *kefalotyri* cheese, or Parmesan or Gruyère
salt	¼ teaspoon grated nutmeg
450 g/1 lb onions, peeled and finely sliced	freshly ground black pepper
	4 eggs
	110 g/4 oz melted butter
	1 450-g/1-lb packet of *fyllo* pastry

It is best to use a large rectangular or square baking dish as in the previous pie recipes, approximately 39 × 28 × 8 cm/15 × 11 × 3 ins or 25 × 25 × 8 cm/10 × 10 × 3 ins.

Rinse and quarter the chicken. (Do not use the livers, keep them for something else.) Put the chicken pieces in a saucepan and barely cover them with cold water. It is best to add more water, if needed, later. Sprinkle with a little salt and slowly bring to the boil. Skim until the water is clear, then add the onions. Cover and simmer for about 1–1¼ hours according to the size and age of the bird, but the meat should easily come off the bone.

Take the chicken out, skin and bone it and shred the meat into small pieces. Continue to simmer the onions until they become pulpy and the contents of the saucepan look like a runny sauce. Add the chicken pieces and simmer together for a further 10 minutes, stirring occasionally.

Remove from the heat, add the cheese and nutmeg, season and mix well. Let it stand and cool slightly for 10 minutes. Beat the eggs slightly, add them to the mixture when cooler and mix well.

Brush the bottom and sides of the oven dish with melted butter and line it with a sheet of *fyllo* pastry. It is best if the edges are lined with the pastry slightly so that they can be folded over the filling later to seal it in, as it may be runnier than a spinach and cheese filling, for instance. Put 8–9 layers of pastry into the dish, brushing each one with melted butter. Spread the filling evenly on top, fold any overlapping edges over it and cover with 7–8 layers of pastry, brushing each with butter, particularly the top one.

Using a sharp knife, roughly cut the remaining side edges of the pastry all round the container, keeping in mind that *fyllo* shrinks quite a lot. Cut the top layers of *fyllo* into elongated strips, sprinkle on some water and cook the pie in a pre-heated oven, gas no. 5 (375°F/190°C), for 45 minutes until the top is crisp and golden. Let it cool slightly and cut it into square or oblong portions – approximately 10–12 pieces.

BOUREKAKIA, TYROPITTAKIA, SKALTSOUNAKIA

Small, Individual Pies

Bourekakia from the Turkish word *borek* (most probably derived from the old word *bürük* or *bür* – to coil) are small individual savoury pies containing any kind of filling from strictly traditional ones of cheese or spinach and cheese, to more elaborate ones such as the chicken filling of *Kotopitta* (Chicken Pie), the meat of *Kreatopitta* (Meat Pie), the delicious filling made with brains described on page 276, or the even more delicious concoction of *glikathia ke jambon* (sweetbreads and ham) all cubed and amalgamated with a thick béchamel sauce.

The shape of these small and intricately surprising parcels could be either that of a small triangle (*trigono* in Greek) as small cheese pies are always made, or a thin cylindrical one resembling a short cigar; or they could be the shape of an oblong or little square parcel, according to the mood of the creator; alternatively for a big family gathering there would be trays of all shapes and most importantly of different fillings to surprise and satisfy the palate with totally secret and unexpected delights.

All these are always wrapped with paper-thin *fyllo* pastry bought ready-made in Greece from specialized workshops (quite often very eso-teric subterranean ones) that only sell two or three different kinds of sim-ilar-type pastry and which nowadays one can easily obtain in most countries abroad, either fresh or frozen. On very exceptional occasions, they are wrapped with delicious homemade pastry called *sfoliata* in Greek, none less than our familiar puff pastry.

Because of the predominant 'extended family' pattern in Greece, as well as the traditional magnificent female spirit of co-operation at an hour of need, even nowadays such luxurious delicacies emerge out of pleasur-able shared hours of female company, interrupted by that other pleasur-able activity of Greek women, reading each other's coffee-cups.

Another very common aspect of *bourekakia* is when they are made with homemade pastry of various sorts but easier than the *sfoliata* (puff pastry), and these almost always are of a half-moon shape with their edges pressed decoratively together, and are either fried or baked. The most common filling of these is cheese or spinach, or a mixture of both, although any of the other fillings mentioned in the previous large pie recipes can be used, as long as one makes sure the filling is in a thicker form, otherwise it may ooze out of this type of pastry.

To the Kretans, these half-moon-shaped cheese and spinach pies in their homemade pastry are known as *kallitsounakia* or *skaltsounakia* and they are particularly delicious since they contain their homemade rich sheep *myzithra*, *xynomyzithra* or *anthotyro* cheese instead of the usual feta. (*Anthotyro* is roughly a cottage-type cheese but by far richer and tastier but also unsalted, while *myzithra* is roughly its salted equivalent.)

Quite often, *skaltsounakia* are made with *horta* (greens) that are gath-ered from the mountains. This is a special category of *horta*, which are cooked *tsigarista* (sautéed) as the Kretans specify, as opposed to *horta* which are boiled and served as salad with an olive oil and lemon dressing. The various *horta* from this category are also cooked in casseroles with meat in similar combinations as in the recipe of lamb with spinach, in the meat section, but without the addition of the egg and lemon sauce. This category of *tsigarista horta* includes *hatzikous*, *maratha*, *koutsounathes*, *tzilibithia* and beautiful heart-shaped, lustrous green *avronies* which are also cooked with snails, in a dish which is a speciality of the island.

The pastry for these can be made from plain ingredients such as flour, salt and water and in some cases a little olive oil or it may be a richer one which contains all these but also some butter and yoghurt.

Bourekakia of any shape render themselves more suitable for small gatherings and also for 'leftovers'. Leftover chicken or meat can be transformed once cubed, dressed with a cloak of tasty béchamel, plenty of grated cheese and wrapped in crisp layers of either *fyllo* or one of the homemade pastries. The quantity of 225 g/8 oz *fyllo* pastry, given below, will produce approximately 30–35 individual savoury pastries; for the filling halve the quantities of any of the fillings described for the large pies, previously in this chapter.

HOW TO WRAP AND ROLL TRIGONA (TRIANGLES)

Use about 225 g/8 oz *fyllo*, approximately ten sheets. Lay it on a wooden surface and, using a sharp knife, cut the whole stack into four elongated rectangular strips approximately 8 cm/3 ins wide. The same job can be done successfully with a pair of scissors if you have a steady hand. Stack three of the piles on top of each other and cover with a damp kitchen towel in order to prevent them drying and becoming brittle and non-pliable before you use them.

Take the fourth pile and brush the whole length with melted butter, place a heaped teaspoon of the chosen filling at one end, about 4 cm/1½ ins from the edge, and fold over the two near corners, forming a small triangle; fold this triangle at an angle, one upwards, one downwards until all the strip has been folded. Then continue until you have used all the pastry. Place the pies on buttered baking containers, trapping the loose end of the pastry underneath and leaving a little space in between them so that they do not stick together. Brush all over their tops with melted butter and bake in a pre-heated oven, gas no. 4 (350°F/180°C), for 30 minutes until they become light golden and crisp.

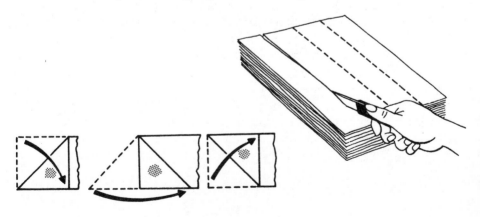

'CIGAR' SHAPES

Slightly easier than the triangle; traditionally used for meat or chicken fillings only.

Use the same quantity of *fyllo* as above but cut it into three slightly wider long strips, about 10 cm/4 ins wide. Stack and cover them as above to prevent them from drying, taking three or four strips out at a time. Brush all over the surface of the top one with melted butter; place a tablespoon of the chosen stuffing widthways at one end, about 4 cm/1½ ins from the short edge of the strip. Fold the two elongated sides about 1.5 cm/½ in at either side over the filling and press a crease all along the two long edges of the pastry, down to the far end, with the tips of the fingers. Then, fold the short edge, near the filling, over it, in the shape of a cigarette or a short cigar, thus trapping the filling securely. Roll it with the tips of the fingers, down to the far end of the pastry. Place in a buttered oven container, trapping the loose end underneath. Brush all over their tops with butter and bake in a pre-heated oven, gas no. 4 (350°F/180°C), for 30 minutes.

MISOFEGARA OR HALF-MOON SHAPES

These are made with any homemade pastry or any kind of shortcrust or puff pastry that one is familiar with. Ready-made frozen pastry is also good, once it has defrosted. Once the pastry is made, divide it into two or three sections and, using a lightly floured rolling pin, roll each one out, on a lightly floured surface, as thinly as you can. Cut with a round-rimmed glass or a round pastry cutter, or even a small saucer, into discs approximately 10 cm/4 ins diameter. Place a tablespoon of the stuffing in the middle and fold half of the pastry over it in a half-moon shape, pressing the two edges together and slightly overlapping them, giving a braid-like or ribbed effect at the semi-circular end; this edge can be decorated further by pressing the open ends of a fork all along the folded semi-circular edge, or pressing a thumb over it at a leaning angle over equal distances.

When puff or shortcrust pastry are used they can be either baked or fried in hot oil; whenever the simpler bread-dough type pastry is used, of flour and water, they are best fried in hot oil.

In the first instance, place them in an oven container that has been wiped with a damp cloth, when puff pastry is used, or a buttered container for shortcrust pastry; brush their tops with a little beaten egg in order to give them a shining and crisp appearance and bake in a pre-heated oven, gas no. 6 (400°F/200°C), for 10 minutes, then turn the heat down to gas no. 4 (350°F/180°C) and bake for approximately 20 more minutes.

KALLITSOUNAKIA OR
SKALTSOUNAKIA KRITIS

Kretan Half-moon-shaped Traditional Savoury Pastries

Driving through the Kretan countryside, or on the outskirts of almost every village, mountainous or not, you will see the strange spectacle of female figures enveloped in black, definite and strict dots against the lacy blue of the uneven horizon, stooped over in a solitary trance.

They are the *horta* gatherers, concentrating on differentiating their favourite slender and sometimes insignificant-looking 'greens' from among the thick and tangled undergrowth, the bushes of the wild thorny brooms and the wild flowers. These greens their family will enjoy as a pungent salad, once they have been boiled, such as *stamnagathia*, *syrithes*, *gourounopothithes* and in March and April wonderful slender wild *sparagia* (asparagus).

Or the ladies may be picking *koutsounathes*, *tzilibithia*, *hatzikous*, *maratha*, or *avronies* or *ovryes* as they are called elsewhere in Greece. These are preferred sautéed and added to meat or used as stuffing with chopped fresh mint (which also grows wild in abundance and is very aromatic), in the traditional Kretan half-moon-shaped pastries called *skaltsounakia* or *kallitsounakia*.

Any one of these wild greens, individually or in combination, can be chopped and sautéed in olive oil with fresh mint and used as a stuffing on their own or alternatively mixed with homemade village *xynomyzithra* (fresh sheep's cheese) and eggs. Either way they are delicious in their homemade rough thick pastry, deep-fried in olive oil.

One of the *horta* in this group, *avronies*, is the companion *par excellence* to snails in a casserole that undoubtedly makes one of the island's esoteric specialities that will not be met elsewhere in Greece. Kretan women know where to look for each variety of wild greens, as some grow more prolifically in one spot rather than the other.

Avronies, a fragile climber with heart-shaped leaves, is common around the village of Agios Vasilis under the Kethros mountains or the village of Melambes facing the mountain of Psiloritis; *stamnagathia* and *gourounopothithes* are found in leafy valleys, in villages such as Episkopi or Roustika near Rethymno; but almost all in season will be found in baskets in the wonderful markets of Hania or Iraklion along with bunches of the slender pen-shaped freshly gathered asparagus. One kind of the Kretan traditional pastries of *skaltsounakia* that are made on Easter Saturday, with a cheese filling, are polished with beaten egg, then sprinkled with roasted sesame seeds and sent to the local baker, in each village.

PITTES

169

KALLITSOUNAKIA KRITIS

Kretan Cheese and Spinach or Horta Pies

*In this recipe for Kretan skaltsounakia, I have replaced wild horta
with spinach for obvious reasons but that does not exclude
imaginative improvisations. The quantities given will produce
approximately 12 small pies.*

Filling
225 g/8 oz fresh spinach
170 g/6 oz feta cheese,
   crumbled with a fork
110 g/4 oz cottage cheese
1 egg, lightly beaten
1 small onion, or 3 spring
   onions, finely chopped
2–3 tablespoons chopped
   fresh mint, or 1 tablespoon
   dried mint

freshly ground black pepper
3 tablespoons olive oil
Pastry
225 g/8 oz plain flour
pinch of salt
1 tablespoon olive oil
5–6 tablespoons water
olive or good vegetable oil,
   for frying

Trim the spinach and discard stalks. Rinse in plenty of water, repeatedly, until the water is absolutely clear. Squeeze gently and drain in a colander. It should be fairly dry by the time it is used, so prepare well in advance. Shred the raw spinach very finely and mix it well in a bowl with the rest of the filling ingredients.

To make the pastry, sift the flour with the salt into a bowl, make a little well in the middle and add the olive oil and half of the water. Work these into the flour with your fingers, adding more water as you proceed until it is gathered into a ball and leaves the sides of the bowl clean. Knead it with your fist a little until it becomes more elastic and pliable, then divide the dough into two. Rest each ball of dough on a floured marble surface or board, flatten each a little with the palm of your hand and roll out to about 50 mm/⅛ in thickness. Cut round shapes, approximately 10 cm/4 ins diameter, with a pastry cutter, saucer or glass.

Put a tablespoon of the filling in the middle of each one, fold and stick the edges firmly into half-moon shapes as described previously. Deep-fry them in hot oil for 2–3 minutes until they are crisp and golden. Take out and drain on absorbent kitchen paper before you serve. They should be eaten hot.

KOTOPOULA KAI KYNIYI
Poultry and Game

There is a plethora of interesting ways and ingredients that Greeks use to transform otherwise bland chicken dishes. Simple ingredients like lemons and fresh basil have glorious results in *kotopoulo lemonato*; a chicken casserole finished with a smooth thick *avgolemono* sauce can be a real delicacy and chicken flavoured by the addition of exotic okra is, to my taste, at least, the best among the chicken dishes.

KOTOPOULO STO FOURNO

Roast Chicken and Potatoes

A free-roaming chicken on the island, roasted in a sparkling, round, aluminium container with quartered potatoes, lemon juice and fresh herbs at hand nearby, stays in one's mind for ever, particularly if it has been roasted in the special beehive oven outdoors, with the women chattering and the men sipping *ouzo* and consuming black, sharp olives at sunset. This is one of the easiest and most delicious ways to prepare chicken.

Potatoes cooked with the chicken in this manner usually do not turn out as crisp as other roast potatoes, but they are absolutely delicious as they absorb all the juices and are penetrated by the lemon juice and the aroma of the herbs.

1 roasting chicken, 1.5–2 kg/3–4 lbs	1 small onion
salt and freshly ground black pepper	1 kg/2 lbs potatoes
	juice of 1–2 lemons
1 tablespoon each oregano and thyme, dried or fresh	4 tablespoons olive oil
	25 g/1 oz butter
	150 ml/¼ pint water

Rinse and dry the chicken. Season the chicken with salt and black pepper all over, as well as in its cavity. Sprinkle some herbs in its cavity and place the onion in it. Place it in the middle of a roasting tin, breast down first. Peel and quarter the potatoes lengthways (quarter-moon shape), rinse them and arrange evenly around the chicken.

Pour the lemon juice and olive oil over the chicken and potatoes, then sprinkle with most of the herbs. Dot the butter all over and carefully pour the water into a corner of the pan.

Roast in a pre-heated oven, gas no. 7 (425°F/220°C), for 30 minutes. Turn the chicken over, breast side up this time, sprinkle with some herbs, baste the potatoes, reduce the temperature to gas no. 6 (400°F/200°C) and cook for a further hour.

A little water may be added if it looks as if it is drying up, no more than 3–4 tablespoons. The chicken should be golden brown by the end and the potatoes a little less so.

KOTOPOULO YEMISTO

Stuffed Chicken

*If you are in a creative mood and you wish to add a hint of
exoticism to an ordinary roast chicken, try stuffing it with either of
the following stuffings and then roast it as described above, with or
without the potatoes. The same stuffings can be used for a turkey,
but increase the quantities of ingredients by half again.*

Stuffing 1
2 medium onions, finely
    sliced
1 clove garlic, peeled and
    crushed
3 tablespoons olive oil
chicken liver and heart,
    rinsed and thinly sliced
    (optional)

55 g/2 oz long-grain rice,
    rinsed and drained
150 ml/¼ pint hot water
salt and freshly ground black
    pepper
55 g/2 oz pine nuts, browned
    in a frying pan
25 g/1 oz sultanas (optional)
1 teaspoon each oregano and
    thyme

Sauté the onions and garlic in the olive oil. Add the giblets and sauté for
3–4 minutes, then add the rice and sauté for a few minutes until it looks
glistening. Add the hot water, salt and pepper and simmer slowly for 2–3
minutes until most of the water is absorbed but the rice should remain
hard. Take off the heat, add the pine nuts, the sultanas (if used) and the
herbs. Mix well and stuff the chicken, leaving a little room for expansion.
I do not find any need for sewing up the opening of the chicken; in fact,
sometimes we seal this opening with half a potato, which seems to work
well. In any case roast the stuffed chicken breast side up and avoid turning it too much.

Stuffing 2
75 g/3 oz pine nuts
170 g/6 oz lean lamb or beef,
    minced
chicken liver and heart,
    rinsed and finely sliced
1 medium onion, finely sliced
1 piece cinnamon stick
2 teaspoons ground allspice,
    or 2–3 whole grains

1 glass white wine, or juice of
    ½ lemon
90 ml/3 fl. oz water
salt and freshly ground black
    pepper
3 tablespoons chopped
    parsley
25 g/1oz long-grain rice,
    rinsed

Put the pine nuts in a dry frying pan and roast them over a medium heat, shaking or stirring almost continuously for 3–4 minutes until they look nicely brown. Keep aside.

Sauté the minced meat, which should produce its own fat so there is no need to add more, and the giblets for a few minutes, breaking down any lumps.

Add the onion and the spices and sauté for a further 3–4 minutes. Pour over the wine or lemon juice and, when the steaming subsides, add the water. Season with salt and pepper, cover and simmer for 20 minutes. Remove from the heat, add the rice, pine nuts, parsley and mix well. Stuff the chicken and roast as above.

KOTOPOULO LEMONATO

Chicken in Lemon Sauce

At home we also used to add quite a quantity of fresh chopped basil, when in season, to this dish which made it particularly aromatic. Dried basil can be used but I feel that dried basil changes its flavour and aroma to a much different substance with too strong and pungent a smell, so I am afraid it does not entirely result in the same luxurious dish.

Pots of basil with various forms of leaf are an indispensable feature in Greek households of every description and rank, from whitewashed island courtyards and mountain villages to small houses, squashed amidst the notorious blocks of flats in larger cities, and particularly in Athens.

On small balconies, or even windowsills, the pots of basil will appear in May and their round fresh leafy growth becomes apparent within two or three weeks. At home we always planted two pots with the larger leaf variety, specially for cooking, apart from the small tiny leafed very decorative one, as my grandmother believed the larger leaf to have more flavour and its aroma to last the cooking better.

One of the most successful ways of cooking chicken, since it harmonizes perfectly with the lemon flavour, which gives an altogether luxuriant taste to the finished dish. In Greece, where lemons go with almost everything and they also come in large numbers, at least two large lemons would be used in this recipe if not more. Younger and smaller chickens become really delicious cooked in this manner.

1 chicken, about 1.5 kg/3 lbs, jointed	1 stick celery with leaves, rinsed, trimmed and thinly sliced
4 tablespoons olive oil	
salt and freshly ground black pepper	some sprigs fresh basil, or ½ teaspoon dried basil
1 small onion, finely sliced	juice of 1–2 lemons
3 carrots, sliced	300 ml/½ pint hot water

Rinse and dry the chicken pieces. Put the olive oil in a wide saucepan and, when fairly hot but not brown, season the chicken pieces and sauté them gently on both sides. They should not get brown. Remove them to a plate.

Put the onion in the same saucepan and sauté until it becomes transparent. Add all the vegetables and the basil and sauté for a few more minutes, until they are all coated in oil. Add the chicken pieces on top of the vegetables and pour the lemon juice all over. It is best to start with one lemon and adjust to taste before you add any more. When the steam from the lemon has subsided add the water and more seasoning, then cover and cook slowly for approximately 45 minutes to 1 hour.

Served with plain white *hylopittes*, a kind of small, flat, square noodles (quite often homemade in Greece), boiled separately, it is absolutely delicious, but is equally good with plain white rice. In either case, serve the chicken and vegetables on top of the pasta or rice and coat with the delicious thick sauce.

KOTOPOULO ME SALTSA KARYTHIA

Chicken with Walnut Sauce

In the islands, the poorest peasant will ask you into his clean and tidy cottage, give you cognac, coffee and a glass of water, after the invariable Greek fashion, and offer you walnuts, which he will crack for you, or whatever else may be in season.

(William Miller, *Greek Life in Town and Country*, 1905, p. 6.)

Walnuts have always been part of the Greek tradition and are intimately intertwined with peasant life on the mainland and particularly so on the Greek islands. It is characteristic of Greek island cooking to incorporate them into sauces in order to enrich their taste and give a velvety smoothness to their texture. Walnuts are primarily added to the Greek *skorthalia*, the rich and sharp, garlic paste assembled from humble ingredients that accompanies fried or boiled vegetables, fried or boiled fish and occasionally boiled chicken.

This chicken dish is said to have originated on the island of Kriti. An almost identical dish is occasionally made with hare. Chicken cooked in this manner has an unusual but delicate taste. Care must be taken to avoid adding too many walnuts which tend to leave a bitter aftertaste.

1 chicken, about 1.5–
  2 kg/3–4 lbs, jointed into
  4 pieces
salt and white pepper
25 g/1 oz flour
4 tablespoons olive or
  vegetable oil

25 g/1 oz butter
1 glass white wine
300 ml/½ pint hot water
55 g/2 oz crushed walnuts

Rinse and dry the chicken pieces. Season each piece, coat it with flour lightly and fry it in the hot oil in a frying pan. Take the pieces out as they become golden on both sides and place them in a wide saucepan, with the butter. Pour the wine into the frying pan and, using a wooden spatula, deglaze it. Pour the contents of the frying pan over the chicken in the saucepan, add the hot water and more seasoning. Cover and simmer slowly for 1 hour, adding a little water if needed. Crush the walnuts either in a pestle and mortar, coarsely, or in an electric grinder. Care must be taken not to make them too fine and powdery. Take the chicken pieces out, add the walnuts to the sauce and gently bring to the boil, stirring. Let the sauce bubble for a few minutes, return the chicken pieces and cook for a further 2–3 minutes.

Serve each chicken piece coated with the sauce together with fried or sautéed potatoes, or *patatokeftethes*, the potato croquettes on page 149, and either a tomato or green salad.

KOTOPOULO ME PILAFI

Chicken with Rice Casserole

Even though sometimes this dish appears a little messy, it is always delectable. The rice cooked in the rich sauce unfolds layer after layer of delicious tastes, in its true oriental capacity of a proper pilau but with a Mediterranean aroma from the typical Greek herbs used instead of the oriental spices. In place of the rice, any of the summer vegetables can be added, such as courgettes, aubergines or green beans, towards the end of the cooking time. Courgettes or aubergines become particularly delicious if they are briefly fried to a pale golden colour first.

1 large free-range chicken, jointed
4 tablespoons olive oil, or vegetable oil
1 large onion, thinly sliced
2 cloves garlic, peeled and thinly sliced
1 tablespoon oregano

1 tablespoon thyme
1 396-g/14-oz can tomatoes
300 ml/½ pint water
salt and freshly ground black pepper
170 g/6 oz long-grain rice, rinsed and drained
some chopped parsley

Rinse and dry the chicken pieces. Place the oil in a wide saucepan and, when hot, fry the chicken pieces on both sides until they become golden. Take the chicken out, add and fry the onion and garlic until they are pale brown. Add the oregano, thyme, tomatoes and water, pressing them with a wooden spoon to break them up. Bring to the boil. Season with salt and pepper, add the chicken pieces, cover and cook slowly for about 1 hour. Stir from time to time and turn the chicken pieces over.

When cooked, take the chicken pieces out and, while the sauce is boiling, add the rice, more seasoning and some of the parsley. Stir to amalgamate the tomato sauce and the rice well, cover and simmer very gently, without stirring and disturbing the rice again, for approximately 10 minutes, until the rice feels cooked but is still a little hard. If needed, add a little hot water during the cooking.

Replace the chicken pieces on top of the sauce, cover the saucepan first with a tea towel and then its lid and let it stand for 5 minutes before serving, so that the rice still cooks in its steam and fluffs up. Then sprinkle with the remaining parsley.

The chicken can be cooked in advance but the rice should be added just before it is to be eaten, otherwise it may become soggy. If the chicken has been cooked in advance, bring back to the boil, place the chicken pieces on a plate, add the rice in the boiling sauce and proceed as above.

CHICKEN WITH SUMMER VEGETABLES

As an alternative to the above, instead of the rice, add 675 g/1½ lbs fresh green beans, trimmed and rinsed, for the last 20–30 minutes. Or add 1 kg/2 lbs courgettes or aubergines, trimmed, rinsed and sliced thickly. Aubergines should be immersed in salted water for 30 minutes first, then rinsed and squeezed gently. For more delectable results fry them first, add them to the casserole and simmer for a further 10 minutes in order to amalgamate the different flavours.

KOTOPOULO ME BAMIES

Chicken with Okra Casserole

Okra, with its wonderfully rich taste and distinguished aroma, adds to a chicken layers of exoticism. It absolutely transforms it into a very special dish, always welcomed and treasured by all (apart from the non-okra lovers). It is my most favourite chicken dish. Follow the instructions for cooking the chicken as in *Kotopoulo me Pilafi* (Chicken with Rice Casserole) on page 177, but cook the chicken for 20 minutes and then add 675 g/1½ lbs of prepared okra on top. The okra should sit in but not be covered by the sauce. Add a little water if needed. Shake the pan and cook slowly for about 30 minutes without stirring, but rotating the saucepan occasionally.

Sprinkle with parsley and serve.

KOTOPOULO FRICASSEE

Chicken Casserole with Egg and Lemon Sauce

*Very light and fragrant and perhaps the best of the chicken dishes.
It is excellent combined with a crisp, green salad.*

1 chicken, approximately 1.5
  kg/3 lbs, cut into 4 joints
25 g/1 oz butter, melted
2 tablespoons olive oil
2 medium onions, finely
  sliced
2 carrots, sliced
½ stick celery, rinsed,
  trimmed and chopped

2 tablespoons chopped dill, if
  available
300 ml/½ pint water
salt and white pepper
Avgolemono sauce
1 tablespoon cornflour
4 tablespoons cold water
2 eggs
juice of 1½ lemons

Rinse and dry the chicken pieces, and sauté gently in the butter and oil.
They should not get coloured. Add the vegetables and the dill, water and
seasoning, cover and cook gently for approximately 50 minutes. Let it
stand for 5 minutes before proceeding with the sauce, which should be
made as described on page 56 (first method). Pour the sauce over the
chicken and rotate the saucepan, until it looks completely amalgamated.

Return to a very low heat for 3–4 minutes, rotating occasionally until
the sauce looks slightly thicker and the cornflour has cooked a little.

Serve the chicken pieces covered with the thick sauce and vegetables, on
top of plain white rice.

KOTOPOULO ME KOLOKYTHAKIA

Chicken with Courgettes and Egg and Lemon Sauce

Make exactly as in the preceding recipe but omit the carrots and celery.
Once the chicken is almost cooked add 1 kg/2 lbs thickly sliced courgettes. Shake the pan, cover and cook for 10 minutes. Remove the pan
from the heat once the courgettes are cooked and let it stand before proceeding with the egg and lemon sauce, which should be made and applied
in the manner described above. There is no need for rice with this dish.

KOTOPOULO KOKKINISTO OR KAPAMA

Chicken Casserole with Tomatoes and Spices

This recipe is more suitable for a free-range chicken or a boiling fowl since, with the rather longer simmering required, the aroma of the spices penetrates the meat and enhances its flavour. Also the truth is that a good hen is much more flavoursome than a chicken. This is almost the equivalent of the bride's island dish, only instead of an elderly goat one should use an elderly hen.

1 free-range chicken, or a
    good boiling fowl, jointed
salt and freshly ground black
    pepper
4 tablespoons olive oil
1 glass red wine
1 stick of cinnamon

3 cloves
3–4 grains whole allspice, or
    a pinch of ground allspice
350 g/12 oz fresh tomatoes,
    skinned and sliced, or 1
    396-g/14-oz can tomatoes
1 bay leaf

Rinse and dry the chicken pieces. Season with salt and pepper and fry the pieces in a large saucepan in hot oil until golden on both sides. You can also rinse and fry the giblets, if using. Slowly pour the wine all over. Add the spices and the tomatoes (if fresh tomatoes are used, add 300 ml/½ pint hot water for a hen or 150 ml/¼ pint for a chicken), more seasoning and the bay leaf, then cover and simmer for 1 hour for a chicken, or approximately 2 hours for a fowl, according to its age and toughness. Stir occasionally. You should have a thick aromatic sauce by the end, quite oily. Serve the chicken pieces on top of white rice or any kind of pasta with the sauce over it, or serve with Greek *hylopittes* as described on page 181.

KOTOPOULO ME ELIES

Chicken Casserole with Olives

Rinse about 16 black or green olives and add them to the chicken and tomato casserole described above. In this case the olives should be added for the last 10 minutes of the cooking time and the rice should be cooked separately. Serve the chicken and olives on plain boiled rice, or on mashed potatoes or plain boiled pasta.

KOTOPOULO ME HYLLOPITTES
Chicken with Noodles

It is common in Greece to serve both meat and chicken, once cooked in a tomato sauce and particularly as in the way described for *Kotopoulo Kokkinisto*, with a square, small, flat pasta called *hylopittes*.

Once the chicken is cooked as described, take the pieces out, and add to the sauce 170–225 g/6–8 oz boiled, but still a bit hard, drained, small pasta. Mix well into the sauce, season with salt and lots of black pepper, place the chicken pieces on top, cover and simmer for 4–5 minutes very gently. The pasta that has absorbed the delicious juices becomes quite memorable when treated in this manner.

KYNEYI
Game

Athens, producing little, draws its supplies from far and near. The early vegetables come from Syra, the best veal from Naxos, the finest oranges from Kalamata. Cart loads of splendid cauliflowers may be seen on their way from Eleusis through the pass of Daphni; and in the season I have never passed Megara station without being asked to buy a fine hare.

(William Miller, *Greek Life in Town and Country*, 1905, p. 194.)

Hares at Marathon, and red partridges at Aegina, are common enough; woodcocks are not too scarce in the ravines that surround Cephissia ... The passage of the wild ducks gives fine opportunities to those in the neighbourhood of Lake Copais. I have seen loads of these aquatic birds brought in to the market of Athens. The quails on their passage give food in Maina during a whole month. The game eaten in Greece is excellent – hares, snipes, thrushes, have a delicious flavour.

(E.F.V. About, *Greece and the Greeks*, 1855, pp. 104–5.)

Game has always been treated in Greece with due respect and reverence, and a meal is considered very special and an honour to the guests who receive it when it contains any kind of game, even when at the very least it is a 'fine hare'.

KOTOPOULA KAI KYNIYI

Rabbits, hares, pigeons and partridges used to be quite common but it is more difficult to come across them in Athens, at least at present.

Wild boar, quails and venison were rather more unusual and included in the menu whenever possible of a specialist restaurant in Athens, called Zafiris, in Thespithos Street in the old quarter of Plaka at the foot of the Acropolis.

This old-fashioned establishment preserved its internal as well as external appearance with tin, accordion-like shutters, exactly as on the first day that it was opened, and supplied its faithful Athenian clientele not only with the best game in town but also with the best *soutzoukakia smirneika* (cummin-scented mince rissoles in tomato sauce). Of course, being seasonal like the menu it offered, it remained closed in the summer months.

Nowadays one is more likely to find an abundance of all kinds of game in the northern Greek cities such as Thessaloniki, Florrina and Verria or Kavalla where it still abounds, whereas the 'ravines that surround Cephissia' that hosted woodcocks and other winged creatures as in E. About's days in 1855 are now filled with affluent villas instead.

The Greeks, of course, are very keen huntsmen by nature. Their most favourite game being ... the female species. Apart from that, in early autumn, groups of virile men fill the plains of Copais, Yiannena, Messolonghi and any other lake districts in western, northern and central Greece.

On flights to Thessaloniki, when I was flying domestic routes with handy DC3s, there was a rather eccentric veteran pilot who, in the right season, would take a slight detour and circle a few times over the marshes just before we approached Thessaloniki in order to find out if the wild ducks and geese had descended so that he could plan his exciting game expedition the following day.

The same pilot, on flights to Lesvos, after landing, as soon as the DC3 came to a standstill, would run down the cabin in his swimming gear, and jump into the sea, to the astonishment of the passengers still dazed by the flight, and he literally had to be dragged out of the sea for the flight back.

The most common way to cook game in Greece, particularly hares and rabbits, is in a *stifatho*, the tomato sweet and sour sauce made with vinegar, rosemary, garlic and an abundance of small sweet onions (page 183). Hares and rabbits are always marinated in a solution of water and vinegar for at least three hours or even better a whole night, preferably in an earthenware bowl.

KOUNELI STIFATHO

Rabbit Casserole with Onions and Wine Vinegar

This is the best way to eat rabbit. The enormous quantities of the small pickling-sized onions add a particular sweetness that match and complement the taste of the rabbit. The same recipe can be used for hare, with excellent results, by increasing the quantities of the other ingredients, since hare is much heavier than rabbit. Rabbit or hare should be treated in exactly the same preparatory way, i.e., being soaked in vinegar. (This only applies to wild varieties.) Served with fried potatoes on the side, this is a very piquant dish, or if you prefer a milder taste to counterbalance the richness of the rabbit, serve with plain white rice. A green salad is always welcomed as it adds a refreshing note.

1 rabbit, jointed
2 bay leaves
4 tablespoons red wine
  vinegar
150 ml/¼ pint olive oil
4 cloves garlic, peeled
small piece cinnamon stick
3–4 grains whole allspice, or
  a pinch of ground allspice
1 sprig of rosemary
1 small glass of red wine

2 tablespoons tomato purée,
  or 4–5 fresh tomatoes,
  approximately 350 g/
  12 oz, chopped
¼ teaspoon sugar
300 ml/½ pint hot water
salt and freshly ground black
  pepper
675g/1½ lbs small onions,
  peeled but left whole

Rinse the rabbit pieces and put them in a salad bowl with the bay leaves. Sprinkle the vinegar over the pieces and let them marinate for at least 2 hours or preferably in the fridge overnight. Heat half of the olive oil in a saucepan, pat the rabbit pieces dry and fry them in it until they are quite brown on both sides. Take out and put on to a plate.

When all the rabbit pieces have been fried, put them back into the saucepan along with the garlic cloves, bay leaves, spices, rosemary and the wine. Then add the tomato purée or tomatoes, sugar and the hot water. Season, cover and cook for about 1 hour for rabbit or 1½ hours for hare.

In the meantime, heat the remaining olive oil in a frying pan and gently fry the onions. Stir them occasionally, in order to make sure they turn golden all over, for about 15 minutes. Add the contents of the frying pan to the saucepan, and shake it so that the onions spread evenly. Then cover and simmer for a further 15 minutes.

LAYOS E KOUNELI LEMONATO

Hare or Rabbit in Lemon Sauce

1 hare or rabbit, jointed
300 ml/½ pint water
4 tablespoons wine vinegar
salt and freshly ground black
   pepper

150 ml/¼ pint olive oil
25 g/1 oz butter
juice of 1–2 lemons
300 ml/½ pint hot water
1 teaspoon oregano

Rinse the hare or rabbit and put the pieces to marinate in the mixture of water and vinegar in an earthenware bowl for at least 3 hours. If the animal is large, it is better to marinate it overnight. If it is a farmed hare or rabbit, omit this step altogether.

Drain and dry the pieces well. Season with salt and pepper. Heat the olive oil and butter in a wide saucepan and fry the pieces in it, until they look golden all over. When all the pieces have been fried, pour the lemon juice slowly over them. Once the steam subsides, add the hot water and oregano, cover and simmer slowly for about 1 hour for a rabbit or longer for hare, until the meat is quite tender and comes away from the bone easily.

A little water can be added if needed, during the cooking, but the dish should be left with a thick and oily sauce at the end and should not be swimming in water. If the sauce needs thickening, take the meat pieces out, boil the sauce rapidly to reduce, adjust the seasoning and lemon and cover the pieces with it.

For a variation, add a dozen or so green olives, rinsed first, for the last 10 minutes of cooking time.

Serve with french fried potatoes or plain rice.

PITSOUNIA KOKKINISTA

Pigeons in Wine and Tomato Sauce

*An excellent way to cook not only pigeons but any kind of bird,
partridges, quails and even pheasants.*

4 whole pigeons, ready-dressed	salt and freshly ground black pepper
150 ml/¼ pint olive oil	2 glasses white wine
25 g/1 oz butter	1 227-g/8-oz can tomatoes
	1 teaspoon tomato purée

Singe excess hair from the birds. Rinse and dry them well. Heat the olive oil and butter in a frying pan, season the birds and fry them in it all over until they become golden. In the case of larger birds, such as pheasants, it is better to have them jointed.

Place the birds in a flameproof casserole, pour the remains of the oil in the frying pan over them, being careful to omit the sediment; place the casserole on the heat and pour the wine all over. Once the steam subsides, add the tomatoes and tomato purée, cover and cook in a pre-heated oven, gas no. 3 (325°F/175°C), for about 1½ hours, checking occasionally in case it is drying up, in which case a little water or wine can be added to keep it moist.

Alternatively, cook on top of the cooker slowly for about 45 minutes or, for pheasant, about 1¼ hours.

PITSOUNIA KAI ORTYKIA STI SHARA

Barbecued Pigeons and Quails

Often, particularly in country or provincial *tavernas*, pigeons or quails are split down the middle and barbecued. A dressing of olive oil and lemon juice is used for basting them, during the 20–30 minutes' cooking time.

PERTHIKES

Partridges

There were coloured rugs, the handiwork of Akrivakes's womenfolk, upon the floor, with reed matting beneath them, and pillows all round the walls, against which we reclined, the chairs were entirely lacking.

After our host's wife had offered us the usual brandy and coffee, a table about fifteen inches high was brought in and we sat on a couple of pillows at this very hospitable board, to eat a dinner composed of partridges, turkey, sardines, chicken, radishes, fish, Thessalian apples, cheese and red *retsinato*.

(William Miller describing dinner with an *archipoimen* (ἀργιποιμὴν) or arch-shepherd near Karditsa in Boeotia, from his book *Greek Life in Town and Country*, London, 1905, p. 216.)

Perthikes, always female in gender in Greek, have entered Greek folklore and peasant verse metaphorically as loved women. So, *perthikostithi* (partridge-breasted) and *perthikomata* (having the velvety eyes of a partridge) are attributes to the beauty of women, either in common everyday speech or in lyrics.

To my astonishment, since I had completely forgotten about the term, a Greek male friend visiting us in London recently called one of my little daughters *perthikomata*, referring to her large, dark brown, velvety eyes.

The most common way that partridges are cooked in Greece is in a casserole with white wine and lemon juice. Occasionally they are roasted in the oven briefly.

PERTHIKES LEMONATES

Partridges in Lemon Sauce

Exactly the same recipe can be adapted to woodcocks (bekatses) or indeed any other bird.

4 partridges, prepared whole	juice of 1 lemon
4–5 tablespoons olive oil	1 glass white wine
salt and freshly ground black pepper	150 ml/¼ pint hot water
2 carrots, peeled and sliced round, thinly	chopped parsley, to garnish

Singe any remaining feathers from the birds, then rinse, dry and season them. Heat the olive oil in a frying pan, and sauté the birds in it until they are light golden. Place the carrots in a saucepan large enough to hold the birds in one layer, and add the birds on top. Pour the juices of the frying pan over them, being careful not to include any burnt sediment, place the pan on the heat and slowly pour in the lemon juice and wine. Add the hot water, cover and cook for 30–40 minutes. Turn them over occasionally and baste them with the sauce.

Sprinkle with the parsley and serve.

PERTHIKES PSITES

Roast Partridges

Partridges cooked in this manner should be fresh and not 'high' otherwise their smell is too overpowering. Prepare the birds as above, pour over them the juice of a lemon and let them marinate for 1–2 hours. Place them in a small roasting dish and season inside and out. Pour any leftover lemon from their marinade over them, together with a mixture of olive oil and butter, and cook for 40 minutes, gas no. 4 (350°F/180°C), basting and turning occasionally.

PSARIA
Fish

Greece is surrounded by the sea and has some two thousand islands (or is it three thousand?). Some of these islands are so tiny and so flat that you can see the sea enclosing you on all sides. Shinouses is one of these tiny gems in the middle of the Aegean.

As a result, the sea is part of a Greek's life, and a major source of his diet. We learn to live in perfect harmony with it and at an early age learn to draw from it all the enjoyment one can.

At the same time as we were learning to swim, we were also encouraged to treat the sea as a large orchard whose fruits were there to be gathered and enjoyed. We learnt to catch little crabs and eat them raw, as we did tiny shrimps that had been caught in still pools of water among the rocks after the morning tide, the cockles, the clovisses (*ahivathes*) and, of course, our favourite, limpets (*petalithes*) which we sucked and ate with great delight on the spot.

Later on we also discovered *ahinous* (sea urchins). We learnt to collect them the hard way, as was inevitable. Their dark purple-black short needles would often get embedded in our fingers or feet, which instantly put an end to the enjoyment and made us seek the vinegar-rubbing remedy implemented by our grandmothers.

The fruits of the sea, not necessarily fish only, were abundant and cheap when we were children and everything was cooked and eaten one way or another – things that have now been totally eclipsed, at least from Greek metropolitan cuisine. I remember clearly my mother coming back from the fish market in Piraeus, with those strange elongated shells – *solines* (razor-shells). My grandmother used to make a pilau with them. Unfortunately no one bothers with them now in Greece and most people cannot even remember their delicious (slightly gritty at times) pilau. A pilau was also made with all sizes of cockles, once they had been parboiled and taken out of their shells.

Squid, small octopus and cuttlefish were fried almost daily as an accompaniment to more frugal vegetable dishes or pulses. On Wednesdays and Fridays, they tended to be cooked in their own merits and made into delicious casseroles with wine, onions, tomatoes or spinach – not, of course, all at once. More commonly they were made into pilaus, in combination with mussels or on their own with an abundance of fragrant, rough, olive oil. We learnt at school, later, that these were the prescribed days for fish eating or anyway, sea products, by religion. At any rate, it was a handy measure at the time, as meat was beyond most people's reach.

Fish was, and still is, interchangeable with shellfish and cephalopods. Greeks have a passion for small fish like *marithes* (brown picarel), *sarthelles* (silvery sardines), and the slim *gavros* (small anchovies). One of these, crisply fried, still makes a main meal for a family, along with a huge bowl of boiled *horta* (hand-picked mountain greens). All these small varieties of fish, still ludicrously cheap, attract a female audience every morning in every neighbourhood with the first cry of the motorized wandering fishmonger.

Fried *barbounia* (red mullet), quite small ones, since the smaller they are the cheaper they are, are the next favourite. Strange fish like small, slim *zarganes* (garfish) and fresh *palamitha* (bonito) were fried regularly but are more rare now.

Fish soups were quite often made at home and were regarded as highly nutritious and light, particularly for children. These were also cooked on national religious occasions such as the twenty-fifth of March – the Annunciation of the Virgin Mary (*Evaggelismou*) – Palm Sunday (*Vaion*), and others, that are traditionally fish-eating days.

Salted cod is eaten quite regularly in the winter and during Lent. The best selection of fish though can be found when one has straight access to a fishing boat on return from its voyage early in the morning. Setting eyes on the fresh, colourful catch, intermingled in the wet nets, can be a pure stimulant.

On such an occasion in Kriti, in the small fishing community of Georgioupolis, between Chania and Rethymno, I recently found some such unusual species, like the dark green, strangely shaped *hristopsara* (John Dory), grey, elongated, slim *litses* (the French *liche*) that looks very similar to a small version of salmon, and *mylokopous* (the French *ombrines*). All these were amongst the more familiar flat, silvery *melanouria* (saddled breams), *skatharia* (black breams) and the regal, orange-red tones of some splendid, fleshy specimens of *skorpines* (scorpion or the French *rascasse rouge*). The choice in such instances is titillating and difficult. On this particular occasion it was solved by choosing the familiar *melanouria*, to be charcoaled in the garden of our friend's house in the tiny, hilly village of Episkopi, and on the spot we had a sumptuous soup made with the mouthwatering *skorpines*, on which we later banqueted in a solitary restaurant at the rocky end of the bay, on a table almost resting in the cold waters.

Fish in Greece is divided into categories for costing purposes, particularly at restaurants. First category fish, *protis katigorias*, include the firm-fleshed, less bony and rarer varieties: *barbounia* (red mullet), *synagritha* (dentex), *tsipoures* (daurade), *lithrinia* (pandoras) as well as *astakoi* (lobsters). This category is so highly priced, particularly at restaurants where it costs about four times the price of spring lamb (which is terribly expensive anyway) per 1 kg/2 lbs, that one has to be quite certain of the excellence of the wares one is paying for.

Thefteri katigoria (second category) includes all the different flattish but sumptuous breams: *melanouria, skatharia, sargous* etc., the splendid *skorpines* (scorpion), all soup-making fish, *litses* (*liche*) etc.

Triti katigoria (third category) includes all the smaller varieties, such as *gavros* (slim anchovies), wonderful *maritha* (picarel), *yopes* (bogue), *sarthelles* (sardines), and *kolious* or *skoumbria* (common mackerel). We have a folkloric saying which goes: '*Kathe pragma ston kero tou kio kolios ton Avgousto*' – 'Everything at its right time and mackerel in August' – and when mackerel are eaten in August, young and fresh, straight out of the sea, and cooked on a charcoal fire, they taste surprisingly different from the heavy, oily, large specimens we are used to in the United Kingdom. We always make a point to have at least one mackerel fishing expedition in August on the island. We go with one of the local fishermen in the late afternoon. When we are lucky enough to hit a shoal, one can almost take them out by the bucketful. It is a very exhilarating experience and makes us all feel more earthy (particularly my husband). Then the little boat speeds towards the small fishing port of Sterni Vala where the freshly caught mackerel are cleaned and cooked in the boatman's family's restaurant.

In Greece it is not unusual to take the fish you have caught to some restaurant and ask them to cook it, for a nominal fee and the usual trimmings to accompany the full meal, particularly if you patronize a restaurant regularly. In any case, when eating fish it is customary to choose your uncooked fish from among the selection that the restaurant presents you with, then it is weighed and you are told the cost before it disappears into the hot steamy kitchen.

When Greeks want to give themselves a treat, on sunny days throughout the year, they go out to one of the coastal restaurants. They choose a table as near the water as possible (if they manage to have their bare feet splashing in the water at the same time, it becomes, almost, a Utopian dream come true), and they choose a wonderful fresh fish, such as *synagritha*, *lithrini*, or slices of *xifios* (swordfish) or more commonly a large *melanoúri* (saddled bream) to have cooked on charcoal.

I have to admit that I am no exception to this rule and as soon as the sunshine warms up our dampened London bodies, I feel deprived of my Greek-style outing to the sea, with the titillating charcoal smells of grilled fish as a background theme.

From the familiar Tourkolimano in Kastella, in Piraeus, to Faliro, Glyfatha, Vouliagmeni, or a small bay in Varkiza and Lagonnisi, no place is considered too far in search of the ideal spot with the ideal restaurant. The whole beautiful coastal road to Cape Sounio is a searching ground. Porto-Rafti, which until recently was a small fishing village, on the opposite coast, through Mesogia, as the inland Athenian suburbs are referred to, used to be a favourite spot but it has become too smart and exhibits its own *polykatikies* (blocks of flats) now.

The most exciting feature of these outings, that I remember from my childhood years, was that as soon as we chose a table and were all seated with my parents, an elderly, thin, stooping figure would appear almost out of nowhere (as far as I was concerned he had almost emerged out of the sea like Aphrodite). He carried a large deep basket on his arm, full of shellfish; the most favoured of all were *kithonia* (praires), but there were also *ahinoi* (sea urchins) and sometimes *kalognomes* (*arch de Noè*).

It was a pure delight to watch him dexterously forcing them open and pushing all their contents on to one side of their shell and offering them to us. We knew that then they had to be tested. We loved to squeeze a little lemon juice on each one and watch for their disgruntled, quiescent movement, which was the sign that we could now safely eat them, as they were still alive.

Years later, in the early 1960s, I encountered a similar figure who seemed to walk out of the past, in the middle of Athens. This time, the wandering, stooping, identical character was frequenting the deliciously old-fashioned establishment of Apotsos, with its quaint, turn-of-the-century advertisements on the walls and its huge barrels of wine on display, at the top of Stadiou Street. Or he might appear among the tables of Orfanidis, rather more grand with its massive dark wood-panelled walls and bars, at the more prominent and eminent corner of Panepistimiou and Voukourestiou Streets, where it used to spread its tables along the pavement. With his almost mythical basket on his arm, the mysterious wandering salesman still tempted us with his wares; along with a glass of wine or an *ouzo* and a small plate of *meze* in either of these places, one could get a plate of beautiful praires or mouthwatering sea urchins, whose bright orange eggs dexterously exposed by the slender, silent figure delighted us with the aroma of the sea, right in the heart of Athens.

My passion for the various fruits of the sea reached the height of its paroxysm (but did not get satiated) when one of my friends became engaged to a young man who owned a small caïque with his father and brother, all of whom were professional shell-fishermen. Every morning, before dawn, they would start from Elefsina. When they arrived at the prescribed spot, not too far away but somewhere within the straits of Salamina, they would get into their *skafanthra* (old-fashioned diving suits with polished brass helmets which made them resemble the much-later astronauts).

With their life lines, a kind of thick tubing, attached to the breathing apparatus permanently fixed in the boat, they would drop into the sea. There, on the sandy promenade of the bottom of the sea, they would start harvesting their fruit as quickly as possible. The sand was shifted into a fine netted basket that kept the precious shells locked in it; when it was full it was quickly pulled up to the surface. This harvesting would last two or three hours every day, so that their wares could be back for the central markets by 9–10 a.m.

Theirs was a very unusual occupation, even by Greek standards of the latter part of the 1950s. But as shellfish were fetching very high prices at the time, they made a very good living, which they badly needed as there were four daughters in the family to be provided for. Their work was not only unusual, but highly dangerous and unhealthy. It left its mark almost day-by-day on their faces. The father's handsome face, dark and roughened by the salty air, was prematurely wrinkled. The two young sons were clearly going the same way. All three of them were extremely thin, dark, svelte and altogether vibrant with energy. It was no effort for them during our occasional Sunday outings, with all the young members of the family and their friends, to jump into their diving suits and into the bright blue sea, in order to include in our intended picnic in some pine-shaded tranquil deserted bay of Salamis the much-loved *kithonia* (praires) and the more rare *strithia* (oysters). All these exhilarating happy outings (I was seventeen at the time) have been compressed into one very memorable 1st of May outing, on a hot, brilliant, sunlit day and the still waters of the straits of Salamis spreading like a vast silvery mirror.

Apart from the outings that left their almost mythical impression on us, we also had some really memorable feasts at home, when our friend brought the best of the catch: the largest, but also the most unusual. Our whole meal then consisted of his various shellfish and all sorts of other sea creatures that he brought and prepared for us. I remember my father getting terribly excited on such occasions. Some of these fish had to be cooked or parboiled, like the huge brown-purple *pinnes* (fan mussels). These were so gigantic and grotesque-looking, and on top of that they had the strongest iodine smell I have ever encountered, that I was not absolutely sure about them.

Large *porphyres* (*Murex brandaris*), that exuded a dark scarlet, evil-looking liquid when they were boiled, were almost always included at these sessions, as well as strangely shaped horn-shells and exotic, fleshy, deep-water anemones that were cooked on charcoal and were tender, juicy and extremely tasty. But mussels were not part of their métier as they were regarded as too common and almost pedestrian.

PSARI SOUPA SKORPINA

Scorpion Fish Soup

Fish soup is a native and very common dish in Greece. Some are more delicious than others according to the kind of fish used, the amount of fish in proportion to the soup required (it is very indifferent when it is watered down) and, most important of all, the freshness of the fish in question.

Traditionally, it is the dish served to mourning relatives and friends after a funeral. This particular dish should be made with *bakaliarakia*, wrongly translated sometimes as cod when, in fact, they are small hake. Hake makes a bland and indifferent soup so it perfectly matches the spirit of the mourners and does not excite the palate.

Almost any fish is made into a soup in Greece and quite often a collection of various small fish are used. This used to be the case when we went to stay with my grandmother's sister, in Voula, in the summer.

Voula is a few miles from Athens airport, which at the time hardly accommodated any air traffic apart from Dacotas (DC3) and perhaps DC4s and had not had the devastating effect on the area as it later did. Voula was on the way to Sounion, but as there was no coastal road opened yet, it was a sleepy rustic village full of pine trees with a virginal clean coast. Early in the morning the few local small fishing boats would be expected with enthusiasm by the housewives perched on the rocks. It is one of my fondest and most exciting childhood memories, waiting there with the women for the surprises these boats would bring. It was also one of the most rewarding spectacles to see the silvery, pink and grey colours glistening in the bottom of the boat, some of the fish being still alive. I vividly recollect the enthusiasm and excitement of the poor fishermen if there was a particularly large fish among the catch of the day.

It was here in Voula that I experienced fish soup in all its aspects and with all kinds of fish. It was also here I had my first eel soup, made from small, svelte eels (about one foot long), which has remained in my mind ever since the day, after my first apprehensions about it. Watching them being skinned, back home, aged twelve at the time, I could not stop thinking that this was going to be 'snake soup'! It was the most delicious fish soup I ever had until 1967.

I have also had a proper *kakavia* on fishing boats, made from the tiny fish in the catch which were not worth selling. They are boiled for a long time, pounded and then drained. But the most magnificent soup of all was that made from *skorpines* on the island of Alonnisos in 1967. It was made with the scorpion fish which is an impressive creature that cannot be bypassed easily. Its glistening, bright orange colour attracts the eye immediately, even in the middle of a large catch. So does its charmingly rounded, fleshy body, until one comes to its gigantic, triangular head which looks absolutely ferocious and bad-tempered, particularly around the large droopy mouth.

It used to be common in Greece during fights between women, for them to call each other a *scrofa*, among other names. Still people talk about such and such a woman as a real *scrofa*, meaning predominantly bad-tempered, aggressive and untrustworthy. I wonder if the epithet owes its origin to the *Scorpaena scrofa* or if it is the other way round? The fish is covered with dangerous thorny fins as the unguarded will easily find out. This is the reason that it is often avoided by housewives since, unlike the western habit, Greek women clean their own fish at home. In any case when in Greece, never miss an opportunity to have a soup made with scorpion fish (*rascasse* in French), as it is a memorable experience. It is better to order your own soup, once you have selected your fish in the restaurant, rather than order portions of an already made soup, which is inevitably watered down.

On Alonnisos, the Karamalis restaurant, on the seafront near the harbour, make it particularly well. Normally you need about 800 g/1¾ lbs of fish for two or three, otherwise, you are told by their cook, the soup will not be flavoursome enough.

We choose our fish in the early evening, usually 2–3 *skorpines*, and then we stroll a little further down the harbour for our *ouzo* and succulent charcoaled octopus, spending the half an hour needed for preparing our soup in the best possible way.

Skorpines come in all sizes. Sometimes they are very small and then very bony and a bit of a waste, I feel; sometimes they are quite large and weigh up to 1 kg/2 lbs, in which case I find them too rich and oily, so it is best to go for the medium-sized ones, about 225–350 g/8–12 oz each. They are classed as second category fish, as explained in the introduction of this chapter, so they are reasonably priced. Once they are chosen and weighed you will be told how much they cost and from there on it is the cook's responsibility. They are then cleaned and rinsed but left whole, as the head contains a lot of delicate bits such as the cheeks and the tongue.

Since I could not find *skorpines* I tried to reconstruct the recipe using red gurnards – *kaponi* in Greek – which vaguely resemble *skorpines*, but the result was not comparable. Gurnards make a good soup but the fish lacks the lusciousness of the *skorpines*, and this kind of thin soup is best with an *avgolemono* (egg-and-lemon) sauce added at the end. Using a mixture of fish such as red breams, gurnards, a piece or two of conger eel (*mougri*), dogfish (*skylaki*), a John Dory (*Hristopsaro*), sea bass (*lavraki*), grey mullet (*kefalos*), or some monk fish (not of course all at once) produces a more interesting result.

For the best results, prepare a good fish stock in advance from the bones and heads. This is then boiled with the olive oil as described by Alan Davidson on 'Bouillabaisse, The Harlot of Marseilles', from his book A Kipper with My Tea *(Macmillan, 1988). Then use something delicious such as a whole sea bass and a couple of red gurnards which you cook in the stock. Or use a whole grey mullet and a red bream, or a John Dory and some gurnards. And always be thrifty with the water.*

1.5 kg/3 lbs whole fish as above and pieces of conger eel, or monk fish	5–6 small potatoes, peeled whole
4 tablespoons olive oil	4 small onions, peeled whole
1.75 litres/3 pints fish stock, or water	2–3 medium carrots, scraped whole
salt	1–2 sticks celery and leaves, trimmed, rinsed and sliced into 8-cm/3-in pieces
3–4 whole black peppercorns	
pinch of thyme	

Clean, rinse and season the fish. Place the olive oil and stock or water in a wide saucepan and boil rapidly for 6–8 minutes in order to emulsify the liquid. Add everything else apart from the fish, cover and boil for 5–7 minutes. Add the fish and if it is not covered by the liquid add a little more water. Cover and boil steadily for 15 minutes by which time everything should be cooked. Carefully take out the vegetables and fish and arrange on a platter.

Serve the soup immediately and let people help themselves to the fish and vegetables at the table. Some people prefer to have these served in their soup and others afterwards.

In Greece, often, a small bowl with a mixture of olive oil and fresh lemon juice is served at the same time for dressing the boiled fish and vegetables according to individual taste if these are eaten after the soup. This dressing is made by beating lightly three parts of olive oil with one of lemon juice, seasoning and a pinch of oregano or thyme.

SERVING ALTERNATIVES

Once fish and vegetables are removed you could add 2–3 tablespoons of rice to the soup and cook for a further 5–7 minutes. Or you could add an *avgolemono* (egg-and-lemon) sauce (page 56), or both rice and *avgolemono*.

KAKAVIA

The Fishermen's Soup

Kakavia is a fish soup named after the pot in which it used to be made. The ancient Greeks called the rounded, mostly earthenware, cauldron-like pot that went on a tripod or was hung over the fire, *kakavi*. There are mentions of this in Aristophanes. These pots are still called *kakavia* in some villages in Peloponnisos. The soup made in this pot is a traditional soup developed by Greek fishermen and bears a unique quality of simplicity and frugality.

Fishermen used the tiny fish in their catch that were not worth anything to make a thick soup. These were cleaned and then boiled with a little sea water, as well as ordinary water, onions, tomatoes and olive oil until the fish fell apart. The soup was strained and the pulp pressed through a sieve. Stale bread, carried by the fishermen on their boats, was then added in the soup to soak the bread and make it edible.

This thick and rough soup was, and still is, made on fishing boats early in the morning, before the sun rises, after a night's fishing. Twice I had this exact ritual on a fishing caïque after a night's fishing in Paros, in the Kyklathes, with local fishermen; and when we went fishing with fishermen from Alonnisos, we went back to their house where this dish was prepared quickly and consumed with quantities of white *aretsinoto* wine. The fish used for an authentic *kakavia* can be anything from *atherinous* (sand smelts), *marithes* (picarel), *salpes* (*Sarpa salpa*) and *sparous* (two-banded breams) to *chanous* (comber), *perkes* (another kind of comber) and small *skorpines* (scorpion fish). This original *kakavia* bears a lot of similarities to the French *bouillabaisse*.

One of the first Greek cookery writers and cook to the then Royal Palace, Nikos Tselementes, in *Valuable Guide to Cooking and Desserts* (Athens, 1925), claims with vigour that it is the same dish of *kakavia* which was introduced in Marseilles by its first inhabitants, the ancient Phocaeans from Asia Minor, an important maritime state between 1000–600BC. He claims that *bouillabaisse* also derives its name from the pot it is made in – the *bouillot* – which is very similar to the ancient Greek *kakavi*. Alan Davidson throws light on the origin of the name in his collection of essays, *A Kipper with My Tea* (Macmillan, 1988). Having chosen four variables, he then opts for the definition in Littré, *Dictionnaire de la Langue Française* (1883): 'The expression of *bouillon abaissé*, literally "froth lowered", i.e. reduced by evaporation.' Jane Grigson in her *Fish Cookery* notes that a lot of writers attempted to find the origin of the dish but that it could only be traced back to the Roman gourmand and writer, Apicius. However, a number of Apicius' dishes originated with the Greek cooks imported to Rome from Athens at the same time as the Greek law experts who went there to compile a code of Roman justice.

Is it possible that *bouillabaisse* originated through Apicius from the ancient Greek *kakavia*? I have no conclusive evidence on the subject ... But I remember how impressed I was the first time I had *bouillabaisse* in 1969, even though it was in Greece, in a unique restaurant built on the sea in the enchanting small port of Passalimani in Piraeus, on the Freattitha side. The restaurant was called Thiasimos, meaning famous or renowned, and was indeed famous for its sea-food and particularly the *bouillabaisse*. It was also much more expensive than any of the other *tavernas* that used to spread their little tables all round the inside of the port on a tiny strip of pebbles, and which served much humbler dishes such as small fried picarel, anchovies and tiny squid.

The affluent addition of lobster in their *bouillabaisse* made me think, at the time, that this had no comparison to the frugal *kakavia* we had at home. But later on I found out that the more gentrified form of *kakavia* that was served at affluent tables in Greece contained large fish such as *synagritha* (sea bream), *lavraki* (sea bass), *rofo* (grouper) or *sfyritha* (*Epinephelus aeneas*).

Once the initial preparation, cooking and straining of the various small fish and vegetables is finished, the large fish is placed and cooked in the rich broth for 10–15 minutes, then it is either taken out and served separately from the soup or large pieces of it are added to the soup, some parsley sprinkled all over and served. Nowadays, almost any fish soup may be referred to as *kakavia* in Greece, which is confusing.

PSARIA SHARAS

Barbecued or Grilled Fish

This is the most common way that fish is cooked in Greece, either at home or next to the murmuring sea, on the promenade as in Kastella, or on a pebbly beach that makes your table unstable and sloping like Faliro or Voula or, in the best of all circumstances, in a small island harbour, sweating under dark blue canvas tents beneath the explosive midday sun.

If you are lucky enough to get whiffs of the barbecued fish intermingled with soft waves of aroma from the bright green, bristly pine trees, the setting becomes perfect.

I regard it as one of the best pleasures in life to have a large, glistening fish, straight out of the depths of the sea and on to the charcoal in a perfect island setting. My favourite fish for this purpose is the 'second category' fish, *melanoúri* (saddled bream), a flat, fleshy, dark silvery fish with a black line down the length of its body, and *skatharia* (black bream), very similar but even flatter than the *melanoúri*, with a hint of golden rays on it. *Tsipoura* (daurade), a pale pink, flat fish, is also very succulent and held in higher esteem than both the above by most people, and it is appropriately classed as 'first category' fish, thus being more expensive.

We never miss an opportunity, though, to have *xifio* or *xifia* (swordfish), from the *Xiphiidae* family, which takes its name from the Greek word *xiphos*, a sword, due to the sharp and long sword-like nose that makes it unmistakably easy to identify even for the uninitiated. *Xifias* is a prime catch in a fishermen's net and when a large one is caught on the island, excitement is prevalent and everybody knows and descends to the small harbour to take a look. We descend in the evening to the Karamalis restaurant to sample it. It is served either as *xifias souvlaki* – chunks of the fish marinated in olive oil and lemon, skewered, sprinkled with thyme and barbecued – or as *feta xifias* – steaks cooked in the same manner.

However, fish tastes even more delectable when one is installed on a tiny isolated pebbly beach, shaded by the olive groves, on the north coast of Alonnisos for the day. They are not only caught by the men in the group who disappear for the whole morning in their pursuit, but also cleaned by them and cooked on a small, primitive fire with small dried branches of the olive trees (but not pine wood as it spits and jumps in all directions like a daemon) and thyme plants that abound everywhere, which make the fish very aromatic.

Any fish, even small and insignificant ones, caught and cooked in this manner and eaten next to the crystal-clear mirrored surface of the Aegean, with a repose under an olive tree to follow, will simply captivate one's senses and memories. Fig trees are always avoided since, according to Greek folklore, they have a bad influence on one's dreams due to the bewitchingly amorous scent exuded by their craggy leaves, causing nightmares and sometimes spells of madness. An indispensable prerequisite to barbecued fish, apart from its freshness that is, is thyme, or oregano, firstly (or a bit of both), lemons secondly and olive oil thirdly.

Once the fish has been cleaned and scaled, rinsed and drained, it is sprinkled with a mixture of two parts olive oil to one part lemon, and then seasoned inside and out with salt, pepper and thyme. The grill is also well oiled so that the fish will not stick on it. It is then put onto a quietly glowing fire so that it does not get scorched and it should not be overcooked. During the cooking it is always brushed several times with a sprig of thyme immersed in the olive oil and lemon mixture, which makes it juicy and succulent. It is served with quartered lemons around it and a separate bowl of olive oil and lemon dressing for individual preferences. Sometimes finely chopped parsley or dill is added to the dressing.

Quite often, particularly in the Aegean islands, fish is wrapped in fresh vine leaves before it is put on the charcoal. This is done particularly in the spring and early summer when vine leaves are soft, tender and particularly aromatic. It is more often done to the smaller and more oily fish such as *yopes* (bogue), *sarthelles* (sardines), and *kolious* (chub mackerel), but also to the smaller *sargous* (*Diplodus sargus*), *melanoúria* and *skatharia*. The vine leaves are not poached – this is the reason that they are selected young and tender – but they are well oiled before the fish is wrapped individually in one or two leaves and then trapped, opening down, in the double grill used in Greece. The fish is primarily prepared as for grilled fish – oiled and seasoned. Fish cooked and eaten with vine leaves, particularly oily fish, gains from the pungency of the vine leaves and from their aroma.

If you do not have access to young vine leaves, poach the leaves briefly in boiling water for 2–3 minutes before you use them. If you do not have access to any fresh vine leaves, you can replace with preserved ones – though this would never happen in Greece – but make sure they are rinsed absolutely clear of any trace of salt otherwise the essence of the dish is lost. (See pages 74–6 for fuller instructions on vine leaves.)

Fish, either wrapped in vine leaves or plain, can be grilled in a conventional cooker with good results, once it has been prepared as above. It should then be put under a low fire. Always oil the grilling pan that the fish is going to rest on. Keep a constant watch on the fish, basting it occasionally with olive oil and lemon, and turn it over after a few minutes. Cooking time depends on the thickness, the oiliness and the weight of the fish. Mackerel, for instance, will need longer than any fish from the *Sparidae* family (sea breams) or the sea bass.

Do not omit the herbs – thyme and oregano – for a particular Mediterranean flavour. Increase the proportion of lemon to the olive oil for oily fish such as mackerel. You will be surprised how infinitely better even mackerel tastes when cooked in this manner. You will also be surprised at the plethora of sunshine memories and clear blue skies that the cooking aroma will invoke.

PSARIA TIYANITA (MARITHES, GAVROS, SARTHELLES)

Fried Fish (Picarels, Anchovies, Sardines)

Apart from vegetables, fried fish account for the most common feature of a Greek meal at home. Sometimes the fish is served along with the thick peasant soups made from pulses; other times it is the main course augmented by a seasonal salad, raw or cooked.

Most commonly the fried fish eaten in Greek homes is one of the smaller, sometimes tiny varieties that abound in Greek waters and that are ludicrously low-priced even today, but most importantly are regarded as more appetizing, when crisply fried, and quite rightly so.

The most favourite of these is the sombre, brown-greyish *maritha* (picarel), followed by silvery *sarthelles* (sardines), and small slim *gavros* (anchovies). *Maritha* hardly needs any preparation except for rinsing, as it is commonly eaten whole, heads, tails, bones *et al.*

Sardines are gutted, but heads and tails are left on. The only fish which is always beheaded is *gavros* since when the heads are left on they tend to give the fish a faintly bitter taste. The head is removed by holding each fish down with one hand and pulling the head off with the other; automatically, it is gutted at the same time.

Yopes (bogue) are also quite common but they are not a favourite as they lack taste compared to the other varieties. *Kolioi* (smaller mackerel) are preferred grilled since they are regarded as oily and therefore are less often fried.

There is a plethora of other small fish that are also fried: colourful but bony *perkes* (*Serranus scriba*), *sparoi* (two-banded bream or the French *sar dore*) and *salpes* (salema or *Sarpa salpa*) with pretty golden horizontal stripes along its body like sunrays. *Salpes* in particular are very common in the spring and early summer on Alonnisos.

But the king of the fried fish is the *barbouni* – red mullet – which comes in various sizes in Greece but is always delicious. Red mullet is seldom grilled but traditionally fried and served with quartered lemons, or less often wrapped in greaseproof paper and baked *en papillote*. The smaller ones, about 5–8 cm/2–3 ins, are quite cheap.

Apart from *gavros*, heads are never removed from fish. The smaller fish, in any case, are eaten whole with heads, bones and tails. In larger fish, and particularly *barboúnia* (red mullet), the heads are prized since they are juicy and sweet. Consequently, they are sucked and chewed in a manner that to the westerner will seem horrific, but to a Greek seems perfectly sensible and normal.

Heads, according to popular belief in Greece, are supposed to be richer in vitamins since they contain larger amounts of iodine and phosphorus than the rest of the body. The first of these, we were told as children, is good for your bones, the second is good for your eyes. So we learnt to love them at a very early age.

Almost all fish are shallow-fried out of habit, always in oil, preferably olive oil; deep-frying is not common. Small fish, such as whitebait and sprats, in England are very successfully deep-fried in hot oil briefly, for 2–3 minutes, until golden and crisp and they are excellent appetizers.

All fish in Greece follow the same preparatory phase. Once it is gutted and descaled, according to its needs (some fish, like picarel, do not need either), it is then rinsed in cold water several times, drained in a colander, a little lemon juice sprinkled over it, seasoned well with salt and pepper and left to stand and drain for at least 30 minutes, or preferably longer. Fish which is to be fried is always tossed in flour – a sheet of paper with 3–4 tablespoons flour for about 1 kg/2 lbs fish is used for this purpose – as flour protects the skin from bursting open and makes it crisper, but also it stops the fish from splashing oil everywhere and also dampens the frying smell from lingering in the house for hours.

Sometimes when the fish is tiny, they are grouped together three or four at a time, by their overlapping tails, and dipped into a thick batter made from water and flour (three tablespoons water to one of flour) in order to be held together before they are dropped into the hot oil. Larger fish should be shallow-fried anyway, as they need a slower and more attentive cooking.

Large, pale golden, juicy Greek lemons are the eternal accompaniment to fish, in any form, and fish cannot be conceived of without them. Most importantly though, apart from the freshness of the fish, is that fried fish, either small or large, is always cooked just before it is to be served and it is eaten crisp and very hot, as in Greek homes, but also in most cases in restaurants and *tavernas*, too. It is always wise though, if you are ordering fish, particularly the small common varieties, in a restaurant, to make sure that it is going to be cooked there and then.

Finally, it is worth seeking and sampling fresh and freshly cooked *maritha*, *gavros* or *sarthelles* as they constitute one of the simplest gastronomic delights in life.

You are bound to find them either in Tourkolimano, or Mikrolimano as it is called nowadays, in Kastella, when you are in Athens, or in one of the small restaurants along the coastal road from Faliro to Sounio. The large and obviously expensive fish, such as *barboúnia*, *melanoúria*, tsipoures, synagrithes, *xifio*, etc., you will be offered anyway as their potential profit margin makes them worth keeping by any restaurateur, so there is no need to seek them out.

PSARI A LA SPETSIOTA

Baked Fish from the Island of Spetsai

Almost any large, thick fish can be cooked this way, resulting in a very Mediterranean taste. The fish can be cooked either whole or in thick slices. Olive oil is an indispensable factor for the true taste. In Greece and more specifically on the island of Spetsai, not far from Piraeus (Aegina, Poros, Hydra, Spetsai), they would use a large tsipoura (a gilt-head bream of the Sparidae family), or a synagritha (dentex) of the same family. The fish is cleaned but left whole with head and tail on.

1 whole fish, about 1–1.5 kg/2–3 lbs, such as sea bass, bream, a grey mullet or steaks of halibut or cod, cut crossways

150 ml/¼ pint olive oil

salt and freshly ground black pepper

2 tablespoons chopped fresh basil (optional)

2 cloves garlic, peeled and finely sliced

½ glass dry white wine

3 tablespoons chopped parsley

1 396-g/14-oz can tomatoes, or 350 g/12 oz fresh tomatoes

55 g/2 oz fresh breadcrumbs

Clean, rinse and drain the fish. Oil a roasting dish well with a little of the olive oil. Place the fish in it and season it all around and inside. Place the basil inside the fish, so that its aroma penetrates it during the cooking.

Prepare the sauce in a separate bowl by mixing the remaining olive oil, the garlic, wine, parsley, tomatoes, salt and pepper. If you are using fresh tomatoes, which makes quite a difference to the dish, they should be peeled first, and chopped quite finely. If you are using canned tomatoes, drain most of the juice away and chop the tomatoes finely.

Make fresh breadcrumbs as they do in Greece. Lightly toast a few slices of stale bread on both sides and break them up. (Alternatively, one can use the light, ready-toasted bread which comes in packets; but never use the synthetic coloured, plastic breadcrumbs. It is better to buy breadcrumbs from any Italian delicatessen, where they normally make their own.) Put a few slices in a grinder or liquidizer and grind them roughly, very quickly. In Greece they would put them in a mortar and pestle and pound them roughly to the desired consistency.

Spoon the sauce over the fish in the roasting dish. Sprinkle half of the breadcrumbs over the fish and cook it in a pre-heated oven, gas no. 5

(375°F/190°C), for 20–25 minutes. Turn the fish over carefully, baste it all over with some of its sauce, sprinkle with the rest of the breadcrumbs and cook for a further 20 minutes according to the size of the fish. If it is sliced, it will need slightly less cooking.

ZARGANES TIYANITES

Fried Garfish

Added to all the above, there are some fish we used to have routinely when we were young and of which I have kept very fond memories. These are unfortunately almost extinct now or, at any rate, difficult to find in Greece.

The first one, an almost exotic specimen, unique in its colour, was the rounded, slim, long-beaked *zarganes* (garfish) with bright green phosphorous lines along its body. I was always fascinated when opening it up, once it was cooked, in order to extract its central and only bone, to find bone and flesh coloured, as I thought at the time, with all the hues of peacock blue to emerald green, like the depths of the sea.

We were always told that the *zarganes* were very rich in phosphorus, which explained their colour, and particularly wholesome as they would strengthen our eyes. We did not need much persuasion anyway, as they were delicious. The garfish in Greece were always small compared to the garfish I have seen in England. In Greece they used to be about 8–10 cm/3–4 ins while the ones I have had in England were about 70 cm/2 ft and quite thick.

At home, once they were initially prepared and rinsed, they were rolled in flour, quickly fried in the hot oil, and served with lemon quarters to be squeezed all over them. I ask the fishmonger to prepare the large ones that I find in England occasionally, and to cut them into thin round slices which I then flour and deep-fry for 3–4 minutes. I serve them with lots of lemon all round.

PALAMITHA TIYANITI

Fried Bonito

My father was obsessed with *palamitha* and as a result he introduced us to the dish when we were very young and taught us to love it as well. This dark fleshy fish belongs to the tuna family and tastes like it.

There were periods, or seasons to be exact (it must have been late autumn or winter as I remember him always in his dark blue naval uniform, rather than the white uniform of summer), when my father went by the local fishmonger's daily on his way home and picked up a small, shiny, smooth and absolutely fresh specimen, which was then cleaned and sliced by the fishmonger into medium steaks and handed over, wrapped in a large newspaper funnel. The fleshy steaks were then rinsed, drained, floured and fried, like all the other fish, by my grandmother.

The almost boneless, sweet-tasting flesh of the bonito had a special appeal for us, the children, as did the tender squid, and these were our two favourites, and also the ones we used to have more often than any other sea creature. Fresh, small bonitos are still available in Greece, but not so common and cheap as I remember them.

PSARIA PLAKI KAI GAVROS PLAKI

Baked Fish with Garlic and Tomatoes

A *plaki* predominantly implies garlic and quite a lot of it, not 1–2 cloves as in other more refined dishes. Sometimes a whole head of garlic is used for a family meal.

We have fish *plaki* or potatoes *plaki* and sometimes the two combined together in the same round container and sent to the local baker's, or mixed vegetable *plaki*. A *plaki* can also be cooked in a casserole with very good results for the potato dish but it bears no comparison with a baked fish *plaki*. Fish *plaki* can be made with a whole fish, fish steaks or, and this is the most delicious for me, with small *gavros*, the silvery flat, slim anchovies about 5–8 cm/2–3 ins long.

When it returns from the local baker's at lunchtime, in the summer, with its crusty brown top dotted by the scorched pieces of tomatoes, it fills the whole house with its sharp garlic aroma. Of course, any fish *plaki* will effuse the garlic aroma but none will match the sharp, peppery, titillating taste of *gavros*.

Matched by a ludicrously cheap price, this is altogether a dish of the people! '*Gavros, freskos gavros*', is still a cry that gets us all out in the street on hot summer mornings, to meet the now motorized, Yamaha-tricycled fishmonger, in the Athenian suburbs.

One inspection and approval will give the signal to the whole neighbourhood who will all be having one or another form of *gavros* for lunch that day but, on the contrary, one scornful, disapproving look will instantly turn all the women's backs to the unfortunate *gavros*-seller who will be left stranded in the middle of the crossroads like an illusionary oasis in the middle of the desert.

If one steps out of line and buys the disapproved goods, one becomes the laughing stock and the subject of gossip for the rest of the women, who in a wonderfully choreographed manner will group themselves chorus-like (*horos*), on one side, with the unfortunate buyer-protagonist totally rejected, on the opposite side, like in a primitive form of tragedy.

Anyway, once the fish is brought home, the head of each fish has to be pulled off. This is done in one movement which brings the guts out at the same time. The clean fish is rinsed in several changes of cold water and drained. Lemon juice is poured over it, it is seasoned with salt and pepper, and left to stand for 30 minutes. It is then spread in an oiled oven container and treated in the same manner as for any other fish *plaki*.

If the dish is meant for a more special occasion, or for relatives or friends visiting who have to be honoured, then undoubtedly a 'first category' fish has to be used, such as *synagritha* (dentex), *lavraki* (sea bass), or *rofos* (grouper, the French *merou*).

Almost any firm fish can be used for this dish, either whole or in steaks, which is the more common in Greece, too. Sea bass, bream, grey mullet or steaks of cod or halibut will do fine.

1 kg/2 lbs fish as above	3–5 cloves garlic, peeled and
juice of 1 lemon	finely sliced
salt and freshly ground black	350 g/12 oz fresh tomatoes,
pepper	finely sliced, or 1 396-g/14-
150 ml/¼ pint olive oil	oz can tomatoes, drained
1 large onion, finely sliced	1 bunch parsley (about a
1 glass white wine	teacup), finely chopped

Clean, rinse and drain the fish. Pour the lemon juice over it, season with salt and pepper and let it stand for about 1 hour on a drainer. Oil a small oven dish or roasting tin and place the fish, whatever size, in it.

Sauté the onions in the remaining olive oil in a frying pan until translucent, then add the garlic and continue stirring for a few more minutes. On no account should they turn brown.

Add the tomatoes, wine and salt and pepper; break the tomatoes with a spoon or a fork and simmer slowly for 10–15 minutes. Add the parsley, mix and spoon the sauce over the fish. Cook in a pre-heated oven, gas no. 5 (375°F/190°C), for 30–40 minutes, or a little longer for a whole fish.

PSARIA MARINATA (E SAVORO)

Fried Fish in a Piquant Sauce

A very definite and strong-tasting dish which dates back to Ancient Greece and the Roman Apicius, and is found all over the Mediterranean. The sauce was used as a kind of preservative when fridges were scarce. Fish cooked and covered in this sauce, stored in earthenware bowls and covered would last for days on end. It has always been quite common in the Greek islands, where quantities of all kinds of fish would have to be preserved and used when the fishing boats came back, otherwise the fish would be wasted as there were no freezing facilities.

It is still used in the same way, since it is not uncommon for small villages perched on top of craggy hills away from the sea not to have electricity. My grandmother, who had a liking for strong tastes, used to make it often and she always called it *savoro*. I remember it also used to be the dish taken for picnics, as it was quite good eaten cold. At any rate, hot or cold, it makes an unusual but extremely tasty appetizer when served on its own, or a robust main course when served with plain boiled rice.

Basically it is the sauce that identifies this dish so one can improvise and use any kind of fresh fish at hand, from fresh herrings, mackerel or sprats, to the more genteel fish steaks of cod, halibut or monk fish. Obviously one of the latter boneless fish will make a dish in a different league altogether. I tend to associate this dish with cheaper bony candidates, such as mackerel, which is exactly the same as we were served recently on Alonnisos by a simple peasant family and what we used to have at home.

1 kg/2 lbs fish, whole or
   steaks as described above
juice of 1 lemon
salt and freshly ground black
   pepper
5 tablespoons flour (3 for
   coating fish and 2 for
   sauce)
150 ml/¼ pint olive oil
3–4 tablespoons white wine
   vinegar
1 tablespoon tomato purée
   diluted in 4 tablespoons
   water

2–3 small fresh tomatoes,
   sliced with their skins
   (optional)
2 cloves garlic, peeled and
   finely sliced
2 bay leaves
sprig of rosemary
4 whole black peppercorns
1 teaspoon sugar
150 ml/¼ pint water

Prepare the fish accordingly, rinse and drain. Lay it on a platter and pour the lemon juice all over. Season it inside and out and let it stand for 1 hour.

Flour the fish lightly in 3 tablespoons of flour. Heat half the olive oil in a frying pan and, when it is hot, fry the fish in batches. Take them out as they become pale golden on both sides. When all the fish is cooked, strain the contents of the frying pan, being careful not to include any burnt sediment, rinse the frying pan and start again. Pour the strained oil as well as the reserved olive oil into it and heat up. Add 2 tablespoons of flour and stir with a wooden spatula for a few minutes in order to amalgamate it in the oil until it turns slightly brown. Add the vinegar, diluted tomato purée, tomatoes if they are used, garlic, bay leaves, rosemary, black peppercorns, sugar and the water and simmer for 10 minutes. Add the fried fish back into this sauce and simmer for about 5 minutes.

ATHINAIKI MAYIONEZA

Fish Athenian Style (with Mayonnaise)

This is a magnificent dish, both in looks and taste, when it is prepared with the appropriate care, the fish is absolutely fresh and the mayonnaise homemade.

In the early 1960s, I went to have lunch with a friend in Athens when a huge platter with a large fish, covered with a mayonnaise sauce and richly decorated, was brought to the table. It had been prepared by their cook, who was quite dexterous and who also made, among other dishes, the most delicious meat, chicken and cheese pies that I have ever sampled.

Athinaiki mayioneza is made with a large fish, preferably a *synagritha* (dentex), which is cooked in court-bouillon briefly, then skinned and boned very carefully, with the head and tail reserved intact. The flesh is broken by hand into small portions and mixed with small cubes of boiled potatoes and carrots. It is then reassembled on a decorative elongated platter into a fish shape with the head and tail in their appropriate positions. The body of the fish, but not the head and tail, is then completely, but smoothly covered with a velvety, thick mayonnaise. The cook is free to exercise imagination in decorating both platter and fish with colours and patterns. Boiled and shaped beetroot, capers and gherkins, boiled carrots, boiled eggs and black shiny olives are all used for this purpose.

Any large but firm fish can be used as long as one has the patience to bone it. If you wish, it can be boiled with the addition of other smaller and insignificant fish and the broth can be served as a fish soup *avgolemono*. Care should be taken not to overboil the large fish as it may fall apart and the flesh will lose much of its flavour.

A lot of expensive Athenian cafés, particularly the ones bordering Kolonaki Square, such as Papaspyrou and Hellinikon, keep it as a standard dish among their other cold buffet dishes that can also be taken away for a cold meal at home. Their version of the dish is quite good, unlike the one I had some years ago in the expensive restaurant, Je Reviens, in Xenokratous Street, which was a real disappointment.

LITHRINIA E TSIPOURES ME SELINO AVGOLEMONO

Pandora or Daurade with Celery and Egg and Lemon Sauce

A wonderfully refined way to cook any firm, non-oily fish or fish steaks, from fresh cod, halibut and haddock to turbot or fillets of any kind of sole. This is traditionally a speciality of Messolonghi on the west coast of Greece and Lord Byron's adopted land. Strictly speaking, it should be made with celeriac, the Greek selinorriza, *which is only available in the autumn in Greece.*

4 fish steaks, or 4 fillets as
    above, about 1 kg/2 lbs
salt and white pepper
2–3 sticks celery, trimmed,
    rinsed and sliced (include
    as many green leaves as
    you can)
1 small onion, finely sliced

3 tablespoons olive oil and
    25 g/1 oz butter
3 tablespoons dry white wine
150 ml/¼ pint water
chopped dill, or parsley
Avgolemono sauce
2–3 egg yolks
1 lemon

Prepare, rinse and drain the fish accordingly. Poach the sliced celery in plenty of boiling, salted water for 4 minutes and drain.

Sauté the onion in the mixture of olive oil and butter in a wide saucepan or frying pan until it looks translucent but not brown. Add the wine and, shortly afterwards, the water, bring to the boil, put the celery in and stir to mix it. Cover and cook for 5 minutes before adding the fish.

At this stage, if you are using fillets of sole instead of fish steaks, empty the contents of the saucepan into a flameproof, shallow oven dish and spread them all over the bottom. Place the fillets on top, season, cover with foil and cook in a moderate oven, gas no. 4 (350°F/180°C), for 30 minutes. Check in case more liquid is needed in the process.

Otherwise, add the fish or fish steaks to the saucepan, season and mix well with the onion and celery, being careful not to break the fish. Add a little more water if needed – the fish should be half-immersed in the liquid – cover and simmer until the fish feels tender but not overcooked. For average size fish it usually takes about 15–20 minutes.

Remove from the heat and let it stand for 5 minutes before adding the *avgolemono* sauce (see page 56). Pour the sauce over the fish, and add the chopped dill or parsley. Shake the pan gently and return on very low heat for 2–3 minutes, in order to thicken the eggs slightly.

BAKALIAROS TIYANITOS ME SKORTHALIA

Fried Salted Cod with Garlic Sauce

Traditionally a Lent dish but also frequently eaten during the winter. Salted cod, even though imported from northern countries, has always been embedded in Greek life and diet; the scarcity of fridges and the cheapness of the cod were the original reasons. Cod is still quite cheap, following roughly the price per kilo as one litre of olive oil or slightly more, which is still half the cost of meat per kilo. (However, meat is very expensive in Greece, by Greek standards, so do not get overjoyed.)

The flat, triangular, wing-shaped, opaque sides of cod, smothered with salt, can be seen in piles everywhere in Greece, in the central market in Athens, or in each individual street market, the *laikes* as they are known. Their strong fetid aroma mingles with the clove-scented bunches of scarlet carnations on the stall next door and the mountains of dill of the stall opposite and altogether transforms the otherwise tranquil gentility of Xenokratous Street in Kolonaki every Friday and manages to overwhelm the waves of the pine aroma from the nearby slopes of Lykavittos.

There is even a subterranean *taverna* with an uneven stone floor called Ta Bakaliarakia (The Small Cods) in Plaka. This simple but colourful place became famous in the early 1960s for serving, as its name suggests, mouthwatering, crisp, fried, puffed-up balls, encrusted morsels of salted cod, covered with a creamy, sharp garlic coat of *skorthalia* and accompanied by the best *retsina* Athens could exhibit at the time, straight out of huge wooden barrels in prime position in the *taverna*.

Ta Bakaliarakia still rooted in the exact spot and still, primarily at least, devoting itself to the same dish, continues its seasonal tradition, only operating in the winter and early spring, until the end of May, like its main dish. But perhaps being on the main tourist trek, right in the heart of Old Athens, it has sacrificed some of its original charms and lost some of the fervour in its original tastes.

Salted cod can be easily obtained in Italian and Greek shops, sometimes already cut up in square pieces and packeted. It must be soaked overnight, changing the water frequently during the evening as well as the next morning. Ideally, it is better skinned and, according to the recipe, sometimes boned. It has a strong and definite taste, so a small quantity goes a long way. Introduced to people as a starter it is quite a success and those who acquire a taste for it fall in love with it sooner or later. Serve it as a first course with a raw or cooked salad.

450 g/1 lb salted cod	freshly ground black pepper
½ teaspoon baking powder (optional)	½ teacup water
	1 egg, lightly beaten
75 g/3 oz flour	vegetable oil, for deep-frying

If the cod is not already cut up, cut it into medium-sized pieces, discarding its fins and tail. Soak the pieces in a bowl of cold water, starting the evening before it is to be eaten. Change the water 2–3 times in the course of the evening. Then, skin the pieces and let them soak in fresh water all night. Change the water 2–3 times during the course of the next day. Rinse and drain the pieces, let them drain for at least 1 hour, then bone them as much as you can. During the process of boning, inevitably the pieces will almost fall apart, or they will have to be cut quite small in order to do this job efficiently.

Mix the baking powder (if using) with the flour and black pepper and then dissolve the flour carefully in the water. It should be quite thick. Add the egg and mix well, beating together with a fork.

Empty all the pieces of cod into this batter. Take one spoonful of fish at a time and deep-fry in hot vegetable oil for 3 minutes, until they look golden; drain. Alternatively, dip each morsel of cod into the batter with a slotted spoon, drain excess batter and lower straight into the hot oil. This way, it will have a much thinner coating of batter.

Serve with the *skorthalia* (garlic paste) on a separate plate so people can help themselves individually to the amount they wish.

AN EASIER ALTERNATIVE

Bakaliaros is also served fried in a larger serving of flat portions. This is a much easier way but it lacks the delicacy of the previous recipe. If you opt for this one, divide the cod into four small flat oblong or square portions, soak it and skin it as described above. It does not need boning, apart from pulling out the obvious bones. Cook and serve as before.

BAKALIAROS PLAKI STO FOURNO

Salted Cod Baked with Garlic, Tomatoes and Potatoes

*This has stayed in my mind as a Friday dish, when it will also still
be found on restaurant menus. It is an unusual dish with a definite,
memorable taste. The most important point is to soak the cod
overnight efficiently in order to get rid of the excessive salt as
described in the previous recipe.*
*In Greece this is always a main course, usually accompanied by
a green raw salad, so the quantities given are for the same purpose,
that is a main course for four.*

675 g/1½ lbs salted cod, or
   4–5 medium-sized pieces
1 kg/2 lbs potatoes, peeled
   and quartered or sliced as
   for roast potatoes
1 onion, peeled and thinly
   sliced
2 cloves garlic, peeled and
   sliced

3–4 tablespoons chopped
   parsley
freshly ground black pepper
120 ml/4 fl. oz olive oil
1 396-g/14-oz can tomatoes
1 teaspoon oregano
12 black olives, not the
   Kalamata variety
   (optional)

Soak the pieces of cod as described on page 213. They do not have to be
skinned for this dish, but trim them slightly and take out obvious bones.
Mix the potatoes, onion, garlic, parsley, pepper and olive oil well in a
roasting dish. Add 150 ml/¼ pint water.

Lay the cod pieces on top and spread the tomatoes all over the surface,
breaking them up with a fork. Sprinkle the oregano all over, add some
more black pepper and place in a pre-heated oven, gas no. 5
(375°C/190°C), for 1½ hours. Take out 2–3 times, gently mix the potatoes
and, tilting the tin, baste well all over the surface. A little water may be
added if it dries out too much. A handful of black olives is often added to
the dish for the last 20 minutes of cooking time.

MITHIA TIYANITA

Fried Mussels

My father was so fond of this dish that it was often included in the Sunday morning repertoire, a sort of Greek equivalent to the English egg and bacon for a late Sunday breakfast, though this was quite eccentric, even by Greek standards.

A delicious meze *(appetizer), worth every bit of the work involved in its preparation. The mussels should be served almost straight out of the frying pan, when they are still perfectly crisp and retaining their sea aroma. This will serve four to six people.*

1 kg/2 lbs mussels
2 eggs
55 g/2 oz flour
½ teaspoon baking powder
5 tablespoons water
salt and freshly ground black pepper

2 cloves garlic, peeled and crushed
3 tablespoons finely chopped parsley
150 ml/¼ pint olive oil, or vegetable oil, for deep-frying
juice of ½ lemon

Prepare the mussels as described in *Mithia Pilafi* (Mussels with Rice) on page 216. When cooked take them out of their shells and drain them in a colander. Discard the cooking liquid and all the shells as they are not needed for this recipe. You can keep a few large shells for decorating the platter later, if you wish.

Beat the eggs in a deep bowl. Mix the flour and baking powder with the water and add it to the eggs. Mix well, making sure there are no lumps. Season, add the crushed garlic and half of the parsley and mix.

Take three mussels at a time, dip them together in the batter and deep-fry them in the hot oil, briefly but briskly, for 1–2 minutes so that they appear slightly golden and crisp.

Take the mussels out with a slotted spoon as they become ready and drain them on kitchen paper in order to absorb excess oil. Spread them on a platter, squeeze the lemon juice all over, sprinkle on the rest of the parsley and serve at once.

MITHIA PILAFI

Mussels with Rice

This is a very common but delicious way to eat mussels in Greece. Almost routinely this makes a Wednesday or Friday dish during the winter, the days that traditionally require people to abstain from meat. Even more often, it is eaten during Lent.

It is a delicious alternative to animal products. The mussels should be absolutely fresh with the inviting aroma of the sea, and they should be properly cleaned and rinsed to remove any trace of sand. They should be eaten on the day they are bought as they are perishable and also lose taste and aroma when they are even a little stale. As their preparation is quite time-consuming, it is not worth bothering with stale mussels or imported mussels from abroad that are bound to have been sitting around for a few days. Trust a good fishmonger.

Mithia pilafi, apart from being a very Mediterranean dish in taste, is also very Mediterranean in appearance, colourful and holiday-evoking. Served in a large, decorative, copper frying pan with a long, thick, iron handle, or a heavy, blackened, cast iron frying pan with fresh green parsley on it, it is even more so. It is also very representative of the new health-orientated trend towards Mediterranean cuisine.

It is a good idea, and quicker too, to half cook the rice for the pilau in a saucepan and then add it to the rest of the ingredients. It is also important that the rice is cooked with some of the mussel liquid once it has been carefully strained through a fine piece of muslin.
The quantities given are for a first course for six people or for a main course for four.

1.5 kg/3 lbs mussels (1.75 litres/3 pints)
1 small onion, sliced
3–4 peppercorns
300 ml/½ pint water
Pilau
1 large onion, finely sliced
2 cloves garlic, peeled and finely sliced
150 ml/¼ pint olive oil
1 glass white wine

1 227-g/8-oz can tomatoes
2 bay leaves
1 teaspoon oregano
200 g/7 oz long-grain rice, or yellow Italian rice
150 ml/¼ pint of the mussels' cooking liquid
parsley, finely chopped
salt and freshly ground black pepper

Put the mussels into a bowl with cold water and scrape each one individually, to dislodge alien substances and grit from their shells. A sharp knife is best for this exercise (and if you can get the man of the household to do, it even better) but a stiff brush can also be used. Try to pull away the hairy beard they have at one end, at the same time. (This can also be done once they have undergone their initial cooking.) Then place them in a sink or a bowl full of water and let the remaining grit sink to the bottom. Lift them out with a slotted spoon and repeat this process several times, until the water appears clear. No matter how well one rinses mussels there is always some hidden grit or sand nesting in them so one has to be particularly meticulous with them.

Place half of the mussels in a large saucepan with the sliced onion, the peppercorns and the water, cover and cook rapidly for 4–5 minutes, shaking the pan gently a few times until they start to open.

Place a colander on top of a bowl and, using a slotted spoon, lift the mussels out, into the colander in order to collect all their juices. Discard the ones that have not opened as they are probably dead ones, not worth risking. Repeat this process with the rest of the mussels. Let the liquid in the saucepan settle and carefully, without disturbing it much, strain the liquid through fine muslin. Do the same with the liquid from the bowl, where the mussels have been strained. Remove the mussels from their shells and discard most of the shells but keep a few large ones for decorative purposes.

To make the pilau, sauté the sliced onion and garlic in the olive oil in the frying pan, until it turns pale golden. Add the wine and, when the steam subsides, add the tomatoes, bay leaves and oregano, stir and cook for 3–4 minutes in order to thicken the sauce.

In the meantime, prepare the rice. Bring the mussel liquid to the boil and add the rice. Cover and simmer gently until all the liquid is absorbed.

Add the rice and the mussels to the frying pan, add half of the parsley, the salt and black pepper, and the reserved mussel shells, and cook gently, stirring from time to time, until the rice is cooked but still feels a little hard. Sprinkle the rest of the parsley on top and serve.

YARITHES SALATA

Prawn Salad

In Greece, prawns are often presented in a simple way as a salad, beautifully arranged on a large platter with their bodies peeled but their heads and tails intact and an olive oil and lemon dressing over them. This sounds simple but it is a perfectly delicious way to eat them when the prawns are not only very fresh but also freshly cooked.

Personally, I love eating them raw when I am sure of their place and time of origin as I adore the aroma and the slightly salty taste of the sea in them. The Aegean island of Limnos is famed for its prawns as well as its fish, not only for their abundance in its waters but their considerable size.

On flights to Limnos when I was an air-hostess, we never failed to order some, while still in the air, through the radio to the Limnos Airport control, who would have them ready whenever possible by the time we landed. Limnos Airport, at the time, was a tiny military airport with a tin hut for the passenger building and a runway that was not even concreted but had a rusty metal mesh covering to keep the grass down.

Nevertheless, it had prawns waiting for all of us in the crew and, at times, even beautiful fish and fresh eggs to take back to Athens; an altogether hospitable ambience. These were very folkloric flights indeed, even the passengers entered the small Dakota planes with livestock as presents for their relatives in Athens. It was not unusual to have a couple of chickens and a few cockerels as well on the flight and almost always large glistening fresh fish tied together by their tails with sea weeds or raffia and, of course, endless bags of prawns. It was on these long flights back to Athens that I developed the habit of eating these pink prawns raw, sitting at the back of the aircraft and looking at the clouds.

Unfortunately, in England at least, it is not easy to buy raw prawns and as a result the cooked prawns one buys lack taste apart from the fact that they tend to be oversalted as a means of preservative.

If you are able to find them raw, rinse them carefully in cold water first. Have a saucepan with enough water only to cover them and some salt, preferably rock salt, boiling, add the prawns into it and boil steadily for 3–5 minutes according to their size. They should be firm when they are cooked. The water left is used for the sauce or the rice when a pilau is made with the prawns, so it should not be very salty.

Peel their bodies, keeping heads and tails intact and arrange them on a round platter, their heads towards the centre and their tails in a fan-shape. Place in the middle a bowl of olive oil and lemon dressing (three parts olive oil to one of fresh lemon juice) for individual serving.

YARITHES YIOUVETSAKI

Baked Prawns with Fresh Tomatoes and Feta Cheese

No one out for a meal in the tiny picturesque port of Mikrolimano in Kastella should miss this delicious, colourful dish. Prawns are always bought uncooked in Greece which makes quite a difference to the taste of the dish since the cooking liquid from the prawns is used for the sauce.

What makes it very distinctive is the addition of thin slices of Greek feta cheese on top which, by the time the dish comes out of the oven, is almost melting in soft whirls with the sweet summer tomatoes. It is a dish which we did not have at home because of the lack of an oven so I always associate it with sunny lunches in the spring or cool summer evenings next to the sea in fashionable Mikrolimano, unfashionable Freattitha in Piraeus, or a run-down picturesque *taverna* in Vouliagmeni (the resort on the coastal road to Sounio), when it was still idyllic with its sleepy emerald interlocking bays bordered by white luminous sandy beaches and the dense pine trees reflected in the still waters. That was before the Greek Tourism Board struck in the early 1960s and developed it into a complex of modern beaches and the ultra luxurious Astera Hotel. Trendy Athenians followed and built even more luxurious and affluent blocks of flats which now reflect in the busy waters of what resembles today, perhaps, a more humane, more picturesque morsel of the Côte d'Azur.

The dish derives its name from the small version of the dull red, round, earthenware dish, very common in Greece, called *yiouvetsi*. Originally these were made in the Athenian suburb of Maroussi, famous for its clay and its waters. Even today people seek those made in Maroussi as they are considered to be the best. *Yiouvetsia* of all sizes can be found everywhere from urban street markets to small island grocer shops (*pantopolia*).

> Yarithes Yiouvetsaki *is a very simple dish to make but very unusual and characteristically Greek. It is lovely as a first course and the quantities given here are intended as such. If you want to make it more picturesque, bake it in four individual ovenproof bowls and serve it in these straight from the oven as, in fact, it is served in restaurants in Greece.*
> *Prawns, of course, are almost always bought cooked in this country, so some of the flavour is lost and, more importantly, they are quite often oversalted so make sure you rinse all traces of salt by immersing them in a bowl of cold water. But, even better, you could buy frozen raw king prawns, defrost properly and boil them as in the previous recipe. Then shell them before using.*

1 pint prawns in their shells
  (285 g/10 oz)
1 medium onion, finely sliced
120 ml/4 fl. oz olive oil
1 teaspoon oregano, or
  thyme
1 glass white wine
350 g/12 oz fresh tomatoes,
  skinned and sliced, or 1
  396-g/14-oz can tomatoes,
  drained and chopped
salt and freshly ground black
  pepper
chopped parsley
110 g/4 oz white feta cheese

Rinse the prawns and drain. Peel away the shell from the body but keep head and tail intact in most of them. Have a few completely shelled, discarding heads and tails in order to add body to the dish, particularly if they are small.

In a frying pan, sauté the onion in the hot olive oil until it becomes translucent; add the herbs, wine and then the tomatoes. At this stage one would add a little of the liquid that the prawns had been cooked in, if they were raw.

Boil the sauce for 5 minutes, season it, mix in the parsley and pour over the prawns. Spread thin slices of feta cheese on top and cook at gas no. 4 (350°F/180°C) for 20 minutes.

Alternatively, just crumble the feta and mix it in the sauce; then bake it as above.

AHINI

Sea Urchins (Echinoidea)

One does not have to search for long in order to find these prickly but delicious creatures. Where there are rocks there are also sea urchins. Whole colonies of them seem to hold the granitic rocks in their embraces just under the water.

Sea urchins make one of the simplest, quickest and easiest gastronomic experiences for anyone that can be bothered to harvest them. They are also hailed as an aphrodisiac and evidently make one euphoric, to say the least! They vary slightly in colour from a lustrous ebony black or dark purple to a dull unusual olive green. They are perfectly round with a forest of thick needle-like spikes all over, apart from the centre of one side where there rests a Cyclopean eye (some people call it a nose, but personally it reminds me more of a Cyclops' eye as fantasized about and described to us in our childhood). This eye is always a lighter rich purple colour. All sea urchins are edible, apart from one kind that even if it was opened would be found empty of the precious star-shaped golden-orange eggs: this is the male sea urchin. It can be spotted from its longer and thicker spikes, but particularly from its dull black colour which does not change round the eye to become purple but it looks even darker and inkier, unlike other specimens.

All our swimming outings include a sea urchin collection; armed with a plastic bar or a net, you have to choose the larger specimens, hold with a very light hand and pull them gently from the rock. (The worst is when you step on one hiding under some seaweed.) Many people in Greece claim that sea urchins and limpets are at their biggest and best in March. I prefer to eat them in the early afternoon when one can enjoy their flavour without the pangs of hunger.

Either slice a round section with a small sharp knife round the eye, or hit gently with a rock around the eye and break this section away. Turn it upside-down in order to drain all its liquid, or dip it in the sea and rinse it. Pull out of each one its golden rays of eggs, either with a knife or with a finger. Some people squeeze a little lemon juice on them before eating them. They are absolutely delicious. They are difficult to open but then what arduous tasks and pressures has one got when lying on a dazzling white pebble beach all day?

KALAMARAKIA

Squid (Loligo Vulgaris) *and How to Prepare Them*

Of all the cephalopods it is undoubtedly squid that occupy first place in the heart, as well as the stomach, of most Greeks.

Fried squid is as commonly eaten in restaurants as it is at family meals. Sweet, and always very tender, the slightly golden rings, that should come to the table almost straight out of the frying pan, are consumed in huge quantities.

Kalamarakia is derived from the Greek word *kalamos*, primarily meaning a bamboo reed and later, metaphorically, an old-fashioned pen. This must have been either because of their long, slim, tubular body or because of the transparent, feather-shaped soft bone down their spine that might have been used as a pen.

Kalamaras, as a result, towards the end of the nineteenth century, became the slightly ironic slang term given to an educated person, and an inkpot became a *kalamari*. Today Greek Cypriots, in the same slightly ironic fashion, address their compatriots from mainland Greece globally as *kalamarathes*.

When I first came to England, in 1966, *kalamarakia* were the things I missed first and longed for most. They were nowhere to be seen in those days, not even in Soho. It was about two years later that they started appearing occasionally. In the meantime, such was my passion for them that I established a squid aero-bridge between Athens and London, with the help of my ex-flying colleagues. My grandmother would get the fresh squid early in the morning, prepare it for me, and my mother would then deliver it to one of my friends scheduled for the noon flight from Athens to London. The Hermes-like courier, having delivered the goods, partici- pated in a squid feast in London the same evening, along with other home- sick expatriates studying here at the time.

Only once the system failed and the unfortunate squid and some red mullet were going back and forth from London airport for a couple of days without being able to trace me, until they had to be thrown away.

On Alonnisos, at about the end of July, there is an abundance of unusu- ally large, but extremely tender and sweet-tasting squid. On quiet nights, when the sea is calm, everyone including the amateurs, goes squid fishing. Their indispensable equipment is a lead weight with lots of hooks on it, about a dozen at least.

The fishing outings end in the early hours of the morning, unless there is a real plethora, when spending one hour is enough. The stories travel from mouth to mouth next morning all along the *kafenia* on the seafront, where the first small cups of black coffee send steaming rings up into the hazy morning dew, with a crescendo of clearing of throats as the droopy- eyed fishermen join the choir of the new day.

It is customary on such mornings after a successful squid-fishing out- ing, for the fishermen to distribute offerings of their fresh catch to their relatives and friends. Small, bright blue, plastic bags, so characteristic of Greek island summer life, can be seen changing hands in a highly con- spiratorial manner, with no verbal exchange between donor and recipi- ent. These small bags circulate through a network of outlets and are distributed not only by the one taxi on the island that might stop in some remote spot for delivery to an isolated stone cottage, but also through the baker's motorcycle and sometimes even by the local postman. At the beginning I was full of curiosity and determined to break the cycle of silence and find out the meaning of these ritual exchanges.

Having entered the communal reciprocity pattern, we now sometimes find the small blue bag waiting on our doorstep first thing in the morning, or one of the children is sent to deliver it. The fishermen always clean the squid before it is sent and they also peel its skin as these squid are the larg- er type and tend to have tougher skins.

To *clean squid*

People who are not familiar with squid are bewildered by the process of their cleaning and sometimes by their texture. But once you have tried to clean them you will realize it is not such a difficult task after all. As for the texture, why not use a pair of plastic gloves? The job can get done equally well with them.

Squid which are going to be fried are more common sliced in thick rings. This does not stop you from initially opening their body, at least, in order to make the cleaning easier. But if you want to use them stuffed, then you need their bodies intact. The principle in either case is to empty the body completely and to extract the eyes and nose from the head.

First, gently pull the head from the body. If you need the body intact, empty everything from inside with your fingers. It is not necessary to peel the red-purply skin off, unless the squid are particularly large, in which case the skin may prove rubbery. You can leave the two fins attached on its sides but make sure to rinse well under them in case of sand. If the squid is large then they are better removed and dealt with separately. The fins, though, look attractive, particularly in the case of stuffed squid, when they make them look like kites.

If you are going to fry them, slice the body in thick rings and rinse them well under running water, removing all traces of sand. Squid, as you may find out, can be very gritty.

If the bodies are going to be stuffed, particular care is needed to rinse them well inside several times. There is a lot of ink contained around the eyes, so be careful you are not splashed with it. Make a vertical slit on one side of the head, normally the one that looks a lighter colour. The head, with the tentacles attached on one side, will open up like a strip of cloth or a curtain. In the middle of it you can see the protruding beak, which you should extract and discard. Then cut horizontally just underneath the eyes, a long strip, from one end to the other, and discard it as it contains the eyes. Cut the strip you are left with into two or three smaller pieces, according to the size of the squid, each piece containing three or four tentacles also. There is no need to cut the tentacles; they curl up when fried. Tentacles tend to spit a lot, so they are always fried, covered, all together at the end.

In the case of stuffed squid you need the strip with the tentacles for the stuffing, and it must be sliced finely. Before you do anything else with the tentacles, rinse them carefully, rubbing their suckers with your fingers. Then drain them and make sure they are quite dry before they are fried.

The smaller squid are always preferred fried, sometimes whole; the slightly larger ones stuffed, or cooked in wine and made into a pilau either on their own or with prawns and/or mussels.

PSARIA

Sometimes in Greece the tiny octopus are sold as *kalamarohtapotha*. These are treated as squid are and mostly fried. As they are much cheaper than squid, they are very popular and I remember having them very often at home. The difference though is quite distinct as they are full of muscle and one has to agonize to chew them properly. So, even as children we could not be deceived as to exactly what they were. Even though we whined we ate them and learnt to love them.

But D.H. Lawrence did not:

> A *calamaio* is an inkpot: also it is a polyp, a little octopus which, alas, frequents the Mediterranean and squirts ink if offended. This polyp with its tentacles is cut up and fried and reduced to the consistency of boiled celluloid. It is esteemed a delicacy: but is tougher than india rubber, gristly through and through.
>
> I have a peculiar aversion to these inkpots. Once in Liguria we had a boat of our own and paddled with the peasant paddlers. Alessandro caught inkpots: and like this. He tied up a female by a string in a cave – the string going through a convenient hole in her end. There she lived, like an Amphitrite's wire-haired terrier tied up, till Alessandro went a-fishing. Then he towed her, like a poodle, behind. And thus, like a poodly-bitch she attracted hangers-on in the briny seas. And these poor polyp inamorati were the victims. They were lifted as prey on board, where I looked with horror on their grey, translucent tentacles and large, cold, stony eyes. The she-polyp was towed behind again. But after a few days she died.
>
> (D.H. Lawrence, *Sea and Sardinia*, 1923, p. 50.)

From this description I am certain that D.H. Lawrence was suffering from exactly the same species as we did when we were children: the *kalamarohtapotha*, the small chewy octopus and not the tender, succulent squid.

KALAMARAKIA TIGANITA

Fried Squid

One of the most appetizing dishes on a Greek table. It never fails to excite the spirits as well as the palates. These squid should always be fried just before they are to be eaten. They are passable cold but they are horrid re-fried: they go leathery and altogether stale. At worst, spread them in an oven dish and re-heat them in a slow oven for 10 minutes, uncovered, if you decide to cook them earlier. The quantity given below will do as a first course for four people.

675 g/1½ lbs fresh squid
vegetable oil, for deep-frying
55 g/2 oz flour
salt and freshly ground black
  pepper

juice of ½ lemon
a little oregano, or chopped
  parsley

Prepare the squid as described on pages 221–23. Rinse, then drain in a colander for at least 1 hour; otherwise, dry them in kitchen paper as they spit like devils when fried.

It is much easier to deep-fry them as long as the oil is not too hot when they get mummified (about 350°F/180°C is the right temperature). In Greece they are almost always shallow-fried and turned over individually in order to get them crisp on both sides, which, of course, is a real labour. Put the flour with salt and pepper in some paper, mix well and add half of the pieces of squid, but do not include any tentacles – leave those for the end. Shake them in the flour, by holding the four corners of the paper, then lift a few pieces up at a time, shake excess flour off and drop them in the hot oil. When they turn a nice golden colour – it takes about 3 minutes – lift them out with a slotted spoon. At the end sprinkle the lemon juice all over, some oregano, or parsley (oregano is more common in Greece), and serve immediately.

KALAMARAKIA YEMISTA

Stuffed Squid

For a unique and unmistakably Mediterranean flavour, I cannot think of a better candidate than this dish. It instantly evokes an image of brilliance, of sunshine and of holidays to most people, but of home to me.

This was the way my grandmother stuffed squid at home and I think it is the best since the taste of spinach enhances the sea-flavoured flesh of all the cephalopods, hence the other exquisite combination of cuttlefish cooked with spinach and white wine (page 232). I have spent numerous mornings with my grandmother, partly in the kitchen and partly working at a table in our small garden, discoursing upon squid and the merits of their spinach stuffing and putting theory into practice, there and then, to the amusement of our neighbours.

This is a rather unusual stuffing as the most ordinary one that the visitor in Greece will come across is that of onions, garlic, rice and herbs. Occasionally some pine kernels are added to the latter. The dish can be cooked well in advance and re-heated just before it is served, or it can be served at room temperature. It even survives deep-freezing well as long as it is given time to thaw properly and is then re-heated gently. According to the size of the squid, they can be sliced into two or three portions when served as a starter. This quantity will serve six people.

2–3 medium-sized squid, about 1 kg/2 lbs (their body should be at least 5–8 cm/2–3 ins long)
450 g/1 lb fresh spinach
150 ml/¼ pint olive oil
2 medium-sized onions, finely sliced
juice of ½ lemon
150 ml/¼ pint hot water for the stuffing, and 300 ml/½ pint for the tomato sauce

salt and freshly ground black pepper
55 g/2 oz long-grain rice
2–3 tablespoons finely chopped parsley
225 g/8 oz fresh tomatoes, sliced, or 1 227-g/8-oz can tomatoes, finely chopped
1 glass red wine

Bearing in mind that you need the bodies of the squid intact, pull out their head with one hand while holding their body with the other. It easily comes away. Empty the inside of the body of its elongated, plastic-like spine. You can leave the outside exactly as it is unless you dislike the purple-pink skin or if it seems particularly membranous and hard. In the latter case pull it away and you will end up with the white body underneath.

Try to leave the two fins on either side of the body in place as it makes it look like Ikaros ready to fly. Rinse the bodies properly, particularly inside, in case they contain sand, and drain them open-side down. Lay the head, with its tentacles down, on a wooden board and slice horizontally just above the eyes. This will leave you with the tentacles and a thin, ribbon-like edge. Discard the rest of the head. Rinse the tentacles well, rubbing them with your fingers. Then lay them on a wooden board and slice them finely.

Prepare the spinach by discarding any damaged or yellow leaves and also all the stalks. You only need the soft leaves for the stuffing. Rinse the spinach in cold water two or three times, until the water is left perfectly clean, then drain. Taking 4–5 leaves at a time, roll them tightly like a cigar and slice them finely. Once this preparatory work is done you can attend to the cooking.

Put 4 tablespoons of the olive oil in a heavy-bottomed saucepan and, when it is hot, add the chopped tentacles of the squid and fry them for 3–4 minutes until their water has evaporated. Stir constantly as they stick rather easily. Tentacles tend to sizzle and spit a lot, which is why when one is frying squid the tentacles are fried last and always covered, but do not let their sizzling noises frighten you.

Next, add the onions and fry until they are transparent. Then slowly pour on the lemon juice. When this has evaporated, add the hot water, cover and cook slowly for 20 minutes. Then add the chopped spinach, season with salt and pepper, cover and cook for a further 10 minutes. Add the rice, stir and cook for a further 2–3 minutes, just until it expands a little, but on no account must it cook. If the rice cooks at this stage it will end up overcooked and mushy inside the squid, which is undesirable.

Once the mixture has cooked a little, mix in half of the parsley, then stuff the squid by putting teaspoons of the filling through the opening. Do not press the stuffing down, instead shake the body and the stuffing will descend. Fill the bodies up to about 1.5 cm/½ in from the top, leaving some room for the rice to expand. There is no need to sew them.

Prepare the sauce that they will cook in by putting the remaining olive oil into a wide saucepan – the squid need to lie in one layer but also bear in mind that their length will shrink once they start to cook.

When the oil is hot, add the sliced or canned tomatoes and bring to the boil, stirring and pressing them. After a few minutes add the wine and, if you are using fresh tomatoes, 300 ml/½ pint hot water, otherwise, for canned tomatoes, 150 ml/¼ pint. Bring to the boil and carefully lower the stuffed squid in it, lying them on their backs, fin side down. They should not be covered by the liquid, they should just lie in it. Season with salt and lots of black pepper, cover and cook slowly for 40 minutes. Baste them with the sauce every 10 minutes so they do not dry out on top, and make sure they do not stick by moving them gently from time to time.

Take the squid out carefully and arrange them on a platter. Boil the sauce down rapidly to a thick consistency, pour over the squid, sprinkle with the parsley and take to the table.

KALAMARAKIA PILAFI

Squid in Rice

Make exactly as for *Soupies Pilafi* (Cuttlefish with Rice) on page 232, substituting squid for the cuttlefish. Much eaten during Lent.

KALAMARAKIA ME KRASSI

Squid Cooked in Wine Sauce

*Absolutely delectable and very tender. Also much quicker
than octopus to cook and, in my opinion, preferable
for its gentler taste.*

Treat exactly as *Soupies me Krassi* (Cuttlefish with Wine Sauce) on
page 231 but cook for 20–30 minutes, slowly, and use the same quantities
for four. Serve on their own with lots of fresh bread, as a first course.
Alternatively, they can be served on top of plain white rice.

SOUPIES

Cuttlefish (Sepia officinalis)

They [snails] must form part of a Greek Lenten dish, much esteemed
by that ancient people, almost as much so, indeed, as the cuttlefish,
which they eat in great quantities during the same season; and the
worthy man who intends a treat of the last-named delicacy for the
family supper, does not shrink from carrying home the loathsome
creature, suspended by a string, with all its livid-looking tentacles
flapping, as he walks along, reflecting on the rich flavour of the 'ink'
sauce with which it is to be dressed. The bag of dark-coloured fluid
which is found in the body of the cuttlefish, and called by the natives
'ink', is the sepia well known to the artistic and commercial world.

(Mrs M. Walker, *Eastern Life and Scenery*, 1886, p. 79.)

Soupia is the modern Greek name for cuttlefish. It is a derivative of *sepia*
– the ancient name, from which the Latin name originated. Also, the rich
brown-red colour of sepia, prepared from the ink of the cuttlefish, derives
its name from the same Greek source.

The cuttlefish one finds in Greece – just take a stroll in the almost
medieval dark, cobbled fish market inside the large central meat market
in Athens in between Athinas and Aeolou Street – are small, unthreatening creatures about 13–15 cm/5–6 ins long and although they look messy
covered in their black ink, they are easy to handle, to clean and altogether to cope with.

The shape of the cuttlefish is different from and lacks the svelteness of the octopus and the squid. Its body is larger in proportion to its short, stout head and its tentacles and is almost totally flat. Cuttlefish have eight short, equal-sized tentacles and two very long ones. Their disproportionate body is not helped by the shiny, slimy, black ink that they are covered with and which makes them look ferocious, particularly when they are a reasonably large size. But do not be put off or scared by their looks! Once you have the creature in the safety and assurance of your own sink at home, mastering them is easy.

Discovering their taste is a very pleasant experience. Perfectly smooth, unexpectedly sweet with a very slight edge at the end, it could mislead the unsuspecting recipient as to the source of this dish. The unique taste is coupled by a tender almost chewy but pleasing texture which is unique, I think, among the cephalopods.

All in all, to me at least, cuttlefish is unfailingly the most delicious creature, cooked or uncooked, among the cephalopods. No wonder that the Japanese have chosen the opaque, smooth, skinned flesh of the cuttlefish to serve raw among their *sashimi* dishes. In Greece, they are more commonly eaten fried, exactly like squid, because of their small size.

In the early 1960s, there used to be a restaurant in Paleo Faliro, called Soupies, which was wholly devoted to serving all kinds of different dishes of this delectable creature. It must have only been operating in the summer as I distinctly remember always sitting on the flat concrete roof of a large one-storey house, under the stars with glimpses of the dark sea in the distance.

Although we often had fried rings of small cuttlefish at home, it was at 'Soupies' that I first tried *soupies me krassi* – cuttlefish cooked with white wine and a sweet pulpy thick sauce made with masses of onions. Of course, the restaurant is extinct now, as Paleo Faliro stopped being the quiet, palm-fringed, decaying-villa suburb, as one after the other the fashionable, luxurious blocks of flats replaced the villas.

Cuttlefish, like octopus and squid, is eaten a lot during Lent. In particular, casserole versions like the one with white wine and onions, or the one with spinach or various pilaus made with them or sometimes in combinations with shrimps and mussels, are eaten regularly in huge quantities by Greek families during this period.

Soupia is also a term used metaphorically for a sly person because of the manner in which the cuttlefish squirts quantities of black ink at the slightest hint of danger.

This polemic side proved amazingly forceful. A couple of years ago I saw a cuttlefish that was on the verge of being caught in a small net, when it suddenly released its ink which landed on the face of a fully dressed girl standing on the beach about fifteen feet away.

To *clean cuttlefish*

Now, to the apparently difficult task of cleaning cuttlefish which, in fact, is not difficult at all. Basically, one must empty their body of all its contents, apart from the two inkbags which add an edgy flavour, reminiscent of the sea, when added to a casserole. Then, one has to get rid of the eyes and the round, ping-pong-ball-shaped beak in the middle of the head.

Rinse the ink from the *soupia* first, so that you can see what you are doing. Pull the head apart from the body; it easily comes away. Cut the body open at its front, find the two thin elongated inkbags (they are not bags actually, but a waxy, glutinous base, covered with thick concentrated layers of black ink), pull them gently away and keep them in a cup.

Discard everything else from inside the body, including the stiff elongated canoe-shaped bone down its spine. (My grandmother always kept these bones, once she had dried them in the sun, for her canary. They are good for pecking at.)

Rinse the body well and pull the grey-brown stripy skin away. Most of it comes away quite easily. Take off the flaps that are attached to the body, in order to facilitate the skin peeling.

Once the skin is peeled, you are left with the attractive opaque flesh, resembling porcelain. Rinse it well. Cut it into elongated strips approximately 2.5 cm/1 in wide and 10 cm/4 ins long and place them in a colander. Cut the head open in the middle, so it unfolds like a strip of cloth with the tentacles attached on one side. Pierce it where the beak protrudes (it is quite an obvious round shape) with a sharp knife, extract the beak and discard it. The upper part of this strip contains the eyes and quite a lot of inky liquid, so be careful you do not get splashed with it. The best way to remove the eyes is to cut horizontally just under them, all along the strip, and discard the thin ribbon-like uppermost part which contains them. Separate the strip into two or three parts and cut the elongated tentacles into smaller sections. Rinse well, rubbing the tentacles with your fingers as it is certain there will be some sand in their suckers. Drain all the pieces in a colander and let them stand and dry out before you use them.

If you are slightly apprehensive about the inkbags and the colour they add to the casserole, omit them. The dish will still be delicious.

Bear in mind that cuttlefish, like octopus and squid, shrink quite a bit when cooked. Cuttlefish, in particular though, is so rich in taste that you do not need huge portions. Also, cuttlefish exude a rather strong 'aroma' when casseroled but do not be put off by this as it is not significant.

Lastly, a word of advice: when they look slimy and black, covered in ink, they are fresh; when they look a little dry and their ink is not there, because they have been sprayed with water too often, do not buy them; they are bound to be a little too 'ripe'.

SOUPIES ME KRASSI

Cuttlefish with Wine Sauce

Cuttlefish is delicious, no matter how it is prepared. Cooked or raw, it has an unparalleled sweetness in taste and a very pleasing and somehow satisfactory texture.
Cooked this way, with the sweetness of the onions added and the smoothness of the white wine, it becomes a delicacy which wins over even the sceptics. Served on its own with fresh bread, it makes an unusual but excellent first course for four, or served on plain white rice it can be a main course for two to three. In the latter case, boil separately 225 g/8 oz long-grain or yellow Italian rice in 600 ml/1 pint slightly salted boiling water, until all the water has been absorbed. (Roughly, it is 2 teacups of rice to 4 teacups of water.) A fresh salad, in order to counterbalance the rich flavours of the dish, is a must.

1.5 kg/3 lbs cuttlefish	1–2 inkbags from the
285 g/10 oz sliced onions	cuttlefish
120 ml/4 fl. oz olive oil	salt and freshly ground black
1–2 glasses dry white wine	pepper
150 ml/¼ pint water	4 tablespoons finely chopped
	parsley

Prepare the *soupies* as described on page 230. Rinse and drain them. Keep the inkbags in a small cup separately.

Sauté the onion in the olive oil, in a saucepan. Add the cuttlefish pieces as soon as the onion starts to change colour. Sauté, stirring all the time (it easily sticks), until all the water it produces has evaporated and the cuttlefish start to change colour. This process takes about 15 minutes in all. Slowly add the wine and, when the steam subsides, add the water and the inkbags and stir to dilute them. Season, cover and cook slowly, stirring occasionally, for about 30 minutes. If it becomes too dry in the meantime and sticky, add a little water. It should be left only with its oil and a sweet pulp that the onions have disintegrated to.

Sprinkle on the parsley at the end of the cooking, stir and serve, either on its own or on top of plain, white rice as above.

SOUPIES PILAFI

Cuttlefish with Rice

Alternatively, we cook the rice with the *soupies*, whereupon the rice becomes impregnated with the delicious sea juices and acquires an almost smoky flavour. In this case there are two versions. One with tomatoes and the other without. Both are good.

Proceed exactly as before up to the stage where you add the wine. Once it has evaporated, add 2–3 small sliced tomatoes (if you want to use them) and 300 ml/½ pint hot water. Cook for 10 minutes and add 110 g/4 oz long-grain rice or yellow Italian rice, the parsley and more seasoning; stir, cover and cook slowly until the rice has absorbed all the water, about 20 minutes.

Inkbags are omitted in pilaus for decorative purposes, unlike in Italian *risottos*, but, of course, you can use them if you prefer to.

SOUPIES ME SPANAKI

Cuttlefish with Spinach

A very unusual but delicious dish, which in Greece is served as a main course and eaten routinely on Wednesdays or Fridays, the days that traditionally call for eating fish. It always surprises people with its merits and absolutely charms them with its taste. It has acquired a great following among our friends. The quantities given would do as a main course for four.

Use the same quantities as in *Soupies me Krassi* (Cuttlefish with Wine) on page 231, but use only 1 large onion and 1 glass of white wine. You will also need 1 kg/2 lbs fresh spinach. Prepare and cook the cuttlefish as before and, while it is cooking, prepare the spinach. Rinse it in several changes of water until the water is absolutely clear, as described on page 140. Drain, squeeze it very lightly and shred coarsely. When the cuttlefish feels tender enough, at the end of its cooking time, add the spinach, more seasoning, stir to amalgamate the tastes and juices, cover and cook for a futher 6–8 minutes. Serve with brown bread and some white feta cheese.

SOUPIES TIGANITES

Fried Cuttlefish

Particularly suitable and really delicious when the *soupies* are smaller, up to 20 cm/8 ins in length approximately. In this case treat them exactly as described in the recipe for *Kalamarakia Tiganita* (Fried Squid) on page 224. As they are thicker than squid however, it is better to open their bodies with a sharp knife and, once they have been cleaned, to slice them in elongated strips. Discard the inkbags completely in this case. They are best shallow-fried in oil, slowly.

Sprinkle them with a little lemon and some chopped parsley before you serve them hot, straight out of the frying pan.

HTAPOTHI

Octopus

Htapothi is a combination of two Greek words: *okto* meaning eight and *pous*, the ancient word for foot. It is one of the family of the cephalopods (*kefalopotha* – heads and feet, or lacking a body) along with squid and cuttlefish.

This eight-legged, or eight-tentacled creature stands in high esteem among Greeks, who rank it amongst the most appetizing of appetizers. *Htapothi liasto* (sun-dried octopus) is the most highly regarded and a line of octopus hanging on a clothes line is only too familiar a spectacle, not only in the Greek islands or coastal resorts, but also in inland spots, and it always fills me with non-specific expectations and joy. It brings memories, too, of innumerable sunsets and seafronts, when the jingling of the glasses of the first evening *ouzo* is echoed, and the earthy smell of the sun-dried octopus quietly scorching on the charcoal, somewhere on the seafront, magnetizes one's steps. Their highly ritualistic killing and tenderizing by beating them on the coastal rocks, as soon as the fishing boats arrived back in the morning, always attracted us when we were children and we used to spend hours watching one fisherman after the other perform the ritual, with magnetic precision and incredible force, until the muscular creature was transformed to a floppy mass.

It really requires a lot of strength and force. I tried beating octopus when friends had caught one and apart from making my arm ache and my heart thump, it had absolutely no effect on the octopus. We had a friend who came from the island of Kalymnos in the Dodekannisa, where traditionally most of the sponge-fishermen came from, and he, true to the tradition, would never fail to bring up from the depths of the sea all sorts of appetizing creatures, octopus being his favourite.

We used to spend numerous weekends at the time on a friend's boat, wandering in the nearby islands from Poros to Hydra to Spetsai and anchoring in tranquil deserted bays. At times our friend would come up with an octopus clenched round his fist, as he had pulled it out of its nesting rock. A white cloth waved in front of their nest is almost always too strong a temptation for them to resist. Once the octopus is wrapped around somebody's fist, it is customary to bite them in between the eyes, where their main nerve is, as soon as they are brought to the surface. Not the gentlest of techniques but I must admit quite efficient.

On clear, still, summer nights one can see fishermen, trousers rolled halfway up their legs, slowly combing the shallow waters of sandy bays, holding a huge brilliant acetylene light in one hand and a long-handled fork in the other. The silent, lightfooted performance is only interrupted by the sudden throw of the rigid implement towards the unsuspecting octopus which, bewitched by the brilliance of the light, becomes a candidate for the next morning's clothes-line parade in the sun.

The same performance is quite often done with the fisherman sitting in his small wooden boat, bending over and looking through the funnelled light in almost identical fashion and with identical results.

The fishermen's favourite *meze*, once they catch an octopus, is to skilfully remove the inkbag and the stomach from the octopus body without breaking it, before they start to beat it on the rocks. *Tholos* or *olos* – the cloudy, as the bag is called by the fishermen, varies in size from that of a large almond in small octopus to that of an egg in the large ones. The very small ones are mostly used for bait but the large ones go straight into the frying pan. The smaller ones are more tasty and they are buried in the glowing embers of the fire. First, though, the centre of an unpeeled onion is scooped out, the small bag is placed in the cavity and sealed with the top end of the onion, then it is buried into the slow embers for 20–30 minutes. The scorched outer layers of the onion are then discarded and some lemon sprinkled on the rest. These have a strange taste as if the whole of the seabed has been compressed in them.

Octopus is cooked in a number of different ways, mostly with wine since wine is considered to add a soothing element to the creature and make it more digestible.

Vari fagito, literally meaning 'heavy food', is a common Greek expression, pronounced with awe and accompanied by equally expressive hand gestures. Octopus almost certainly is considered the *vari fagito par excel-*

lence in Greece and as such it is served in small quantities, unlike Greek habits, and avoided as a main course in the night.

Htapothi krassato, htapothi stifatho and *htapothi pilafi* are quite common. Most common of all though, is a little plate of mouthful morsels of boiled tender octopus, dressed with olive oil and vinegar, that arrives at the table automatically with the order of an *ouzo*.

Octopus not only has to be beaten against a rock but also it has to be forcefully rubbed against the rock, like a piece of cloth, in order to get it even more tender. Sometimes housewives rub it against a kitchen marble slab for a while as a safeguard of tenderness.

Salt is never added as it is supposed to make it tough and more indigestible and in any case it seems to hold in its flesh a lot of the saltiness of the sea, even after it has been cooked.

When the octopus is small, it is cooked and presented at the table whole, as it resembles a pretty large bloom with its petals curled intricately. Octopus should be rinsed well (see advice on cleaning squid, pages 223–4), then it must be parboiled and the liquid thrown away. The octopus can also be just covered with water and boiled steadily for 10-15 minutes and then drained. When cooked this way it becomes very easy to slice it into smaller portions and to peel its skin off as some people prefer, but peeling the skin is not necessary unless one has an aversion to the creature.

If the octopus is larger, the second method is to slice it raw and put it in a saucepan on its own. It will produce quite a lot of liquid and it must be stirred around until all the liquid has evaporated, then one adds the olive oil and other ingredients as the recipe calls for, in the same saucepan.

The first method of cooking the octopus is easier but the second method has a slightly tastier result.

HTAPOTHI VRASTO

Octopus Salad

A very simple and very Mediterranean appetizer which is always hailed with excitement. It is smaller octopus which are cooked this way and almost always served cold. Once the octopus has been cleaned and boiled until perfectly tender, it should be skinned and sliced into thin rounds for the tentacles and thin short strips for the body. Prepare a dressing by beating 3 parts olive oil and one of vinegar or lemon juice with a little oregano or chopped dill and seasoning. Arrange octopus on a platter and pour the dressing over it.

HTAPOTHI TOURSI

Pickled Octopus

In case the octopus you have cooked for the previous recipe, *Htapothi Vrasto*, is not consumed, it can be preserved by putting the octopus pieces in a jar and covering them with vinegar. Store in a cool place. Rinse the pieces before you serve and cover them with olive oil and some oregano.

HTAPOTHI KRASSATO

Octopus in Wine Sauce

1 kg/2 lbs octopus
120 ml/4 fl. oz olive oil
2 medium onions, sliced
150 ml/¼ pint red wine
285 g/10 oz fresh tomatoes,
    sliced, or 1 227-g/8-oz can
    tomatoes

1 teaspoon oregano
1 bay leaf
freshly ground black pepper
150 ml/¼ pint water

Prepare the octopus (see page 235) and rinse it well under running water, rubbing it to make sure there is no sand in the suckers on its tentacles. Drain it. Cut it into 3–4-cm/1–1½-in pieces and put them in a saucepan, on medium heat. They will turn almost scarlet and produce some liquid. Keep turning them with a wooden spoon until all the liquid has evaporated. (If it is too tough to slice follow the alternative method and boil it beforehand as described on page 235.) Add the olive oil and sauté the octopus in it for a few minutes, then add the sliced onion and sauté together until it turns lightly brown. Slowly pour in the wine and, when the steam subsides, add the tomatoes, oregano, bay leaf, seasoning and water. Cover and simmer for about 1½ hours, or if using a pressure cooker for 15–20 minutes. It should be left with a thick oily sauce at the end but if it looks too watery, boil the sauce down uncovered, until it thickens.

HTAPOTHI STIFATHO

Octopus Braised with Vinegar and Small Onions

1 kg/2 lbs octopus
4–6 cloves garlic, peeled
   whole
120 ml/4 fl. oz olive oil
1 227-g/8-oz can tomatoes,
   or 2 tablespoons tomato
   purée diluted in water
2 bay leaves
1 glass red wine
sprig of rosemary

3 tablespoons red wine
   vinegar
300 ml/½ pint water
4–5 black peppercorns
1 cinnamon stick
¼ teaspoon ground allspice
½ teaspoon sugar, preferably
   brown
450 g/1 lb small pickling-size
   onions

Prepare the octopus as in the previous recipe. Sauté the octopus and garlic in half the olive oil. Once the garlic starts to change colour add all the other ingredients, apart from the little onions, cover and cook for about 1 hour.

In the meantime, peel, rinse and dry the small onions whole. Fry them slowly, in a frying pan, in the remaining olive oil, stirring and turning them occasionally, until they look brown all over. This takes about 15 minutes.

Pour the contents of the frying pan into the saucepan, sprinkle with the sugar, cover and cook for 30 minutes, or until the octopus feels tender.

Serve with lots of fresh bread because the sweet and sour sauce always attracts a big following.

HTAPOTHI PILAFI

Octopus with Rice

A delicious and substantial dish, often eaten during Lent. Being also quite economical, it is very commonly cooked and eaten by island communities. Quite often, rice is replaced by short thick macaroni, but in either case it is cooked with olive oil and is often eaten cold.

Follow the recipe for *Htapothi Krassato* (Octopus in Wine Sauce) on page 236 but reduce the amount of wine to half. When the octopus feels quite tender, about 20 minutes before the end of its cooking time, add

150 ml/¼ pint hot water, stir it and add 110 g/4 oz long-grain or arborio rice. Add some salt and black pepper, stir, cover and cook as slowly as possible until the rice has absorbed all the liquid and feels cooked but not overcooked. It should be dry like a risotto by the end.

HTAPOTHI ME MAKARONAKI
Octopus with Pasta

On Alonnisos, at times, there is such a profusion in the supply of octopus, it feels as if the island is under their attack and they almost walk themselves to the restaurants! At such times, apart from the favourite *stifatho*, or *htapothi krassato*, octopus with pasta also appears at the restaurants, which makes a delicious and cheap alternative.

In Greece the short, thick macaroni (*kofto makaronaki* as it is called) is used but any favourite shape of pasta will do. I prefer to parboil the pasta for 3–4 minutes in plenty of water, drain it and then add it to the dish and continue to cook it, in order to get rid of the excessive starch, unlike most Greeks who cook the raw pasta in the same dish, with the octopus, from start to finish.

Follow instructions as for *Htapothi Krassato* (Octopus in Wine Sauce) on page 236 but reduce the amount of wine to half. Drop 175 g/6 oz small shaped pasta into a saucepan with plenty of salted boiling water and boil for 3 minutes. Drain it. Add 300 ml/½ pint hot water to the octopus towards the end of its cooking time, when it feels very tender. When bubbling add the pasta and a lot of freshly ground pepper, stir, cover and cook very slowly for 10 more minutes, or less, according to the size of the pasta, until the pasta feels done and all the liquid is absorbed.

Alternatively, once the pasta is mixed with the octopus and the extra water has been added, empty the contents into a flat, medium-size oven dish and cook slowly in the oven, gas no. 3 (325°F/170°C), stirring occasionally, for 20–30 minutes. A little more hot water should be added in this case, if it looks dried out. A little finely chopped parsley sprinkled on top just before it is served adds a hint of freshness.

KREAS
Meat

Food at Greek country inns consists mainly of variations on the theme of lamb. How the Hellenic lamb is ever allowed to grow up to mutton state is one of those problems which the wit of the 'European' cannot solve.

Wherever you go, unless it be during the season of fasting, lamb always figures on the bill of fare, usually in more forms than one. Roast lamb is the favourite dish; but the advance of western ideas has not yet suggested the addition of mint sauce. Boiled lamb is also common – in fact, the animal is to the Greeks what beer is to the German student, or water to the teetotaller.

(William Miller, *Greek Life in Town and Country*, 1905, pp. 236–7.)

William Miller was right, of course! Tender, young, succulent lamb is the king of every Greek feast, preferably roasted whole on an outdoor spit, or stuffed with rice, fried onions, minced meat and pine nuts and roasted in a huge, shallow oven dish in the local baker's.

But if lamb is the king of the Greek feasting, goat – young, still milk-fed goat, as Greeks are quite precious about this – is the regent! There would not be Greek Easter – quite the occasion in a Greek calendar – without the succulent goat or lamb, roasting slowly over vine branches and capturing completely everybody's senses with tantalizing scents. Similarly, there would be no Greek weddings, baptisms or other highly celebratory meals without the roasting of a lamb.

Here is another description of a formal dinner given in the honour of Lord George Cochrane, head of the British forces, in the triple alliance formed by Britain, France and Russia for the liberation of Greece from Turkish occupation, after the loss of the battle of Athens on 6 May 1827. The dinner was on the island of Hydra, in the house of George Koundouriotis, the powerful nautical family which commanded most of the shipping commerce at the time.

> The house possessed a great luxury for the east – the floors being of marble and the walls of great thickness, consequently imparting a coolness and freshness to the air within, that no one but a resident in a hot climate can appreciate ...
>
> The table groaned beneath the viands: an immense Turkish pilau was at the head of the table; at the bottom a lamb roasted whole, with a lemon in its mouth; in the middle was a large tureen of soup. Several dishes were at the sides, composed of cucumbers that were scooped out and filled with chopped mutton; and there was a particular veg-etable about the size and form of gherkins, which I have often since eaten in Greece and which imparts to the ragouts, an indescribably pleasant flavour. [Courgettes, I think.]
>
> (George Cochrane, *Wanderings in Greece*, 1837, p. 88.)

Rocky hillsides of Greece, covered with wild, scented, purple thyme are always spotted with the white fleece of lamb and sheep and filled with the lazy jingling of the goat-bells, reverberating from rock to rock and impregnating the air with a strong sense of nostalgia.

It is only strong-footed animals that can survive and conquer these rocky lands. The Greeks often use the expression: 'He runs like a goat', for the slim and fast animals have to go miles daily to find greenery and to travel to the nearest well in the dry summer months. In comparison to their life, a cow's life seems endlessly luxurious and lazy and by mere logistics a cow would not be able to carry her weight up a hill, survive the heat and feed herself from purple thyme. This is the reason that there are more goats to be seen in Greece than anywhere else.

In fact, William Miller observed from national statistics in 1905 that:

> In proportion to its population, Greece has more goats than any other country; there are 119 goats to every 100 Greeks, which brings up their numbers to over 2½ million and in the country they are ubiquitous.
>
> (William Miller, *Greek Life in Town and Country*, 1905, p. 231.)

> Despite its modern houses, Athens still has oriental characteristics. There are flocks of goats – the Athens milkmen – strolling about the streets with the inquisitive eye which the Greek goat, a true Hellene, always possesses.
>
> (William Miller, *ibid* pp. 185–6.)

Even to the present day, every family in a village or an island possesses at least one goat, which gives them milk daily and the desired young kids for the Easter ritual.

During the rest of the year a Greek family does not consume much meat, even though recently I have observed that these eating trends are slowly changing. Four to five years ago a village family would depend on their own grown vegetables and pulses and their protein would be their homemade cheese and fish, that mostly changed hands through relatives and friends in an eternal pattern of reciprocity. Meat was eaten only on festive days, not necessarily Sundays, as the poverty-stricken peasants could not afford such luxuries. Now, at least, wherever tourism descends (and it is almost everywhere in Greece – there are even organized treks on the high remote slopes of the mountain of Pindos, in central western Greece), it creates a seasonal affluence, so that people can afford to buy meat. Also in the last decade they started raising cattle in the north of Greece; but despite this most of the beef is still imported.

In Greece, they call beef *moshari*, which is wrongly translated as veal. Veal, in the proper sense of the word, a milk-fed calf, does not exist and in fashionable westernized Athenian restaurants, dishes which call for veal, such as veal *à la crème*, are quietly substituted with fillet of pork.

This is the reason that various books on the subject misinterpret dishes such as beef *stifatho* as calling for veal. A *stifatho* needs the body of beef to amalgamate with the vinegar and strong scented rosemary. If, instead, one uses veal with its delicate but almost bland taste, which is instantly killed by the vinegar, the result is simply catastrophic. The same applies to *moshari kapama*, the Peloponnisian beef casserole with wine and spices. Substitute anaemic veal for beef, cook it with cloves, allspice and cinnamon sticks and you end up with a dish as authentic as a *gâteau Saint-Honoré* coated with blackberry jam.

Pork in Greece is very tasty and very popular in the winter, appearing in its most glorious form as a whole roast suckling pig, honey-coloured and deliciously crisp. In the summer months pork is considered dangerous and sometimes banned altogether in the month of August. Pork is always sold more cheaply than any other meat in order to attract the difficult and suspicious Greek customer from his life-long loyalty to the Greek lamb or goat.

Frugality has made Greek cooks stretch and plan with ingenuity. This is the reason that 500 g/1 lb 2 oz minced lamb or beef, made into stuffed vine leaves, or *soutzoukakia* or *keftethes* or the glorious summer stuffed vegetables – tomatoes, peppers, courgettes, aubergines – will often feed a whole family, and, of course, nothing is wasted: lambs' heads are roasted, intestines are highly prized and made into delicacies like *kokoretsi*, *splinantero* or *yarthuba*; tripe is made into a soup or a spicy casserole; lambs' feet are served with an *avgolemono* sauce, etc.

There are also special dishes made from older animals, such as *nyfiatiko*, the bride's dish of the Sporathes islands which requires an older goat – a *yitha* as it is called in Greek; and the boiled lamb or sheep, the traditional celebratory meal of the island of Kriti and also of many of the mountain communities.

ARNAKI PASHALINO TIS SOUVLAS

Easter Lamb on the Spit

Easter in Greece is the major event in the whole year. To the Greeks, Easter is what Christmas is to the westerners. Combined with ritualistic spring elements and garlanded by almost pagan, exhilarating events, the festival finds its climactic expression on the morning of Easter Sunday when almost every Greek family devotes itself to the preparation and roasting of the traditional *ovelias*, young spring lamb, on a fire preferably made of a combination of vine branches – permeating the atmosphere and most importantly the meat with their fragrance – and charcoal.

There must be more lambs and young goats consumed on that day alone, in Greece, than all the other occasions put together.

There is an amusing description of this ritualistic event in E.F.V. About's *Greece and the Greeks of the Present Day.*

> The lambs are all destined for Easter. The day of that great festival, which the Greeks name, to distinguish it, the *Lambri*, or the brilliant, there is not a family in the kingdom that does not eat a lamb.
>
> On Good Friday, the town of Athens is invaded by fifty long devils, dressed in the most picturesque rags, escorted by two hundred big curly dogs and followed by ten thousand bleating lambs. All this crowd, animals and men, install themselves in the open spaces in the town, or in the uncultivated fields in the neighbourhood. The citizens are treated, during two nights, to a vast concert of bleating. On Saturday all the men to be met in the street carry, like the good shepherd, a lamb upon their shoulders. Each father of a family, on returning home, cuts the throat of the animal in the midst of his sons and daughters, empties it in as clean a way as he can, seasons it with aromatic herbs and passes a stick through its body. The bowels are carefully preserved for frying. The meat thus spitted, is set before a large flaming fire of faggots in the courtyard or before the door.
>
> (E.P.V. About, 1855, p. 102.)

Things did not look very different in recent years. But there is one slight difference. Easter lamb is normally slaughtered on the Thursay before Easter as an allegorical parallel to the religious aspect of the day, the death of Christ. The practical explanation is that the meat has to be hung for a day or two in order to be tenderized, or as we say in Greek *yia na honepsi*.

The other thing that About would not know is that the 'bowels' as he calls them, are carefully preserved for making the traditional soup of *mayiritsa*, finished with egg and lemon sauce, that breaks the long fasting after the midnight liturgy on Saturday night with a plethora of excited cries of *Hristos Anesti* – Christ has risen – and the reply of *Alithos Anesti* – He has risen indeed.

In small village communities the lambs are roasted communally, so one could have six or seven lambs roasted one next to the other over the same charcoal pit. Even in the armed forces the custom of the day is observed.

For an engaged couple the custom is that the husband-to-be provides the lamb and he, himself, takes it to the girl's house, but not before he gives it a good bath and possibly ties a pretty ribbon round its neck.

On Sunday morning, the fire is started early to ensure that the wood is reduced to glowing embers by the time the roasting starts. The lamb or goat, having been properly cleaned, is rubbed with lemon all over its skin and seasoned with salt and pepper and any mountain herbs at hand, usually one or two different kinds of oregano and wild thyme, both outside and inside.

Then the *souvla*, the long, round, iron stick, is passed through the animal from one end and out through the head. The back feet are secured by passing one through the muscle of the other and are then tied with wire. Two iron poles with forked ends for the spit are inserted in the earth by the fire. At the beginning the lamb is quite a distance from the fire, about 60–70 cm/2 feet; later the two poles are lowered so the meat rests at a distance of 30–40 cm/1 foot.

The long iron spit ends in a handle and members of the family take it in turns to sit and turn it almost continually while the animal is cooking, and to sprinkle on a mixture of olive oil and lemon with a bunch of twigs of thyme plants, which they immerse in the dressing and then brush on the meat.

A lamb roasted like this takes around 3 hours or less, presuming that it is of the desirable weight of 3.5–4.5 kg/7–9 lbs maximum. A larger family would opt for two lambs instead of a larger animal as that would not be regarded as suitable for a traditional Easter lamb. It is vital that the lamb cooks very slowly, even if it takes longer than three hours. A clear indication that it is nearly cooked is when the flesh shrinks away from the bones.

A point to keep in mind is that its fleshy parts – that is, legs and shoulders – take longer to cook, so in Greece they draw most of the glowing embers to the two ends, making two small piles of them under the fleshy parts which succeed in giving these parts the extra heat they require, while the thin body is cooking at a slower speed.

'THE GODFATHER' AND A TREATISE ON INTESTINES or ENTHOSTHIA LATHORIGANI

Lambs' Livers, Kidneys and Hearts with Oregano and Lemon

This is considered a full-hearted *meze*; not just something to nibble at absent-mindedly but something to tingle and titillate the palate. When the men get together in the early evening in Greece, in their local *taverna* or *kafenio*, they will enquire at the tops of their voices (particularly if there is good reason for showing off), if there is a *theriaklithikos mezes* to accompany their *retsina*. *Therio* means a ferocious beast, so literally they are asking for a *meze* fit for ferocious beasts or, metaphorically, for men! This will give you a picture of a Greek man's image of himself and the society that goes with it. I remember my father sometimes even asking for a *theriaklithiko* coffee and one can hear this routinely in a Greek *kafenio*.

Having said this, but wishing to be kind to my father and other Greek men, I must add that it might also be taken to mean something that has been prepared by somebody full-heartedly, devoting their heart and soul to it. Anyway, this dish is definitely considered in this league. In fact, the smaller the animal the intestines come from, the more *theriaklithikos* the *mezes* is considered and no time is wasted in cooking and sampling it.

In April 1977, just after Easter, there was going to be a baptism in the village on the island, with a feast to follow in the local *kafenio*. Excitement was prevalent in the air! The narrow, whitewashed cobbled alleys were echoing with the whispers and giggles of the women rushing to and fro with their aprons, gathered in the unique way only village women have, sheltering secrets of the cooking in process. Days were spent in the sunshine, all of us shelling almonds in order to make the delicious sugar-melting, star-shaped and crescent-shaped sweets called *amygthalota* – *amygthala* are almonds in Greek – that are traditional in island communities in Greece for feasting days. Particular effort and care was invested on this baptism as the godfather, we were proudly told, was going to be a wealthy businessman from Athens.

Anyway, the 'wealthy businessman from Athens', who was quite clearly a crook, dark-suited with dark Mafiosi glasses, a golden ring on the little finger, fat wife, fat little daughter *et al.*, arrived on the ferry on Saturday. As it became clear during the course of his stay, he was interested in establishing friendly local connections as his interests lay in embezzling the monks out of a nearby deserted island for his own 'unspecified' use for the next twenty years. Historically, the group of deserted islands, further east in the chain, is supposed to have been the amphitheatre of a lot of shipwrecks in antiquity as most of the ships from Makedonia to Athens and Kriti went through these straits. So, the whole area abounds in archaeological finds and thus draws the interest of Greek and international smugglers. Anyway, the last I heard of the 'godfather', he was spending time in a Greek jail.

But back to the island feast! The main course of the celebratory meal after the baptism was going to be two enormous *yiouvetsia*, made with two milk-fed goats that were kept specially for this occasion, and the traditional *kritharaki*, an almost tear-shaped pasta that had been rolled specially this time by the elderly grandmother.

Early on Thursday afternoon the butcher and his virile entourage arrived from the harbour. The cobbled alleys reverberated with the heavy steps of the 'execution' squad going by. The atmosphere became electrified as the sulky 'heavies' walked on, armed to the teeth with knifes, ropes and iron hooks. The children followed at a distance silently and the women watched standing at their doors.

Shortly, the Iphigenian-like sacrifice took place under the thick mulberry tree on the periphery of the village, watched by all the bloodthirsty men including those in my family, that is my husband and our friend Sami.

Mitsos the butcher and his entourage consumed quite a few glasses of *tsipouro* before and after the execution, which impressed Sami and made us all think that perhaps the 'heavies' were not so heavy after all.

The main point of the afternoon for us was that as soon as their duties were completed and the little goats hung triumphantly from the mulberry, the butcher and his helpers demanded their *theriaklithiko meze*. Half an hour later they were all sitting enjoying what looked to my husband and Sami like a frying pan full of scrambled eggs and short macaroni! They laughed and laughed when I told them this and asked us all to join them and try it. It turned out to be the most delicious *meze* we ever tasted; the fresh intestines cleaned, chopped and quickly thrown into the frying pan with the eggs. Simple, but with what perfection!

Aided by drink, the sulky masks fell and the spirits rose higher and higher, some 'heavy' songs sung to go with the occasion, interrupted by a lot of '*aman, aman*', a popular heavy sigh, and our little street was hosting a wonderful gathering until the early evening.

In the actual party which followed the pious baptism, in the early evening on Sunday, in the Kafenion, Graeme and Sami were so titillated by this dark-suited cliché figure of the 'godfather' that they took it in turn, throughout the course of the evening, to jump to attention, like a jack-in-the-box, every ten minutes and toast him loudly in Greek with a '*Stin ygia soukoumbare*' – 'To your health, godfather' – trying to get him drunk and shake his heavy performance a little. The poor man must have been muttering under his teeth: 'Talk of mad dogs and Englishmen.' But by the end of the evening he was unfolding to us his grandiose plan of the *coup d'état* he was preparing for the deserted island across the sea.

ENTHOSTHIA LATHORIGANI

At last, here is the long-awaited recipe for the enthosthia lathorigani. *Bear in mind that in Greece one buys lamb's liver as a package of all the internal organs as they come out of the animal. This contains the liver, lights, heart, the spleen and some sweetbreads. Ideally a Greek would then buy separately some intestines, but these are not vital for the dish. The intestines are turned inside out and rinsed meticulously, then made into a thick plait which is plunged into boiling water and kept boiling for 2–3 minutes. Then it is drained and cut into 2-cm/1-in portions. If these are difficult to obtain, I suggest the following. One can vary the combination of the meat any way you prefer.*

335 g/12 oz fresh lambs' liver
1 lamb's heart
3 lambs' kidneys, skinned
 and split in the middle
 lengthways
4–5 lambs' sweetbreads

5 tablespoons olive oil
1 large lemon, or 2 smaller
 ones
salt and freshly ground black
 pepper
2 tablespoons Greek oregano

Rinse all the meat and drain it. Cut it into small cubes and spread it on a small oven dish. Combine the olive oil and lemon in a bowl and beat it with a fork a little to amalgamate it. Pour over the meat. Season with salt and pepper and sprinkle oregano all over. Place in a pre-heated oven, gas no. 4 (350°F/180°C), and cook for 30 minutes, taking it out once or twice to mix everything, turning over with a spoon.

Serve on its own, in its sauce, as a starter with bread. Try not to re-heat it as it will dry out. If you think you will need to cook it long in advance and you do not like it cold then it is better to go for the casserole version which is safer but not so piquant.

CASSEROLE VERSION
Combine all the above ingredients plus 150 ml/¼ pint hot water in a saucepan, cover and cook slowly for 15–20 minutes, until almost all the water has evaporated and a thick oily sauce remains. If it is going to be re-heated, cook for slightly shorter to allow for the re-heating.

SOUVLAKIA

Lamb Kebabs

The favoured meat for souvlakia *is always a leg of lamb. The meat is boned and cleared of any hard gristle or muscle; it is then cubed in rather large portions and marinated. The meat should preferably be rinsed before it is cut, otherwise it will produce too much moisture for barbecuing.*
Alternatively, souvlakia *are made with lean pieces of tender pork, or very tender pieces of* moshari – *beef.*

½ a leg of lamb, or 1.5 kg/
   3 lbs lean pork
4 tablespoons olive oil
juice of 1 large lemon
2 tablespoons oregano
1 tablespoon thyme, either
   fresh or dried

1 clove garlic, peeled and
   crushed
salt and freshly ground black
   pepper
5 bay leaves

Prepare the meat as described above. Trim excess fat if pork is used. Dry the meat before it is put into the marinade. Make the marinade by beating together the olive oil, lemon juice, oregano, thyme and garlic. Put the meat pieces in it, cover and place in a refrigerator for 2–3 hours.

Lift the meat out and thread it on skewers. Break the bay leaves in two and thread 2–3 pieces on each skewer, in between the meat. You can cook them under a hot grill but the best results, I think, are achieved by barbecuing on charcoal. If grilling, cook them briefly for about 3 minutes on each side, basting them often and turning them once; they are better slightly underdone and juicy. If barbecued, they take a little longer, about 15 minutes, depending on the strength of the fire.

ARNAKI STO FOURNO

Roast Lamb

Roast lamb in Greece invariably means a leg of lamb. Shoulders are more often used in casseroles with various seasonal vegetables, aubergines, okra, courgettes, etc.

Even to this day the leg of lamb surrounded by quartered potatoes will be taken to the local baker's. Then it gets overcooked by western standards until it is virtually falling off the bone. Because of the way it is prepared it never dries out. It is not firm like a roast in England, but succulent and virtually melting in the mouth. Serving any kind of 'pink' meat to Greeks would be considered a failure, and it would not be touched.

A roast's main feature is that it is always smothered with mountain herbs, at least one sort of oregano and perhaps one or two different aromatic sorts of thyme. A shoulder of lamb can be treated in exactly the same way but cooked slightly less, 1½ hours would be enough for a medium-sized one.

1 leg of lamb, approximately 2 kg/4 lbs	4 tablespoons olive oil
2 cloves garlic, peeled and cut in two lengthways	300 ml/½ pint water salt and freshly ground black pepper
1 kg/2 lbs potatoes, peeled and quartered lengthways	2 teaspoons oregano
juice of 1 lemon	1 teaspoon thyme

Rinse the meat. Make four deep slits with a sharp knife at various fleshy points and insert the garlic. Lay the meat in a container and surround it with the quartered potatoes. Pour the lemon juice and olive oil over the meat and potatoes, then pour the water into a corner of the dish. Season and crush the herbs all over the meat and potatoes.

Cook in a pre-heated oven, gas no. 7 (425°F/220°C), for the first 20 minutes then turn down to gas no. 5 (375°F/190°C) and cook for 1 hour. Take out halfway through to stir the potatoes and baste the meat and add a little water if needed. After this, take out and turn the meat over on its uncooked side and season with salt, pepper and more herbs. Turn the oven up to gas no. 7 (425°F/220°C) again and cook for a further 20 minutes. It will be different from an English roast and the potatoes will not be so crisp but they will have absorbed all the meat juices and they will be delicious. A green salad served along with it will make the meal perfect.

ARNAKI YIEMISTO ME KOUKOUNARIA

Stuffed Lamb with Pine Nuts

This was a recipe that came from my mother's side and as my mother originally came from Constantinople (Constantinou-Polis – the City of Constantine, the Emperor) it became a standing joke in our family to call this dish *lamb à la polita* which pleased her quite obviously and made her giggle in a nostalgic way. Very often, she would recall bright incidents from her childhood and describe them in a very animated way. We were quite familiar with her grandparents' wooden bungalow on the Bosporus coast, on the sea of Marmara, and we could almost capture the vastness of the umbrella-shaped pine tree *Pinus pinea* behind their house.

There, summer after summer, we could visualize and hear the running and the laughter of the numerous children as they chased each other threateningly, brandishing the heavy, tight, swollen pine cones, which were laid out in the brilliant sunshine every morning ceremoniously by their grandmother, in order to dry them and cause them to open up like innumerable petals round an exotic flower. We could almost hear the cracking of the pine nuts, once they were extracted from the cones, under the small marble stones that even the children could use in this exuberant *panegyris* (a merry assembly of people with some ritualistic element usually in it). The small marble stones were kept from year to year as they were considered the best method for cracking the tiny shells and leaving the elongated kernels unblemished.

Then the ivory-coloured nuts were spread on a dazzling white linen tablecloth and left in the sun to dry a little for two days. Once that was done successfully, everybody felt satisfied and secure as the nuts were stored in clean jars – secure with the thought of the delicious stuffed turkey for Christmas, as well as the crisp, exotic-tasting stuffed lamb which could be had immediately.

What was even more exciting for us was my mother's description of the wonderful homemade swing with thick nautical rope that was thrown over the strongest branch of the 'motherly' embracing pine tree.

Anyway, these wonderful dense pine trees grow all over Greece, some with more successful results than others, for the size of the pine nuts can vary from tiny to quite substantial and the quality also varies. Some are more fragrant, more oily or sweeter than others. There are two huge pine trees of this variety in a remote spot on the island and they are the only ones, so everybody knows them and our village friends – the family of Karakatsanis – claim to own them. When my husband first found them years ago he was overwhelmed by their majestic grandeur.

This dish is delicious and fit for special occasions. The lamb used is part of the saddle, boned, and it should be as lean as possible. This is a recipe for six people as it is quite an elaborate dish and not worth making for less. The saddle should contain six chops on either side, that is twelve altogether, and as you slice it you serve two chops per person. Your butcher will bone it if you give him some notice.

Stuffing
55 g/2 oz pine kernels
55 g/2 oz blanched and
  peeled almonds
3 tablespoons olive oil
1 medium onion, finely
  sliced, about 150 g/5 oz
1 clove garlic, peeled and
  finely sliced
55 g/2 oz long-grain or
  Basmati rice, soaked for 10
  minutes, rinsed and
  drained
½ teaspoon cummin seeds,
  but ground cummin will
  do
3 spring onions
175 ml/6 fl. oz hot water
½ teacup chopped parsley

1 tablespoon chopped fresh
  basil, or 1 teaspoon dried
  basil
salt and freshly ground black
  pepper
Meat
a saddle of lamb containing 6
  chops on either side, as
  described above, about
  2 kg/4 lbs, boned
4 pieces of uncoloured string
juice of 1 lemon
salt and freshly ground black
  pepper
1 teaspoon thyme
3 tablespoons olive oil
Gravy
bones from the meat
1 onion
450 ml/¾ pint water

First make the stuffing. Put the pine kernels and the almonds in a frying pan and gently fry them dry for 5 minutes, stirring, so they become golden. Take them out. Add the olive oil to the frying pan and sauté the onion gently; add the garlic and sauté together for a few minutes. Add the drained rice, cummin, almonds, pine kernels and spring onions and fry gently until the rice becomes golden, 4–6 minutes. Then add the hot water and stir until it is absorbed, approximately 2 minutes. The water will be gone but the rice should be hard and almost uncooked but it will contain sufficient liquid for it to cook and expand during roasting in the oven. If the rice is overcooked and has become a solid mass, the dish loses its flavour and crispiness. Turn the heat off, add the fresh herbs and seasoning.

In order to prepare the meat, first wipe it with a damp cloth externally only (skin side) and lay it open on a table, skin-side down, on the pieces of string; season with salt and black pepper. Place the stuffing all along the centre of the meat like a thick sausage. Fold one side over the stuffing and then the other one overlapping but not too tightly so the rice has room to expand. Bring the string over and tie as for a roast of beef.

Place in a small oven dish, pour the juice of the lemon and the oil over it, season with salt, pepper and the thyme. Pour 3–4 tablespoons of water in the dish and place in a hot oven, gas no. 7 (425°F/220°C), for the first 15 minutes, then turn down to gas no. 5 (375°F/190°C) and cook for a further 45 minutes, basting the meat from time to time. Turn the oven up to gas no. 7 (425°F/220°C) again and cook for a further 15 minutes so that the skin becomes rather crisp. Take the meat out on to a hot platter and keep it warm while you prepare the gravy.

While the meat is cooking, prepare the stock by boiling the bones of the meat with the onion in the water for approximately 30–40 minutes. This should be reduced to about a cupful by then. If you feel this is too much work you may replace it with a small glass of white wine and 3–4 tablespoons of hot water – the gravy will still be delicious so do not worry. Add whichever of the two you prefer to the juices of the meat in the pan and boil down a little. Season to taste and serve in a pre-heated sauceboat.

Slice the meat thinly at the table just before you serve, otherwise it will get cold. Serve with roast potatoes and hand the gravy separately.

YIOUVETSI

Roast Lamb with Pasta and Tomatoes

Yiouvetsi is a typically Greek dish, favoured in particular by island communities. It derives its name from the dull red, round, terracotta dish that it is baked in. However, nowadays it is very often cooked in the round shallow aluminium dishes that can be seen at any baker's in any city or village; despite this the dish is still called *yiouvetsi*.

A *yiouvetsi* is the marriage of lamb or goat with tomatoes and the small tear-shaped pasta called *kritharaki* – orzo – which results in the most delicious combination. From this safe base, however, a *yiouvetsi* can be varied; it can be made with any kind of pasta, usually with spaghetti, and the meat also might be tender boneless portions of beef. When intended for a family meal, the meat is always a leg of lamb, or two goat legs, as they tend to be tiny. Greek families, remember, tend to be rather large because of their 'extended' character, primarily.

Apart from this, they take account of a possible visitor or two, as the aspects of *filoxenia* (hospitality) are strictly observed in everyday life.

Lastly, with such a delicious and rather special dish, the typically Greek *myrothies* (samples) that will possibly be sent to a favoured neighbour or a relative in the vicinity, or simply to an ageing solitary neighbour who would welcome such a feast, must be taken into account. (A *myrothia* or a *meze* is very often a cloak for a more humane kind of 'meals on wheels', for the lonely elderly, in Greece, particularly so in small village communities where social patterns are so intertwined and secrets don't exist.)

Despite the 'pasta' aspect of the dish, there are hardly any similarities to any of the Italian pasta dishes. A real *yiouvetsi* has its pasta deliciously overcooked and impregnated with the meat juices and the sweetness of the sugary fresh tomatoes. Whenever we had a *yiouvetsi* at home, usually on a Sunday, or on a special saint's day, the leg of lamb, with cloves of garlic stuck into it in prime positions, was smothered with fresh, peeled tomatoes, olive oil and oregano, and then it was taken to our local baker's early in the morning. A packet of the special pasta *kritharaki*, was carried in the handy huge pocket of my grandmother's dark, grey-striped apron and deposited with the baker.

Once the meat was half cooked, the baker pulled the container out of the huge hot oven, using his long wooden stick that ended in a large flat round surface whereupon the container sat. Then he added a lot of hot water, the pasta all round the meat, and some salt and pushed the container back among its other aluminium companions, into the oven.

Even to the present day, this ritual is enacted in exactly the same way by my parents, and we still eat our *yiouvetsi* cooked by their local baker in Athens. Of course, a *yiouvetsi* is even more delicious and memorable when cooked by any of the village women on Alonnisos, in one of the outdoors ovens in somebody's garden, or on crisp spring days in the dark opening behind the home hearth, specially designed for baking, that will be found in the downstairs room of stone village houses everywhere.

This roast will serve six people.

1.75-kg/3½-lb leg of lamb, or a shoulder about 2 kg/ 4 lbs, boned, trimmed of fat and sliced into large serving portions

4 cloves garlic, peeled and halved

1 396-g/14-oz can tomatoes, or 450 g/1 lb ripe tomatoes, chopped finely

5 tablespoons olive oil

1 tablespoon dried oregano (*rigani*)

150 ml/¼ pint hot water

salt and freshly ground black pepper

400 g/14 oz orzo – the Greek *kritharaki* – or spaghetti, broken a little

75 g/3 oz grated Parmesan, or Greek *kefalotyri* cheese

Rinse the meat and place it in a large roasting dish. If using a whole leg of lamb, make 3-4 deep slits with a small sharp knife and insert a piece of garlic into each one. Scatter the remaining garlic around the meat. Pour the olive oil and the tomatoes over the meat, then add the seasoning and the oregano. Pour the water into the dish.

Place in a pre-heated oven, gas no. 7 (425°F/220°C), and cook it for 50 minutes, basting from time to time, and turning the portions over. (If cooking a whole leg, just baste it a couple of times and, after 50 minutes, turn it over.) After 50 minutes, pour 600 ml/1 pint more boiling water into the dish and add the pasta, together with more seasoning. Turn the oven down to gas no. 6 (400°F/200°C) and bake for a further 40 minutes, stirring occasionally, until the pasta is cooked to your taste. Keep testing it to catch it at the right time. If needed, add a little more hot water. Serve immediately sprinkled with the cheese.

If using beef for this recipe, it would need to be cooked longer initially and with more water, until tender, before the pasta is added to the dish.

REPLACING LAMB WITH BEEF

Even in Greece this has become the trend in recent times (partly because of the high price of young lamb), especially in restaurants. I have had excellent versions of beef with globe artichokes and egg and lemon sauce, as well as beef fricassee (casseroled with cos lettuces and egg and lemon sauce), in Athenian restaurants. Beef, of course, is not as fatty as lamb, so it will need a larger proportion of butter or oil, particularly in the casseroles with tomato sauce and vegetables. It will also need longer cooking.

All the following lamb casserole recipes can also be made with beef; all the recipes with egg and lemon sauce added at the end in particular are very successful when cooked with stewing steak or any tender cut of beef, which should be sliced thickly.

ARNAKI ME BAMIES

Lamb and Okra Casserole

A rather unusually exotic casserole that is always received with enthusiasm at a dinner party. Make sure, though, that the okra is not overcooked otherwise it appears mushy and it tastes predominantly glutinous.

In Greece it is cooked with the meat on the bone as long as it is cut professionally and expertly by the butcher and not just chopped with an axe, which results in thousands of bone splinters. Of course, if you prefer to have the meat boned and cubed for appearance's sake, do so, but there is no real need. Ask the butcher to cut the meat into serving portions. A shoulder or a leg is traditionally used, for this kind of casserole. Cheaper cuts can be used but since okra is quite an expensive commodity, it would seem like down-grading the whole dish to me – a bit of a waste.

2 kg/4 lbs lamb shoulder or
   leg, cut into thick slices
675 g/1½ lbs fresh okra, or 2
   400-g/14-oz cans okra
4 tablespoons olive oil
1 medium onion, thinly sliced
1 clove garlic, peeled and
   thinly sliced
450 g/1 lb fresh tomatoes,
   peeled and sliced, or 1
   396-g/14-oz can tomatoes

300 ml/½ pint water
salt and freshly ground black
   pepper
pinch of sugar
some chopped parsley (about
   2–3 tablespoons)

Rinse and drain the meat. Prepare the okra as described on page 138. Pat the meat dry and sauté in the olive oil in a large heavy saucepan until it is nicely brown all over. Take out and put on a plate. Add the onion and garlic to the same saucepan and sauté until transparent, then add the tomatoes and the water and bring to the boil, stirring and pressing the tomatoes. Return the meat to the pan, season with salt and black pepper, cover and cook slowly for 50 minutes.

Then add a pinch of sugar, the okra and most of the parsley and shake the pan (do not stir) to spread the okra evenly around the meat. The okra should just sit in the water, rather than being immersed in it. In any case do not add any more water at this stage as the okra are bound to produce some moisture. Season them, cover and cook slowly for 30–40 minutes until the okra seem soft but not falling apart. Check during the cooking in case a little water is needed after all.

If canned okra are used, it should be drained and rinsed under running cold water. As it needs less cooking than fresh okra, do not add to the meat until the last 15 minutes; that is, cook the meat for 1 hour and then add the okra.

Sprinkle on a little parsley before serving.

MOSHARI ME BAMIES

Beef and Okra Casserole

Prepare exactly as above, but replace the lamb with 1 kg/2 lbs chuck steak or stewing beef, add 600 ml/1 pint water and cook it for at least 1 hour and 20 minutes before you add the okra, or until you are certain that the meat is very tender.

ARNAKI ME ARAKA

Lamb with Fresh Peas Casserole

When fresh peas are in season, try cooking them with lamb as we do in Greece in the spring. The result is very delicate and unusual. The peas should be young and tender since towards the end of their season they become full and hard as bullets and taste almost as unpleasant as processed peas. All in all I do not think they are worth bothering with, at that stage. One could also try this dish with frozen garden peas, particularly if you search around for a good brand, but even then there is no comparison to the real genuine Greek dish. So, be seasonal instead! The dish can be made with or without tomatoes. It is worth trying both versions. When the peas are young and fresh my preference is to have it au naturel, *that is without the tomatoes so that one can enjoy the delicate taste of the peas.*
This dish can be cooked with cheaper cuts of lamb such as breast, as long as it comes from a really young animal and any excess fat is trimmed off. Alternatively it could be cooked with lamb chops, either loin or best end, allowing two per person, but of course the best is always a leg or a shoulder of young lamb.

2 kg/4 lbs fresh young peas in
   their pods
1 shoulder of lamb, about
   2 kg/4 lbs, cut in thick
   slices on the bone
4–5 spring onions
1 medium onion, thinly sliced

4 tablespoons olive oil
juice of ½ lemon
450 ml/¾ pint water
3 tablespoons fresh dill,
   chopped
salt and freshly ground black
   pepper

Shell and rinse the peas. Sauté the meat in the hot oil until lightly brown, add all the onions and sauté together for a few minutes until the onions are transparent. Add the lemon juice, water, seasoning and half the fresh dill, cover and cook for about 45 minutes, stirring occasionally, until the meat is almost tender. Add the peas and a little hot water to just cover them, cover and cook gently for 30–45 minutes according to their size. Sprinkle on the remaining dill just before serving. For the tomato version, omit the lemon juice and add instead a 396-g/14-oz can of chopped tomatoes and 300 ml/½ pint water. Then follow the above method.

ARNAKI ME FASOLAKIA

Lamb with French Beans Casserole

Prepare exactly as above, but replace the peas with 675 g/1½ lbs French green beans or bobby beans. French green beans are very tender and hardly need any attention apart from topping and tailing them. If they are long, cut them in two. Bobby beans may need to have their strings removed, apart from topping and tailing them. In this case, peel their stringy edges with a sharp knife. Rinse beans in a bowl of cold water and drain. Also replace the dill with parsley.

On no account could one replace with runner beans as they are always leathery, hard and tasteless and would make very suitable fodder for goats.

ARNAKI ME KYTHONIA

Lamb with Quince Casserole

The ochre, pear-shaped, sour-tasting quinces are very common in Greece in the autumn. They are a northern fruit as they prefer a moist atmosphere and cool weather. They thrive in places such as mountainous, leafy Pilion, among the bright green foliage of the walnut trees. As such, it is surprising that they are not more common in England, although I have met people who claim to have them growing successfully in their gardens. One can find fresh quinces in London during October and November, when they are flown in from Greece and Cyprus. For those English gardens that contain the 'golden' fruits, this is an exotic casserole to exhibit them in.

Quinces are very much part of my autumnal memories from Greece. Very often, when we were children, we had them grated in a small heap and sprinkled with sugar and a little cinnamon. As quinces are supposed to be constipating because of their acid content, this was doubling up as a Hippocratic remedy of the oral tradition against upset tummies.

For the same reasons, when my grandmother made this casserole, she believed that by adding their pips, which have softening qualities, she gave the dish an agreeable balance.

The quinces are also part of the autumn ritual of jam-making for almost every household, as well as other delicious preserves.

A cheaper cut of meat such as lean breast of young lamb goes well with quinces for a family gathering but if there are guests, a shoulder of lamb is more suitable. The same casserole is occasionally made with tender beef or boned pork.

1 small shoulder of lamb on the bone, about 1.5 kg/ 3 lbs, cut into serving portions
1 kg/2 lbs quinces
juice of ½ lemon
3 tablespoons olive oil
1 medium onion, thinly sliced
900 ml/1½ pints hot water
1 cinnamon stick
salt and white pepper
1 teaspoon sugar, preferably demerara

Rinse the meat, removing loose splinters, and drain. Cut the quinces in half lengthways and then cut each piece into 3–4 slices lengthways in half-moon shapes. Peel and core the pieces of quince and discard the trimmings. Have a bowl of cold water with the lemon juice ready. Drop them in the acidulated water to prevent them from discolouring.

Heat the oil and lightly sauté the meat in it. Take out the meat and then sauté the onion until transparent but not brown. Put in the hot water and bring to the boil. Add the meat and cinnamon, cover and simmer for 45 minutes. Drain the quinces and rinse them with cold water. Add them to the meat, season with salt and white pepper and rotate the saucepan in order to spread them evenly. Sprinkle the sugar on top, cover and cook for a further 30–40 minutes, until the quinces feel soft.

MOSHARI ME KYTHONIA

Beef with Quince Casserole

Prepare exactly as above but replace the lamb with 1 kg/2 lbs stewing steak or tender chuck steak and cook for at least 80 minutes before adding the quinces.

ARNAKI FRICASSEE ME MAROULIA

Lamb with Cos Lettuce in Egg and Lemon Sauce

This one is a great success, both with Greeks and with our English friends. It is traditionally a spring dish, as this is the time when spring lamb is available as well as the cos lettuces and anithos – dill – which is very much used in Greek cooking and salads. That is why this dish is always identified with Easter and for me it always has a festive aspect that remains from childhood, even when I cook it in the cold winter months in this country.

2 kg/4 lbs lamb shoulder or leg, boned and trimmed of fat
3 tablespoons vegetable oil
1 medium onion, finely chopped
4–5 spring onions, trimmed, rinsed and coarsely chopped
600 ml/1 pint hot water
2 cos lettuces
½ cup dill
salt and white pepper
Avgolemono sauce
3 eggs
2 lemons
1 tablespoon cornflour, diluted in a little water

Cut the boned meat into serving-size pieces and trim excess fat. Rinse and drain. Heat the oil in a wide saucepan, put in the meat with all the chopped onions and sauté gently for a few minutes. Then add the hot water and let it simmer for about 1 hour, or until the lamb is cooked.

In the meantime, rinse the lettuce leaves and drain. Chop them coarsely and add to the meat almost at the very end, with the dill, salt and pepper, and cook for a further 10–15 minutes.

Prepare the *avgolemono* as described on page 56, pour over the meat, rotating the saucepan; heat gently for 1–2 minutes and serve.

ANGINARES ME ARNAKI AVGOLEMONO

Lamb with Artichokes in Egg and Lemon Sauce

This is another spring dish with an air of Easter about it. It is one of the most delicate dishes in Greek cooking. When the artichokes are in season, in late April and May, one finds them in all the street markets, laid out in mountain-like heaps along with cos lettuces and an abundance of dill. At that time they are so cheap that everyone cooks them by the dozen.

The lamb should be very lean and ideally off the bone for this dish. A shoulder or a leg of lamb boned and cut into thick chunks are the cuts used in Greece. Again, you can vary the number of artichokes according to their availability and, of course, their price, but allow at least one per person. This dish will serve six people.

Prepare exactly as for *Arnaki Fricassee me Maroulia* (Lamb with Cos Lettuce) on page 259, but instead of the lettuce add 6 prepared fresh artichokes (see page 124) after 50 minutes, and cook for a further 30 minutes. Then add the egg and lemon sauce and dill as previously.

ARNAKI ME KOLOKYTHAKIA AVGOLEMONO

Lamb with Courgettes in Egg and Lemon Sauce

Another unusual and refreshing casserole. The lamb should be very lean otherwise a greasy sauce may cause the avgolemono *to curdle – if a shoulder is used then trim carefully any excess fat and ask the butcher to bone it and cut it into large serving portions. Of course, one can replace the lamb with beef, such as braising steak, with excellent results.*

The ingredients and preparation are the same as for *Arnaki Fricassee me Maroulia* (Lamb with Cos Lettuce in Egg and Lemon Sauce) on page 259, but replace the lettuces with 1 kg/2 lbs courgettes. Trim, rinse and slice each courgette into 3–4 pieces, lengthways. Once the meat is tender – about 1 hour – add the courgettes, cover and cook for a further 15 minutes. Then proceed with the egg and lemon sauce as described.

ARNAKI ME KOUKIA AVGOLEMONO

Lamb with Broad Beans and Egg and Lemon Sauce

Prepare exactly as above, replace the courgettes with 2 kg/4 lbs fresh broad beans. Treat them according to the description on page 127, rinse and drain. Add them to the meat for the last 45 minutes of the cooking time and either add the juice of the lemon at the same time and serve *au naturel*, or finish with the egg and lemon sauce and serve, as above.

Alternatively, it can be made with fresh shelled peas and finished with an egg and lemon sauce. In this case, use 1.5–1.8 kg/3–4 lbs peas in their shells. Prepare as above.

ARNAKI ME ANDITHIA AVGOLEMONO

Lamb with Curly Endives in Egg and Lemon Sauce

Endives in Greece have the same curly appearance as Italian endives but in an elongated form. They are stalkier and harder and almost exclusively eaten cooked as here, or as a boiled salad dressed with olive oil and refreshing lemon. It is best to have a shoulder boned and then cut into serving portions or, even better, a small leg of lamb boned first. Again, use the same ingredients and method as for *Arnaki Fricassee me Maroulia* (Lamb with Cos Lettuce) on page 259, but add 2 heads of curly endive, rinsed, drained and coarsely chopped, and cook for 10–15 minutes.

ARNAKI ME SPANAKI AVGOLEMONO

Lamb with Spinach and Egg and Lemon Sauce

Another exquisite dish of the *avgolemono* family. The fresh spinach gives the dish a unique flavour.

Proceed exactly as in the *Arnaki Fricassee me Maroulia* (Lamb with Cos Lettuce) on page 259, but replace the lettuce with 1 kg/2 lbs fresh spinach. There is no need to blanch the spinach, just shred it a little. For instructions on cleaning and preparing spinach, see page 140.

KREAS ME PATATES

Lamb and Potato Casserole

When we were children, if we were asked what we were having for Sunday lunch the reply was, 'Kreas me patates.' This was a real favourite even when the potatoes had disintegrated, as they usually had, for they were inevitably overcooked due to the large quantities in the saucepan. We much preferred it when on some more special occasions the potatoes would be fried first and then added to the meat. When we were slightly older and considered, by our grandmother, more refined and worth lavishing attention on, she would serve it to us with delicious chips.

Personally, I like the sweetness of lamb in this dish, but it can be replaced with stewing beef, in which case it should be cooked slightly longer. In the latter case, replace lamb with 1 kg/ 2 lbs chuck or stewing steak.

1 shoulder of lamb, about
    2 kg/4 lbs, cut into serving
    pieces
3 tablespoons olive oil
2 tablespoons vegetable oil
1–2 medium onions, finely
    sliced
2 carrots, peeled and thinly
    sliced

1 396-g/14-oz can tomatoes,
    chopped, or 450 g/1 lb
    fresh tomatoes, peeled and
    sliced
salt and freshly ground black
    pepper
2 tablespoons finely chopped
    parsley
1 kg/2 lbs potatoes, peeled
    and thickly sliced

Rinse the meat and remove any loose splinters. Drain. Heat both the oils in a large saucepan, and fry the pieces of meat in it, browning them on both sides and taking them out as they are ready. When all the pieces are fried, add the onions and the carrots and sauté them. Add the tomatoes, bring to the boil and return the meat pieces to the pan. They should be covered with the liquid. If not, add a little hot water.

Cover and cook until the lamb is almost tender, approximately 50 minutes. Season with salt and pepper, add the parsley and the raw potatoes. Add enough water to cover them, then cover and cook for a further 20–30 minutes, until the potatoes are soft.

If you want the more special version, cut the potatoes thickly and fry them first, then add them to the meat and cook for a slightly shorter period, about 10 minutes. Or you can serve chips with it.

MELITZANES ME KREAS

Aubergine and Meat Casserole

An interesting alternative to the standard casserole. Prepare as above, but instead of potatoes add 1 kg/2 lbs thickly sliced aubergines for the last 15–20 minutes. As with all the aubergine dishes you are presented with the dilemma yet again: 'To fry, or not to fry?' Much more delicious but also heavier if you fry the aubergines first. Also, they will only need 5–10 minutes' cooking with the meat. (See page 129 for method of preparing.)

Alternatively, instead of aubergines, one can add 1 kg/2 lbs thick round slices of courgettes which have been lightly fried first.

MOSHARI STIFATHO

Beef Casserole with Baby Onions

A stifatho is always made with meat, beef in particular, game, or snails and it contains a little vinegar and a large amount of small onions (the pickling size), normally an equal quantity with the meat. The onions, which are fried whole first and then simmered with the meat, contribute an unusual sweetness to the dish which, combined with the slightly sour taste of the vinegar, produces a very definite and memorable result. In the islands, where they like their tastes strong and definite, they add different spices. Cinnamon is the most universal, but then it may also have 4–5 grains of allspice, or 3–4 whole cloves.

4 tablespoons olive oil
1 kg/2 lbs tender beef, such as top rump, brisket, or braising steak, cut into large cubes
3 tablespoons red wine vinegar
small glass red wine
5-cm/2-in cinnamon stick
5 grains allspice, or ¼ teaspoon ground allspice

1 small sprig of rosemary
900 ml/1½ pints water
2 tablespoons tomato purée
salt and freshly ground black pepper
4–6 tablespoons vegetable oil
675 g/1½ lbs onions, peeled and left whole
1 teaspoon demerara sugar

Heat the olive oil in a large saucepan and brown the meat in it. It will produce a lot of moisture but persevere until it has all evaporated and the meat starts to turn golden. Slowly pour the vinegar over it and, when the steam subsides, add the wine. Then add all the remaining ingredients except the vegetable oil, onions and sugar, cover and cook slowly for 1 hour or until the meat is almost tender.

Heat the vegetable oil in a frying pan and add as many onions in one layer as it will take. Sauté them gently for about 15 minutes, shaking and turning them over until they brown lightly. Lift them out with a slotted spoon and spread them over the meat, distributing them evenly. Repeat until all the onions are done. Sprinkle the sugar over the onions, cover and cook very gently for 30 minutes, until the onions are soft but not disintegrating. Do not stir once the onions have been added, but rotate the saucepan occasionally to coat them in the sauce. Serve with fresh bread.

PASTITSATHA

Spicy Braised Beef from Corfu

This is the celebratory meal in Corfu, reserved for special occasions and large family gatherings. It is the recipe of Spyrithoula Zohiou, who is praised among her relatives for the excellence of her Pastitsatha. *This quantity will serve six people.*

3–4 cloves garlic, peeled and
   finely sliced
½ teaspoon ground cinnamon
¼ teaspoon ground cloves
salt and freshly ground black
   pepper
1.75-kg/3½-lb piece of top
   rump, or rolled brisket
4 tablespoons olive oil

15 g/½ oz butter
450 g/1 lb onions, finely
   sliced (4–5 onions)
2 tablespoons tomato purée,
   diluted in a little hot water
3 tablespoons red wine
   vinegar
450 g/1 lb spaghetti, to serve

In a small bowl, mix together the garlic, cinnamon, cloves, salt and pepper. Make frequent deep slits around the meat and fill them with some of the garlic mixture, pressing it down inside the meat until it is all used up.

Heat the oil and butter in a large ovenproof casserole and seal the meat until lightly brown all over. Take out the meat, add the onions and stir until they start to colour. Put the meat back into the saucepan and add enough hot water to come just below its top surface; then add the tomato purée and salt and pepper. Cover and cook slowly, turning the meat over frequently and stirring the onions to prevent them sticking, until the meat is tender – about 1½ hours.

Alternatively, cook in a pre-heated oven, gas no. 3 (350°F/170°C) for 2 hours, turning the meat and the onions occasionally.

When the meat is tender, put the dish on the hob, slowly pour the vinegar over the meat and let it bubble uncovered for 5 minutes, guarding against the onions sticking. By then, there should be a deliciously reduced sauce, smooth and sweet with the melted onions. If not, take out the meat and cook the sauce, uncovered, rapidly until it is reduced. Discard the string, slice the meat and put it back into the sauce.

Cook the spaghetti in plenty of boiling water until *al dente*. Serve immediately with the sauce over the pasta and the meat on the side.

MOSHARI LEMONATO

Beef Casserole with Lemon

Any kind of stewing beef is suitable for this dish, or brisket. It is equally tasty when cooked with lamb and any kind of stewing lamb can be used, but it is always best with pieces from a shoulder. Serve with plain white rice, or fried or sauté potatoes.

1 kg/2 lbs stewing steak, cut into serving portions	bay leaf
3–4 tablespoons olive oil	salt and freshly ground black pepper
1 medium onion, thinly sliced	3 carrots, scraped and sliced
juice of 1 lemon	chopped parsley
300 ml/½ pint water	

Rinse and drain the meat. In a large saucepan, sauté the meat in hot oil until it looks golden, then take out and add the sliced onion. Sauté the onion until transparent. Add the meat and slowly pour the lemon juice all over. Add the water and the bay leaf. Cover and cook slowly until the meat is tender – between 1–1½ hours. Add the carrots 10–15 minutes before the end of the cooking time. Season to taste, sprinkle with parsley and serve.

Alternatively, add 1 kg/2 lbs prepared potatoes with the meat towards the end of the cooking time. Add the juice of one more lemon and enough hot water to cover the potatoes and cook for a further 20–30 minutes.

HIRINO ME FASOLIA

Pork with Cannellini Bean Casserole

*A very filling and warming dish that is always eaten in the winter,
and a simplified but flavoursome predecessor of the French
cassoulet. Any cut of pork can be used and it should contain
some fat in order to give the beans their rich sweet taste,
characteristic of the dish.*

225 g/8 oz cannellini beans
3 tablespoons vegetable oil
1 medium onion, sliced
1 kg/2 lbs pork, thickly sliced
   and preferably boned
   because of splinters

900 ml/1½ pints hot water
3 tablespoons tomato purée
salt and freshly ground black
   pepper
3 tablespoons finely chopped
   parsley

Pick the beans clean of any grit and soak them overnight in a bowl of cold
water. Rinse and drain them before using. Rinse the meat and drain.
Cover the beans with cold water, and cook until they start to soften, about
45 minutes, or if using a pressure cooker about 5 minutes.

Heat the oil in a large saucepan and fry the onion until it turns slightly
brown. Add the meat and fry together for about 5 minutes, then add the
hot water and the tomato purée. Cover and cook for about 40 minutes.
Season with salt and black pepper, add the parsley and the beans and cook
for a further 40 minutes or until the beans are very soft, almost mushy, and
the whole casserole looks thick and wholesome.

Alternatively, once the beans have been added, cover and cook slowly
in a pre-heated oven, gas no. 2 (300°F/150°C), for about 2 hours.

FASOLIA GIGANTES ME HIRINO

Pork with Giant Beans in the Oven

A delicious alternative to the preceding recipe is to cook pork with the eccentrically named *fasolia gigantes* – the giant beans. This is the trend followed at Hánia, high up in the snow-capped tops of mountainous Pilion, in the winter. There it is cooked either with local, rough, spiced village sausages, or with pork, or even with a mixture of both; either way, it is something to look forward to at lunchtime, after skiing.

This version does not end up in a thick, almost creamy casserole, but in a crisp baked one with the occasional bit of scorched meat and beans.

The ingredients are the same as in the preceding recipe, but instead of cannellini beans use giant beans (or butter beans) and add 2 cloves of garlic, peeled and thinly sliced, 1 stick of celery, thinly sliced, and lots of chopped parsley.

Clean and soak the beans overnight. Drain and rinse them and then boil them in plenty of cold water for approximately 30 minutes, or if a pressure cooker is used, for 2 minutes. Giant beans cook quicker than haricot beans and they should still be a bit hard at the end of this initial cooking. Ideally, they should not overcook and fall apart. Cook the meat as in the preceding recipe, for 40 minutes.

Mix the beans, meat, garlic, celery, parsley, 150 ml/¼ pint hot water, and more seasoning in a large baking dish and spread them out evenly. Bake in a pre-heated oven, gas no. 4 (350°F/180°C), for 40 minutes, without stirring. Check halfway through cooking in case it looks too dry. If it does, add a cupful of hot water and 2–3 more tablespoons of olive oil by sprinkling this all over its surface and shaking the container a little. The amount of evaporation depends on how spread out the beans are. If it is a really large container they will need additional liquid.

HIRINO ME SELINO AVGOLEMONO

Pork with Celery in Egg and Lemon Sauce

This is an outstanding, delicate dish. Some people with fixed ideas about Greek food who think that it is a variation on the theme of 'garlic and tomatoes' find it rather hard to believe that such a delicacy could have been produced in the same arid lands.

As this is a rather special dish, it deserves a better cut of meat, preferably boneless, such as loin of pork, chops or fillet of leg, cut into serving portions. Celery in Greece is completely different from the stalks of celery we are used to in the west. It comes in thin bunches of slender greenery, resembling the continental parsley in appearance and colour. Its taste and aroma are more prevalent than those of the thick-stalked variety. As a result of its texture, a family in Greece would use kilos of it in this dish and, of course, the appearance of the dish in Greece would be different.

1–1.25 kg/2–2½ lbs lean boneless pork, or 4 medium-sized pork chops	600 ml/1 pint hot water salt and white pepper
1 large head of celery	2 eggs
3 tablespoons good vegetable oil	1 tablespoon cornflour diluted in 3 tablespoons cold water
1 medium onion, finely sliced	1–2 lemons

Rinse the meat and drain. Discard the root end of the celery, separate into stalks, trim and rinse individually under cold running water. Using the sharp point of a knife, dislodge any suspicion of grit in between its ribbed back. Cut the celery into 5-cm/2-in pieces, using its leaves as well. Drop the celery into salted boiling water in a large saucepan, about 22–25 cm/9–10 ins, and boil for 5 minutes, then drain and keep aside. In the same saucepan, heat the oil and sauté the meat and then the onion. Neither should get brown but just be slightly transparent. Add the hot water, cover and simmer for 45 minutes, or until the meat is tender. Season with salt and white pepper, add the celery and cook for a further 10–15 minutes until the celery is very tender. Turn the heat off and let it stand for at least 5 minutes before you add the sauce.

Prepare the *avgolemono* sauce as described in *Arnaki Fricassee me Maroulia* (Lamb with Cos Lettuce) on page 259. Pour it slowly all over the meat, rotating the saucepan at the same time. Put back on a very low heat for 5 minutes only, in order to cook the cornflour and thicken the sauce, but on no account let it boil.

This dish, served with a fresh green salad and fresh bread, should be enough, but if you are feeding someone with a large appetite, potatoes are inevitable, either roast or mashed.

HIRINO ME ELIES

Pork Casserole with Olives

An unusual change with the rather brave addition of the black olives that provide a pungency to the tongue that pork dishes normally lack. One should use round, black, fleshy olives, rather than the Kalamata variety which have been soaked in vinegar. Olives that come from Amfissa are ideal for this dish. (There is more information on olives on page 95.)

1 kg/2 lbs lean boned pork
    from the shoulder, or leg or
    fillet, cubed
25 g/1 oz butter
2 tablespoons vegetable oil
1 clove garlic, peeled and
    crushed

1 glass red wine
salt and freshly ground black
    pepper
150 ml/¼ pint hot water
10–12 large black olives

Rinse and drain the meat then pat it dry.

Combine the butter and oil in a frying pan, or a large saucepan, and, when hot, fry the meat rather briskly until it is brown. Add the garlic, fry for 1–2 minutes and pour the wine slowly over the meat. Season with salt and pepper and add the hot water and the olives. Simmer for approximately 40 minutes or until the water has evaporated and a thick sauce remains. Serve with french fries or sauté potatoes.

LIVER, SWEETBREADS, BRAINS, FEET, FRIES, ETC.

In 1972 I went to live with my husband in a flat, overlooking Highbury Fields, in Islington. Soon after that, he introduced me to Chapel Street market and I instantly fell in love with it and over the years made friends with various stallholders. The fishmonger, the fruit stall, the Greek vegetable stall, etc., always look after us very well, but I was particularly thrilled to discover the Offal Shop, halfway down the market, frequented by old-age pensioners and, from then on, by me. They were there because of the amazing low prices, I was there out of choice.

It reminded me a lot of Athens market and so made me feel at home, but, most importantly, it contained all the various internal bits of the animal that are considered the *meze par excellence* in Greece. Daily, there were trays of lambs' and calves' brains, wonderfully fresh sweetbreads, much esteemed by Greeks, lambs' or cow spleens, kidneys, hearts, tongues, pigs' feet and tripe, occasionally lambs' fries (the testicles which the French appropriately call *frivolités d'agneau* and the Greeks, *ameletita*, meaning the unmentionables), lambs' and pigs' heads, etc. One could also order particular things such as lambs' feet or intestines.

Offal, to a foreigner like me, sounded 'awful' so I looked it up in a dictionary. It was defined as 'that which is removed from a thing as worthless, particularly the inedible parts of a butchered animal, and in general meaning refuse or rubbish'. Since then I have felt almost embarrassed to use the word, but we feasted and feasted and introduced our friends to delicacies such as sweetbreads and brains, even though they resisted some of the others, but then, around 1977, high rates forced the shop to close, to the great disappointment of all its followers.

In Greece, there is a whole tradition involving different dishes of *meze*, some more delectable than others, but most of the internal parts of the animal, particularly lamb or young goat, are more highly esteemed than the flesh itself and fetch high prices. Some, like spleen and liver which contain a lot of iron, are considered strength boosters and/or aphrodisiacs, particularly given to people recovering from an illness. Brains, we were always told as children, would put more brains in our heads!

One could argue that Greece being a poor country could afford to waste no parts of the animal. True, perhaps, but what about France where most of the same things are as highly prized? At any rate, who could file sweetbreads under the offal category once they have tried them?

SIKOTAKI ARNISIO

Lambs' Livers

If one ventures into the meat market in the central market in Athens or, indeed, into any Greek butcher's shop, one will see the whole lambs' livers, with other various bits, hanging from iron hooks and most probably dripping blood if they are fresh. This, to the Greek, is a *sikotaria* which basically means liver but which, in reality, contains the lights or lungs, the heart, thymus glands or sweetbreads and the spleen. It all comes out of the animal in one and this is the way it is sold and the way it is eaten. One has to buy the whole package. The younger the animal, the more delicate the taste of the *sikotaria* and the more highly considered. Normally it weighs about 450 g/1 lb. When it is heavier it is not so desirable. In reality then, when a Greek is talking of liver, he really means offal, as a lot of other things are included in the term.

The *sikotaria* is even more highly prized if it comes from a young goat, as it always does on our island, and particularly if it has been an almost wild roaming goat being raised in one of the small deserted islands across the sea such as Yioura or Kyra-Panagia. Then the taste is absolutely delectable. Some parts of the *sikotaria* are more highly prized than others to different people. So, the tiny spleen is treasured with as much regard as the French have for their truffles! I remember years ago I used to be taken out by a friend who would drive miles out of Athens to Varibobi to a tiny *taverna* where their speciality was to serve a *meze* of spleens barely cooked on charcoal. Their taste was so delicious that it still makes my mouth water sixteen years later.

Some people love lights rather than liver, as I do; some with stranger tastes go for the more membranous texture of the heart and some are addicted to even the glutinous, soft, bone-like oesophagus. So, if you order liver in a restaurant in Greece do not be surprised when a plate of a mixture of all the above comes. This is the norm.

SIKOTAKIA TIYANITA

Fried Lamb's Liver

The *sikotaria* is firstly separated into its different parts which are rinsed under cold running water and drained. Then they are sliced into large mouthful portions, coated in seasoned flour and fried quickly in olive oil (ideally) or vegetable oil, but not butter. They are turned over individually, allowing 2 minutes on each side, perhaps a bit longer for lights, but they should not be fried over too high a heat and allowed to dry out or burn. Lights are a terror to fry as they spit a lot, so they are done right at the end (all together) and possibly covered. When the frying is finished, the oil contents of the frying pan are emptied on top of the meat, the juice of a lemon poured over, and more salt and black pepper and a sprinkling of *thymari*, Greek wild mountain thyme, added.

Fresh bread soaked in this oily sauce is wonderful and always large quantities of it are consumed with fried liver etc., particularly in homes where the olive oil is not spared.

SIKOTAKIA ME KRASSI

Calf's Liver in Wine Sauce

For years, when my sister lived in the green suburb of Psychiko – ten minutes' drive from Athens – we used to go to a couple of *tavernas*, almost identical and one right next to the other, in nearby Neo Halanthri. They were particularly pleasing in the summer, when tables were spread all over their large garden overhanging with leafy vines and heavy dark red bunches of grapes and soothed by the fragrant waves of the sweet-scented jasmine, sprawling and merging with the undisciplined and unattended creamy honeysuckle, but also convivially familiar as well as familial, in the winter. When the wind was blowing in the right direction, one would also get whiffs of delectable suspicions from the large barbecue at the back of the kitchen.

The starters were excellent: *melitzanosalata* with the genuine taste from being roasted on charcoal, homemade *horiatika loukanika* – spiced sausages peasant-style, barbecued on charcoal, *taramosalata*, crisp long slices of fried courgette dipped in *tzatziki*, small triangular cheese pies, etc.

Among their even more excellent main meat dishes, were succulent pieces of calf's liver quickly barbecued with the singeing straight marks of the grill visible but still full of juices sealed in them, which I always hurried to order. This is the most common way that one will come across calf's liver in Greece, particularly in the countryside.

My other memory of calf's liver is when I was pregnant with twins a few years ago and feeling as anaemic as *La Dame aux Camellias*, my Greek girlfriend rushed to her Kretan butcher nearby and pleaded with him to make sure that he could provide her with quantities of fresh calf's liver daily, so that she could build me up on delectable liver.

Day by day, she either fried it or cooked it in this delicious white wine sauce and served it as a starter, followed by a selection of wonderful dishes and ending with the juiciest summer fruits that the *laiki* market would exhibit, to make the most gargantuan meals I have ever consumed.

Calf's liver in Greece, surprisingly, is excellent. It is tender and wonderfully tasty.

450 g/1 lb calf's liver	3–4 tomatoes, peeled and
25 g/1 oz flour	sliced (under 225 g/8 oz)
55 g/2 oz butter	salt and white pepper
1 glass white wine	a little chopped parsley

Rinse the liver and cut it into long strips. Drain and dry it, then dip the strips in the flour. Heat the butter in a wide saucepan or frying pan, add the floured strips of liver and sauté quickly on both sides, but do not fry it on too high a heat. This should take about 3–4 minutes altogether. Slowly pour the white wine over the liver and, when it evaporates, add the fresh sliced tomatoes, season, and cook gently for 4–5 minutes.

Sprinkle with the parsley and serve.

FRYGATHELIA

Little Liver and Garlic Parcels

The beautiful Ionian island of Lefkas, still quite traditional with village ladies enwrapped in the dark local outfits, offers Frygathelia, which is one of the most enticing mezethes I have ever tried. The name is derived from the Italian word for liver – fegato. These small parcels of liver are wrapped in caul – the Greek bolia – which is the lining of the stomach; they are served either fried, grilled on charcoal, or roasted in the oven.

285 g/10 oz calf's liver,
    thickly sliced
2 cloves garlic, peeled and
    crushed
salt and a lot of freshly
    ground black pepper

2 tablespoons finely chopped
    parsley
2–3 large pieces lamb's caul,
    rinsed
sunflower oil, for frying
lemon quarters, to serve

Slice the liver into pieces about 10 cm/4 ins long and 5 cm/2 ins wide. Mix the garlic with the seasoning and parsley and place a thin line of this mixture down the centre of each slice of liver. Place the caul in a bowl of warm water to make it pliable; cut large pieces off the caul and gently stretch each one, to avoid it tearing. Roll up each slice of liver and wrap it as neatly as possible in the caul to form a short cigar shape. Secure it with a toothpick and keep in the refrigerator until needed.

Heat a little oil in a frying pan and fry the parcels gently but briefly, for about 2–3 minutes altogether until they are light golden. Take out and discard the toothpicks. Slice each parcel thinly, sprinkle lemon juice over them and serve.

YLIKATHIA

Sweetbreads

*In Greece, it is rather rare that one is able to buy lambs'
sweetbreads on their own as we are fortunate enough to be able to
in the west; they are normally sold along with the liver as I
explained previously. They are easy to prepare and produce a most
delicious appetizer. They look better if soaked in cold water for 30
minutes or an hour before cooking, since this helps them exude
blood and acquire a paler creamy colour and to brown
homogeneously when fried. I have found that it makes no
difference to their taste, but only to their looks.*

675 g/1½ lbs sweetbreads
55 g/2 oz seasoned plain
  flour, for frying
5–6 tablespoons vegetable or
  olive oil

juice of ½ lemon
salt and freshly ground black
  pepper
little chopped parsley, or
  oregano, to garnish

If the sweetbreads are fresh they tend to have attached to them small
pieces of meat, membranous muscle-like bits and, worst of all, the animal's hair. It can all be easily pulled off by hand; then rinse the sweetbreads
in several changes of water.

If frozen, let them defrost first. Immerse them in a bowl of cold water
for at least 30 minutes, drain and then dry them before frying. I have
found that gentle shallow frying achieves the best results, though it is
more troublesome. Deep frying, which is more difficult to control, tends
to destroy some things by making them leathery, or simply overcooks
them to the point of making them look like *apolithomata* – fossils.

Put the seasoned flour on a sheet of paper, place the sweetbreads on it,
get hold of the four corners of the paper, lift it and just shake it about, until
they are all properly coated.

Heat the oil in a frying pan and when quite hot, but not burning or
smoking, lift the sweetbreads one by one, shake off excess flour and place
them in the oil. Give them about 3–4 minutes on each side, turning them
over individually, once only. Lower the heat a little once you have turned
them all over, so they cook slower on the other side. Turn up the heat again
for the last 2 minutes, so that they crisp and brown nicely before they
come out. Lift them out of the frying pan individually with a fork or a slotted spatula, place them on a shallow dish, pour the lemon juice over them,
season with salt and pepper and sprinkle with the parsley or oregano.

NEFRA

Fried Kidneys

Allow two sets per person for an appetizer. Slit and take off the outer membrane they are covered with. Slice each one in half, lengthways, and cut away as much as you can of the white muscle core. Rinse and drain them, then fry and serve them exactly as the sweetbreads above. They should still be a little juicy inside when cooked and not totally dried out.

MYALA

Brains

In Greece, brains are easily available and they can be either lamb's, sheep's or calf's. They are considered a delicacy and a very nourishing one too, so they are always given to children or adults recovering from an illness. For this purpose they are first poached for a few minutes and then a knob of butter is added to them while they are still hot. They are very light and easily digestible when cooked this way.

When used as a *meze* though, once they have been poached, they are either fried whole or sliced thickly, immersed in beaten egg, rolled in flour and breadcrumbs and then fried. Sometimes they are also made into delicious small *fyllo* pastries.

The most important point about brains is that they should be absolutely fresh. When they start looking slightly grey they are undesirable. They all have to be soaked in lukewarm water first for 30 minutes in order to remove the blood, otherwise once they are cooked the blood turns brown. Always handle them gently, and rinse them under cold running water.

At this stage some people laboriously try to take their outer membrane off but I do not bother. If somebody objects to the membrane they can take it off before eating the brains. In any case it is hardly noticeable. Other people try to take it off once they have been boiled.

Bring a saucepan with water, some salt and a tablespoon of wine vinegar to the boil and lower the brains into it one by one. Reduce the heat and simmer – for lamb's brains approximately 4–6 minutes, or for calf's brains 8–10 minutes. Then carefully take out with a slotted spoon. The easiest way to finish them now is to fry them, as below. Alternatively, they can be sliced and served with a dressing of olive oil, lemon and some capers.

MYALA TIYANITA

Fried Brains

Once they have been poached, brains can be rolled in seasoned flour, whole, and fried in a mixture of butter and oil until they are golden all over. The juice of half a lemon is then poured over them and some parsley sprinkled on before they are served. If they have broken into pieces, it makes no difference, you can still proceed the same way with the pieces.

Alternatively, slice them carefully into thick slices, dip them into 1–2 beaten eggs, roll them in seasoned flour and then breadcrumbs and fry them as above. Serve on a platter with the slices overlapping, parsley sprinkled on top and some quartered lemons around. Some sharp vegetables, such as watercress or the Greek *ylistritha* or *roka* (purslane, rocket) or small round, red radishes are occasionally used as garnish.

BOUREKAKIA ME MYALA

Brain Patties

Once the brains have been treated and poached as above, take out with a slotted spoon and, using a sharp knife, try to get as much of their membrane off as you can. Break them into a bowl with a fork, mix with 1 beaten egg per set of brains and 25 g/1 oz grated *kefalotyri*, Gruyère, or Parmesan cheese, season with salt and black pepper and add some finely chopped dill if available, otherwise a little grated nutmeg. Proceed to roll this stuffing with *fyllo* pastry and bake as described on page 167.

GLOSSES ARNIOU LEMONATES

Lambs' Tongues in Lemon Sauce

I know some people have got an aversion to the texture of tongues or to their definite taste. Well, nothing can be done about the texture but a lot *can* be done about their taste. Treated like any other respectable piece of meat and not like pariahs, they respond and reciprocate. Combined with fresh vegetables and herbs or spices, the way we eat them at home in Greece, they produce wonderfully tasty casseroles that are bound to impress and convert the uninitiated. My husband and our twin daughters have been my most celebrated converts, to be followed by various friends.

If you are not particularly squeamish about their skin there is no need to first boil the tongues and skin them. Cook them for 15 minutes longer in the final casserole. Tongues produce quite a glutinous sauce and this is the reason I do not like to cook them only in butter.

675 g/1½ lbs fresh lambs'
    tongues
25 g/1 oz butter
3 tablespoons olive oil, or
    good vegetable oil
1 large onion, finely sliced
3 carrots, peeled and thickly
    sliced
approximately ½ cup
    chopped celery

juice of 1 lemon
3–4 sprigs fresh basil,
    chopped, or if unavailable
    1 teaspoon dried thyme
salt and freshly ground black
    pepper
450 ml/¾ pint hot water
1 kg/2 lbs potatoes, peeled
    and quartered

Rinse the tongues. Cover them with cold water in a saucepan and boil slowly for approximately 10 minutes. Drain and when cool enough to handle peel off their skin and slice them thickly.

Combine the butter and oil in a heavy saucepan and when hot sauté the onion until transparent. Add the tongue pieces and continue to fry fairly quickly for 5 minutes. Then add the carrots and celery and fry, stirring continuously, until the onions turn brown. Slowly add the lemon juice, herbs, salt, pepper and the hot water. Cover and cook slowly for 30 minutes. Add the quartered potatoes, more seasoning, cover and cook slowly for a further 20 minutes, or until potatoes are cooked.

You can cook the tongues without the potatoes, in which case add only 300 ml/½ pint hot water, cover and cook the tongues for 45 minutes. In this case they can be served with plain boiled rice.

GLOSSES RAGOUT

Lambs' Tongues Ragout

The allspice and cinnamon offset the richness of the tongues.

1 kg/2 lbs lambs' tongues
1 large onion, finely sliced
3 carrots, peeled and thickly
    sliced
5 tablespoons olive oil, or
    good vegetable oil
1 227-g/8-oz can tomatoes,
    or 350 g/12 oz fresh
    tomatoes, peeled and sliced
    and 150 ml/¼ pint water

2 cloves
2 grains of allspice, or ¼
    teaspoon ground allspice
small cinnamon stick
salt and freshly ground black
    pepper

Prepare and cook the tongues as for *Glosses Arniou Lemonates* (Lamb's Tongues in Lemon Sauce) on page 277. Add the tomatoes and spices at the stage where the lemon is added above and cook for 45 minutes. Serve with plain boiled rice and a green salad.

SOUTZOUKAKIA SMYRNEIKA

Minced Meat Rissoles with Cummin

This is a very popular Greek dish – a classic. It is one of the most exciting dishes that can be produced from minced meat. With its rich sauce it can make a lovely main course, served with plain white rice, or mashed potatoes. It also makes a popular starter for a dinner party. My grandmother, who came from Smyrna, had a particular knack for *soutzoukakia*, not surprisingly, as they were particularly famous in that region.

When *soutzoukakia* are being fried they produce such a tantalizing aroma that we were always given one out of the frying pan as a special treat, so we always made sure we hung about, like bees waiting for honey!

The following quantities will produce enough for four people as a main course, if served with white rice or potatoes, or they can be served as a starter on their own.

3 thick slices of bread, soaked
in water
450 g/1 lb finely minced beef,
or lamb
1 egg
2–3 cloves garlic, peeled and
crushed
1–2 teaspoons ground
cummin
salt and freshly ground black
pepper

1 glass white wine
25 g/1 oz flour, for frying
3 tablespoons vegetable oil
2 tablespoons olive oil
2 tablespoons tomato purée,
or 1 227-g/8-oz can
tomatoes, preferably
liquidized roughly first
some chopped parsley, to
garnish

Soak the bread in water for 10 minutes and discard the crust. Squeeze the water from the bread and mix with the mince, egg, garlic, cummin, salt and pepper and 3 tablespoons of the wine. (The best results for mixing are always achieved by using your hands.) When properly mixed make long thin shapes, like fat cigars, about the length of your finger (around 15 of them), roll them in the flour and fry in the vegetable oil on medium heat, making sure that they are crisp all over.

In the meantime, put the olive oil in a saucepan and, when it is warm, add the tomato purée dissolved in a cup of water, or add the tomatoes, and the rest of the wine and cook slowly for 5 minutes, stirring and making sure it does not stick. Add the *soutzoukakia* as they come out of the frying pan, roll them in the tomato sauce, add a little more water if needed, cover and cook slowly for 10 minutes. Garnish with chopped parsley.

SOUTZOUKAKIA ME PATATES

Minced Meat Rissoles with Potatoes

It is quite common to add potatoes to the above dish and cook them on top of the *soutzoukakia*. In this case you will need more liquid in the saucepan and double, at least, the olive oil, and need to add a 396-g/14-oz can tomatoes and 150 ml/¼ pint water.

Slice the potatoes thickly and spread them on top, making sure they are rolled in the sauce first. Add more seasoning, cover and cook for 20–30 minutes until the potatoes are done. Shake the pan occasionally but do not stir too vigorously, as the *soutzoukakia* may break.

It becomes really delicious if the potatoes are quickly fried first and then added to the casserole and cooked further in the sauce.

MOUSSAKA

This is without a shade of doubt the best-known Greek dish abroad. Unfortunately, it is usually served, either abroad or in restaurants in Greece, notoriously oily. Primarily, *moussaka* relies on the taste and flavour of the aubergines; if the aubergines look of dubious freshness and quality, it is not worth embarking on making *moussaka*, as it involves a lot of work. People wrongly assume that dubious aubergines can be disguised with a layer of minced meat and a milky white sauce and served to the unsuspecting as a 'glorious' *moussaka*; it will be a waste of time. Having seen and eaten various concoctions of what was called *moussaka*, I now recoil in horror when threatened with it at a dinner party or a restaurant in a Greek tourist resort. *Moussaka* from Makedonia may contain a layer of thinly sliced round potatoes which have been fried first.

Moussaka *should be baked in the oven and by the end it should have a golden crusty top, resembling a thick pie; it is then cut into square or oblong-shaped pieces, about 8 cm/3 ins thick, in order to be served. It should be quite dry by then and the pieces should ideally stay intact. Use a roasting container, either square or oblong, approximately 25 × 25 cm/10 × 10 ins or 39 × 28 cm/15 × 11 ins. Spread the work involved over two days for your convenience; one can easily cook the meat the day before, without the* moussaka *suffering at all. Do not do the same with the aubergines though, if it can be helped; they should be fried on the day. This amount will serve 6 people as a main course.*

1 kg/2 lbs aubergines (large round or elongated variety)
150 ml/¼ pint vegetable oil (about 1 teacup)
1 large onion, finely sliced
450 g/1 lb minced lamb for authenticity, or otherwise beef
1 glass white wine (not *retsina*, but *aretsinoto*)
350 g/12 oz fresh tomatoes, or 1 396-g/14-oz can tomatoes, drained of some of their juice and chopped
½ teaspoon ground cinnamon
¼ teaspoon ground allspice (optional)
salt and freshly ground black pepper
1 teaspoon oregano
25 g/1 oz grated Parmesan, *kefalotyri*, or Gruyère cheese
some chopped parsley

Béchamel sauce
75 g/3 oz butter
75 g/3 oz flour
600 ml/1 pint warm milk
salt and white pepper
25 g/1 oz grated Parmesan or
    Gruyère cheese
2 egg yolks

Topping
55 g/2 oz grated Parmesan,
    Gruyère or *kefalotyri*
    cheese
4 tablespoons toasted
    breadcrumbs (optional)

There is no need to peel the aubergines, just top and tail them. Rinse the aubergines, cut them lengthways in 75-mm/¼-in thick slices and immerse them in salted water, for 30 minutes (as described on page 129). Take them out, squeeze gently, rinse, then squeeze them again. Drain them in a colander and pat dry. Fry them in hot vegetable oil until they become pale golden on both sides; you can either deep-fry them, which is easier but they absorb a lot of oil, or shallow-fry them. In either case, drain them on absorbent paper on a flat platter before serving, so that most of their oil will dribble away.

Meat
Sauté the sliced onion in 2 tablespoons vegetable oil, until it looks glistening. Add the meat and sauté together, stirring, until all the lumps are broken down and the meat starts to change colour. Pour in the wine, add the fresh tomatoes, sliced finely, or the can of tomatoes, the spices, salt and pepper and the oregano. Cover and cook for 20 minutes, stirring from time to time in case it sticks. Then mix in the grated cheese and parsley.

Béchamel sauce
Melt the butter and, away from the heat, gradually add the flour and stir to amalgamate. Return to the heat and gradually add the milk and seasoning, stirring continuously. Simmer for 8–10 minutes, stirring, until it has thickened considerably. Withdraw the pan from the heat, let it stand briefly, then add the cheese and the egg yolks. Stir to amalgamate them. Do not let the sauce boil after this. It should by now be a thick béchamel, to enable it to sit on top of the meat mixture and form a kind of crust.

To assemble, cover the base of the roasting dish with half of the fried aubergines, then spread half of the meat mixture evenly on top of them and cover neatly with the remaining aubergines. Spread the remaining meat and sauce evenly over the top and cover neatly with the béchamel. Sprinkle the grated cheese all over the top, and the breadcrumbs if they are used. Bake in a pre-heated oven, gas no. 4 (350°F/180°C), for 1 hour, until a golden crust is formed all over the top. Let it stand for 5 minutes before serving, in order to be able to cut it more easily.

KEFTETHAKIA SHARAS OR BIFTEKIA

Hamburgers with Herbs

These are always very aromatic with the two mainstay Greek herbs, rigani *(oregano) and* thymari *(thyme), which are collected from mountains and hillsides in the summer and dried in the sun. They are at their best when made with tender and lean minced lamb. They are succulent, absolutely enticing and the best among any other kind of barbecued meat.*
Minced beef can be used, providing it is tender, but somehow it never matches either the flavour or the mouthwatering taste of lamb. Quantities of keftethakia *are easily consumed, so always allow more than usual, particularly if they are to be barbecued.*

2 slices of bread, soaked in
   water for 10 minutes
1 kg/2 lbs minced lamb
1 large grated onion
1 egg
1 tablespoon oregano

2 tablespoons thyme
some freshly chopped parsley
salt and freshly ground black
   pepper
1 lemon, to garnish

Squeeze excess moisture from the bread and discard the crusts. Mix together all the ingredients, in a bowl, by hand. Let this mixture stand for about 1 hour if you have the time.

Make large, round, flattened hamburgers and grill under a hot grill, approximately 3 minutes on each side; or even better place them on an oiled grid and barbecue them approximately 5–6 minutes on each side, according to the strength of the fire. They should be slightly undercooked inside and moist; turn them over once, but do not let them get scorched.

Serve them with quartered lemons on the side of the platter.

SFOUGATO

Courgette and Meat Pie

1 large onion, finely sliced
3 tablespoons olive oil
450 g/1 lb minced beef, or lamb
juice of ½ lemon
150 ml/¼ pint water
1 kg/2 lbs courgettes
salt and freshly ground black pepper
4 tablespoons chopped parsley
2 tablespoons chopped dill, if available
4 eggs, lightly beaten
5 tablespoons milk
55 g/2 oz self-raising flour
75 g/3 oz grated Parmesan cheese
2 tablespoons oil, for the base of baking dish
55 g/2 oz toasted breadcrumbs

Heat the olive oil and sauté the onion until it glistens. Add the meat and sauté, stirring with a wooden spatula and breaking any lumps, until all its water evaporates and the meat browns slightly. Pour the lemon juice all over, add the water, cover and simmer for 20 minutes until almost all the water is gone and the meat is tender.

Top and tail the courgettes and clean them under a running tap. Slice them into thin rounds and add them to the meat. Add some seasoning, stir, cover and cook for approximately 15 more minutes or until the courgettes feel soft; as courgettes produce moisture, avoid adding more water, but if needed add a few tablespoons. The courgettes should not be overcooked though, as they are also going to cook in the oven. Remove from the heat and add the parsley and dill. Beat the eggs with the milk and flour until amalgamated.

When the meat and courgette mixture is slightly cooler, mix in half the grated cheese, as well as the egg mixture. Oil a medium-sized baking dish, approximately 25 × 25 cm/10 × 10 ins, or an oval dish 39 × 28 cm/15 × 11 ins, dust half of the breadcrumbs all over its base and pour the meat and courgette mixture in it evenly. Flatten its surface, sprinkle the remaining grated cheese all over and the remaining breadcrumbs on top and bake in a pre-heated oven, gas no. 4 (350°F/180°C), for 30–40 minutes. Cut into square pieces and serve.

GLYKA
Pastries, Cakes and Preserves

The best introduction to the pantheon of Greek cakes is a visit to a *zaharo-plastio* (a cake shop), particularly a large and reputable one. Every small town possesses one nowadays, even the smaller islands. It was not so long ago when on holiday on islands such as Serifos, Sifnos or Tinos that we all eagerly awaited the arrival of the boat from Piraeus for the replenishing of the empty containers of *baklava* and *kadaifi*, the two basic sweet com-modities that can travel without being affected by the heat. These two cakes are jointly referred to as *glyka tapsiou* – sweets of the special shal-low, flat, large containers, which they are baked in and from which they are sold by the piece. When the boat arrived, blackened, rectangular, empty containers were marched on, and the freshly made contingents were marched out, triumphantly, to the island's grocer shops – the *Pantopolia* – that sell everything as their Greek name suggests.

A visit to a *zaharoplastio* in any of the large cities, Athens, Piraeus, Thessaloniki, Patra, or Volos, is impressive and unforgettable. In Athens there are whole suburbs that are renowned for the quality of their *zaharo-plastia*, like Nea Smyrni or Kiffisia or even Agia Paraskevi. In these shops there are row after row of large impressive glass-fronted cabinets filled with delights of all kinds, shapes, colour and size, which resemble luxuriant courtesans in repose.

Petits fours made of marzipan in pastel colours faithfully copying tiny pears, strawberries, tomatoes, onions or even garlic on one side and tiny animals such as mice, piggies, etc., on the other, excite and delight the imagination of children and some adults. While behind are the chocolate cabinets, filled with tray after tray of mouthful-sized dark chocolates – coated toasted almonds, walnuts, glacé cherries, or chocolates containing sweet liqueur fillings such as Cointreau, Benedictine, Grand Marnier, or Framboise.

On the opposite side is a cabinet glittering with colour, for everything in it is wrapped individually in soft silver, gold or metallic red and blue foil, all resembling participants in an extravagant *bal masquer*; these contain small individual pieces of traditionally honey-coated cakes such as *baklava* or *kadaifi* or wonderfully rich, sugar-melting *marrons glacés* and all kinds of other sugared follies.

On shelves on the walls there is a rich display of golden flat boxes with see-through covers that exhibit elongated sticks of warm honey-coloured caramelized pistachio nuts, almonds and hazelnuts.

Further on, you can see cabinets with trays of *koulourakia*, or *voutimata* as they are called – literally something to dip in coffee or tea. These are lightly sweet, shortbread-variety cakes in neat round shapes. There are also trays of snow-white *kourabiethes* – little shortbread cakes containing almonds and dusted liberally with icing sugar, traditionally made in Greek homes during Christmas, Easter or for celebrating someone's nameday.

Brioche-type cakes, freshly made, of all shapes are tastefully displayed on top of cabinets and sold by the weight; and, of course, trays of *loukoumia* – Turkish delight as it is known abroad – which is supposed to have originated from the Aegean island of Chios, and was originally made with mastic, the main produce of the island. The best *loukoumia* in Greece are those made on the island of Syros and William Miller writes on the subject that the *loukoumia* industry there was: 'Established by a refugee from Chios in 1822; the superiority of the Syra *loukoumia* is due to the water on the island and even there only the water of certain springs is suitable. *Loukoumia* was originally made of otto of roses and Chian mastic; at present it is composed of sugar (imported from Austria), starch, vanilla, mastic from Chios and pistachio.' (W. Miller, *Greek Life in Town and Country*, London 1905, p. 288.)

There is also the inevitable cabinet with all kinds of *bâtons salé*, some of these fragrantly spiced with coriander seeds or cummin and others with a salted almond in the middle; all, slightly salted and extremely appetizing, are offered with drinks in the early hours of the evening.

Right in the middle of a *zaharoplastio* lies the heart of the place: the large refrigerated, glass-fronted unit with the supremely rich fresh-cream cakes that are referred to as *pastes* in Greek. These range from the pure white almond follies called *nougatines* – which are my favourite – the dark *sokolatines*, the *chicagoes*, the *milles feuilles*, profiteroles in individual bowls, éclairs, cakes made with fresh oranges or with peaches, or apricots, strawberries and fresh cherries, all of them exquisitely decorated with lashing of thick *crème chantilly*. Next to these individually sliced cakes are always a few large round *gâteaux*, soft and creamy and a delight to the eyes.

On special Saints' days like St George's, or St Nicholas's, or Peter and Paul's day, Greeks celebrate the equivalent of western birthdays – their own namedays. On such days the house is open to friends and relatives who can come and go at any time they like through the afternoon and evening without prior arrangements, to give their good wishes. Those who cannot make it phone or send telegrams or send cakes through a *zaharoplastio*. One can imagine the pandemonium in a Greek household on such a day. All day the telephone is ringing interrupted only by the door bell. Everybody comes loaded with large colourful boxes of all sorts of wonderful *gâteaux* or a collection of individual cakes or any of the sugared follies that a *zaharoplastio* exhibits. All the *zaharoplastia* are making frenetic preparations on such occasions, trying to meet the special demand of the day. For us, the children, these days were quite blissful and exciting.

One was bound to have at least two or three friends named Maria, so on the fifteenth of August, when their nameday was celebrated, this added up to quite a number of fresh cream cakes or home-made slices of *karythopitta*, or *baklava*. *Hronia Polla* – many happy returns – was the password on such occasions.

In Greece it is customary, in general, for people just visiting each other to bring boxes of cakes, and all happy events in one's life are celebrated with cakes and sweets. A birth, an engagement, a baptism, one's entrance to university or a promotion at work, they all call for cake-feasting.

Inevitably a *zaharoplastio* always exhibits large containers of the Greek honey-coated nutty cakes of *baklava* and *kadaifi* and one of fresh *galaktoboureko*. One of the earliest references to a celebratory meal in Ancient Greece – a symposium – is: 'Seven couches and as many tables crowned with poppy cakes and linseed and sesame and among the flagons, honey cakes.' (*Early Greece*, Oswyn Murray, London 1980,

p. 199.) Could these honey cakes be a distant relative to our *baklava*?

Lastly, a *zaharoplastio* always possesses a glass-fronted, refrigerated unit specially for ice-cream, *parfaits*, *granitas*, *cassata* and *pralina*.

Some *zaharoplastia* are very popular for their cream cakes, Delice, Bokolas, Flokas, Papaspyrou, Elliniko in Athens, Vitis in Nea Smyrni, Varsos in Kifissia; others are famous for their ice cream – the most famous and popular of all is Stani in Piraeus, renowned for its wonderfully rich and sticky *pagoto kaimaki* flavoured with quantities of mastic (see page 322). Of course, Athenians have their own little esoteric places in some remote corner of Athens or the suburbs that dedicate themselves completely to the art of ice-cream-making and use a lot of seasonal fresh fruit.

Unlike western habits, Greeks do not finish their meal with cakes but with fresh fruit. Cakes are kept for social occasions in between meals and served with black coffee.

Early afternoon, when waking up from a siesta, is the most common time for cake-eating. At the same time people arrange to meet their friends in their favourite *zaharoplastio*, where an assortment of cakes may be consumed, and a shopping trip always includes a visit to a *zaharoplastio*. Almost all of them having sitting arrangements spread all over the pavements, squares or public gardens for the spring, summer and autumn, and inside for the winter. It is simply the Greek way of life, to sit in a *zaharoplastio* and watch the world go by. An outing to a *taverna* is almost always followed by a visit to a favourite *zaharoplastio*, either for some special cake or a cool ice-cream followed by coffee. Sometimes we travel for miles from one corner of Athens to the opposite or down to the coast in order to have the *zaharoplastio* 'fling'. Pahos in Paleo, Faliro, near the sea, was our favourite place for an *ekmek kadaifi* – *kadaifi* with a layer of thick cream and a portion of their special ice-cream on top, at two or three o'clock in the morning. Later on, Sweet Home was opened a little further down the coast with an excellent ice-cream, so our loyalties were divided. A visit to cool Kifissia for a dramatic ice-cream Alaska that arrived at the table blazing alight was not considered unusual in the middle of the night; or a visit to Bokolas in Kolonaki Square for a plate of hot, honey-drenched *loukoumathes*. Greeks are late-nighters and it is in the course of the night that large quantities of cakes are consumed in the way other people in other countries would consume drink. Athens, Piraeus, suburbs and coast, as well as other major cities, Thessaloniki, Patra, etc., are bustling with life until the early hours of the morning. Greeks are very high spirited in the night but naturally not so in the morning! In order to appease my husband I admit publicly that I also belong to this category, and suffer with typically Greek bad temper in the mornings.

In the course of the day, one may visit a slightly different *zaharoplastio*, a *galaktopolion* as they are called – a shop for milk and milky products. There is still a whole range of them crowning Omonia Square in Athens. These were originally connected to small farms in Maroussi or Kifissia, as public outlets for their products. Here, one primarily has that other Greek speciality, strained, thick, wholesome yoghurt – *yiaourti sakkoulas* – served coated in thick, glowing honey and dotted with walnut halves, an altogether delicious combination. The same almost instant dessert is eaten quite a lot at homes and it is also served to visitors in the Greek villages and the countryside where they would be proud not only of their rich, deliciously creamy yoghurt, but also of their own walnuts, and some families also of their own honey.

My favourite place for yoghurt and honey is a little place called Doris in Praxitelous Street in Athens. My most recurring dream throughout my childhood and my youth was of a Utopian visit to a *zaharoplastio* where I was let free to indulge in devouring whatever took my fancy; I am also certain that Hans Christian Andersen was inspired by a typical Greek *zaharoplastio* in writing his fairytale, *The Gingerbread House*.

GALAKTOBOUREKO

Custard-type Pie

Since I spent my infancy in the years during the German occupation drinking powdered milk I have acquired an aversion to it; its mere smell makes me turn yellow. As a result I avoid milky things, milky puddings in general. *Galaktoboureko* came under this category until, in the summer of 1963, I went to the beautiful island of Paros, in the Kyklathes. Every early evening when we came down to the waterfront through the cobbled whitewashed alleys, the atmosphere seemed to be permeated with a wonderful hot, vanilla-scented baking aroma. It did not take me long to discover that the aroma belonged to the large black rectangular containers – the *lamarines* – of the hot, freshly baked, golden-topped *galaktoboureko* as it came out of the local bakers' ovens.

The temptation was too great; I tried the local *galaktoboureko* and I became a convert. This was obviously the speciality of the island and I have never had such splendid *galaktoboureko* since, unless it was homemade.

Paros was famous in the antiquity for its beautiful, strong, white marble; modern Paros exhibited uncountable charms; among them hundreds of tiny, dazzling white churches (almost each family possess their own little church), its traditional Aegean architectural simplicity, crystal-clear, literally emerald waters, an eccentric boatman with the name of Kombos (the Knot) a tiny, humble restaurant, frequented by the local fishermen every evening, with a large, awe-inspiring owner who, if he liked you, served you beautifully fried fresh squid from the catch of the day, in silence, along with other homemade dishes that his wife cooked behind the counter, and if he did not like you, always in silence, he just showed you the door; and now it had also become the island of splendid *galaktoboureko* for us.

> On Alonnisos and other Aegean islands they make a similar version called galatopitta. This is made with cinnamon and nutmeg powder sprinkled in between the layers of pastry instead of with the metropolitan vanilla flavouring.
> Galaktoboureko *is at its best eaten fresh, preferably when it is still warm, but is still good the next day. No need to keep it in a refrigerator unless the weather is particularly hot. For more detailed information on* fyllo *and how to handle it see the recipe for Spinach and Cheese Pie on page 157. This quantity will serve 8–10 people.*

850 ml/1½ pints creamy milk
1 vanilla pod, or 3–4 drops
   vanilla essence
100 g/4 oz semolina
25 g/1 oz unsalted butter
6 eggs
225 g/8 oz caster sugar
Pastry
1 450-g/1-lb packet *fyllo*
   pastry

110 g/4 oz unsalted butter,
   melted
Syrup
170 g/6 oz caster sugar
150 ml/¼ pint water
1 cinnamon stick, or some
   lemon peel
1 tablespoon lemon juice

Bring the milk with the vanilla pod to the boil gently. (If using vanilla essence do not add it yet.) Withdraw from the heat, take the vanilla pod out and gradually add the semolina to the milk while stirring continuously with a wooden spatula. Return to a gentle heat and cook for about 5 minutes, stirring continuously, until the mixture has thickened. Take off the heat, mix in the butter and let it cool for 10 minutes.

Beat the eggs with the sugar until pale and fluffy and gradually add to the cooled mixture while stirring. If using vanilla flavouring add it at this stage. Return to a gentle heat for a further 2–3 minutes, stirring continuously, then withdraw from the heat. While working with the pastry, stir the mixture occasionally to prevent a crust forming on top.

Butter a roasting dish approximately 39 × 28 × 20 cm/15 × 11 × 8 ins. Prepare the *fyllo* pastry and fill in exactly the same way as on page 157. Bake in a pre-heated oven, gas no. 4 (350°F/180°C), for 45 minutes until pale golden. Take out and cool for 10 minutes while you make the syrup.

Dissolve the sugar in the water, add the aromatics and lemon juice and boil gently for 5–7 minutes until slightly thickened. Let the syrup stand for 5 minutes, then remove the aromatics and slowly pour all over the *galaktoboureko*. Once the syrup has been absorbed, cut and serve.

BAKLAVAS

Honey and Almond Cakes

Baklavas or something very similar is described by the 2nd century AD Greek writer Athinaeos, from the Greek colony of Nafkratis in Egypt – modern-time Alexandria, in his famous work *Deipnosophists*. Considering the fame and popularity of Attic honey and almonds it is not surprising that these would have been used in a multitude of dishes.

GLYKA

This is a sumptuous cake, suitable for a large gathering and not difficult to make. Left covered at room temperature, it will keep for days even if it does become a little drier. This quantity will make approximately sixteen medium-sized pieces. Allow two per person.

Filling
450 g/1 lb walnuts, coarsely
   chopped
55 g/2 oz sugar
1 teaspoon ground cinnamon
Syrup
225 g/8 oz caster sugar
   (approx. 2 teacups)
300 ml/½ pint water

2 cinnamon sticks
1 tablespoon lemon juice
some lemon peel
2 tablespoons Greek honey
Pastry
450 g/1 lb *fyllo* pastry (1
   packet)
170 g/6 oz unsalted butter,
   melted

Mix all the filling ingredients in a bowl.

Liberally butter the base and sides of an elongated or round, as is more familiar in Greece, baking dish. Measure the length of the *fyllo* against the baking dish roughly and, allowing 2 cm/1in extra approximately for shrinkage, cut to length with a sharp knife.

Brush each layer of *fyllo* with melted butter and spread over the base of the container as evenly as possible. (A few folds here and there will not mean the end of the world or your cooking career!) Once you have used 5 layers of pastry, sprinkle a thin layer of filling all over the surface and add 3 more layers. Sprinkle a thin layer of filling and place 2 more sheets of *fyllo* on top. Sprinkle on all the remaining filling, spreading it evenly, and cover with 7–8 more layers of *fyllo*, brushing individually with butter. Fold any excess pastry on either of the sides over the filling and brush it with butter.

(Alternatively, spread 8–9 sheets of pastry on the base and sprinkle all the filling evenly on it. Cover with 7–8 sheets of pastry.)

Brush the top layer liberally with butter in order to get it crisp and golden. Trim any excess pastry with a small sharp knife, keeping in mind that it will also shrink. Cut the top layers of *fyllo* carefully, either diagonally into diamond shapes or straight, which will result in square or elongated pieces. Be careful not to cut right down to the base, but only the top layers. This is done in order to make cutting and lifting the pieces out, once it is cooked, much easier and efficient.

Using the tips of your fingers, sprinkle drops of water all over the surface, in order to prevent the pastry from curling up, and cook it in a pre-heated oven, gas no. 5 (375°F/190°C), for 15 minutes; lower the heat to gas no. 4 (350°F/180°C) and cook for a further 20 minutes.

In the meantime, prepare the syrup. Place all the syrup ingredients, apart from the honey, in a saucepan and stir to dissolve the sugar. Simmer for 6–8 minutes, add the honey and simmer for a further 5 minutes until it thickens slightly. Let the *baklava* cool down then pour the hot but not boiling syrup slowly all over, through a strainer. Let it stand and absorb the syrup.

KADAIFI

Nut Pastry

Kadaifi, in Greece, is almost always rolled in individual servings resembling portions of shredded wheat, and then baked, rather than cooked in one large unit like the *baklava*, which is sliced in individual portions later. There is only one exception to this rule: *Kadaifi Yiannotiko*, a variation of this recipe, named after the old provincial town of Yiannena in western Greece, well known for its beautiful lake. *Kadaifi Yiannotiko* is really a cross between a *baklava* and a *kadaifi* as it contains both kinds of pastry: *fyllo* used at the base and the top and sandwiched in between the thin, thread-like dough of *kadaifi* with a layer of whatever type of filling is used, walnut or almond, spread right in its middle.

If you find rolling individual portions too intricate and time-consuming, you can spread half of the pastry on the buttered base of the container, spread the filling evenly all over, and cover with the rest of the dough.

Filling
350 g/12 oz walnuts or
  almonds, coarsely chopped
55 g/2 oz sugar
1 egg, slightly beaten
2 tablespoons brandy
1 teaspoon ground cinnamon
  if walnuts are used, or
  1 tablespoon grated lemon
  peel for almond filling
Pastry
450 g/1 lb thread-like *kadaifi*
  pastry

170 g/6 oz unsalted butter,
  melted
1 tablespoon ground
  cinnamon, for the top
  (optional)
Syrup
450 g/1 lb caster sugar
450 ml/¾ pint water
1 tablespoon lemon juice
1–2 pieces of lemon rind

Mix all the filling ingredients well, in a bowl. Brush a large baking dish with butter. Pull a small handful of pastry lightly and spread it flat on a wooden board or a marble slab. Place a large tablespoon of filling at one end of the pastry and roll the pastry tightly over it, making sure the filling is securely enclosed. The result should resemble a cylindrical fat parcel, about 10 cm/4ins long maximum.

Place these parcels in rows in the baking dish, leaving a little space between them, otherwise they do not crisp on the side, they stick to each other and become soggy once the syrup goes on them. There should be approximately 15–20 pieces by the time you finish. Heat the butter and pour 1–2 tablespoons over each piece of *kadaifi*.

If you decide to follow the alternative method, divide the pastry in two and spread one half lightly and evenly over the base of the dish. Spread the filling evenly on top and cover with the rest of the pastry, handling it lightly again. Flatten the surface without pressing down heavy-handedly. Pour the melted butter all over the surface.

Bake in a pre-heated oven, gas no. 4 (350°F/180°C), for 30 minutes; increase the temperature to gas no. 7 (425°F/220°C) and cook for a further 10 minutes. The pastries should have a crisp and pale golden appearance. Let them cool while you make the syrup.

Dissolve the sugar in the water, add the lemon juice and rind, and boil gently for 8–10 minutes, until the syrup thickens slightly. Pour the hot syrup slowly over the cool *kadaifi* and let stand in the dish until the syrup is completely absorbed. Sprinkle a little cinnamon on each piece.

KARYTHOPITTA

Walnut Pie

We sat in a row under his tent, drinking coffee and rum and eating walnuts... Though not so rich as Akrivakes, he gave us water in a silver cup, which was a marvel of art. The Byzantine double-eagle, two snakes, a lion and other emblems were embossed round the rim on the bottom...'
(William Miller visiting an arch-shepherd in Boiotia, from his *Greek Life in Town and Country*, London 1905, p. 218.)

A traditional Greek gesture, as soon as a visitor arrives, particularly in country or island households, is to offer him a tiny glass of brandy, engulfed in the aroma of the muscatel grape, a small plate of walnuts and a thick, revitalizing, small, black coffee.

At the height of the summer, when the glorious fresh fruit preserves have just been made and sealed in their jars, this may be alternated with a perfectly round, fresh, green walnut in its heavenly sweet syrup, balancing expertly in the middle of a silver spoon, and accompanied by a cool, large glass of fresh water.

Walnuts in one form or another, are everywhere in Greece, but their most splendid appearance is in this regal, honey-moist pudding. Karythopitta *is undoubtedly the most representative of Greek desserts, either heavily spiced with the presence of cloves and cinnamon or with the light aroma of the grated peel of sweetly scented oranges. Light and springy, it is almost always crowned with the velvety thick, nectar-like syrup at the end.*

150 g/5 oz unsalted butter
110 g/4 oz caster or
  granulated sugar
4 eggs, separated
150 g/5 oz flour, or 150 g/
  5 oz toasted breadcrumbs
  (1½ teacups)
1 teaspoon baking powder
½ teaspoon ground cinnamon
¼ teaspoon ground cloves
  (optional)

4 tablespoons brandy
grated rind of 1 orange
285 g/10 oz walnuts,
  coarsely chopped
Syrup
225 g/8 oz sugar
300 ml/½ pint water
orange or lemon rind
3–4 cloves
1 tablespoon brandy
2 cinnamon sticks

Cream the butter and sugar until light and fluffy. Add the egg yolks one by one, beating between additions so they are well incorporated. Sift the flour with the baking powder, cinnamon and cloves, if using, or mix the breadcrumbs with them. Add the brandy, grated orange rind and walnuts to the butter mixture and mix well. This step should be done by hand, otherwise if a food processor is used it will pulverize the walnuts and the *karythopitta* will lose its essence.

Whisk the egg whites until they become stiff, then, with a metal spoon, start folding them in, alternating with tablespoons of the flour or breadcrumb mixture, until they have all been incorporated. Butter a flat oven dish or a round cake tin and empty the thick mixture into it. Traditionally *karythopitta* is baked in a flat dish and cut into diamond or square shapes. Cook in a pre-heated oven, gas no. 5 (375°F/190°C), for 40 minutes.

Meanwhile, prepare the syrup as in the previous recipe, bearing in mind that the syrup must be poured hot over the hot *karythopitta* in order to be well absorbed. Strain it. Take the pie out of the oven and cut the shapes you want but leave it in the container. Pour the hot strained syrup slowly all over and let it stand for at least 20 minutes so that it can be absorbed.

Leave the *karythopitta* in its container, placing the two cinnamon sticks diagonally, side by side, on the centre – it will look quite dramatic.

LOUKOUMATHES

Cinnamon and Honey Fritters

Golden and crisp but feathery *loukoumathes*, perfectly round and walnut-sized, coated with rich amber honey and sprinkled all over with cinnamon, can be seen served steaming hot in *zaharoplastia* (cake shops) at all hours of the day. No shopping expedition is complete unless it includes a break with a visit to a favourite spot for *loukoumathes*. Or quite often an evening outing starts with a plate of *loukoumathes*, at a *zaharoplastio*, while a group of friends gathers and then spends an hour or two discussing the merits of this or that favourite restaurant that should be visited for dinner later on the same evening. (Greeks are very late diners.)

The best place for *loukoumathes* in Athens is still the one that my mother would take us to when we were children and to which we now take our own children. Krinos (The Lily) at 87 Aeolou Street, near the main market in Athens, devotes itself almost wholly to serving *loukoumathes*, and from the back of the shop you can catch a glimpse of their huge cauldrons bubbling with the hot oil as morsels of the elastic dough are dropped into it and within seconds emerge puffed up like airy bubbles on to the surface. Apart from the old-fashioned Krinos, where a very characteristic sample of Greeks and Greek life can be observed, there is another small place a little further away in narrow Praxitelous Street, the old shop Doris, where the *loukoumathes* are also wonderful, but ring-shaped.

Loukoumathes are basically made from leavened bread dough, and one wonders how such cheap ingredients as flour, yeast and water, and such a simple process can produce such a sumptuously pleasurable result. They should be light and crisp and not doughy and sticky inside, and they should always be eaten hot. Their hour of glory, though, comes from their platonic relationship with thyme-scented honey. As a small ladleful of golden honey is quickly poured all over them on their way to your table, they are transformed from perhaps an insignificant and bland fritter, to their true self. Eaten immediately, while each of the two participants (*loukoumathes* and honey) still holds to its own status and identity, before they have the time to get better acquainted and amalgamated (thus becoming wet and soggy), crunched and swerved in the mouth in small doses, they reaffirm what they are, the glorious *loukoumathes*.

In most of the Aegean islands, *loukoumathes* are also made traditionally for the workers, when the foundations of a building are laid. On Alonnisos they are called *fouskakia* – little bubbles – and they are also offered at local weddings on large trays which are passed around among the guests, who pick one at a time with their fingers.

Loukoumathes *should never be dipped in honey or any other liquid and thus drowned in sogginess; also they should not be left waiting once the syrupy honey has been spread on them.* Loukoumathes *that are served cold and soggy have no relationship with real* loukoumathes.

14 g/½oz fresh yeast, or 6 g/
¼ oz dried yeast
300 ml/½ pint warm water
½ teaspoon sugar
225 g/8 oz plain flour
¼ teaspoon salt
300 ml/½ pint corn oil, for
frying
1½ teaspoons ground
cinnamon

Syrup
6 tablespoons honey (thyme-
scented Greek honey for
authenticity), or a mixture
of 4–5 tablespoons honey
and about 75 ml/2½fl. oz
water

Dissolve the fresh yeast in half a teacup of the warm water, add the sugar to it, to activate, and let it stand for about 15 minutes in a warm place, until it starts to froth. The liquid must not be too hot as it will kill the yeast cells.

Sift the flour and salt into a bowl and empty the dissolved yeast or the dried yeast into it, mixing continuously. This can be done with an electric mixer. Start adding the warm water, beating all the time. The mixture should be thick but elastic. When almost all the water has been added (it may take 2–3 tablespoons less than the 300 ml/½ pint, beat it for a few minutes until it starts to bubble. Cover it with a thick towel and leave in a warm place for about 2½ hours, until it rises and almost doubles in size.

Have a cup of cold water ready into which you can wet a teaspoon and also the fingers of your hand each time. Heat the oil until very hot but not smoking. Wet the teaspoon so that the dough will not stick on it, take a teaspoon of the dough, and, using your hand, push it down into the hot oil. Within seconds it puffs up and rises to the surface. Repeat this process, wetting the spoon each time, for about 6–7 *loukoumathes* at a time. Turn them over so they become golden all around – it only takes 1 minute. Take them out with a slotted spoon and drain on kitchen paper.

Serve 4–5 *loukoumathes* on each plate, pour a tablespoon of honey all over them and sprinkle on a lot of cinnamon. They should be eaten immediately. Alternatively you can make a lighter syrup by mixing honey and water; stir it well, and simmer it for 4–5 minutes, until the ingredients have been amalgamated. The syrup should be prepared in advance, and does not have to be hot. In fact I prefer the contrast of the cold syrup on the hot *loukoumathes*.

HALVAS

Semolina and Almond cake

This was the pudding that saw us through our childhood. When the huge, blackened frying pan came down off the nail it hung from on the wall, we knew this was going to be *halva* day. My grandmother had a particularly majestic gesture when she stretched to reach for her frying pan: she did it in complete silence.

On such days we were so delighted that we almost flew to school like birds with exhilaration and flew back home again at lunchtime; there we virtually devoured our lunch without any complaints, even though it might have been yet another bean soup, or one of the dishes we dreaded most, leeks and rice, or spinach with rice, and waited for the big moment.

Halva, let me say, is almost miraculously assembled out of very common and cheap ingredients which existed routinely in every household, even in those frugal days that followed the dark years of the German Occupation: olive oil, semolina, sugar and a little cinnamon. Blanched almonds were a bit of a luxury and as such only included for special occasions.

After lunch the frying pan went on the fire with the olive oil. When the olive oil started to smoke the semolina was added while grandmother stirred and stirred and the wonderful aroma rose and filled every corner of the house as the semolina got gradually pale golden, golden and then rich brown. My grandmother had a certain way of taking matters to extremes; and as far as cooking went, she liked her tastes robust and very definite. 'Pale golden' would have been a term that she would have frowned upon with the familiar Greek word *nerovrasto* – insipid! On the same stream of thought she encouraged us never to do things with *misi karthia*, literally – half a heart. 'A pleasure,' she used to say, 'is a pleasure, and it cannot be half a pleasure.' So, in went the olive oil, in this full-hearted way. (Needless to say that her favourite reading was the *Odyssey* which we knew by heart by the age of four. Sometimes, of course, she found herself in trouble when she confronted us with the Aristotelian *pan metron ariston* – moderation in all things. The bridge between the two points was a fragile and difficult one to cross.)

However, back to the *halva*; when the semolina had turned a dangerously deep brown colour, the pan was withdrawn from the fire and the syrup that had been simmering for 4–5 minutes with all the aromatics was poured into the semolina with a very triumphant hissing noise which filled the kitchen with steam and smoke and made our mouths water as the crucial moment we had waited for, all day, approached.

When the syrup had all been absorbed, the deep honey-coloured *halva* was served into small bowls, straight out of the frying pan; no refinements of moulding and unmoulding it, in fanciful shapes.

We sat in the steamed kitchen or outside in the winter sunshine and ate the glorious *halva*, bowl after bowl, with our friends from across the road as no household could possibly consider such a feasting without including all the friends; and bowls of *halva* covered with clean dish towels were sent with us to the immediate neighbours for the unavoidable Greek notion of a *myrothia* – a small sample for the neighbours to enjoy.

Everyone in Greece will recite the golden formula for halva, *which is counting 1, 2, 3, 4. What this means is: 1 cup olive oil, 2 cups semolina, 3 cups sugar and 4 of water. For tradition's sake I will give the quantities in the same manner. Nowadays, people reduce the amount of sugar and also instead of olive oil they may use sunflower seed oil or a mixture of both. My sister Maria who makes an excellent halva uses only 2½ cups of sugar and she keeps half a cup undiluted which she adds at the end as you will see below. This quantity will make enough to serve six to eight people.*

1 cup olive oil	2½ cups sugar
2 cups coarse rather than	4 cups cold water
smooth semolina, if	1 cinnamon stick
available	1 teaspoon ground cinnamon,
55 g/2 oz blanched almonds	for sprinkling on top

Put the oil in a large, heavy-bottomed saucepan over medium heat and when it is almost smoking hot gradually add the semolina, stirring continuously until it turns light brown. Reduce the heat, add the almonds and brown together, stirring – it is a matter of taste and courage how brown you will let it get.

In the meantime, dilute 2 cups of sugar in the water, add the cinnamon stick and boil for 3–4 minutes. Withdraw the semolina from the heat, remove the cinnamon stick and add the hot syrup while stirring. Return to a gentle heat and keep stirring until the mixture looks smooth. When almost all the moisture has been absorbed add the remaining sugar. (This trick will make the *halva* stay grainy and not lumpy.)

Cover the *halva* with a clean tea towel and let it stand for 10 minutes to absorb moisture. Empty it into a fluted mould or a cake tin, and when cold unmould onto a platter and dust all over with cinnamon.

HALVAS RINA OR HALVAS FOURNOU

The identity of Rina remains a mystery. Was she a village girl or a village? It is occasionally called halvas fournou – *baked halvas – which is exactly what it is and, to my eyes, it is identical to the small slices of samali we used to buy from wandering sellers. This recipe which is the best among the ones I have tried comes from my friend Vera Kyriakou.*

¼ cup ground nut oil
110 g/4 oz demerara or
    ordinary sugar
4 eggs
5 tablespoons milk
3 teaspoons baking powder
3 tablespoons *anthonero* –
    lemon blossom or rose
    water

½ teaspoon ground cinnamon
225 g/8 oz semolina
110 g/4 oz skinned almonds
Syrup
170 g/6 oz caster sugar
300 ml/½ pint water
1–2 tablespoons *anthonero* –
    lemon blossom or rose
    water

Beat the oil and sugar in a food processor. Add the eggs one at a time, beating between each addition, and then the milk and all the remaining ingredients except the almonds. Beat well. Reserve 18 almonds and add the rest to the mixture. Mix briefly so they are chopped coarsely. The mixture will appear quite liquid at this stage.

Oil a small Pyrex or roasting dish and spread the mixture evenly in it. Decorate with the whole almonds and bake in a pre-heated oven, gas no. 5 (375°F/190°C), for 20–25 minutes.

In the meantime, prepare the syrup by diluting the sugar in the water and boiling gently for 8–10 minutes until lightly thickened. Add the lemon blossom water and let it cool a little.

Take the halva out of the oven, cut it into diamond-shaped pieces, pour the syrup all over and let it be absorbed before serving.

FLOYERES ME MILA

Flute-shaped Cakes with Apple Filling

Floyeres – flutes – are usually small individual pastries filled with walnuts like a *kadaifi* and bathed with syrup.

These unusual *floyeres*, made by the mother of a friend who comes from the island of Sifnos, have an apple filling. They are never bathed in syrup, and can be eaten hot or cold. Cover them with a clean tea towel or place them in a biscuit container. Never place anything wrapped in *fyllo* pastry in the fridge as it absorbs moisture and becomes soggy.

If you want to make the walnut-filled kind, use the same filling and syrup as for *Kadaifi* on page 293 and fill them as described below. Pour syrup over them and sprinkle with chopped pistachio nuts.

Filling
675 g/1½ lbs cooking apples
juice of 1 lemon
55 g/2 oz sugar (3–4 tablespoons)
3–4 drops vanilla essence
25–55 g/1–2 oz raisins, rinsed and drained
½ teaspoon ground cinnamon
110 g/4 oz coarsely chopped walnuts

Pastry
110 g/4 oz melted butter
225 g/8 oz *fyllo* pastry (about ½ packet)

Decoration
25 g/1 oz icing sugar
1 teaspoon ground cinnamon (optional)

Peel, quarter and core the apples. Drop them in acidulated water to prevent them from discolouring. Drain and place in a saucepan with the sugar. Stir over a very gentle heat until they produce liquid. Avoid adding any water as the final result should be quite thick. Simmer until soft, about 6–8 minutes, then add the vanilla, raisins, cinnamon and walnuts.

Cut the *fyllo* pastry down the middle, lengthways, and cover half of it with a clean tea towel to prevent it from drying out. Brush each sheet of pastry with melted butter and fold it in the middle, lengthways and brush again the new half strip. Place a large tablespoon of the apple filling at one end. Fold the elongated sides slightly over the filling and roll it up in a cylindrical thin parcel, sealing the filling in securely. Place them in a buttered baking tin, leaving a little space between them. Brush the top of each with a little melted butter and cook in a pre-heated oven, gas no. 5 (375°F/190°C), for 30 minutes, until they look golden.

As soon as they come out of the oven, sprinkle them with sifted icing sugar, and with a little ground cinnamon if you wish.

MELOPITTA SIFFNOU

Sifnos Honey and Cheese Pie

An Easter speciality from this beautiful Aegean island. Sweet pastries using fresh unsalted cheese – *myzithra* – are traditional in the Kyklathes. In Santorini for instance the Easter speciality is *militinia* – small pastries filled with *myzithra*, sugar and mastic (see page 322). However, the thyme-scented honey makes the Sifnos *melopitta* unmistakable.

Use quark, or Greek Cypriot anari cheese or Italian ricotta mixed with cream cheese in equal proportions. This pie will serve six to eight people.

Shortcrust Pastry
110 g/4 oz unsalted butter
220 g/7 oz plain flour, sifted
   with a pinch of salt
45 ml/3 tablespoons cold
   water
Filling
4 eggs, beaten

55 g/2 oz sugar
500 g/1 lb 3 oz *quark* cheese
   (see above for alternatives)
3–4 tablespoons Greek,
   thyme-scented honey
1 teaspoon ground cinnamon

Rub the butter and flour to the consistency of breadcrumbs. Add the water and knead briefly. This can be done successfully in a food processor. Let the pastry rest in a refrigerator for 10 minutes, then roll it out thinly on a floured surface and use it to line the base and sides of a 25-cm/10-in tart dish.

Beat the eggs, add the sugar and beat together until light and fluffy. Add the cheese, honey and half the cinnamon and beat briefly until well incorporated. Spread evenly in the pastry flan, place on a baking sheet in a preheated oven, gas no. 4 (350°F/180°C), and cook for 50–60 minutes until light golden. Take out and sprinkle with the remaining cinnamon while still hot.

AMYGTHALOTA

Almond Pears

There cannot be a feast on a Greek island without large trays filled with snow-white, pear-shaped or sometimes star-shaped, freshly made little sugared almond cakes. They appear at weddings, baptisms, namedays and also on important religious holidays, which may vary from island to island according to its patron Saint; however, they are Panhellenic on the 15th of August – the Virgin's Day – which is celebrated from one corner of Greece to the other, with its focal point on the Aegean island of Tinos, where the faithful pilgrims arrive in thousands on over-crowded boats and sleep around the church waiting for a miracle to happen.

It is a pure delight to watch the island women sitting on their doorsteps on sunny days, skilfully shaping in their palms the little pears or stars or occasionally other improvised shapes.

Almond trees are like olive trees – they are everywhere in Greece; they flourish with little attention and are sprayed once or twice in early summer to help them keep their green fruit. Green, fresh almonds – *tsagala*, as they are called – are also delicious; once their green skin is peeled either with a knife or broken with a flat stone, the soft, brilliant white almond inside is crunchy and very juicy and aromatic. These can be seen for sale in baskets in the Greek shops in London, in the spring, as they are flown from Cyprus. At about the end of July the almonds are ready to be picked; this is when their green skins start to split, unveiling the golden coloured shells inside.

Picking them is not such an easy task, as they have to be hit rather hard with a strong, very long and straight wooden pole, normally the upper part of a cypress trunk. At the beginning of August, Greek families unite under their almond trees and the silent hills come alive with the chattering and the laughter of the pickers – a very similar operation to the olive picking that starts in October, only on a smaller scale.

Once the almonds have been picked they must be peeled of their green skins. They are then our familiar almonds in their woody, porous, golden shell as we find them in the shops. The almonds are spread out for 3–4 days in the sun in order to dry before being stored. At this time of the year, Greek courtyards and balconies are covered with almonds and our balcony on the island is also filled with almonds and all the collection of our herbs, as we are desperately trying to dry them before returning to London. As soon as we arrive back in Athens we fill my parents' flat roof terrace with them, for a last spell in the hot sun. It is considered a friendly gesture to give a bag of freshly picked almonds to a departing friend.

GLYKA

303

*Amygthalota are made with a paste of ground almonds, sugar,
vanilla and rose water, in the ratio of 2 parts almonds to 1 of sugar.
They are more interesting when, as on the island of Alonnisos, the
blanched almonds are toasted slightly before they are put in the
mortar and pounded to a powder.*

225 g/8 oz ground almonds
110 g/4 oz caster sugar
3–4 drops vanilla essence, or
    ½ teaspoon ground
    cinnamon

½ teacup rose water
75 g/3 oz icing sugar, to
    decorate

Mix the ground almonds with the sugar and the vanilla or cinnamon and
gradually add the rose water, kneading the mixture to a pliable paste.

Wipe your hands clean, take tablespoons of the paste and shape into little pears or flat stars, or whatever shape you fancy. Arrange them on a tray
and when they are all finished, slowly sift the icing sugar all over them.

Store in a tin, in layers, divided by rounds of greaseproof paper in order
to prevent them becoming too hard.

MELOMAKARONA OR PHOENIKIA

Honey-dipped Biscuits

These are made by all Greek families in the week preceding Christmas.
Great quantities are made in order to have enough for the large Greek
families not only during Christmas and New Year, but for weeks after.
Also platefuls of these as well as *kourabiethes* would be exchanged with
neighbours for the inevitable comparisons and praise.

At home we used to store them in layers in two small earthenware pots
– *pitharia* – in a dark and cool corner of the house but easily accessible to
the children. Huge platters were filled decoratively and stood in prime
positions in the living room, which actually is not a living room at all but
a kind of set piece or showcase in most Greek houses, even today.

*There is also a version of these biscuits which encloses a filling of
chopped walnuts and spices. These are called* Melomakarona
Smyrnis *– a tradition of Greeks from the city of Smyrna on the
Asia Minor coast. The quantities given will make approximately
20 melomakarona.*

150 ml/¼ pint olive oil
75 g/3 oz sugar
4 tablespoons brandy
juice of 1 orange
½ teaspoon ground
   cinnamon
400 g/14 oz self-raising flour
pinch of salt
½ teaspoon bicarbonate of
   soda

Syrup
1 teacup honey
110 g/4 oz sugar
150 ml/¼ pint water
Topping
1 teaspoon ground cinnamon
150 g/5 oz shelled walnuts,
   coarsely chopped

Beat the oil and sugar well, with an electric beater or in a blender. Add the brandy, orange juice and cinnamon and blend. Sift the flour with a pinch of salt and the soda and add it gradually into the oil and sugar mixture, mixing it with a spoon. Knead the dough well for about 10 minutes. If too sticky, add 1–2 tablespoons more flour and mix it well. Knead until it feels soft and pliable.

Flour your hands and take egg-sized portions of dough. Roll and shape them into small oval shapes. Place on an unbuttered baking sheet, and flatten them with the palm of your hand. When all the dough is finished, wet a fork and, pressing it on the surface of each *melomakarono*, draw lines or ridges lengthways.

Bake in a pre-heated oven, gas no. 4 (350°F/180°C), for 25 minutes. Let them cool and harden before dipping them in the honey syrup.

Prepare the syrup by mixing in a saucepan the honey, sugar and water. Bring slowly to the boil, skim with a spoon, then simmer for 4–5 minutes.

Dip the cold *melomakarona* in the hot syrup, three or four at a time only. Let them stand for 1 minute and take them out with a slotted spoon. Place on a decorative platter and immediately sprinkle with a little cinnamon and chopped walnuts. If they are not consumed during the next 3–4 days they should be kept in airtight tins, like biscuits.

KOURABIETHES

Shortbread Snow Cakes

Snowy kourabiethes, half-moon shaped or little round shapes, are traditionally made at Christmas, to symbolize or to substitute that rare, for Greek homes, Christmas luxury, the dazzling white snow. Nowadays, they can be found ready-made in a zaharoplastio all year round and they are also made at home for other occasions, such as namedays, and in the villages and the islands they are encountered even more often at baptisms and weddings.

225 g/8 oz unsalted butter
110 g/4 oz caster sugar
2 egg yolks
1 teaspoon vanilla essence
3 tablespoons brandy
110 g/4 oz almonds

450 g/1 lb flour
1 teaspoon baking powder
1–2 tablespoons rose water
    (optional)
350 g/12 oz icing sugar

Cream the butter, gradually add the caster sugar and beat together until light and fluffy. Beat in the egg yolks one at a time, then the vanilla and gradually add the brandy.

The almonds can be skinned or not, whichever way you prefer. Toast them lightly and chop roughly.

Sift the flour with the baking powder and add to the butter mixture with the almonds. Knead it lightly; it should be quite a firm consistency. Take walnut-sized pieces, pat them into a ball and then flatten slightly between your palms and place them on a floured baking sheet. Alternatively, flatten half of the pastry on to a board, about 2.5 cm/1 in thick, and press half-moon or star shapes out of it with pastry cutters. Repeat until all the pastry is finished.

Bake in a pre-heated oven, gas no. 5 (375°F/190°C), for 20–25 minutes. Sprinkle with the rose water as soon as they come out of the oven. Sift about a quarter of the icing sugar onto a large platter, place the *kourabiethes* on it, while still hot, and sift the remaining icing sugar all over the top.

In a dry climate they survive well for 2–3 weeks, but in a damp climate, where they may lose their crispness after a week, they are best kept in a biscuit tin.

VASILOPITTA

New Year's Eve Cake (St Basil's)

> On the same night, too, [New Year's Eve] takes place the ceremony of cutting 'St Basil's cake' – a large circular mass of *brioche* with almonds and walnuts upon it, which is solemnly cut open, shortly before midnight, by the head of the house. Sometimes a franc or a gold piece is put into the cake, and the person receiving the piece which contains the coin, is supposed to be going to have a lucky year. In the country, after cutting the cake, a fine pomegranate is thrown violently on the ground, so as to scatter the seeds.
>
> (William Miller, *Greek Life in Town and Country*, London 1905, pp. 99–100)

New Year's Eve and New Year's Day celebrations are far more elaborate than Christmas for Greek families. Folklore intertwines with superstition and find their climactic expression in the two-day ritual. The Greek equivalent to Father Christmas or Santa Claus is Aghios Vasilis – St Basil – and he arrives on New Year's Eve as the clocks strike midnight. This is when we, as children, received all our presents which usually also included a pair of new shoes.

All day, during New Year's Eve, there is a definite excitement in the air as people rush about town, doing their shopping and buying presents, allowing themselves folly-buying and entering little smart shops that they will not enter for another year. All the shops, including large markets, stay open until almost 11 p.m., until it is time for everyone to rush home and get ready for the traditional *reveillon*.

People greet and kiss their friends in the brightly lit streets, among the mountains of luxuriously wrapped parcels that everyone is carrying. Everybody stays up on this night, not only to wait for the New Year's arrival, but most often till dawn; even we, the children, were allowed to stay up and join in the light gambling that customs prescribe, the tombola, the *parta ola* – a kind of simplified roulette – until each one of us quietly collapsed with fatigue in various corners. As midnight approached, everyone got more excited and nervous as the various customs have to be observed at that precise moment. Everyone's ears stretched with tension for those unmistakable sounds that announced the arrival of the majestic New Year, the cannons fired from the hill of Lykavittos and the sirens of all the boats in nearby Piraeus, creating pure pandemonium.

With the first signs of these sounds, the head of the family rushed to open the front door in order to allow the old year to make his exit graciously and the New Year to enter triumphantly. At the same time, our mother would turn the lights off and on at the mains, three times.

A bright scarlet pomegranate is always hung by the front door in October, waiting for this exact occasion. As soon as the front door was opened, the by now dried pomegranate would be thrown against the front step, causing it to break and scatter its red seeds like rain everywhere, thus demonstrating metaphorically the myriads of riches, wealth and happiness that will be bestowed on the family during the coming year.

This custom has rooted itself in me so much, as it was dramatically displayed by our father each year, that whenever I set eyes not only on pomegranates but also on their vividly exotic scarlet flowers against the glimmering leaves of the pomegranate trees that grow all over the island in the summer, there is only one predominant image in my mind, that of the innumerable New Year's Eves from our childhood.

Even the wicked *kalikantzaroi* did not dare to appear that night. The *kalikantzaroi* were tiny ink-black, demonic figures, with limping goat-legs, always upright, and semi-human faces, but with little horns on top of their heads and a coiled tail at their back; in fact we always thought of them as little demons are depicted at the bottom of icons. I suppose we diminished their size and rendered them unthreatening, or perhaps our grandmother had purposely described them so. They always had a big naughty smile on their faces as they went rampant in the period between Christmas and Epiphany, when they retreated to their hellish home.

Pots that were broken and things that were spilled inexplicably during this period were always attributed to these spiteful creatures. The Cambridge don John Cuthbert Lawson, in his *Modern Greek Folklore and Ancient Greek Religion*, examines them at length and traces them back to the Pilion Centaurs, where they are supposed to have originated. They piss on fires and they scatter the ashes and other litter; they break the traditional cakes – *kourabiethes* and *finikia* – that are specially made for this period; they steal the meat or they cause the traditional lunch or dinner of goose or turkey to be burned, or to be dropped on the floor. (If this is burned by the local baker, then appropriately he is cursed as a real *kalikantzaros*.) Whenever we were naughty as children, we were referred to as *kalikantzarakia*, and unfortunate babies that are born with congenital malformities are still whispered about among the women as *kalikantzarakia*. Unfortunate ugly men are also referred to as *kalikantzaroi*, since they are always male, and in village communities I have often heard the expression uttered by stubborn girls who are refusing to marry someone suggested through a *proxenio* – marriage match – 'I am not marrying this *kalikantzaro*.'

The *vasilopitta* – St Basil's cake – is the *pièce de résistance*, waiting at a prominent position on the table for the arrival of the New Year, when it should be cut. A coin (a golden English sovereign in affluent households), was always inserted in the pie before it was baked. As soon as the pomegranate has been broken and New Year has come in, the *vasilopitta* is sliced. First and foremost, a piece for *Panaghia*, the Virgin Mary, then a piece for the patron saint of the household (in sailor's families it is most certainly St Nicholas, and even the bakers have got their own saint, Saint Panteleimon, while opticians have Saint Paraskevi), then a piece for our house, and lastly one for each member of the family, including members who happen to be abroad or not present, and a piece for each guest.

All the mystical pieces, those for the various saints and the house, were kept in the *ikonostasi* – the ikon corner – and I remember this used to mystify me so much that I would get up in the middle of the night and watch in case the ikons were finally 'eating' their portions; to my disappointment I was never lucky enough to observe at the right moment...

Whoever found the hidden coin in his piece of *vasilopitta*, amidst the teasing and laughter, was hailed as the luckiest person in the year to come. (I always felt a certain disappointment when no one could trace the coin, which meant that it had gone to the ikons, a bit of a waste I thought as 'they' certainly did not need the luck.)

Considering all the necessary pieces that a *vasilopitta* has to provide, one realizes that it is quite a substantial affair. Quite often there are two or more made if there is a number of guests. They are also successfully made by various respectable *zaharoplastia* (cake shops) not only for the New Year but also through the year, in large plaited shapes as opposed to the traditional round shape of the *vasilopitta*. The best ready-made ones to my taste are those made by Varsos in Kifissia.

The first person to actually enter the house on New Year's Day was very significant according to how lucky this person was considered, or in some cases how unlucky and so unwelcomed. In order to eliminate this risk altogether, my grandmother used to send me out through the back garden very early in the morning. I would then run around to the front door, knock and be let in, thus ensuring the *kalo pothariko*, as it is called, literally a *'lucky footing'*.

On the morning of New Year's Day all the children go around to friends or relatives in small groups and sing outside the door the *kallanda*, ringing their triangles excitedly. *Kallanda* are very similar to the English carols, only they are different for Christmas and New Year. For the occasion of the New Year, the emphasis in the song is on the wishes to the family for a very lucky and happy year – *'Arhiminia ki' Arhihronia ki' Arhi kalos mas Hronos'* – the little voices sang outside, waking us up in the most melodic way that anyone can ever be woken up. Money and cakes dispensed, the little group would fly away to their next stop while its place had already been taken by a new little singer, waiting for his turn.

There are various kinds of different vasilopittes, *but the most successful one I believe is the brioche type with fresh yeast, some attributed to the Greeks of Constantinople and so called* Vasilopitta Politiki. *The shortbread type, made with baking powder but no yeast, is attributed to the Greeks of Smyrna in Asia Minor and so called* Vasilopitta Smyrneiki.

25 g/1 oz fresh yeast
200 g/7 oz caster sugar
150 ml/¼ pint warm milk
1 kg/2 lbs plain flour
½ teaspoon salt
225 g/8 oz butter, melted
7 eggs

1 tablespoon each grated
    orange and lemon rind
1 egg yolk beaten with 1
    tablespoon water
75 g/3 oz flaked almonds
25 g/1 oz raw sesame

Dissolve the yeast with a little sugar in the warm milk. Wait until it is activated and starts to bubble at the surface, then add 3 tablespoons flour and mix well to make a batter. Cover it with a clean tea towel and keep in a warm place for about 1 hour or until it rises.

In the meantime, sift the rest of the flour with the salt in a large bowl, add the melted butter, the 7 eggs, the rest of the sugar, and the grated rinds. Add the risen yeast mixture to it, and knead it in order to amalgamate all the ingredients like a bread dough. It should be rather firm but elastic by now. Cover it again and put in a warm place for about 1½ hours, until it rises and doubles in size.

Butter a large round cake tin, about 26–28 cm/10–11 ins, and line the bottom and sides with greaseproof paper, which you should also butter to avoid sticking.

When the mixture has doubled its size, knead it again to break it down, keep a piece for decorating the top of the cake, and pour the rest into the cake tin. Insert a coin. Make sure the mixture only comes halfway up the sides, so that it has space to rise. Cover and let it stand in a warm place until it again doubles in size.

Brush its surface with the beaten egg yolk and decorate, either by using the reserved dough to write the numbers of the new year in the middle of the cake, or by making a few rosettes, or by simply sprinkling the almonds and sesame all over. You could make a few nominal cuts using scissors.

Bake in a pre-heated oven, gas no. 4 (350°F/180°C), for about 1 hour until the top looks golden. Let it cool and shrink slightly, then unmould and remove the greaseproof paper.

TSOUREKIA PASHALINA

Easter Cakes

50 g/2 oz fresh yeast
5 tablespoons warm water
1 kg/2 lbs plain flour
a little salt
6 eggs, separated
225 g/8 oz caster sugar
150 ml/¼ pint warm milk
225 g/8 oz butter, melted

3–4 drops vanilla essence
1 teaspoon *mahlepi*, ground
   to a paste in a mortar
Topping
1 egg white, lightly beaten,
   for a light finish, or 1 egg
   yolk for a dark

Dissolve the yeast in the water; leave to rise for 30 minutes in a warm place. Sift the flour and salt into a bowl and make a well in the centre. Beat the egg yolks and sugar together until smooth. Beat the egg whites until they form soft peaks.

Pour all the ingredients into the centre of the flour and draw in the flour to make a dough. Gather into a ball, sprinkle with flour, cover and leave in a warm place to rise for 2–3 hours. When almost doubled in size, knead it again for 5–10 minutes, take small pieces from it, roll them on a floured surface and shape into round shapes, or make three 18-cm/7-in strips and plait together. Scarlet Easter Eggs (see below) can be stuck upright in their middle. Place them on a greased baking sheet and leave to rise in a warm place for 1½ hours. Brush with the beaten egg white or yolk and bake in a pre-heated oven, gas no. 5 (375°F/190°C), for 40–45 minutes until golden.

PASHALINA AVGA

Scarlet Easter Eggs

'Underneath their diary along with their little school secrets, they also hide other secrets together with ochre-studded old recipes for honey-drenched cakes, for the Phoenikia, the almond marzipan and crunchy shortbread, and more of those of the spoon preserves, mastic, citrus, fig, bergamot, bitter orange, watermelon and tiny aubergine, together with the tiny sachets of scarlet paint for the prescribed eggs of Easter.'

(*Monemviassiotises* by Yiannis Ritsos.)

Ritsos's 'prescribed eggs of Easter' can be seen in mounds in every house and every cake shop, bright and shining scarlet. Traditionally these are painted on the Thursday of Holy Week. These hard-boiled eggs are cracked among friends and relatives round the Easter table with a lot of teasing and merriment and the cries of *Hristos Anesti* – Christ has risen. Together with *Kalo Pasha* – Happy Easter – they are the two phrases one hears resounding everywhere as people embrace each other.

25 brown eggs (for best results brown is better than white)
1 sachet of scarlet paint (obtainable from Greek shops), enough for up to 50 eggs
1 cup of red malt vinegar
olive oil, for polishing them

Rinse the eggs in warm water. Dissolve the paint powder in a cup of boiling water. Fill an old (it may get stained), large saucepan with cold water, add the vinegar and paint and mix well. Put it on a very gentle heat and, using a spoon, place the eggs in carefully, one by one.

Let them boil very gently, uncovered, for about 30 minutes. Cover a platter with kitchen paper. Take out the eggs with a slotted spoon and drain on the paper. As soon as they are cool enough to handle, dip some cotton wool in the olive oil and polish each egg for a really glossy effect.

YIAOURTI

Yoghurt

Rich, thick, sheep's yoghurt, with a delicious creamy-colour crust on top, is a daily 'must' in Greek homes. Luckily, the watered-down, insipid fruity varieties have not invaded us yet.

It is 'natural' yoghurt and I think no yoghurt in the world can be more natural in all senses of the word than Greek yoghurt, particularly that found in small provincial towns or the islands. The yoghurt of Kriti, for instance, can make one an addict to its creamy charms.

In the old-fashioned covered market at Chania, or in the plane-shaded village of Vrysses, or high up in pure shepherd's land, in mountainous Omalos on the western side and impressive Lasithi on the Agios Nikolaos side, yoghurt is still as my generation knew it.

We all mellow at the thought of the melancholic cry 'Yiaourti – Silivriano yiaourti' echoing in the empty streets at dusk, of the wandering yoghurt seller. *Silivria*, my grandmother had explained to us, was a town in Asia Minor famous for its wonderful yoghurt. Long after the Smyrna catastrophe, the Greek refugees still lived and nurtured fragile thoughts of the life left behind; and the yoghurt makers of Silivria were supposed not only to have brought their secrets of yoghurt making but also the small sample needed in order to recreate identical yoghurt.

Yoghurt is not only eaten on its own, between meals or with thick fragrant honey and sometimes walnuts spread on top, or served with vegetables, particularly stuffed vegetarian ones such as *dolmathes*, but it is also used to make a light and moist cake, unusually unsweetened by Greek standards, a *yiaourtopitta*.

Yoghurt does not vary much in the way it is made but in the quality of its basic ingredient, milk; it is the rich sheep's milk that makes wonders.

YIAOURTOPITTA

Yoghurt Pie or Cake

110 g/4 oz unsalted butter, or margarine
170 g/6 oz caster or granulated sugar (1½ teacups)
4 eggs, separated
150 g/5 oz natural yoghurt
grated rind of 1 lemon

225 g/8 oz flour (if self-raising flour is used, reduce the baking powder to 1 teaspoon)
2 teaspoons baking powder
55 g/2 oz icing sugar, for the top

Cream the butter or margarine and sugar together until light and creamy. Add the egg yolks, one at a time, beating in between additions. Add the yoghurt and lemon rind and mix them in well. Sift the flour and baking powder together. Whisk the egg whites until stiff. Using a metal spoon, fold tablespoons of flour, alternating with the egg whites, into the butter mixture until they have all been incorporated.

Butter a ring mould, or a springform tin, pour the mixture evenly into it and bake in a pre-heated oven, gas no. 4 (350°F/180°C), for 45 minutes.

Let the cake cool in the tin. If a ring mould is used, slip a sharp knife all round the edge and invert it onto a flat platter. Unclip the springform tin. Sprinkle the surface of the cake with sifted icing sugar.

WHEAT AND ITS ROLE IN GREEK LIFE

From Bread to Kolyva

Grain of one kind or another has been the staple on which communities relied throughout the ages.

Barley – *krithari* – was the most popular grain in ancient Greece until around 6000BC when wheat made its appearance from the Near East and became a favourite. There is historical evidence that the Greeks had a special aptitude and preference for bread. (They still have the preference but not the aptitude any more.) Originally this was made with barley flour mixed with wine or water and olive oil into a kind of dried biscuit which was called *maza*. Aristophanes mentions it in the *Frogs* and also compares *maza* to an excited crowd in his *Peace*. In modern Greece we still use the same term in a slightly contemptuous tone to describe an amorphous and diverse crowd.

Bread was given different names either according to the way it was cooked or its shape. For instance *esharitis* was a thin flat bread that was cooked on a grid; *krivanitis* was the bread that was cooked in a *krivanos* – a primitive oven built either from mud or metal and which gave the bread a particularly attractive and identifiable flavour; Aristophanes praises explicitly this kind of bread. *Apopyrias* was bread cooked over an open fire as the word suggests.

According to shape, there was a square loaf which was called *blomiaios*; *imiartion* which was a half-moon shape; *plakitis* was a small flat loaf; *mystili*, was the full-hearted pregnant round loaf, etc. Needless to say there also existed the equivalent of our wholemeal or granary which was called *aftopyros* or *aftopyritis* which, in real terms, had a high fibre content. Its opposite was a pure flour content bread called *Semidalitis*. Bread from Attica was much superior by any standards. Coarsely ground wheat was also boiled with milk and made into *tragos* – modern-day *trahanas*, which once cooked and dried is kept as a winter staple, when it is made into a soup.

All these, however, were meant for the living. In ancient Greece, according to Aristophanes' *Acharniai*, they cooked a special dish called *panspermia* which, as the word implies, was a selection of grains and seeds. This was offered to the dead as well as the living members of the family. Moreover it was offered to the god of the Underworld, Hades. In modern Greece a similar dish called *kolyva* is specially made for the dead. This, although primarily made of wheat, contains all kinds of grains and nuts like its ancient equivalent. The Turkish *assuré* is very similar and probably based on *panspermia* or *kolyva*.

When I wanted to know more about *kolyva* I rang up my mother in Athens and she, having assembled all her friends for a session, sent me a long and laborious recipe, the result of their combined wisdom.

Their recipe would make suitable reading as at least a piece out of *The Golden Bough* for its pagan and ritualistic element. For instance the impurities found in the wheat are not to be thrown into a dustbin but into the sea. Water from rinsing and cooking the wheat is to be used for watering plants and thus provide further life rather than be disposed of down a sink.

Kolyva is prepared for a funeral and distributed in handfuls to the participants at the end of the service. Forty days after a death it is made and distributed to neighbourhood houses and the local church. But it is also prepared at prescribed times in the year, such as the equivalent of the Greek Orthodox All Souls Day – *Ton Psihon* – which occurs during three consecutive Saturdays in the Spring before and during Lent.

And it is also made yearly to commemorate somebody's passing away. It is prepared on Fridays and the finished dish is taken to the local church to remain overnight and to be blessed by the priest the following morning. A spare plate is prepared at the same time and distributed to at least three, six or nine households in the neighbourhood in order to remember the dead of the family and to attribute peace to their souls. Multiples of three are also important in the recipe, an allegory of the Holy Trinity. For instance the wheat should be rinsed three times.

Kolyva that is prepared on the first Friday of Lent is not sweetened with either sugar or nuts and has a very special significance for young girls. They attend the Saturday morning service and after the *kolyva* has been blessed it is distributed to them by the priest. That night unmarried girls place three grains of the *kolyva* wheat under their pillow and according to popular belief they will then dream of the man who is to become their husband.

In this way *kolyva*, or its main ingredient, wheat, perpetuates life in an infinite circle. Staple for the living, the dead and the dreaming.

KOLYVA

Kolyva is an extremely pleasing dish – a kind of rich muesli *– with different textures from all the nuts – flaked almonds, walnuts, sugared almonds, sesame seeds – against the smoothness of the boiled wheat. It is aromatic with ground cinnamon, coriander and cummin. We used to love it as children. The addition of juicy crunchy pomegranate seeds made it almost into a festive dish for us.*

450 g/1lb whole wheat
3 pinches of salt
110 g/4oz small currants
110 g/4oz raisins
110 g/4oz coarsely chopped
   walnuts
150 g/5oz shelled and flaked
   almonds
1 pomegranate, shelled and
   seeded

1 teaspoon ground cinnamon
1 teaspoon ground coriander
1 teaspoon ground cummin
3 tablespoons flat-leaved
   parsley leaves
Topping
350 g/12 oz plain flour
450 g/1 lb caster sugar
10 sugared almonds
handful of raisins

Pick the wheat clean. *Repeat three times.* (A touch of *The Golden Bough* here.) Keep any impurities and dispose of them into the sea. Rinse the wheat *three times* and dispose of the water by watering a plant. Strain, cover with fresh water, add *three* pinches of salt and boil gently for about 40–50 minutes. It is important to keep testing at this stage as the grains should not go mushy. They should be intact and although they will feel hard on the outside they will be tender inside. Strain, keeping the water for the plants. Spread the wheat on a clean cloth and dry for 5–6 hours.

Before assembling the dish you have to prepare yourself *spiritually*. For this purpose light a candle and think of the dead that the *kolyva* is to commemorate, accounting their names.

Mix the dry wheat with the remaining ingredients, keeping some pomegranate seeds for decoration. Spread evenly on platters. Put the flour into a frying pan and roast dry on gentle heat, stirring continuously, until light golden. Let it cool. Spread a thin layer of flour all over the surface of the wheat, pressing down lightly. This will absorb any remaining moisture. Spread a thin layer of sugar on top (using as much sugar or as little as you like) and press it down with a piece of paper so that it becomes quite solid.

Now comes the important task of decorating. Anything goes – particularly crosses and flowers. Use sugared almonds and raisins, pomegranate seeds and/or ground cinnamon to make attractive patterns. Some people use silvered almonds or silvered pinenuts but that is pure bad taste.

GLYKA TOU KOUTALIOU

Spoon Preserves

'It was about midday and we were served with the customary compliment. The lady of the house had been one of the most beautiful
Sciotes, nor had her daughter any inferior pretensions. More native
politeness and gay complacency could scarcely have been shown than
in their reception of us.

    According to the universal custom amongst the Greeks, soon after
our arrival, a servant appeared, bearing a silver salver, upon which
were placed several spoons filled with conserves, which the young
lady [daughter] presented to us severally, with a grace and attitude
worthy the antique. Small glasses of water succeeded, and lastly, coffee prepared in the eastern manner. In every visit that may be made
during the day, this compliment is repeated. Should the mistress of
the house be young, she shows her respect to her guests by this ceremony; if otherwise, her eldest daughter or some other lady present
takes her place.'

(From a visit to the island of Chios by James Dallaway from his *Travels*,
London 1797, p. 279. Dallaway was chaplain and physician of the British
Embassy to the Porte, in Constantinople.)

The same custom prevails even nowadays. Spoon preserves are the common stand-bys for welcoming an unexpected visitor.

Reminiscent of the early soft spring are the tiny aromatic perfumed
lemons, the green bitter oranges, and the soft but strong-scented petals of
the April roses. Jars of these treasures (always hidden from the children),
would instantly sweeten and warm the blood in the coldest of winter days.

While the glorious summer fruits are the juicy dark purple cherries, the
golden soft and sweet grapes, the bright green unripened figs, the pears,
the sweet and rosy apricots, the fresh green round walnuts and, in May,
the lovely tiny strong-scented strawberries from Kerkyra. At the same
time on flights from Kerkyra to Athens, when I was an air-hostess, the
whole aircraft, once in the air, was totally enwrapped in the concentrated
perfumed waves of sweet strawberries that had been loaded in the hold,
and this made work more pleasant and life brighter altogether. Apart
from all these fruits there were also the tiny purple aubergines and the special shaped Santorini-type tomatoes that were also transformed into the
sweetest of preserves.

NERANTZAKI GLYKO

Bitter Orange Preserve

> In Andros it is the custom to regale the visitor on delicious local jams
> (*rothozachari*), or 'sugar of roses', and bergamonte, a small young
> fruit, like a lemon in colour and an orange in shape, which has a
> strong scent, and has the effect of rendering its recipient temporarily
> speechless by entirely filling his mouth.
>
> (William Miller, *Greek Life in Town and Country*, London 1905, p. 213.)

Bitter orange trees adorn pavements, small squares and parks, right in the
middle of Athens, as well as the suburbs, and also most of the provincial
towns, and in the spring the aroma is almost bewitching.

*Any of the citrus fruits can be preserved in the same way,
particularly lemons. The fruit is picked when very young, before it
matures, so it is of dark green colour, round like a walnut, and still
very aromatic, being closer to the perfume of the orange or lemon
blossoms, which is the sweetest and most overwhelming of all
perfumes, rather than that of the developed fruit.*

1 kg/2 lbs fresh small green bitter oranges, or lemons	1.5 kg/3 lbs caster sugar
450 ml/¾ pint water	1 teaspoon fresh lemon juice

The fruit should be fresh and of equal size. Open a small hole at one end
with a small sharp knife and remove the pips. (In Greece, there is a special
implement for this job.) Immerse the fruit in cold water and when they
have all been processed, wash and drain them.

Place the fruit in a large saucepan, or a special jam pan, cover with plenty of cold water and cook until they become soft. Drain them and immerse
in cold water. Leave to soak for 48 hours, changing the water 7–9 times in
the meantime, in order to get rid of their bitterness completely.

Bring the water and sugar to the boil, stirring, and simmer for about 5
minutes. Strain the bitter oranges, add to the syrup and simmer for a further 5 minutes. Remove from the heat and let them stand in the syrup for
24 hours. Bring to the boil again, skim, add the lemon juice and boil rapidly without stirring until setting point has been reached. Let it cool. Store
in sterilized jars and seal.

Care must be taken not to overcook the fruit in the first stage of cooking. Keep in mind the additional stages of cooking in the syrup.

NERANTZI GLYKO

Bitter Orange Peel Preserve

This is one of the most exotic and easier preserves to make and it will keep for one or two years. You could substitute Seville oranges with the ordinary navel kind which have quite a thick peel. This quantity will make about 30 pieces.

1 kg/2 lbs Seville oranges	150 ml/¼ pint water
(8 or 9)	juice of ½ lemon
1 kg/2 lbs caster sugar	

Rinse and dry the oranges. Grate them lightly with a zester. Slice each orange vertically into four segments, take the peel off and drop it into a bowl of cold water. Discard the flesh.

Using a tapestry needle with a double thread, roll each piece of peel and thread it. Once you have threaded about 10 pieces, tie the two ends to form a small 'necklace'. Immerse them in fresh cold water for 24 hours, changing the water 3 or 4 times, in order to extract their bitterness.

Place the strings of peel in a saucepan with about 2.8 litres/5 pints of fresh water and boil, half-covered, for 15 minutes, then strain and discard the water. Cover with the same amount of fresh water and cook for about 10 minutes until the peel is tender but not falling apart. Strain, discarding the water, and leave the strings to drain for 1 hour.

Dilute the sugar and water in a large saucepan over a gentle heat, stirring continuously. Once the sugar is dissolved, boil gently for about 4 minutes until it bubbles and starts to set. Cut the threads and release the fruit into the sugar; cook for 5 minutes. (By this stage they retain their cylindrical shape which makes them easier to serve.) Withdraw from the heat and leave overnight.

Next day, boil the syrup gently for 4–5 minutes, uncovered, until it starts to set. Add the lemon juice, withdraw from the heat and, when cool, pack into sterilized jars.

The pieces of peel are offered a piece at a time on a spoon, resting in a little saucer, with a glass of water.

SYKALAKI GLYKO

Figs and Fig Preserve

Bright green, small figs (*syka*), tight and unripened, are picked from the trees in early July for the purpose of preserving. Fig preserve is my most favourite and since fig trees seed themselves they grow on the island everywhere – on cobbled paths, in gardens, out of stone walls (a very persistent one is almost bringing our garden wall down), and they are difficult to resist.

Fig trees go through a fascinating cycle each year. Even though I feel quite familiar with all its details now, I still find it interesting to watch and to discuss with the local people at the precise time every summer. It's a kind of intimate relationship of people and trees that produces a blooming of life. What is more, it all happens quietly each year as a matter of course. Wild fig trees are male; cultivated or grafted ones that produce edible fruit are female. However, if the fruit of the 'female' trees is not fertilized by the fruit of the 'wild' male ones by the end of June, it cannot be kept on the trees and consequently it is dropped.

Devotedly then in about the middle of June, one sees local people wandering in solitude on the hillsides, with a sack over their shoulder, early in the morning. By this time, the 'wild' figs are quite large and developed; obviously more so than the tiny female edible figs. Nevertheless, they never become edible. The firmest and biggest of the male figs are collected and taken home. There, the lady of the household sets to work.

The figs are tied in pairs, with a short piece of string, sometimes even with the help of a darning needle. In the early evening, or early next morning (it has to be done during the cool part of the day, otherwise the heat of the sun may kill the little exposed aphis), the pairs of figs are thrown over the branches of the trees that are to be fertilized. Five or six pairs per tree are enough. If too many are put on the same tree, the figs become over-fertilized, they darken inside, they become dry and sugary thus losing most of their wonderful flavour. The male fruit is called *ornos*, from the ancient word *erinos* – male, and on closer investigation they appear to be full of tiny black aphis. These aphis that penetrate each of the female figs are their most important friends. Without them there will not be moist, aromatic fruit later. Once their mission is completed the *ornos* dry and look shrivelled but they are not removed.

Throughout my life, I had been seeing these dried, brown shrivelled figs, tied in pairs, and I had always presumed rather readily (according to my Greek upbringing) that this was some spell of bewitchment, perhaps a token against the notorious evil eye.

Apparently, if a female tree is left unfertilized to drop its fruit for five or six years, it slowly gets used to finding other means of fertilization, like from the aphis of the *rigani* (oregano) flowers, or bees, etc. However, everybody agrees that such figs cannot be compared to the glorious results of the properly fertilized fruit from the aphis of the male figs. And so, the ritual of the dried shrivelled figs can be seen each summer, on fig trees, all over Greece.

Fig trees, either male or female, as well as their unripe fruit, if cut, produce a thick milky sap that is terribly caustic and should never be touched. It is this natural caustic milky element in figs that requires the elaborate process of cooking in various changes of water.

1 kg/2 lbs small, unripe green figs (about 40–45)	300 ml/½ pint water
	1 teaspoon fresh lemon juice
1 kg/2 lbs caster sugar	4–5 drops vanilla essence

Wearing kitchen gloves, cut off the small stem of each fig with a sharp knife and drop the figs into cold water. Let them soak for 3 hours. Strain them, cover with plenty of fresh water, bring to the boil and simmer for 10 minutes. Strain again, cover them with fresh water, bring to the boil, and simmer for a further 10 minutes. Strain them and soak in fresh cold water for 30 minutes.

Dilute the sugar in the water, bring to the boil and simmer for 5 minutes, stirring to prevent it sticking. Strain, add the figs and simmer them together for 5 minutes. Remove from the heat and let them stand in this syrup for about 12 hours.

Then add the lemon juice to the syrup, bring to the boil and skim it. Boil rapidly, without stirring, for a further 1–2 minutes. Remove from the heat, add the vanilla and let it cool before storing in sterilized jars and sealing them.

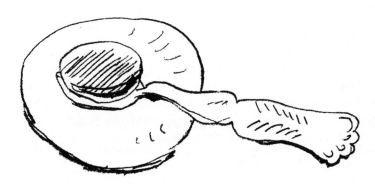

LEMONANTHOS CHIOU

Chian Lemon Blossom Preserve

Chios is a beautiful and diverse island. It is known as the home of *mastic*, the resin of the eponymous trees which grow on the south of the island around the fourteen villages which are called *Mastihochoria*. *Mastic*, with its refreshing taste (it smells like freshly ironed linen), is used as a flavouring in the local drink and in baking, not only in Greek but also Middle Eastern cuisines.

Unlike the arrid south where the mastic trees grow, in the middle of the island and near the main town there is an area called Kambos which resembles the Garden of Eden with its orchards of lemon, orange and clementine trees. It was here that we were introduced to all best things Chian by our lovely hosts Maria and Michalis Voulamanthi who have converted their beautiful house and orchards into the most enchanting hotel. It is natural that local tradition makes good use of these fruits in different ways.

This is the recipe of Isabella Kallisperi from Chios. Everyone on this beautiful island has access to lemon trees – even if not their own, then those of friends and relatives. They gather only the petals straight from the trees in order not to damage the fruit as it forms.

450 g/l lb lemon petals	1 kg/2 lbs sugar
4 lemons	450 ml/¾ pint water

Rinse the petals in cold water and strain. Bring a large saucepan of water to the boil, add the petals and, once it comes back to the boil, strain, discarding the water. Repeat this twice more. The last time add the juice of one of the lemons and simmer for 5 minutes. Strain and spread the petals on a large platter. Pour over them the juice of two lemons and place it in the sun for 2–3 hours.

Dilute the sugar in water over a gentle heat and boil gently for about 6–8 minutes, skimming it with a slotted spoon until it bubbles and starts to set. Rinse the lemon petals thoroughly with cold water and strain. Add them to the syrup with the juice of the remaining lemon and boil gently but steadily for 5 minutes or until setting point is reached. Withdraw from the heat and, once cool, pack into sterilized jars.

VYSSINO GLYKO

Sour Cherry Preserve

The most common of the spoon preserves and also the most traditional. Long sessions are required by each family for stoning the kilos of sour cherries, and in early August, on the island, we all suffer from over-exposure to cherry preserve as everyone is required to try each other's successful or sometimes unsuccessful efforts, as soon as the cherries are safely in their jars.

Vyssinatha, a cherry drink, beautiful in colour, which is diluted with water and served with ice when possible, is also made from the excess juices of the preserve. The same thick extract of the preserve is always poured on top of vanilla and the special Kaimaki ice-cream, and then it makes an absolutely delectable combination.

Homemade or even ready-made cherry preserve (there are very good brands in the market, the best one is Anthos Kifissias, made by the well-known large cake shop in Kiffissia) is delicious mixed with thick plain yoghurt and one of the best ways that it can be consumed.

1 kg/2 lbs firm sour cherries	1 kg/2 lbs caster sugar
300 ml/½ pint water	1 teaspoon fresh lemon juice

Wash and stone the cherries. There is a special implement for this, or you can use a forked hairpin. Their stoning has to be done carefully in order to leave them intact. Place the stones in the water as they are taken out; at the end remove the pips from the water and discard them. Do not discard the water.

Place the cherries and sugar in alternating layers in a wide saucepan. Add the water strained from the stones, bring to the boil and simmer for 20 minutes. Withdraw from the heat and let it stand for 24 hours. Bring back to the boil, skim, add the lemon juice and boil rapidly, without stirring, until it reaches setting point. Store in sterilized jars and seal tightly.

KYTHONI GLYKO

Quince Preserve

In October almost everyone occupies themselves with the beautiful fruit of the quince tree. They are eaten raw, peeled, grated and sprinkled with sugar and cinnamon, cooked with meat and, best of all, they are preserved and bottled or made into jellies with the most exotic taste and aroma.

Quinces vary a lot in size and they are quite heavy. Allow at least two or three medium ones for preserving. This is the method that Maria Karakatsani uses on the island of Alonnisos.

Wipe the furry coat of each quince clean and rinse them. Slice the quinces into quarters to make them easier to handle. Peel and core each piece and cut into small cubes. Have ready a bowl of cold water with a little lemon juice and drop them in to prevent discolouring.

Strain them and measure the quantity of fruit. For every 2 cups of quinces you need 1 cup of caster sugar (or even better *golden caster* which is unrefined sugar with a lot more taste). Put them into a saucepan, sprinkle sugar on top, add 3–4 tablespoons of water and simmer without stirring for 20 minutes, half-covered.

Add a teaspoon of lemon juice. Also at this stage people add a little bunch of an aromatic plant called *ambaroriza* – a kind of rose or lemon geranium – or 3–4 drops of vanilla and slithers of flaked almonds.

Stir and boil uncovered at a steady pace for a further 10–12 minutes in order to set it. Skim with a slotted spoon. Test for setting by dropping a little liquid onto a cold saucer and if it forms a skin on top and does not run it is ready. Let it cool, then bottle in sterilized jars.

KYTHONOPASTO

Quince Paste

Wipe and rinse the quinces. Cut them into quarters or smaller, peel and core them. Put them into a saucepan with 150 ml/¼ pint water per quince and a small bunch of *ambaroriza* (see above). Simmer until soft – about 30–40 minutes. Discard aromatics. Strain through a fine strainer, squeezing the pulp through.

Measure the thick liquid and add half its volume in golden caster sugar. Boil gently but steadily in a heavy-based saucepan (being careful not to get splashed), stirring continuously for 8–12 minutes until it thickens like dough, becomes elastic and comes off the sides of the pan easily.

Pour evenly into an oiled quiche dish or small roasting tin – ideally to a thickness of about 4 cm/1½ ins – and let it cool and set completely. Cut into small squares or diamond-shaped pieces, and dribble a little brandy on each one, if liked. Dust the tops with icing sugar and stick half a flaked almond on each one.

Let them dry for 1–2 days – in Greece they would be put in the sun – and store in a tin which has also been dusted with icing sugar. Delicious.

MOUSTALEVRIA

Grape Must Dessert

This is a wonderful, seasonal, old-fashioned creamy dessert made with fresh must when the grapes are being pressed for wine-making. Its limited season is late September and October. I long for its sweet and sour taste all year round and if occasionally I am in Athens at the right season my sister takes me to Varsos – the wonderful cake shop in Kifissia – for a pilgrimage to *moustalevria*.

When small *tavernas* with huge barrels filled with draught wine were the landmark of every Athenian neighbourhood it was easy to find fresh *moustos* (must) for the making of *moustalevria* and *moustokouloura* – sweet must and cinnamon-scented biscuits. I still remember how embarrassed I used to be as a child to have to walk into this den full of men drinking and smoking when I was sent to our local *taverna* carrying a container to have it filled with must or a bottle to have filled with wine. Now the local *tavernas* have disappeared, draught wine from barrels is rare and so is must.

When fresh must is boiled down its sugar content is concentrated and becomes syrupy like honey. This is called *petimezi* and it is stored and used for the making of biscuits, such as *moustokouloura*, and also served with yoghurt. *Moustalevria* is made by boiling the must with a little soda and leaving it overnight for the sediment to settle. It is then strained through muslin and brought to the boil again. Semolina is added gradually at this stage while stirring continuously until it thickens and bubbles. It is then emptied into small bowls and dusted with chopped walnuts and cinnamon or roasted sesame seeds. This is one of those landmark tastes that leave their imprint on you permanently. I can savour its taste vividly even while only writing about it.

KAFE
Coffee

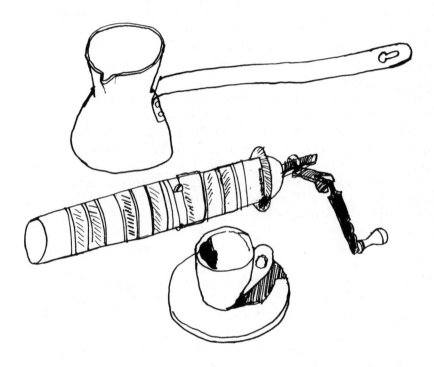

Making, serving and drinking coffee, like so many other things in Greek life, is highly ritualized. Greek life would not be complete without the little tray crowded on one side with the small thick white cups, frothing and steaming, and on the other the cold glasses of water, appearing at prescribed times of the day: the morning, the mid-morning and mid-afternoon.

Weather permitting, coffee is always taken in the open air (nine months out of twelve), a small shaded balcony, a little garden shaded with vines, under a tree, or just in front of the house in a street or alley. If you walk through a backstreet in any Greek town or go through any village between 5 and 6 o'clock in the afternoon, you will see the ritual with all its splendour. Or walk through the main street and observe the inimitably wonderful coffee houses, the *kafenia*, with their little round tin tables, occasionally marble-topped, and their rigidly upright wooden chairs with rush seats, spread on the shaded pavements. There the waves of lethargy are exorcised by the tiny white steaming cups of coffee and the monotonously stark noise of the amber beads of the *komboloyia* (worry beads) rushed among the dexterous fingers of the sleepy men.

A very different image is exuded by the afternoon 'coffee hour' compared to the animated, if not heated, atmosphere of the mid-morning session over a game of *tavli* (backgammon) or the evening session over a little square glass of unadulterated *ouzo*, *tsipouro*, or *raki*, depending on custom and location.

Coffee is ordered in a *kafenion* by shouting one's desired formula, usually in monosyllabic terminology. *Sketos* is without sugar; strong and bitter it can give such a jolt to your nervous system that it could almost breathe life back into a dead body. *Metrios*, medium, usually with one teaspoonful of sugar, is the most common. *Glykys* or *vari glykos*, is almost honey-sweet and, I find, it couples beautifully with the usual honey-coated cakes such as *baklavathes*, *kadaifi* and *galaktoboureka*. *Glykys vrastos* is sweet but without the froth; if coffee is left to boil it loses most of its froth and whereas most people, including myself, regard the lacy froth as valuable and indispensable, there are some who prefer their coffee without it.

Greek coffee is always served black, in small and preferably thick cups; it is made in a *briki*, a narrow, tall, small container with a long handle and a lip, which makes pouring out easy. *Brikia* used to be made of copper or brass in the old days, but are almost always made of aluminium or stainless steel nowadays. Stacks of these varying in sizes can be seen hanging round the entrances of shops or from the ceilings, like bunches of grapes, and always in the *laikes*, the street markets.

There, in the *laiki*, you will also see the small, thick white cups with the massive coiled handles that are the most common and which will be found in most *kafenia*. For me these are the best and the ultimate for drinking coffee from.

Greek coffee is easy to make. It is customary and advisable not to attempt to make more than 3–4 small cups of coffee at a time, as quantity throws the balance out of order and then it is more difficult to bring the coffee to the desired frothing point without letting it boil; consequently it tastes more like a stewed brown liquid, losing a lot of its flavour.

First, choose the right-sized *briki* for the right cups of coffee; it is no good making one coffee in a *briki* that is meant for 3–4. Then measure the required cups of water into the *briki*: the measure should be one of the cups that the coffee is going to be served in. Then measure and add the coffee. A teaspoonful of coffee per cup, not too heaped, is the best. You can really tell the difference when more coffee is used, as it almost drowns everything in its own thickness. Add the sugar, about a teaspoonful per cup for a medium coffee; the best balance is to add the same amount of sugar as coffee.

Put the *briki* on a low heat and stir its contents a little, until the coffee looks diluted in the water. Hold the *briki* by the handle all the time as it can be unstable but, most importantly, it boils so quickly and spills everywhere. Watch it starting to rise with a bubbly foam. Let it rise and rise, keeping your cool (do not panic), until it reaches the lips of the *briki* and then immediately withdraw from the heat. Even if it spills a little there is nothing to worry about as according to Greek folklore, 'some money is on its way to you'; this is the phrase that Greek women console themselves and each other with, when coffee spills. If one of the cups spills a little as it is handed to a guest, the general exclamation is again that there is extra money, an unexpected fortune or inheritance perhaps, on its way to this particular guest.

Once the coffee has been made, let it stand for one minute to allow the coffee grounds to settle at the bottom of the *briki*. Then pour a little in each cup, thus distributing the valuable froth in all the cups. Then proceed and just fill them up to the brim. Forget western beliefs of politeness, as Greeks like their cups of coffee overfilled, almost spilling over the top.

If you find distributing the froth a little difficult, you can do it with a teaspoon. Greek coffee is never stirred once it has been made and served. It is drunk in minute sips as it is quite strong and also the enjoyment is extended.

However, the most important thing about Greek coffee is the mystique that surrounds it and fortune-telling and which accounts for one of the most pleasurable pastimes of Greek women. Apart from joking sessions between friends and neighbours, there is not a woman in Greece who has not gone on a special visit to a renowned *kafetzou* – a fortune-teller who reads and translates, intuitively and imaginatively, the images formed by the settled coffee grounds in the cup after the coffee has been drunk.

For the purpose of coffee-reading, once the coffee has been drunk but still with a little liquid at the bottom, it is swirled around to dislodge most of the coffee grounds from the bottom (otherwise it means bad luck when a black mountain of coffee grounds stay in the cup). Then it is inverted, pouring the remaining contents out, preferably from the side that it has been drunk, as this is the immediate future, on to the saucer. The cup is left inverted on the saucer for a few minutes to dry; it is believed that it is best left undisturbed at this stage, instead of constantly being looked into, as the truths get muddled and adulterated. Then comes the glorious moment of its reading. We used to collect our pocket-money for days until the prescribed fee had been reached and then our little group would skip school one afternoon and run to some remote spot in Piraeus or Athens to some famed *kafetzou* who would first deliver a short sermon on the dangers brooding over our youth and immediately afterwards would proceed to unfold the mystiques of her art, to our delight.

One will almost never see men inverting their empty coffee cups in this fashion as coffee-reading is considered as 'women's follies' and far below their masculinity. Only a foreigner, like my husband, would be so intrigued and get so much enjoyment from our happy afternoon sessions in my sister's house in Psychiko, that he was only too happy to participate.

There, on the cool veranda, among sweetly scented white jasmines and perfumed creamy gardenias, shaded by a flaming red bougainvillea, my mother and lovely old Penelope, my sister's wonderful helper, once they had finished sipping their coffee, would combine their efforts, complementing and correcting each other, sometimes arguing on the finer details, while concentrating on translating the images from each of our coffee cups into words, while the usual Greek exclamatory noises were resounding around the house. The 'Po, po, po, have you seen this wonderful bird, it looks like a peacock to me!' (A peacock was always considered a sure sign of happiness.) Or: 'Ou, ou, look at this lovely big tree!' (The tree always meant the acquirement of something solid, a house, a car, etc., according to its size and denseness.) And then, an anti-climatic 'Pa, pa, isn't this a little snake down there?' (This meant, watch out among your friends, one of them is envious and insincere.) And the wonderful duet carried on, in this fashion, amidst the teasing and the giggles that my two sisters and I could not hide.

VOTANA
Herbs, Tisanes and Medicine

'Which is the essence found from wild herbs?' said an aesthete, 'Which essence made according to prescriptions of ancient Helleno-syrian magicians that for one single day (if its powers cannot prove stronger), or even for a short time could bring back my twenty-three years; my friend in his twenty-two years; bring back again – his beauty, his love?'

(K.P. Kavafi, *According to Prescriptions of Ancient Hellenosyrian Magicians*, 1931.)

Votana is a mother word that embraces herbs which grow wild: herbs used in cooking, for tisanes, medicinally or not, in homemade beauty potions, or simply folklore.

Greeks are intimately attached to the microcosm of wild plants that thrive everywhere from spring to autumn – mountains, fields, stony ground, ruins, either majestic marble ones from the antiquity or humble recent ones, on rocks and beaches.

More than six thousand wild plants have been accounted for, quite a number of them being endemic in Greece. Hippocratis, foremost ancestor of medicine, made good use of a lot of them in ancient Kos. Greeks regard and treat all these as their umbilical cord with nature and they always incorporated them in their lives in various ways as they still do; from the ancient Greeks burning the common *thymari* (*Thyme serpyllum*) – the ancient *thymos* (*oupos*) – on the altars to the Olympian Gods, to present-day feasting, where there could not be a roast lamb amidst the scents of the hillsides, or fresh fish barbecued, without a few *thymari* (thyme) flowers sprinkled all over. Most herbs still carry botanical Latin names that are derived from the ancient Greek. The most indispensable of Greek herbs are the two primary ones used in all cooking, *thymari* and *rigani* (*Origanum dictamnus* – oregano), the ancient *origanon*. Wild mint and feathery fennel (*maratho*) also grow in abundance.

Rigani and *thymari* grow in a number of varieties, one more aromatic than the other. Picked at the right time, dried and stored, they lose none of their beautiful scent and with a sprinkling of nostalgia can transport one even on the darkest of winter days instantly to a Greek hillside, with its ringing sound of goatbells.

After the cooking herbs follow the ones that are used as tisanes. The most representative of these is called *agrio tsai tou vounou* (wild mountain tea – if translated literally). Every mountain in Greece seems to grow its *sui generis* tea; a very esoteric affair that can be identified down to an area by its special aroma. So, the Kretans have got their own, a particularly aromatic *thiktamo*, often called *stamnohorto* which is sometimes brewed with one or two cloves as they served it to us in the little village of Selia, after Sfakia.

The Pelloponnisians have their own tea from the proud mountain of Taygetos, near Sparti; a silvery furry-leaved one with little yellow flowers nesting in each branch at the top. This is very popular with Greeks everywhere and particularly with Athenians. The Greek poet, K. Ouranis, in his travels, said that once he gazed at Taygetos he could understand the ancient Spartans better, and that a race who daily gazed at such a titan of a mountain, and breathed its cold air breezing down from the steely, pyramid-like tops, could have become nothing else but the proud war-riors with the steel discipline that they were.

A different type of tea grows on Parnassos and, as in a number of Greek islands, they refer to tea as *lisfakia*, the ancient *elelisfakos* or common *fraskomilo* – a beautifully aromatic type of sage. *Fraskomilo* is so prolif-ic in the countryside, so aromatic and easy to identify, with its bright, light green, fleshy leaves that turn silvery when dried, that even a child could collect it. It is collected from June, throughout the summer. The top of its stalks are cut, about 20 cm/8ins or more, tied into bunches, and are then hung inverted in the shade for three or four days.

It is common in Greece when ordering tea in a village to be served auto-matically one of these wild growing specimens, according to the pecu-liarity of the area.

Next in the line come those that are still drunk as tisanes but with slight medicinal qualities attached to them.

Sweet-scented, golden chamomile is the first and most important since it will be found in every Greek household. Chamomile is known to be soothing for acid stomachs, upset tummies, nervous tension and insom-nia; a magical sedative in every respect.

There is a standard word among Greek women when it comes to cop-ing with colic or simply unhappy babies: *hamomilaki* – a little chamomile. I do not think there has been a Greek baby that at some point of his or her life has not been quietened down and sent to sleep with the magical weak infusion of chamomile flowers, considered in Greece to be a mother's ally.

The medicinal qualities of chamomile have been also proved scientifi-cally and are credited to two vital substances they contain, bisabolol and chamazulene. Chamomile infusion is also used by eczema sufferers for bathing the skin or any skin inflammation, as well as bathing a wound in its healing stage, as it relieves itchiness. Excess chamomile drinking may relax the heart to such a degree that it can cause fainting.

Chamomile is everywhere in Greece in April and early May, even at the modern airports like a greeting to one's arrival. It makes a beautiful sight, and to lie on a scented bed of chamomile flowers in a field, under the hot sun, accounts for one of the most exhilarating and happy moments in life. Chamomile flowers are collected towards the end of April or even the beginning of May, if the weather has not been too dry and hot, after it has been flowering for some time. Some people prefer to collect it with the stalks as well. It is then spread and dried in the sun for about three or four days, before it is stored. It is never crushed into a powder.

In the same league there is *menta*, the ancient *minthi*, from which it derives its name, or our common peppermint. *Menta*, which has dark purple flowers and effuses a strong aroma of what its name suggests, is very similar to common *thymari* plants and it should not be confused with it. Its leaves are darker green and the plants taller and stronger than *thymari*. It has a particularly soothing effect on tummy aches and sore throats.

Glykaniso (anise – from the ancient *anitho*) is another favourite infusion of the seeds of the anise or the dill plants that grow profusely and it is also given to babies as a sedative like chamomile. Anise seeds are also used in flavouring the favourite Greek drink *ouzo*, particularly preferred in the summer as it can be refreshing served either with cold water or with ice cubes in it. Cold and translucent like alabaster it is then evasively alcoholic, particularly to the innocent recipient. Anise seeds are considered a digestive, a tonic, and are also supposed to help the lactation in nursing or expectant mothers. They were used by the ancient Greeks like most of these herbs were and they are mentioned by Theofrastos and Dioskourithis. Athenaios refers to anise as *anisso*.

Infusions of purple thyme are also believed to having soothing qualities, particularly for nervous tension and unsettled stomachs. I have a friend who will have nothing else for his morning drink but infused wild thyme with its stalks, mixed with a spoonful of homemade honey from his elderly neighbour down the hill; he insists that it not only soothes his acid stomach and the pains from his gallstones, but that it also gives him a soft jolt to the start of a strenuous day.

MAKING TISANES

In Greece, a small quantity of the desired herb, very often still on its stalks, like chamomile or thyme, is put with the appropriate amount of water and brought slowly to the boil. Then it is taken off the heat and left to stand for 2–3 minutes before it is served through a fine strainer. Two or three stalks are normally enough for two teacups, unless it is preferred much stronger. For herbs that come off the stalk or as a powder, a small teaspoonful per cup is enough. These you can treat like ordinary tea, pour hot water over them and let them stand for 1–2 minutes.

GATHERING COOKING HERBS

Every Greek family will combine an outing to the countryside with gathering a bunch of something aromatic, depending on the month. Herbs are gathered from spring to autumn, but each one must be collected at precisely the right time and not indiscriminately. It is no good collecting *rigani* (oregano) before the middle of July; and even then it has to be assessed on the precise spot in order to decide whether it is ready; *rigani*, which is picked mainly for its flowers, not only has to be in full bloom but some of the bloom must have started going to seed in order for the plant to be at its most aromatic and so assessed to be worth picking.

Beautifully aromatic *rigani* is the Greek herb *par excellence* and is used in all the casseroles that contain tomatoes, which is also particularly characteristic of the whole of the Mediterranean. It is also used in a lot of stuffings, and in a number of lemony casseroles when it gives its name to the whole dish, like in *Arni Lathorigani* (lamb cooked with olive oil and oregano) and *Entosthia Riganata* (lamb's liver and intestines cooked in the same manner) but it is never used when an *avgolemono* (egg and lemon sauce) is to be added at the end.

It is used with roasts and grills even though *thymari* would be the king of the occasion, and lastly in all kinds of hamburgers, particularly the fried *keftethes*. Considering its importance, it is not surprising how particular people are about its 'ripeness', especially the elder village women.

Having decided last summer that the time had come for our first *rigani*-picking outing in the village, we reached the village square and the outing was discussed (one cannot go through the heart of a village, normally a *kafenio*, without being asked as to the full extent of the purpose of the outing, in case useful advice has to be dispensed). I was told quite categorically by the eighty-eight-year-old granny of the *kafenio* that the *rigani* was not ready to be picked as it really needed two or three more days of sun! This is the extent of the seriousness of these matters in Greece.

This is the field *rigani*, whose plants grow approximately 30–36 cm/12–14 ins high, bear small, dark green leaves all along each woody stem and eventually burst into tiny white flowers all along each top. This kind likes earth as opposed to stony ground and some moisture, so it is more prolific in shady places, near or under fruit trees, particularly large fig trees, fields with low-trained vines that are watered regularly, and shallow and damp green ravines that burst with foliage and fruit. Of course, it grows in any disused field, totally exposed to the hot summer sun as well.

At the right time of its maturity, the woody stems are cut about 7.5 cm/3 ins from the root and gathered neatly into huge pretty bunches. These are tied with string and hung upside down on an external wall or from a branch of a mulberry tree or from a vine in the garden, exposed to the heat and the sun for four or five days. If it rains – quite an unlikely event in the middle of a Greek summer – they are taken inside, as they turn black and lose some of their aroma once they get wet.

When they are considered dry enough, leaves and flowers are crumbled by rolling between the palms of your hands all along their stems, over a sheet of newspaper. Then they are stored in jars for the winter. This is what some would call ordinary *rigani*, but for me it is the most enticing and aromatic. Others prefer what they call mountain *rigani* (*rigani tou vounou*) – or wild *rigani*. This kind comes from a totally different plant which grows in the mountains, as the name suggests, and specifically on stony ground. It prefers dry places exposed to the heat, and therefore mountains or hills – bare of trees, and with the heat reflected on the grey stones making such places hotter than they should be – are ideal.

The plants of this *rigani* bear the signs of a 'strenuous' wild life. They are shorter than the common *rigani*, woodier, with less leaves and a colour that never seems to be really green but carries the undertones of all the shades of brown even when 'fresh', but at the end of each stem come the magical and pretty clustered umbrella-like layered flowers, in unusual profusion. This *rigani* is exclusively collected for its flowers, made into beautiful bunches and dried.

Within this type there are also variations from place to place and island to island; so in the islands of the South Aegean for example, in Kriti or Kos, it is greener and the flowers hang in a more elongated fashion, miniature catkin-like and apetalous.

On Alonnisos, the flowers are much smaller, rounder, resembling miniature roses, in plethoric clusters; and while everywhere else *rigani* of either kind goes into most casseroles and meat dishes, the local people on

Alonnisos are quite specific about their usage of the wild *rigani*: it only goes into lentil soup and nowhere else. They are quite categorical about this and every household possesses its decorative umbrella-shaped bunch that hangs from a nail in the kitchen throughout the winter.

About 20 metres from our house in the village is the tip of a huge cliff; underneath it lies one of the most magnificently sculptured ravines, quite awe-inspiring. The hard effect of the stony mountain that borders it on the opposite side and which ironically is called *kalovolos* (the kindly one) is softened by thick silvery clusters of symmetrically embroidered olive trees and the dense green of thousands of almond trees lower on the mountain side down to the lacy border of the tiny blue pebbly beach. On the edge of this cliff originally lay huge anomalous rocks that give the clear impression of a citadel which is exactly what the original village was in the 13th century; when one stands on this rock, one feels suspended from a cloud; it certainly feels like the kind of spot that must have filled Icarus with the desire to fly.

Anyway, it is on the precipitous edge of this spot that a couple of plants of wild *rigani* grow, and every year we and our ninety-year-old neighbour use them as barometers in order to know how the main crop up on the mountain peak is maturing.

This is my husband's favourite yearly task; he chooses the hottest day in the summer (that is once the *rigani* has been assessed ready to be picked by the old lady, Moshanthaki) and then the hottest time of any day in Greece, at about 2 p.m., when he goes off to ascend the mountain in the blazing heat. Coffee time brings him back, glowing with sweat and exhilaration, and his beautiful big bunches of *rigani* are the envy of the village. The first time he went up to the mountain years ago after specific instructions from the old lady as to where exactly the best crops were, he came back proudly parading his huge pretty bunch through the village streets only to find the next day this thin and fragile-looking elderly lady coming down herself with an even bigger and prettier bunch.

These bunches should also hang in the sun outside for 2–3 days, even though they are dry on arrival, but on no account should they get wet as their golden looks are dampened, the flowers are destroyed and their aroma is totally diffused.

This is the kind of *rigani* that one could not buy from an ordinary shop, even specialist ones that sell nothing else but *votana*.

Thymari (Thyme serpyllum) is wild thyme and as far as I know the only kind in Greece. It grows everywhere in Greece, even next to the sea, while *rigani* does not like the sea air, and the Greek countryside seems to be enwrapped in the fusing scents of the various thyme plants in the early morning and the late afternoon. One does not have to look far in order to find at least three or four different varieties growing in the same area; they like stony ground and will grow under pine trees where not many other plants would grow. When there is such an abundance of this wild and beautifully aromatic specimens, why grow some gentrified version of it?

Thymari is a small plant varying in height and denseness. All varieties have woody stems with almost miniature greyish leaves and purple flowers on the top. The range of the shades of purple varies according to the different varieties. It can be very light purple, sometimes reddish-purple, very dark, to an unusually dark, that seems to be dusted on the outside of its petals with a white dusty cotton-wool substance. This is one of the most aromatic and easy to pick as it bears a lot of flowers on each branch.

While *rigani* is collected mainly for its flowers, *thymari* is collected for both flowers and tiny leaves. *Thymari* that grows on particularly stony ground is more aromatic and also more difficult to collect as the bushes are very small and insignificant looking, about 15 cm/5–6 ins while at other times it can be double this height and much larger and significant.

Thymari attracts honeybees and in return inevitably Greek honey almost always bears that unmistakable aroma that for me invokes the scented mountain air in an urban setting even on dark winter days. Honey in Greece was particularly famed when it came from the mountain of Hymmitos near Athens and that was attributed to the specially scented type of thyme that grew in profusion there. For me, honey that is not thyme-scented is not the real thing.

When dried, *thymari* is the only herb that loses or alters none of its aroma, while on the contrary dried *rigani* seems to develop a more concentrated scent, once dried. The notion of fresh 'thyme' then makes no sense in Greece as it does not realy exist; either you use a branch of thyme straight from its bush or you first dry it for a few days, it makes no difference, and the aroma will still penetrate and enwrap your whole kitchen. Like *rigani*, when it has dried, it is crumbled over a sheet of newspaper, before it is stored for the winter.

As thyme stalks are harder, they are quite difficult to cut, without pulling the roots of the plant apart, so we have devised a new system: we simply pull leaves and flowers off with one movement of the hand along the stalk, and deposit them in a basket. The next day we put the basket in the sun for two to three days, turning its contents over occasionally. This is easy and efficient and even our two daughters got the hang of it when they were only two years old; now they are five they are real experts! They know exactly which is thyme and which is oregano, not only by their sight but also by their aroma.

In the early evening, at about 7 o'clock, joined by a couple of their little village friends, we take a walk to a nearby place, where the thyme we prefer is particularly prolific and the views particularly beautiful and dramatic. With the sun setting on our left side of the mountain like a huge disc blazing with fire, exploding into myriad segments of mauve and pink tones, it seems to abstract the weight of the mountains opposite and of the small islands below on the horizon that appear to float over the still sea in a cloud of diffused light.

The whole hillside is folded in the scented waves of the dense thyme plants. It is the hour of stillness and peace; a peace that is interrupted only by the laughter of the children and their animated cries when a particularly dense and large bush is spotted, which makes them dance about like miniature Nereides on the deserted hillside. It is also an hour of happiness and makes one think that herb collecting is more about the joys one experiences during it that has made it such a delightful and favourite task thoughout the centuries.

There cannot be a barbecue of meat or fish or a whole lamb roasted outdoors, without twigs of thyme being immersed in olive oil and lemon juice and then rubbed gently all over it.

Greeks, being particularly superstitious, believe it is bad luck to take a bunch of freshly picked oregano or thyme into a cemetery.

HERBS IN FOLKLORE MEDICINE AND WHERE TO FIND THEM

The obvious place to find herbs that are believed to have therapeutic elements, one would say, are fields and mountains. Which fields though and what mountains? There is a bewildering variety of these wonderfully strange looking specimens, with some of them coming from a mountain in Peloponnisos, others from mountains in Kriti and others yet from Parnassos or Olymbos, the mythic mount of Gods, Pillion or Pinthos. It would take a long time and special tuition for amateurs like me to learn to identify the endless varieties. Instead, we can visit specialist shops run by devoted people who have spent sometimes a lifetime on the subject and who get very animated about their wares, which stretch quite far east to include exotic spices. Some of these people do the gathering themselves which makes them all the more interesting to talk to; others just supply a market through local outlets from villages scattered all over Greece.

In Athens, if you crossed Athinas Street, leaving the central market behind, walked down Evripithou (Euripides) Street, or Sofocleous Street, that run parallel to each other, you would find a plethora of subterranean places with overloaded hessian sacks of dry herbs and tisanes bursting up their stone steps and out on to the narrow pavements, and aromatic bunches garlanding their narrow entrances.

This is where Athenians go for their cooking herbs, their tisanes and their ailments: those who missed the chamomile season for one reason or another, those with a craving for some aromatic wild tea from Kriti (*thik-tamo*), those suffering from gallstones, or kidney stones, from high blood pressure, from ulcers, nervous tension, insomnia, migraines, laryngitis, excess period bleeding, prostrate, rheumatism, arthritis, constipation or simple excess hair loss and other beautifying purposes.

My favourite such shop in Athens is at No. 89 Evripithou Street, run by the enthusiast Mr Pantelios who comes from the Ionian island of Keffalonia, which has been there for over twenty years. He will prescribe and instantly supply what is needed and give exact instructions as to the method of infusion and the daily dosage.

Lagokimithia which looks very much like thyme, is prescribed for stomach ulcers and excess sugar in the blood; lemon scented *melissohorto* is for headaches, nervous disorders and insomnia; Egyptian leaves against constipation; *agathoura* for excess period bleeding; angelica for ailing kidneys; *skorpithohorto* and *trivoli* against stones; *taraxakos* for high cholesterol sufferers (I overheard this being prescribed as 20g to 1 litre water, boiled for 20 minutes and 2 teacups of the infusion to be drunk daily); something that looks almost like a witch's tangled brown hair, the innocent corn-beards (*fountos apo kalamboki*) is a diuretic; *menta* (peppermint) is for tummy aches, etc.; *arkouthopsomo* (bear bread), which looks like a potato with only two small leaves at the top and which grows in Thessalia and Makethonia, is made into powder which is sprinkled on eczema spots.

Infusions made with *thenthrolivano* (rosemary) or thyme left to stand in boiling water will strengthen the hair and make it lustrous; while nettle infusions are good for oily hair, and infusions made with *politrihi*, which looks like loose pine needles, are used to rinse the hair and to prevent hair loss.

Infusions made by boiling rosemary for 5 minutes are very good against nervous tension and I remember not so long ago my mother also using it to rub down suits, dresses and particularly my father's uniforms, as a home dry-cleaning method.

Infusions made with the dried leaves of Louisa – the ancient vervain – are good for losing weight. (Most of my Greek friends are devoted to it.)

Apart from the herbs mentioned already, the Greek hillsides offer some for simple practical household purposes. Best and foremost are the saucer-like flowers of the wild tall silvery verbascums that can be seen everywhere; these, once dried, are used as *fytilakia* (little wicks) lit in a glass with water and some olive oil, perpetually burning in front of the inevitable *ikonostasi*, a mystical corner, sometimes draped with little white linen curtains, where the ikons of each household are housed.

(When I was small, I used to read under the flickering light of the *ikonostasi* that happened to be on top of my bed, when the lights were out and my grandmother was fast asleep.)

A small but very pretty bunch of *amarantos* or *nyhaki*, that look like dried, bright yellow little flowers, is hung in rooms or cupboards in order to keep moths away, particularly during the hot months, a kind of natural *naphthaline* – mothballs.

Infusions are often taken with the addition of a spoonful of honey as a special tonic; others are pounded into pastes and used for cosmetic or medicinal purposes.

Somebody we met in Kriti knew exactly where to find the scarce *mandragoras* plants (mandrake) whose large roots, he confirmed, when chewed made one feel euphoric, to say the least; he ended up walking to the nearest village alone, sitting at the only *kafenion* and ordering three coffees for him and his invisible friends, which bewildered its black-scarfed owner.

There is another tiny shop of the same kind run by a real devotee, in Monastiraki Square, behind the church at the edge of the old quarter in Athens and near the central food market again, which has been here for over forty years. Another one is at Rethymno in Kriti, but one will find them in every town and they are always worth visiting.

VOTANA

Index